MW00983703

MISSISSIPPIAN WOMEN

Florida Museum of Natural History: Ripley P. Bullen Series

MISSISSIPPIAN WOMEN

EDITED BY

Rachel V. Briggs,
Michaelyn S. Harle,
and Lynne P. Sullivan

Foreword by Sheila Bird

UNIVERSITY OF FLORIDA PRESS

Gainesville

Published in the United States of America

29 28 27 26 25 24 6 5 4 3 2 1

Library of Congress Cataloging-in-Publication Data
Names: Briggs, Rachel V., editor. | Harle, Michaelyn S., editor. | Sullivan, Lynne P., editor.
Title: Mississippian women / edited by Rachel V. Briggs, Michaelyn S. Harle, and Lynne P. Sullivan ; foreword by Sheila Bird.
Other titles: Ripley P. Bullen series.
Description: 1. | Gainesville : University of Florida Press, [2024] | Series: Florida Museum of Natural History: Ripley P. Bullen Series | Includes bibliographical references and index.
Identifiers: LCCN 2023050550 | ISBN 9781683404149 (hardback) | ISBN 9781683404545 (ebook) | ISBN 9781683404316 (pdf)
Subjects: LCSH: Women—Mississippi—History. | Women pioneers—Mississippi. | Indigenous women—Mississippi—History. | Frontier and pioneer life—Mississippi. | BISAC: SOCIAL SCIENCE / Archaeology | HISTORY / Women
Classification: LCC HQ1438.M7 M57 2024 | DDC 305.409762—dc23/eng/20231108
LC record available at https://lccn.loc.gov/2023050550

UF PRESS
UNIVERSITY OF FLORIDA

University of Florida Press
2046 NE Waldo Road
Suite 2100
Gainesville, FL 32609
http://upress.ufl.edu

All author royalties from this volume will go to the Northeast Oklahoma Chapter of the Missing and Murdered Indigenous Women (MMIW), which is committed to advocating for missing and murdered Indigenous people of Oklahoma.

CONTENTS

FIGURES

TABLES

FOREWORD

Growing up in the foothills of the Ozarks, near the Oklahoma and Arkansas border, I had the pristine opportunity to grow up in the secluded community of Chewey, Oklahoma. At the time of my childhood, I didn't realize that the story of my people was anything close to what I understand it to be right now.

Looking back, the activities, the ceremonies, the community gatherings, the language, the songs, the stories, the planting, and the prayers were the norm. I never asked myself how or why we were so fortunate enough to live on one of the most beautiful landscapes that the Creator had made. The Illinois River runs in front of my childhood home, and a lively creek ran behind our home, and there were many more families within the community that lived and relished this life. They still do.

But outside of the loveliness, one day I got old enough to begin asking my mother questions, questions that would lead me on a lifetime search of the whos, the whys, and the hows on how our family came to be here, in the middle of Eden, or so I have compared it to. Life was full, and it was vast in this part of the world. I was the youngest of eight; me and my sister were the two youngest girls with a heap of brothers, and then there were many more cousins and play cousins, and we all lived in a communal way, just as the old ones did.

In our small community, we had an elementary school named Skelly. If you know the Oil and Gas history of Oklahoma, Skelly was a big name, and so it was told to me that Mr. Skelly had donated that land to build a school. My mom said that occasionally, you would see a big, long, black car come down the road, and a tall man with a coat and a hat would get out of his car, take a long look around and then leave. I've always wondered what was going through his mind, and I often wondered why such a man would give away this prime piece of land to build a school for us Cherokee kids. Except for a few farmers' kids, most students that attended Skelly School, was my family.

It was in this K–8 school that I recall one of the first books that donned a picture of people who looked like me, with the brown skin and the long dark hair, but the image showed them wearing head wraps with a feather sticking out. The picture showed covered wagons, horses, and people walking. The men on horses looked stern, and in a place of authority, but they were dark like me too; I didn't understand why they were on a horse, and there was an elder lady walking, and she had a discerned look on her face of hardship. I remember going home thinking about this book. I didn't dare check it out, and I didn't want to open the book because my headspace wasn't right, and I was trying to decide if I wanted to go past that image and see what was behind it. I must have been in the fourth or fifth grade when I found this book in the school library. I remember the title vividly, though. It was called "The Trail of Tears." Talk about a confused little girl. I was thinking to myself, why would they have such a book with a sad story like that in the library—was it real? I couldn't wait to see my mom and ask her if she had ever seen such a book. My mom was active in our school. She couldn't help but be active in the school, she had eight children go through it, and she had more challenges than one with the administrators and how they governed the children of the community. You see, Chewey was thirty miles from everywhere. That's why we were so secluded in Eden. Who would want to leave? We had everything we needed. My brothers would fish and hunt regularly. We had a river in front of us for catfish, perch, bass, and recreation. We had a creek behind us that yielded our seasonal goods, Wishi (mushrooms), wild onions (no, not Ramps, there is a difference), crawdads, watercress, poke salad, berries, squirrel, rabbits, and deer. You name it, we had it, what we didn't have was Native educators. Teachers drove the thirty miles to get to teach us, you would think, that if someone was that dedicated to teaching us, they would be nice to us, but that wasn't always the deal. So, when one of our mamas came to the school during class time, something was going to happen. We would all get quiet and listen.

My oldest brother learned how to speak English in school, as did many other children from our community. The teachers were hard, and their corrections were even harder; it was a battle that our mothers faced daily, as well as the children, but we made it through. I remember we had the best cooks, and they so loved the students; they were like grannies to all of us.

I asked my mom about the book that I had seen, I asked her about the book called "Trail of Tears" and I could tell by her expression that it was going to be a hard story to share with me; she didn't quite know how to tell me in detail about the history that took place, so all she could start with was "this isn't our real home." Talk about confusion. I remember telling her that I didn't understand, and I remember her struggle to find a way to best tell me why Eden (Chewey) wasn't our real home, when that was the only home that I knew. All she could do was tell me that the white people had taken our land from "way back there" and moved us here. I wanted to know where "way back there" was exactly. She told me that it was a far place in the East, where our families had to move from. She said that the picture that I had seen was someone's painting, and it was their idea of what it was like when the old ones had walked here from our homelands. She said they didn't have a choice, and many people had died on the journey, and that's why they call it the "Trail of Tears."

My mom is a strong woman. She was raised in a single-parent household, in a day and time when the day was long and full of hard work, only to wake up to another day of long and full day of hard work. My mom could survive in the woods better than any man that I know, but as strong as I have known her to be, I can remember the tone in her voice was one of great sorrow. I don't know what broke my heart more, the fact that I was just told that the stressful image of the elder lady on the cover of that book was because she had to leave her home, or the fact that I had seen that same look from the image of the elder, now on my mama's face when she was struggling to tell me the story.

As a parent, reflecting on the day that I asked my mom about the "Trail of Tears" and learning that this place that I knew to be home was not really our home, it would make me face the same level of grief, knowing that the day, my own children would ask me the same question. I, too, struggled with the thought of how I explain it in a way that it would not make them as mad as it made me that day as a child. No mother should have to worry about that day, or what even your child would face, that would lead to having this discussion. I grew up the better part of my life being mad at these facts. After I left the community school, I went straight to an Indian Residential School and lived there for my high school years. It's odd to say that on my first day in the Sequoyah High School library, I came across a book with that same cover. You can see it now on many covers, posters and displays. You can't run from it; we are forced to embrace it.

I did become a mother, and I did have to have these conversations. Yes, it was difficult, but after I raised my children, I vowed to seek a higher level of education so that I could advance my understanding of this lifelong impact that this one picture had placed on my life. I had carried it for so long; the historical trauma that was attached to it had already taken the best years of so many of my friends and family, mainly because they, too, couldn't make sense of it and learn to live with it. So, I vowed to leave my job just as soon as my children completed their high school years, and I was going to learn about the laws and the actions that allowed such a thing to happen. So, I did go to school, and I did learn the processes that took place, and it didn't make it any easier on me. If anything I became angrier.

I had a choice to make with my new understanding, and I followed in the path that my Great-Grandfather Osie Hogshooter had made for me to follow. He as the Secretary of the Keetoowah Nighthawks, alongside Chief Redbird

Smith, led one of the greatest resistance to the Dawes Roll, an action of the federal government where our communities would now be split up and divided into parcels in an effort to further domesticate us from our communal and traditional ways, but it didn't work, it didn't break our spirits, we would prove that it would take more than a line drawn in the dirt to separate a living culture.

I didn't know what I knew until Creator put me on this pathway. It took years of learning and heartache to motivate me to do more than just accept that my Great-Grandfather's work was finished. It was not. It wasn't my secondary education that taught me my greatest value, but it did take a lived experience for me to look back and see the true value of my upbringing. Like my Great-Grandfather, I sought out the same diplomatic spirit that my Great-Grandfather fostered; though the Nighthawks decided to form a government out of resistance, it was this level of diplomacy that created a pathway for them to sit in the Nation's Capital with the president of the United States and then have an opportunity to speak in front of Congress, in an effort to plead a case that would allow our people to be together collectively, not divided. In the end, it didn't work. They divided the land, and my family was allotted land where my childhood home remains. My 87-year-old mother, Marie Tsa-ge-yu Bird, still lives there today in 2022.

My grandfather stood his ground, and now I know where I get my hard-headedness. He would never sign the Dawe's Roll—he was witnessed into the Roll—and was issued his allotted land. Years after his death, we would see a publication in the newspaper about how his land had been petitioned by squatter's rights. I remember that my mother told me that Osie had never taken his land; he wandered and lived with his family until he took his final journey, staying true to his creed that he would never take part in this allotment.

When I was asked to comment on several papers on Mississippian women at a meeting in Augusta, Georgia, I had to ask myself, why me? And what did I have to offer? But as I began to read the papers that these individual scholars had put hours and hours of research into, the things that I had learned through my education in my home, in Indian Boarding school, in college, and in my work at a Tribal Historic Preservation Officer, would all come full circle. Now, things started to make sense to me on why my journey was as challenging as it was up to this point. There was much to learn and a lot to take in over this period.

When I was reading these papers and looking at the pictures, I saw myself, my family, my community, and my ancestors in all of them. The lifeways that were presented, the footprints that our ancestors had left for us to follow, were easy to identify because we still practice many of these things in our present-day communities. It's like I was able to take a string, tie a knot at the end, and weave it through each individual writing, pull that string, close the gap, and combine these words together to paint an image of how these findings were related to today. As I watched the presentations in the room with the lights dim, you could hardly see the tears rolling down the side of my face. Even though it was not my mama telling a little Cherokee girl a story this time, someone else was, but I received it in a spiritual way, without anyone knowing. My ancestors were speaking to me with these words, giving me a glimpse of how this period presents itself. I was so thankful that someone took the time to master this research. My people are gone from those lands now, but for me, ever since the day my mama told me that Eden (Chewey) was not our real home, I had a longing in my heart to visit this space. It took forty years of my life to come to the homelands, and when I did, I carried the Oklahoma spirit of our ancestors who had longed to make the pilgrimage to our homelands and never did, and I joined those that remained to remind them, that we haven't forgotten them. The women of the Mississippian time period are still the women of today in my world. My resolve was to be able to remove those time stamps that have been placed on our lives through these papers. It was a pleasure and an honor to speak to all who came to that discussion and personally proclaim that we are a living, breathing culture. The Mississippian culture is so far down the list in archaeological terms, but somebody had to figure out a scientific way to prove our existence and support the fact that we have been here since time immemorial. I'm just happy that I can live and learn right alongside the rest of you. We are not just a story with a sad cover. We are here, we are relevant, and our women continue to make their mark as we strive to create a new narrative for our next generations to follow.

Wado, Ga-li-e-li-gi-si, Sheila Bird

Acknowledgments

I dedicate this writing to my grandchildren: Rylie, Hadley, Nash, Acy, Valor, Ever, Liam, and those that may come later, I hope to leave footprints that are easy for them to follow. I honor my mother in this writing for taking up the challenge of living through her own time and surviving. Eighty-seven years ago from today was a hard place to come from, but she too had to go through her life cycles to be able to tell us the stories that I will someday pass down. I pray for my children, Nathan, Mitchel, and Alyssa, that when it comes time to tell our stories to my grandchildren, it comes from a place of strength. I dedicate the longevity of my words to my husband, Bob, who supported me when I packed up my bags at forty years old to move three hours away to get the education that I needed to enhance my understanding and strengthen my voice. No, my Great-Grandfather's work isn't done. It's still a viable work in progress, and I am honored to carry the torch in memory of my nephew Ricky James Bird who carried it up until his journey crossed over.

1

The Current State of (Mississippian) Women

Archaeology, Gender, and Indigenous Feminism

Rachel V. Briggs and Michaelyn S. Harle

On August 8, 1920, after a long battle with the courts, with the public, and most of all, with Western ideas of "femininity," women across the United States of America gained the federal right to cast a vote in both state and national elections. The Nineteenth Amendment to the United States Constitution granted the right of women's suffrage, marking a significant event in the history of feminism and sexual equality. Less well known, but just as significant, is the passing of the Snyder Act four years later. While all American men regardless of race were granted the right to vote in 1870, the Fifteenth Amendment specifically excluded Indigenous people, and both Indigenous men and women were legally disenfranchised until 1924. In other words, American Indians, the descendants of the first people to populate the vast area of what would become the United States of America, were among the last of its citizens to gain the right to voice an opinion in its political affairs.

The marginal status of both Indigenous peoples and women in Western colonial North America since the sixteenth century has produced a myopic, and often inaccurate, understanding of Indigenous history prior to and after European colonialism. Well into the twentieth century, this short-sighted view contributed to a popular perception of Indigenous groups as passive, low-level societies that were shaped *by,* and not those that actively *shaped,* their environment, their worlds, or their histories. And yet, while the general agency of Indigenous peoples was downplayed, the particular roles of Indigenous women were all too often dismissed entirely (Conkey and Spector 1984). Studies of political leadership, social organization, and even the dietary significance of hunting activities all focused on the importance of masculine players and activities while relegating Indigenous women to supporting players at best, while at worst, writing them out of history completely. Even as scholars began highlighting the impressive scope of Indigenous lifeways across North America, from the complexity of the Chaco Canyon culture to the urban center of Cahokia, men were still presumed to be the architects, political leaders, and social masterminds; women were nowhere to be found (Smith and Wobst 2005).

Today, this wrong is slowly being righted as North American archaeologists collaborate with Indigenous communities and incorporate Indigenous ontologies and ideologies into our investigations (e.g., Fritz et al. 2001; Lightfoot 2005; Panich and Gonzalez 2020; Purcell 2023). And yet, Western history continues to repeat itself for Indigenous women—despite the growing recognition of Indigenous agency and power in landscape modification (Sherwood and Kidder 2011), religious enactment (Alt 2020; Deloria 2003), colonial entanglements (Voss 2008), and resiliency to Western hegemony (Kelton 2015; Schneider 2021), discussions of Indigenous women and femininity are noticeably missing. Though every branch of North American archaeology is guilty of this dismissal, only some have the necessary research infrastructure for a thoughtful and purposeful exploration of Indigenous feminine power and agency: research into Mississippian societies in the US Southeast is one (Gougeon 2017; LeMaster 2014: 22; Levy 2014; Sullivan 2014; Rodning 1999).

Mississippian societies are diverse late pre-contact and early post-European contact societies generally characterized by social stratification, a reliance on extensive agriculture (including maize and starchy seeds), and communities designed with relationship to regional temple/mortuary mound and plaza centers (Anderson and Sassaman 2012: 155; Fritz 2019). Mississippian societies span a broad geographic as well as temporal range (approximately AD 900 through the seventeenth century) and are found from the Deep South up the Mississippi River to the American Bottom, northeast into central Ohio and east to the Atlantic Coast (Anderson and Sassaman 2012: 155). Mississippian societies have received considerable archaeological attention (Anderson and Sassaman 2012: 155). Combined with a florescence of Indigenous authors and researchers (e.g., Bauer 2022; Cooper 2022; Lowery 2018; Peasantubbee 2005), collaborations with Indigenous groups (e.g., Fritz et al. 2001; Nelson et al. 2023; Purcell 2023), and a critical read of the ethnohistoric record (e.g., Ethridge 2009, 2010; Hudson 1976; LeMaster 2014; Swanton 1946), Mississippian researchers now have the capability, and perhaps the moral obligation, to reconstruct Mississippian gendered roles and institutions. And the emerging picture from the handful of studies that have undertaken this endeavor demonstrates that Mississippian women and femininity were socially powerful agents and institutions driving their societies (e.g., Alt 2020; Briggs 2017; Briggs et al. 2023; Fritz 2019; Gougeon 2012; Mueller and Fritz 2016; Trocolli 2002).

We know Mississippian women were powerful leaders (Briggs et al. 2023; Hudson 2005; Snyder 2009; Sullivan 2014; Trocolli 1999, 2002). In 1540 in the South Carolina Piedmont, Hernando de Soto and his entrada met the impressive Tali Mico (or the Lady of Cofitachequi), paramount chief (or cacique) of the town of Cofitachequi, a powerful Late Mississippian chiefdom (Snyder 2009). Tali Mico assumed the position from her aunt and expected to pass the position onto her niece, reflecting the important transmission of authority through the matrilineage (Rodning et al., this volume; Snyder 2009). Tali Mico was only the first of a handful of female micos and oratas recorded by Europeans during the sixteenth century, reflecting the normalized practice of Indigenous females attaining high social positions within Indigenous US Southeastern societies (Trocolli 1999).

We also know that Mississippian women were powerful even if they were not chiefs; Indigenous authors and researchers clearly indicate that Indigenous women drew power from everyday activities (or those practices prescribed by their gender roles), which were instrumental for maintaining all aspects of Native life (Bauer 2002; Cooper 2022; Edwards 2018; Levy 1999; Mankiller 2001; Sullivan and Rodning 2001; Worth 2000). As Karen Coody Cooper remarks, "Women were the givers of life through birthing and horticulture, while men were the takers of life through hunting and warfare" (Cooper 2022: 6). Women cared for, grew, harvested, and transformed important plants into fundamental social products, like baskets used for gathering and storage (woven from rivercane; King et al. 2019), to meals consisting of hominy (made from maize and woodash; Briggs 2015) with hickory nut oil (Fritz et al. 2001) or bear grease (Altman et al. 2020); to the "Black" drink (a hot tea made from yaupon holly) used in ritual and social ceremonies (Hudson 2004). Women also crafted the tools required for their work and identity, including cooking pots, spoons, awls, cloth, aprons, and sandals (Alt 1999; Briggs 2016; Drooker 2017; Hudson 1976). Reverence for these materials is reflected mythically (Lankford 2008), iconographically (Mueller and Fritz 2016), and verbally (Briggs 2023), with women's tools and products commonly employed to understand central and important abstract ideas. For example, the lived reproductive experiences of females were used as metaphors for fertility and transformation (Bengtson and Alexander, this volume; Sharp, this volume; see also Cooper 2022; Mueller and Fritz 2016), while the omnipresence of hominy and cooking pots served as symbols of creation, resilience, and tradition (Briggs 2015, 2023).

Finally, we know maternal lineages and feminine relationships were a fundamental principle of social organization. Not only was descent, and for some, ascendancy, determined by the mother's lineage, but those familial and social relationships tying together communities separated by rivers, mountains, and great distances were based on maternal networks (Bauer 2022; Cooper 2022; Lowery 2018; Hudson 1976: 185–191; Sullivan, Chapter 6 in this volume). Sisters, mothers, aunties, grandmothers, and female cousins bound communities and fostered intra-community relationships that moved materials, ideas, and people throughout the US Southeast (Perdue 1998).

Imagine if these understandings of Indigenous feminine power were applied to late pre-contact and early post-contact Mississippian societies, and considered in relation to the emergence of ceremonial centers like Cahokia and Moundville (respectively: Fritz, this volume; Briggs, this volume), to power production through crafting at Mississippian mound centers like Carter Robinson (Meyers, this volume), to the meaning of sacred stone statuary recovered throughout the Middle Cumberland region of Tennessee (Sharp, this volume), to the layout and understanding of social space of the Mississippian town of Little Egypt in northern Georgia (Gougeon, this volume), to the gravity of motherhood and womanhood in social affairs and landscape construction in pre-contact Cherokee, Muskogean, and Osage sites (respectively: Harle et al., this volume; Sullivan, Chapter 6 in this volume; Bengtson and Alexander, this volume), to the social and political events of sixteenth-century Fort Walton sites in Florida (White, this volume), and to the unfolding of Spanish colonial entanglements in the North Carolina Piedmont (Rodning et al., this volume). What might the Mississippian world begin to look like if Indigenous femininity were considered formidable and not inert, and if femininity was treated as an energy steering social transformation? How would our understanding of this dynamic world change? And, more importantly, what would happen to our perception of Indigenous women, both present and in the past?

This volume answers these questions by exploring the transformative social power of women and femininity in Mississippian societies (Figure 1.1). Each chapter uses archaeological evidence supplemented by biological, ethnohistoric, ethnologic, historical, geographic, and other complementary lines to demonstrate that women were essential actors in the construction, maintenance, and transformation of the Mississippian world prior to and through European colonial entanglements. Uniting each chapter is a common thread: for too long, we, as archaeologists focused on Mississippian sites, have undermined the social power of Indigenous women, from the strength of their voice in political, ritual, and economic matters, to the formative practices of

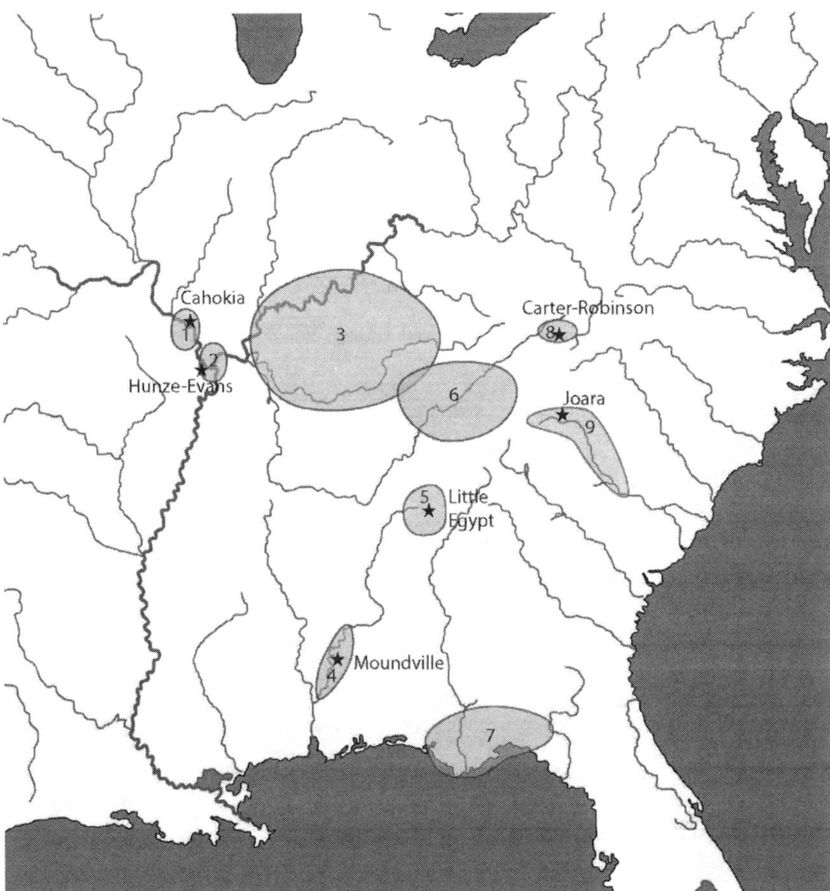

Figure 1.1. Map of the sites and areas discussed in this volume. Key for each area: Area 1, discussed by Fritz in Chapter 2; Area 2, discussed by Bengtson and Alexander in Chapter 5; Area 3, discussed by Sharp in Chapter 8; Area 4, discussed by Briggs in Chapter 3; Area 5, discussed by Gougeon in Chapter 7; Area 6, discussed by Harle, Betsinger and Sullivan in Chapter 4, and by Sullivan in Chapter 7; Area 7, discussed by White in Chapter 11; Area 8, discussed by Meyers in Chapter 9; and Area 9, discussed by Rodning, Briggs, Beck, Fritz, Lapham, and Moore in Chapter 10.

their everyday domestic activities, to the significant role they played in crafting the histories of their communities. Further, the authors of this volume believe that considering the power of femininity in the Mississippian world is a necessary application if we not only hope to understand the past, but also if we hope to make the systemic changes necessary to our discipline to diversify it and make it more inclusive.

Gender and Mississippian Studies

This is not the first work that explores gender in Mississippian societies (e.g., Claassen 2016; Eastman and Rodning 2001; Gougeon 2012, 2017; Thompson 2008). However, neither gender nor sex are popular research trends within Mississippian research, substantially lagging behind other topics like identity, landscape, social status, iconography, and craft production, all of which are capable of, and should, include a gendered focus (see Blitz 2010; Gougeon 2017). The reasons for this oversight are multifaceted, but there are three overlapping factors worth highlighting: first, there are methodological and ideological issues inherent in studying gender in Mississippian societies; second, there are inherent questions of authority and ownership regarding who can do this kind of research; and third, there are still systemic biases within the discipline that reinforce a Western construction of femininity and women. These concerns are addressed below. The first step in this discussion is to disambiguate terms and concepts central to this volume: we need to know what gender is and how we use it here.

Gender Identity and Roles

"Gender" is a misnomer. There are two concepts routinely referred to when most people use the term "gender:" gender roles and gender identities. Gender identity refers to how a person understands themself and how they identify. Gender identities are declared by individuals, and are not imposed by society, though they can be socially influenced. Gender roles, on the other hand, are patterned, artificial social constructions that organize societal responsibilities and expectations into specific categories. As an example: an ultrasound technician does not tell you the gender of a baby; they inform you of the presentation of a baby's biological sex (is a penis identifiable or not?). That child's gender identity is revealed when they identify with specific gendered concepts and share that with others. Their gender role may be either imposed (as it is in Western societies) or chosen based on the social rules of the society they are born into. While some argue that gender is genetically determined based on the presence or absence of a Y chromosome (and thus that gender is an expression of biologically determined behaviors), this is wrong (Fine 2017). Women are not kinder, more nurturing, or more compassionate because they are female (possessing two X chromosomes), and men are not more aggressive, more competitive, and engage in riskier behavior because they are male (possessing an X and Y chromosome) (Fine 2017; Gilchrist 2009). "Gendered" behaviors are conditioned from an early age based on social expectations, social perceptions, and individual agency.

Archaeology is more concerned with gender roles than it is with gender identity. Because gender identity is personal and idiosyncratic, and because the archaeological record is overwhelmingly a study of pattern recognition, it is challenging to effectively isolate a person's gender identity. Gender roles, on the other hand, are widespread social institutions that are regulated and patterned, making them far more visible in the material record.

Have all societies throughout human history used gender roles? Yes, according to Claassen (1992, 2013) and Joyce and Claassen (1997). Both argue that "gender" was one of the first and most fundamental ways society was organized. Here, Claassen and Joyce are referencing the necessity of the social function of gender roles—as a form of categorization, they ensure that key practices and responsibilities related to subsistence and survival are met. That females are often "women" and that males are often "men" does not reflect inherent behavioral differences, but instead is a general product of the biological investment in reproduction. Females have a non-transferable mandate to their offspring, from approximately nine months of gestation to birth to postpartem responsibilities like breastfeeding (which happens multiple times a day and can continue for two or more years), with this process potentially repeated several times in a female's lifetime. Because of these non-transferable responsibilities, over time, females tend to participate in essential social practices that keep them close to their communities, children, and families, like gathering wild plants, cooking, and crafting domestic materials, thus creating "femininity." Males, on the other hand, with greater spatial flexibility in their responsibilities to their children and communities, can leave the immediate vicinity and travel further to procure important resources, creating "masculinity." The result is a general pattern of gender roles that supports the association of females with femininity and males with masculinity. Beyond this basic model, there are no other universal rules that guide gender roles.

The artificial and historical nature of gender is poorly understood in Western society: Western gender ideologies, and in particular the systemic oppression of women, is thought to be natural, stemming from the false idea of innate gendered behavioral differences as well as significant physical differences. This misconception is perpetuated both publicly and within the academy, where essentialized ideas of what it means to be a woman or a man inform pedagogy (i.e., making STEM programming more accessible to girls who are thought of as more "right-brained" than "left"), hiring practices (i.e., hiring more women to work on Wall Street or in corporate positions so they can change the "hyper-masculine" landscape of these professional arenas with their "feminine nature"), and the design of professional spaces (i.e., academic buildings that are designed to appear cold, objective, and pragmatic to deter the expression of emotions, subjectivity, and partiality which disproportionately disadvantages women and people of color) (Fine 2017).

A further misconception perpetuated by Western gender ideologies is the conflation of gender identity and sexuality, an unfortunate habit clearly displayed in European records of Western colonial entanglements in the US Southeast. French, Spanish, and English colonists, when they encountered Indigenous males living as women, referred to them as *berdache,* derived from the Arabic term *bardaj* referring to "kept boys" or "male prostitutes" (Smithers 2014: 631). European adaptations of the term led to the English *berdache,* the French *bardache,* and the Spanish *barbaxa,* which were used to refer to males who had sex with other males conflating gender identities (living as women) with sexuality (having sex with males) (Smithers 2014: 632–633). *Berdache* was used as a derogatory term applied to non-gender or non-sex-conforming Indigenous males, with the blanket assumption being that these were males who dressed or acted as women and had sex with other males. This was problematic for Western gender ideologies, which only recognized one sexual pairing as socially permissible: male and female. Male homosexuality was ridiculed and categorized as feminine, female homosexuality was ignored completely, and transgendered individuals did not exist because they were, socially speaking, inconceivable (Manion 2020; Smithers 2014).

Historically, Western gender institutions were, and still are, structured in such a way to encourage gender conformity while actively discouraging (and punishing) non-conformity. In other words, males are strongly encouraged to fulfill masculine roles, and females are strongly encouraged to fulfill feminine roles, with rather severe consequences for deviant individuals, such as stigmatization, ostracization, socially permissible violence, and even legal punishments. This is an important point because while feminine and masculine may be two categories used by all societies throughout human history, conformity to these categories based on biological sex is not always strictly enforced. Within many Indigenous societies in the US Southeast, both males and females had the option to live as men, women, and potentially third-gendered individuals, with few to no social consequences (for a possible exception among the Choctaw, see Greenberg 1988: 50).

This leads to one further historical construct of Western gender ideologies often misconstrued as a universal truth: while there are only two formally recognized gender roles in Western society, it is not uncommon for a society to have three or more gender roles. Many non-Western societies have two primary gender roles, masculine and feminine, but also other gender roles that fulfill important social responsibilities. However, the exclusive responsibilities vested in third-gender roles, while important, are not those vital for the maintenance of the biological life of a group. Instead, they tend to involve responsibilities like social mitigation (performed by *ihamana* among the Zuni) and specific ritual performance (like those performed by *hijra* in South Asia). Alternative gender identities, like *ma'hu'* among Polynesian societies and *two-spirit* among many Native American societies, are not commonly given exclusive social responsibilities specific to their gender identities; instead, fluidity is exercised in the practice of feminine and masculine practices.

Following the discussion above, this volume assumes that first, within Mississippian societies, there were two fundamental gendered categories that structured all patterned activities: feminine and masculine (Adair 1930 [1775]; Hudson 1976; Perdue 1998), with third-gendered categories available but not strongly represented archaeologically (White, this volume); and second, that masculine and feminine activities are not synonymous with male and female actors. We follow the terminological guidelines common in the biological and humanities fields today—when referring strictly to the outward presentation of biological sex, individuals are identified as female, male, or intersex; when referring to the material culture produced by patterned gender roles, we use the terms woman or feminine, man or masculine, and nonbinary or third-gendered; when appropriate, we strive to use socially specific terms like two-spirit. Unless explicitly known, discussions of sexuality and gender identity are avoided.

Archaeology of Gender Roles

The archaeological analyses presented in this volume each draw to varying degrees on three lines of complementary evidence for assessing feminine gender roles in the Mississippian US Southeast: material culture, biological analysis of skeletal material, and the ethnohistoric record.

Bioarchaeological Studies of Gender

Biological sex (i.e., the genetic composition of an individual that determines their sexual organs and reproductive capabilities) has been the primary source of data used by archaeologists to study gender in Mississippian societies (e.g., Bridges 1989; Hally 2008; Sullivan 2001, 2006, 2014; Sullivan and Harle 2010; Sullivan and Rodning 2011; Thomas 1996). The most common method for sexing skeletal material in the US Southeast has been measuring and comparing morphological features. Morphological sexing is far less costly than DNA testing, though it is also less precise: recent studies of previously sexed skeletal material offer revised interpretations of sexing assignments made in the early to mid-twentieth century (see Emerson et al. 2016). Skeletal sexing for human populations is based on a gradient of sexually dimorphic skeletal features, that, though strongly informed by biological factors, are also conditioned by ancestry, age, and nutrition, as well as the cognitive bias of those researchers conducting the analysis (Spradley et al. 2008; Walker 1995; Weiss 1972). The smaller the population size, the less precise the assignment. However, larger populations produce more precise results; this, combined with standardization in the field and greater understanding of researcher bias, suggests that current revisions are indeed more accurate and trustworthy (Buikstra and Ubelaker 1994; Spradley and Jantz 2011).

DNA testing, though a more precise indicator for biological sex, is used less frequently on probable Indigenous skeletal material recovered in the US Southeast. This invasive procedure requires taking a sample of bone from an Indigenous skeleton, which violates accords laid out by the Native American Graves Repatriation Act. Further, both morphological analysis as well as DNA analysis are considered violent transgressions by many Indigenous groups in the Eastern Woodlands (see White, this volume).

One of the important consequences of recent revisions in skeletal sexing is that more biological females, previously missexed as male, have been identified in the Mississippian record (Emerson et al. 2016). As Claassen (2001) notes, inaccurate skeletal sexing leading up to the 1980s both created and perpetuated a male-centric view of Mississippian societies. It seems that males were not only over-represented in high-status, high-prestige burials (meeting the androcentric expectations of researchers) (Emerson et al. 2016), but that they were over-represented in Mississippian populations *generally*, giving the appearance that Mississippian females were accorded different, and less important, death rights (Hudson 1976). This researcher-biased underrepresentation not only marginalized the contributions of Mississippian females, but it exaggerated the achievements of Mississippian males. The data generated from these studies served to bolster political and economic models for the emergence and social structure of Mississippian societies, using inaccurate data to justify disproportionately placing Mississippian males and their achievements at the top of the social hierarchy (see Sullivan 1995, 2001).

Social status, a common dimension still explored by Mississippian archaeologists, is commonly determined by the inclusion of socially valuable, rare items within graves, items such as copper axes (found among some burials at Moundville and within the Fort Walton culture), copper plates (found at Etowah), or shell cups (found at Spiro). As noted above, incorrect assignment of many Mississippian people as male, particularly those buried with high-status materials, created the illusion of *sexually* stratified societies, with males holding the highest social and political office and females either socially below them or socially invisible (Sullivan 2001). Skeletal assignment revisions, like those conducted by Emerson and colleagues (2016), who reanalyzed skeletal material recovered from Mound 72 at Cahokia, have helped topple these images. Mound 72 played a significant role in shaping many models of Mississippian power and social structure, and the initial assignment of exclusively males in high-status burials interred in the mound encouraged researchers to place males at the summit of the Mississippian political, social, and cosmological orders (e.g., Emerson and Pauketat 2002; Fowler et al. 1999; Goldstein 2000; Reilly et al. 2011). However, Emerson et al. (2016) demonstrated that several central burials were populated with male/female pairs, and that the mound itself was populated with significantly more females in high-status burials than initially recognized. Males no longer appeared to be alone at the top of the social order; instead, males and females shared that honor equally.

Morphological skeletal sexing is an important entry for research into Mississippian gender roles; for example, some researchers have explored gendered practices based on the expectation that repeated motions consistently performed over a person's lifetime may leave skeletal marks (Bridges 1989; Harle et al., this volume). One of the greatest strengths of bioarchaeology is that it combines osteological data with material culture, highlighting demographic, spatial, and social patterns. A number of studies on Mississippian societies use morphological skeletal sexing as a way to explore intra- and inter-community social relationships (Sullivan, this volume, Chapter 6) by comparing mortuary materials recovered from Indigenous people within and between burial populations (e.g., Hally 2008; Hatch 1975; Harle et al., this volume; Peebles and Kus 1977; Rodning 1999; Sullivan 1995, 2001, 2006; Sullivan and Harle 2010). Finally, bioarchaeological studies typically add health dimensions to their analyses, exploring differences in general nutrition and life histories between males and females at various points in their lives, highlighting the dynamic lived experiences within patterned, gendered social systems (e.g., Betsinger 2002; Betsinger and Smith 2018; Harle 2003; Schoeninger and Schurr 2007; Harle et al., this volume).

Material Culture Analysis and the Ethnohistoric Record

For decades, morphological sexing was the primary metric used to explore gender in Mississippian societies, perhaps because this was one of the only areas where females were unequivocally present. However, in the last few decades, the visibility of Mississippian women has grown as researchers, many inspired by bioarchaeological studies of Indigenous females, have actively searched for patterns of gendered behavior in the material culture record based on the assumption that masculine and feminine were two fundamental categories organizing many Indigenous Eastern Woodland societies (Briggs 2015, 2016; Claassen 2016; Eastman and Rodning 2001; Gougeon 2017). However, gendered behaviors and activities cannot be assumed, but need to be demonstrated, and for Mississippian researchers, the post-contact European ethnohistoric record is a rich source of information for delineating Indigenous gendered behaviors (LeMaster 2014).

The body of ethnohistoric literature for the Indigenous US Southeast begins in the sixteenth century and is composed of documents written by European men and a number of scholarly surveys and critical readings of these materials. The two most respected ethnohistoric scholars of US Southeastern Indigenous groups in the early to mid-twentieth century were John R. Swanton (1946) and Charles Hudson (1976), both of whom produced reference guides based on extensive surveys of primary sources documenting centuries of European colonial entanglements. Historians such as Theda Perdue, Michelle LeMaster, Robbie Ethridge, Greg O'Brien, and James Taylor Carson have built from these seminal works by interrogating primary sources and historical accounts and applying critical theoretical perspectives to produce nuanced works that highlight how Indigenous groups responded to persistent, sustained European contact.

Both Swanton and Hudson describe many Indigenous Southeastern groups as sharply divided along gender lines. According to Hudson, ". . . men and women kept themselves separate from each other to a very great extent. They seem, in fact, to have preferred to carry out their day-to-day activities apart from each other" (Hudson 1976: 260; see Perdue 1998). Hudson goes on to say that men were generally involved in hunting, political, and militaristic affairs, and were socially ranked and segmented among themselves with regard to their exploits within these venues. Men were not confined to a single social rank; age, family, and experience impacted their social position as well as their gendered practices, suggesting there were nuanced divisions of masculinity within the overarching concept. Men generally socialized in public spaces within their communities, including plaza areas, gaming grounds, and in forests surrounding towns and villages, as well as more private spaces like townhouses. Numerous European male colonists noted socializing with Indigenous men in townhouses, where they would share pipes filled with tobacco and drink cups of yaupon tea (Hudson 1976: 226, 260; 2004).

Women, on the other hand, spent much of their time socializing with other women in or near their homes (Briggs, this volume; Hudson 1976: 226; Saunders 2000: 34). Like men, women were socially ranked with regard to age, lineage, and experience, suggesting further categories under "femininity" (see Harle et al., this volume). Though the ranking system used by women was not recorded by European observers (likely because, as men, they largely socialized with Indigenous men), Indigenous women had several important sources of social power vested in them. For one, matrilineal descent was practiced in most Indigenous US Southeastern societies: descent was traced through the mother's lineage, with matrilocality the common marriage pattern (meaning men, not women, moved from their natal homes upon marriage). Matrilineal descent ensured that more than just a mother's genealogy was preserved; matrilineal descent also prescribed that ritual sacra, domestic materials, agricultural fields, and horticultural gardens pass from mother to daughter, not father to son. Women performed virtually all agricultural and horticultural activities, from sowing and planting to harvesting and storing. Men only occasionally assisted women in their agricultural duties, lending a hand to field clearing and harvesting when needed (Scarry and Scarry 2005). Women were also the cooks of their communities, transforming raw materials into beloved dishes of hominy with bear fat, hickory nut soup, and dried venison (among others), as well as the principal ceramists and craftspeople, making cooking pots and weaving baskets (Bauer 2022; Briggs, this volume; Swanton 1946; Thompson 2008). These duties were not taken for granted; women's work was celebrated within many Indigenous communities, bestowing women referential status that could be used as social currency to attain positions of social and political leadership as well as to elevate the social standing of their families. Femininity was not universally subordinate to or subjugated by masculinity; in many Southeastern groups, men and women were social equals, both necessary and vital for the continuation of the world (Etienne and Leacock 1980; LeMaster 2014; Levy 1999; Perdue 1998; Smits 1982; Sullivan 2001). Though this balance shifted in many groups by the late seventeenth and early eighteenth centuries in response to colonial entanglements, Indigenous women still maintained considerable power and freedom compared to their European and Euro-American counterparts (Sattler 1995).

Though the ethnohistoric record is a promising and underutilized source for reconstructing Mississippian gender roles, it is not without issue. Undeniably, the ethnohistoric record is a documentation of rapidly adjusting and transforming groups, responding to European colonial systems (Ethridge 2010; Miller 1994; Moss 1993). European colonial entanglements had a profound impact on Indigenous lifeways throughout the Western Hemisphere. European diseases decimated Indigenous populations, altering settlement patterns and social networks as they regrouped and restructured (Ethridge 2010). Additionally, persistent colonial entanglements encouraged (and at times forced) Indigenous groups to adapt to a Western economic system of colonial interdependence that actively undermined Indigenous sovereignty in favor of dependence on European colonial powers (Beck 2013; Kelton 2015; Lowery 2018; Marcoux 2010; Thompson 2008; Wilson 2005). For example, Indigenous groups were folded into European economic systems that favored patrilineal, not matrilineal descent, with inheritance passing from father to son. Further, European masculinity was fundamentally different from Indigenous masculinity: European men tended agricultural fields and conducted most economic transactions for the home; men were the only militaristic, political, and religious leaders; and men were the only gender permitted to attain a profession or an education outside of the home.

European colonial disruptions to Indigenous lifeways ensured the loss of important people, knowledge, places, and sacra. However, despite these losses, Indigenous groups persevered, navigating imposed Western systems of economics, politics, descent, religion, and gender that helped ensure the continuation of their lifeways (Ethridge 2010; Lightfoot 2005; Thompson 2008). Importantly, though Indigenous gender roles did change, the principles underlying Indigenous gender ideologies remained the same (LeMaster 2014; Perdue 1980). For example, though Western political activities silenced women, some Indigenous communities (such as the Cherokee) responded by entrusting Indigenous men with the responsibility of representation but continued to consult and rely on the experience and expertise of women (Cooper 2022; Harle et al., this volume; Lowery 2013). Though women were alienated from ownership and control over agricultural fields and their products, they were emboldened by Indigenous constructions of femininity, and many did not adopt the idea that women were subordinate to men (LeMaster 2014; Perdue 1980). Instead, they found ways to control and enter European colonial economic systems by engaging in black market exchanges with African and Caribbean slaves as well as marginalized European colonists to continue to provide for and elevate their families and communities (Shoemaker 1995; Usner 1992) as well as by cultivating and selling culinary and craft goods, like bacon and cooking pots (Bauer 2022; Briggs and Lapham 2022; Carson 1997; Ross 1938). Though from the European gaze, it appeared Indigenous women were learning to behave and act like European women, they were instead finding novel ways to enact Indigenous femininities within the European ideological system, ways that are often underappreciated and frequently dismissed (Briggs et al., 2023; LeMaster 2014).

Not only is the ethnohistoric record a documentation of European-Indigenous colonial entanglements, but the record itself is inherently biased, a product of the European male gaze (LeMaster 2014). Some of this bias can be mitigated—for example, we know the dearth of information about Indigenous women's activities is primarily a product of European men uninterested in documenting their work. We also know that both European men producing the ethnohistoric record and Euro-American men analyzing it were dismissive of Indigenous women's social power, practices, and even their biological activities, like menstruation and birthing. For example, according to Hudson, during both menstruation and labor, a woman was considered polluted (*sensu* Douglas 2002 [1966]) and was required to seclude herself from the rest of her town in a menstrual hut (Hudson 1976: 320). Though social isolation was an important medicine used for purification among many US Southeastern groups, we should be critical of the term "menstrual hut" and the meaning and purpose behind social isolation (Bauer 2022: 26–27; Bengtson and Alexander, this volume; Galloway 1997). Hudson suggests, for example, that menstrual isolation was a product of the hormonal mood swings females experience during menstruation, suggesting menstrual isolation was a form of social control over (monthly) deviant individuals (Hudson 1976: 320). This view of menstrual activities is common in psychological anthropological interpretations; however, for the US Southeast, it is not supported by the archaeological or ethnohistoric record, which both suggest women's houses were not "huts" but instead sacred social structures and spaces where women practiced important medicine central to femininity and the community (Bauer 2022; Bengtson and Alexander, this volume; Galloway 1998).

Not all biases in the ethnohistoric record are apparent, and many are perpetuated unquestioned (LeMaster 2014; Pate 2004). However, this does not mean the ethnohistoric record should not be used by archaeologists exploring Mississippian societies to produce gender formal analogies (Gougeon 2017). The ethnohistoric record is a key source of information for identifying materials and patterns indicative of gendered roles (*sensu* Deagan 1983). For one, the ethnohistoric record suggests many classes of materials, specifically cooking ceramics; horticultural and agricultural plants; culinary tools, foods, and spaces; maize agricultural implements and spaces; and domestic spaces are overwhelmingly representative of feminine tasks and responsibilities (Hudson 1976; Swanton 1946; see Briggs, this volume; Fritz, this volume; Gougeon, this volume; Meyers, this volume). Further, the social importance and power of femininity within post-European contact Indigenous societies suggests greater attention should be paid to the manifestation and expression of femininity in the construction of space, in ritual sacra, in social networks, and in cosmologies (Mueller and Fritz 2016; see Bengtson and Alexander, this volume; Briggs, this volume; Sharpe, this volume; Sullivan, this volume, Chapter 6; White, this volume). Women were important agents of social preservation in the post-contact period, helping to assuage colonial disruptions, and this social role may have been active in Mississippian societies as well

(Bauer 2022; Braund 2011; LeMaster 2014; Worth 2000; see Harle et al., this volume; Rodning et al., this volume).

Those studies that used the ethnohistoric record to explore gender roles in Mississippian societies produced surprising results that challenge cherished notions (in addition to those listed below, see Rodning 2011; Sullivan and Rodning 2001; Sullivan 2001). Paleoethnobotanical studies of the Eastern Complex plants, for example, demonstrated that at the site of Cahokia in the American Bottom, maize (or corn) was not the dietary staple supporting the emergence and florescence of what some have referred to as America's First City (Fritz 2019). Instead, maize was adopted and only slowly intensified within an endemic agricultural system established on the exploitation of oily, starchy seeds, such as sunflower, marshelder, and chenopodium, highlighting the significance of women's labor in and contributions to the emergence of Cahokia (Fritz 2019; Fritz, this volume). Further, Indigenous oral and written materials combined with ethnohistoric sources recording myths, stories, and cosmologies of Indigenous US Southeastern groups have also been used to reinterpret Mississippian materials, highlighting the cosmological importance of femininity in the Mississippian world (Bengtson and Alexander, this volume; Briggs 2015, 2023; Brown 2011; Diaz-Granados and Duncan 2004; Dye 2013; Emerson 1989; Knight 1986; Mueller and Fritz 2016; Pauketat et al. 2017; Sharp, this volume).

Studies using the ethnohistoric record to explore Mississippian gender roles have generally been well-received, but critics caution against using simplistic, static, or uninterrogated models (Hill 1998; Kehoe 1983; Pate 2004). Entire material classes, like stone or shell, should never be assumed to represent one gender role over another; many classes, tools, and activities may represent practice produced by overlapping gender roles (Brumbach and Jarvenpa 1997; Claassen 2016; Spector 1993). To associate specific tools, materials, or spaces with a particular gender role, the relationship has to be well-supported using several lines of evidence such as ethnohistoric documents, modern-day analogies drawn from descendant groups, biological, archaeological, experimental, or ethnoarchaeological evidence (Gougeon 2017).

Today, those lines of evidence least used to explore gender in Mississippian societies are ethnographic, ethnologic, or ethnoarchaeological research findings (Gougeon 2017; for exceptions, see Gougeon 2012; Smith 1978; Sullivan 2001; Sullivan and Rodning 2001). Each is a kind of modern-day study and record, produced by an anthropologist, who documents the lifeways of a particular group using participant observation (watching), interviews (asking), and surveys (on a scale of one to five . . . ?). Ethnoarchaeological research goes a step further by concentrating on the relationship between people and materials, paying special attention to how materials are crafted (what kind of clay is used to make a cooking pot?), the spatial layout of activity spaces (how is space organized in a culinary area?), and even participating in the activities (how hard is it to grind maize in a large wooden mortar with a five-foot pestle?). Ethnological research compiles material on various groups from across the world and through time to explore possible correlations between social institutions and practices. Mississippian researchers have also been reticent to draw on experimental archaeology. Experimental archaeology attempts to understand the processes, both natural and artificial, that produce the archaeological record.

No authors in this volume draw on ethnological, ethnographic, ethnoarchaeological, or experimental archaeological material to understand Mississippian women, but it is worth noting the possible opportunities for future researchers. Research from the ethnologic and ethnographic records suggests cross-cultural patterns among matrilineal, agriculture societies that could guide research questions and interpretations generated by Mississippian archaeologists (Peregrine 1996). Drawing on the Human Area Relation Files (HRAF), Melvin and Carol Ember (1971) offer testable insights into what conditions might be more or less suitable for the practice of matrilineal descent, the form of kinship most widely practiced throughout the indigenous Eastern Woodlands (Hudson 1976). Further, experimental archaeology is gaining considerable traction in the US Southeast (Fritz et al. 2001; Hart 2021; King et al. 2019; Mueller et al. 2017; Whyte 2019), with some studies explicitly exploring feminine gendered practices (Fritz et al. 2001; King et al. 2019). Experimental archaeology has proven an important entry point for Indigenous practitioners into the field, satisfying an interest in preservation and heritage while addressing a considerable research gap (King et al. 2009)

Gender as a Heuristic Device

Regardless of the approach, what the handful of Mississippian gender studies have demonstrated is that the exploration of gender roles in the past is not simply an exercise in "finding women," but instead a meaningful way to understand the emergence, growth, and transformation of late pre-contact and early post-European contact Mississippian societies (Nelson 2006: 6; see Briggs 2017; Fritz 2019; Gougeon 2012; Rodning 1999; Sullivan 2001, 2006). Without a doubt, the success of gendered studies is due to the way gender was and is constructed in many Indigenous societies in the US Southeast—unlike Western gender ideologies, which render all non-masculine actors socially inert, Indigenous gender ideologies vested power in all gendered categories, permitting each the ability to drive social change. Thus, while it may be challenging to research women landowners in sixteenth-century Spain or the power of nuns in Medieval France, and while women categorically may have been excluded from entering political negotiations, economic exchanges, and practicing matrilineal descent within Western colonial networks, Indigenous women did not define or understand their femininity based on Western models, and both pre- and post-European contact, they did not understand themselves as socially inert forces. During the post-contact period, they did not accept that they were not powerful, but instead found ways around Western policies intended to subjugate women so they could continue to provide for and guide their societies. They were not Western women, and we should not study them as if they were.

This means that, in the study of US Southeastern Indigenous societies, gender is a powerful heuristic device that can be used to gain greater understanding about the social, economic, political, and religious structures that shaped the development, maintenance, and decline of Mississippian societies. The chapters in this volume repeatedly demonstrate this point. They reinforce the premise that Mississippian societies were categorized along two primary gender roles, feminine and masculine, and *both* were powerful. From there, they each apply various methods and theories for exploring Mississippian women and femininity, creating a volume of embodied, Indigenous feminist work.

The Embodied Feminist Approach

Each chapter in this volume employs an embodied feminist approach (for the only exception, see White, this volume, who uses a diacritical feminist framework). An embodied feminist approach marks one of the most recent iterations in the feminist movement, stressing concepts of intersectionality, allyship, and stewardship, and deviates from previous feminist ideologies in that the lived experiences of women, and particularly women of color, are understood to be a defining characteristic impacting their femininity.

Late nineteenth and early twentieth-century Western feminist movements were spurred by the socialist writings of Karl Marx (2017 [1867]) and Friedrich Engels (2010 [1884]) and the existentialist works of Simone de Beauvoir (2011 [1949]). Marx was one of the first to question the "natural gendered order" of the Western world, proposing that women were not created inferior, but, instead, were subjugated by historical processes designed to ensure the social "superiority" of a small, powerful group of men. The basis of Marxist feminism is that within non-egalitarian, socially stratified societies, power is unequally distributed, resulting in the oppression and subjugation of marginalized classes, social groups, and economic groups. This system of oppression is a historical process, one that reinforces itself through the institutionalization of social systems that replicate the power structure, resulting in systemic, structural inequalities that are expressed ideologically and materially. Marx and Engels both insisted that women, as well as other marginalized social segments, who together represented the overwhelming majority of Western society, needed to recognize the artificial constraints that oppressed them and take control by seizing the resources and materials that fueled stratified social systems.

For future feminist movements, the key point from Marx and Engels was that women did not have to be oppressed or subjugated; this was not natural order, just an imposed one. This point resonated with Simone de Beauvoir and inspired the historical research central to *The Second Sex* (2011 [1949]). In this classic work, Beauvoir outlined the Western historical narrative of gender oppression, from the Hebrew Bible to Ancient Greece and Rome to Judeo-Christian Europe, arguing that culture, and not biology, was a strong force driving the Western social order that forced females to work in the home, be financially dependent on their male relatives and husbands, and to dedicate their lives to taking care of their children. In other words, Beauvoir presciently recognized that females do not possess innate behaviors (like being more nurturing, kinder, or gentler) that make them different from males; these are social behaviors encouraged in young girls and women to make them more docile and more likely to accept Western gender and sex ideologies. Beauvoir proposed that the historical origin of this system was the need for sexual domination over females in order to ensure masculine heirs. While a baby's mother may be obvious, prior to DNA testing, a baby's father is a less concrete matter. And while paternal insecurity was not a significant social factor in many parts of the world, in the nascent patriarchal West, paternal inheritance was the foundation of society. Political, legal, and ideological measures were taken to control women and their sexual activities, eventually disenfranchising them from all social matters. Though females had experimented with birth control measures to varying degrees in the past, Beauvoir believed that oral contraceptive birth control (better known as "the pill") would liberate women from Western social oppression by giving them control over their reproductive cycles and thus making it possible to more plan a family while enjoying sex.

Beauvoir's ideas were fundamental to the second-wave feminist movement in the West. The first wave of Western feminism was launched in the late nineteenth and early twentieth centuries when white, Western women gathered and marched for the political right to cast a vote in federal elections. For many first wave feminists, once the Nineteenth Amendment was passed, their work was complete. Second-wave feminism, on the other hand, recognized that disenfranchisement was more than the right to vote; voting was not the same as having a voice in social matters or having power to direct social change. Second-wave feminism, led by such icons as Shirley Chisholm, Betty Friedan, and Gloria Steinem, focused on identifying and dissolving the social structures and materials that oppressed and subjugated Western women. These included domestic work, childcare, cooking, cleaning, excessive attention paid to a woman's appearance, emphasis on pleasing men, marriage, as well as the social pressures exerted to ensure conformity to these institutions like stigmatization and social ostracization if a woman did not marry, if she engaged in sex before marriage, if she chose a profession over a family, and if she rejected stifling women's fashion like high-heeled shoes, tight dresses, and toxic cosmetics.

By the 1980s, however, it became clear that a one-size-fits-all model of feminism did not work for all women. First, women of color faced different systems of oppression based on their skin color than did white women; the obstacles and social barriers erected to keep them from various jobs, academies, and social institutions required different strategies to dissolve them than those faced by white women. This inspired Kimberlé Crenshaw to coin the term "intersectionality," leading to the intersectional feminist movement (or third wave feminism). However, for many Indigenous women whose ancestors lived in the US Southeast, third wave feminism suffered from the same problems as second and first wave—again, third wave feminism focused on dissolving social institutions that were historically mobilized in Western society to subjugate women but were a source of power and respect within many Indigenous communities (Mankiller 2001). Femininity was celebrated, not exploited, and cooking, caregiving, and domestic activities were sources of power, not subjugation.

Many activists say that we are currently living through a fourth feminist wave, with the signature elements of this wave being intersectionality, use of digital networks to promote social issues, and greater inclusivity of gender-related issues. While embodied approaches are not a hallmark of fourth wave feminism, they are growing in popularity, and importantly, they embrace Indigenous women in novel ways. An embodied feminist approach does not position masculinity and femininity in relation to one another, nor does it assume a power imbalance exists between them. Instead, an embodied feminist approach appreciates the lived gendered and sexed experiences of individuals and how these experiences in turn shape the social realities in which individuals are conditioned. Embodied feminist approaches are founded on the body of work produced by Pierre Bourdieu (1977, 1984; see Moi 1991), which establishes that gender, while artificial, is a strong social force constructing biological realities and lived experiences of individuals, affecting mental health, spiritual health, physical health, and life outcomes. Through an embodied perspective, femininity as well as the biological experience of being a female are explored not in their relation to masculinity but instead in relation to the social systems in which they are enacted. This final point is particularly important because it resonates with a fundamental idea of Indigenous feminism.

Indigenous Feminism

Using an embodied perspective, Indigenous feminism focuses on the lived experience of being Indigenous and living by Indigenous gender ideologies within a Western world driven by Western gender ideologies. There are several themes central to Indigenous feminism: first, that Western ideologies systematically devalue the lives of Indigenous women, who are at shockingly greater risk to experience sexual harassment, sexual violence, rape, and violent murder compared to other women, including other women of color (Deer 2015; García-Del Moral 2018). Second, that because Western ideologies are inherently based on power differentials, it is impossible to elevate Indigenous people, especially Indigenous women, within the dominant social system, fostering a call to decolonize legal, knowledge, educational, social, and professional institutions. Decolonization efforts stress that dominant Western social systems, or ones that encourage the ownership of private property, incentivize unsustainable progress and growth, establish the fundamental social category as a nuclear family (father, mother, and children), and categorically delineate the world we live in from the "wilderness," and are founded on Ancient Grecian and Roman ideas of "civilization" and "patriarchy" (Green 2017). Further, these systems are inherently broken and are designed to keep social equality and environmental sustainability from actualizing. This leads to the third theme: Indigenous feminism calls for Indigenous sovereignty, stressing that only when Indigenous groups and nations can establish the social and physical infrastructure necessary to encourage and promote Indigenous food supplies, educational opportunities, and legal systems, will Indigenous peoples truly be able to thrive in the post-contact Western Hemisphere (Green 2017).

To this end, a core mission of Indigenous feminism is to reclaim narratives and histories that have been stripped from them. This is why it is important to do more than "find Indigenous women" in the past; it is important to understand that Western ideologies only dictate the behaviors and actions of Western individuals. While Indigenous groups may have been forced into colonial economic systems, political arenas, systems of valuation, and gender-stratified societies, they continued to enact Indigenous ideologies and categories, and thus continued to be Indigenous. At times, their Indigeneity was reinforced by colonial systems that prohibited social mobility while at other times, Indigeneity was fought for when social systems demanded Western conformity.

Recent feminist approaches applied to the institution of North American archaeology highlight two general facts: first, that women archaeologists are perpetually lagging behind their masculine colleagues in virtually all metrics used to measure career success, including number of publications, tenure-track positions held, and salary and job benefits (Bardolph 2014, 2018; Bardolph and VanDerwarker 2016; Claassen et al. 1999; Fulkerson and Tushingham 2019; Sullivan 2014; Zeder 1997), speaking to systemic issues within the field and the academy itself (Meyers et al. 2018; White et al. 1999: 20–23). Second, that past and current oppressions cripple our field by stymying research questions, limiting research designs, and producing narrow interpretations of the archaeological record, resulting in the systematic dismissal of entire populations, like Indigenous women (Conkey and Spector 1984; Wobst 1978).

The general response to over-representation of white men in the academy is to promote the hiring of more women and people of color. However, many women and academics of color find higher education an uncomfortable, if not hostile, place, one that tokenizes, disproportionately calls on them for service (which is professionally undervalued), and generally expects conformity to Western social and pedagogical institutions (Carter and Craig 2022; Leighton 2020). For women in particular, research, teaching, and service expectations often conflict with maternal responsibilities, forcing them to choose—do I want to be a good professor or a good mother? Sexism is rampant in the academy, while archaeology as a discipline is structured in such a way that masculine qualities are overtly encouraged (Meyers et al. 2018; Voss 2021a; White et al. 1999): field work is often expected to be strenuous and challenging, with social capital awarded to those who ignore their discomfort; access to clean facilities for changing menstrual products are few and far between; and alcohol consumption, which has been correlated to sexual harassment and assault, is encouraged (Meyers et al. 2018). Further, sexual harassment and assault are difficult to discourage when many projects are underfunded and use temporary, poorly supervised, mixed-gender and mixed-biological sex field accommodations in unfamiliar locations; when there is little institutional or disciplinary overhead; when there is limited access to clean bathrooms; and when reporting channels and procedures for sexual misconduct are non-existent (Colaninno et al. 2021; Meyers et al. 2018; Voss 2021b). In short, archaeology has not, and continues not to be, an inclusive environment for women and/or people of color, meaning that hiring more women may not be a panacea for this broken system.

What is? Changing the infrastructure of the discipline in ways that support, encourage, and bolster women and people of color (Voss 2021b). This includes encouraging and championing more feminist and Indigenous feminist research that draws attention to the systemic inequalities inherent in the academy and helps to normalize non-Western approaches to professionalism, research, pedagogy, and the work-life balance. To some, this is backward—to make the academy more inclusive, we need more diverse viewpoints, and the way we encourage those viewpoints is to first and foremost hire more marginalized and underrepresented voices. The inherent flaw in this logic is the assumption that *only* Indigenous women can or should conduct nuanced, intersectional feminist research. Like all social justice movements, Indigenous feminism is not exclusive to Indigenous women—allyship is essential and necessary to the vision of the movement. As Fryer and Raczek note (2020), in a field historically dominated by white men, and one where women of color are all too often expected to carry the heavy and ghettoized mantle of feminist theory, "the burden should not fall predominately on the few archaeologists of color to bring nuanced, intersectional, and intersubjective analyses to the foreground" (Fryer and Razcek 2020: 16). If the onus of doing Indigenous feminist research falls only on the shoulders of the few Indigenous female and feminine scholars within US Southeastern archaeology (who, at the time of this publication, number less than a dozen), and if women and people of color are the only researchers doing nuanced, intersectional studies, then our field will continue to overly produce and promote androcentric, Western viewpoints and present a male-dominated view of the past. We will continue to alienate women and people of color, perpetuating gate-keeping measures that systematically strip them of power and voice. All archaeologists can and should be feminists, and all US Southeastern archaeologists studying Mississippian societies can and should do Indigenous feminist research; only then will our field become a more inclusive space for the diverse perspectives we desperately need.

Mississippian Women

This volume is composed of twelve chapters highlighting the social power of Mississippian women. The volume begins with a foreword by Sheila Bird, member of and former Tribal Historic Preservation Officer for the United Keetoowah Band of Cherokee Indians in Oklahoma, and she speaks to the importance of Indigenous feminist studies of the past. Archaeology began as a hunt for unique, "forgotten items," permitting the plundering of sacred sites and spaces. It was legitimized in the early twentieth century as a subdiscipline of anthropology (in North America) and history (in Europe and Asia), establishing core values, professional rigor, and methodological standardization. However, archaeology never has, nor will it ever be, an "objective investigation of the past": objectivity is a Western fallacy. Archaeology actively shapes and contributes to present-day conversations about human worth, potential, and value, and denial of this impact only perpetuates narrow and ignorant understandings of historically marginalized people while passively (if not actively) championing narratives that justify the current social order. Archaeology is most impactful when it is employed as activism, recognizing how our research is intertwined with Indigenous lives. Sheila Bird's foreword is an important reminder of this relationship.

While we are honored to have Sheila Bird as a contributor to this volume, it is imperative to state that her foreword should not be read as a statement of permission for the ideas and the authority exercised here—while we value the working relationship we have with Sheila and the impact of that relationship on this volume, responsibility for the ideas and concepts expressed here belongs solely to the editors and authors. All mistakes and transgressions are our own.

Finally, this volume stands *with* Indigenous women in the US Southeast, but does not stand *for* them. Similarly, while each chapter highlights the social impact of Mississippian women, no chapter speaks *for* Mississippian women. This volume amplifies the voices of Indigenous women, past and present, weaving together multiple lines of evidence to demonstrate to archaeologists, activists, and the general public that Indigenous femininity is a powerful, generative social force, and that Indigenous femininity will continue to drive history even if history continues to ignore it.

References Cited

Adair, James

1930 [1775] *History of the American Indians.* Promontory Press, New York.

Anderson, David G. and Kenneth E. Sassaman

2012 *Recent Developments in Southeastern Archaeology: From Colonization to Complexity.* Society for American Archaeology, Washington.

Alt, Susan

1999 Spindle Whorls and Fiber Production at Early Cahokian Settlements. *Southeastern Archaeology* 18(2): 124–134.

2020 The Implications of the Religious Foundations at Cahokia. In *Cahokia in Context: Hegemony and Diaspora*, edited by Charles H. McNutt and Ryan M. Parish, pp. 32–48. University of Florida Press, Gainesville.

Altman, Hedi M., Tanya M. Peres, and Matthew Compton

2020 Better Than Butter: *Yona Go'I,* Bear Grease in Cherokee Culture. In *Bears: Archaeological and Ethnohistorical Perspectives in Native Eastern North America,* edited by Heather A. Lapham and Gregory A. Waselkov, pp. 193–216. University of Florida Press, Gainesville.

Bardolph, Dana N.

2014 A Critical Evaluation of Recent Gendered Publishing Trends in American Archaeology. *American Antiquity* 79(3): 522–540.

2018 Controlling the Narrative: A Comparative Examination of Gendered Publishing Trends in the SCA and Beyond. *California Archaeology* 10: 159–186.

Bardolph, Dana N., and Amber M. VanDerwarker

2016 Sociopolitics and Southeastern Archaeology: The Role of Gender in Scholarly Authorship. *Southeastern Archaeology* 35: 175–193.

Bauer, Brooke

2022 *Becoming Catawba: Catawba Indian Women and Nation-Building, 1540–1840.* University of Alabama Press, Tuscaloosa.

Beauvoir, Simone de

2011 [1949] *The Second Sex.* Vintage Books, New York.

Beck, Robin A.

2013 *Chiefdoms, Collapse, and Coalescence in the Early American South.* Cambridge University Press, Cambridge.

Betsinger, Tracy K.

2002 Interrelationship of Status and Health in the Tellico Reservoir: A Biocultural Analysis. Unpublished master's thesis, Department of Anthropology, University of Tennessee, Knoxville.

Betsinger, Tracy K., and Maria O Smith

2018 Regional Differences in Caries by Sex and Social Status in Late Prehistoric East Tennessee. In *Bioarchaeology of the American Southeast: Approaches to Bridging Health and Identity in the Past*, edited by Shannon C. Hodge and Kristina Shuler, pp. 54–68. University of Alabama Press, Tuscaloosa.

Blitz, John H.

2010 New Perspectives in Mississippian Archaeology. *Journal of Archaeological Research* 18: 1–39.

Bourdieu, Pierre

1977 *Outline of a Theory of Practice.* Translated by Richard Nice. Cambridge Press, Cambridge.

1984 *Distinction: A Social Critique of the Judgement of Taste.* Translated by Richard Nice. Harvard University Press, Cambridge.

Braund, Kathryn E. Holland

2011 Reflections on 'Shee Coocys' and the Motherless Child: Creek Women in a Time of War. *Alabama Review* 64(4): 255–284.

Bridges, Patricia S.
1989 Changes in Activities with the Shift to Agriculture in the Southeastern United States. *Current Anthropology* 30: 385–394.

Briggs, Rachel V.
2015 The Hominy Foodway of the Historic Native Eastern Woodlands. *Native South* 8(1): 112–146.
2017 From Bitter Seeds: A Historical Anthropological Approach to Moundville's Origins, A.D. 1050–1120. PhD dissertation, Department of Anthropology, University of Alabama, Tuscaloosa.
2023 Edible Metaphors and the Mississippian Phenomenon: A Case Study from the Black Warrior River Valley Alabama, AD 1070–1250. In *Ancient Foodways: Integrative Approaches to Understanding Subsistence and Society*, edited by C. Margaret Scarry, Dale Hutchinson, and Benjamin Arbuckle, pp. 183–207. University of Florida Press, Gainesville.

Briggs, Rachel V., and Heather Lapham
2022 Chewing the Fat: Native Eastern Woodland Edible Metaphors of Pig and Bear. Presented at the 78th Annual Southeastern Archaeology Conference, November 9, 2022, Little Rock, Arkansas.

Briggs, Rachel V., Christopher Rodning, Robin A. Beck, and David G. Moore
2023 Fear the Native Woman: Femininity, Food, and Power in the Sixteenth-Century North Carolina Piedmont. *American Anthropology,* 1-15. DOI:10.1111/aman.13918

Brown, James
2011 The Regional Culture Signature of the Braden Art Style. In *Visualizing the Sacred: Cosmic Visions, Regionalism, and the Art of the Mississippian World* edited by George Lankford, F. Kent Reilly, and James Garber, pp. 37–63. University of Texas Press, Austin.

Brumbach, Hetty Jo, and Robert Jarvenpa
1997 Ethnoarchaeology of Subsistence Space and Gender: A Subarctic Dene Case. *American Antiquity* 62(3): 414–436.

Buikstra, Jane, and Douglas H. Ubelaker
1994 *Standards for Data Collection from Human Skeletal Remains.* Arkansas Archaeological Survey, Research Series 44, Fayetteville.

Carson, James Taylor
1997 "From Corn Mothers to Cotton Spinners: Continuity in Choctaw Women's Economic Life, A.D. 950–1830." In *Women of the American South: A Multicultural Reader,* edited by Christie Anne Farnham, pp. 8–25. New York University Press, New York.

Carter, TaLisa J., and Miltonette O. Craig
2022 It Could Be Us: Black Faculty as "Threats" on the Path to Tenure. *Race and Justice* 12(3): 569–587.

Claassen, Cheryl
1992 Questioning Gender: An Introduction. In *Exploring Gender through Archaeology,* edited by Cheryl Claasen, pp. 1–10. Monographs in World Archaeology:11. Prehistory Press, Madison, Wisconsin.

2001 Challenges for Regendering Southeastern Prehistory. In *Archaeological Studies of Gender in the Southeastern United States*, edited by Jane M. Eastman and Christopher B. Rodning, pp. 10–26. University Press of Florida, Gainesville.

2013 Fertility: A Place-Based Gift to Groups. In *Género y Arqueología en Mesoamérica. Homenaje a Rosemary Joyce*, edited by María Rodríguez-Shadow and Susan Kellogg, pp. 198–215. Centro de Estudios de Antropología de la Mujer, Las Cruces, New Mexico.

Claassen, Cheryl, ed.

2016 *Native American Landscapes: A Gendered Perspective.* University of Tennessee Press, Knoxville.

Claassen, Cheryl, Michael O'Neal, Tamara Wilson, Elizabeth Arnold, and Brent Lansdell

1999 Hearing and Reading Southeastern Archaeology: A Review of the Annual Meetings of SEAC From 1983 through 1995 and the Journal *Southeastern Archaeology. Southeastern Archaeology* 18: 85–97.

Conkey, Margaret W., and Janet D. Spector

1984 Archaeology and the Study of Gender. *Advances in Archaeological Method and Theory* 7: 1–38.

Colaninno, Carol E., Emily L. Beahm, Carl G. Crexler, Shawn P. Lambert, and Clark H. Sturdevant

2021 The Field School Syllabus: Examining the Intersection of Best Practices and Practices that Support Student Safety and Inclusivity. *Advances in Archaeological Practice* 9(4): 366–378.

Cooper, Karen Coody

2022 *Cherokee Women in Charge: Female Power and Leadership in American Indian Nations of Eastern North America.* McFarland and Company, Jefferson, North Carolina.

Deagan, Kathleen A.

1983 *Spanish St. Augustine: The Archaeology of a Colonial Creole Community.* Academic Press, New York.

Deer, Sarah

2015 *The Beginning and End of Rape: Confronting Sexual Violence in Native America.* University of Minnesota Press, Minneapolis.

Deloria, Vine, Jr.

2003 *God Is Red: A Native View of Religion.* Fulcrum Publishing, Golden, Colorado.

Diaz-Granados, Carol, and James Duncan

2004 Reflections of Power, Wealth, and Sex in Missouri Rock-Art Motifs. In *The Rock-Art of Eastern North America: Capturing Images and Insight.* Edited by Carol Diaz-Granados, and James R. Duncan, pp. 145–158. University Alabama Press, Tuscaloosa.

Douglas, Mary

2002 [1966] *Purity and Danger: An Analysis of Concepts of Pollution and Taboo.* Routledge, London.

Drooker, Penelope B.

2017 The Fabric of Power: Textiles in Mississippian Politics and Ritual. In *Forging Southeastern Identities: Social Archaeology, Ethnohistory, And Folklore of the Mis-*

sissippian to Early Historic South, edited by Gregory A. Waselkov and Marvin T. Smith, pp. 16–40. University of Alabama Press, Tuscaloosa, Alabama.

Dye, David

2013 Snaring Life from the Stars and the Sun: Mississippian Tattooing and the Enduring Cycle of Life and Death. In *Drawing with Great Needles: Ancient Tattoo Traditions of North America*, edited by Aaron Deter-Wolf and Carol Diaz-Granados, pp. 215–252. University of Texas Press, Austin.

Eastman, Jane M., and Christopher B. Rodning, eds.

2001 *Archaeological Studies of Gender in the Southeastern United States.* University Press of Florida, Gainesville.

Edwards, Tai S.

2018 *Osage Women and Empire: Gender and Power.* University Press of Kansas, Lawrence.

Ember, Melvin, and Carol Ember

1971 The Conditions Favoring Matrilocal Versus Patrilocal Residence. *American Anthropologist* 73(3): 571–594.

Emerson, Thomas

1989 Water, Serpents, and the Underworld: An Exploration into Cahokian Symbolism. In *The Southeastern Ceremonial Complex: Artifacts and Analysis*, edited by Patricia Galloway, pp. 45–92. University of Nebraska Press, Lincoln.

Emerson, Thomas E., and Timothy Pauketat

2002 Embodying Power and Resistance at Cahokia. In *Medieval Mississippians*, edited by Timothy Pauketat and Susan Alt, pp. 54–61. School for Advanced Research Press, Santa Fe, New Mexico.

Emerson, Thomas E., Kristin M. Hedman, Eve A. Hargrave, Dawn E. Cobb, and Andrew R. Thompson

2016 Paradigms Lost: Reconfiguring Cahokia's Mound 72 Beaded Burial. *American Antiquity* 81: 405–425.

Engels, Friedrich

2010 [1884] *The Origin of the Family, Private Property, and the State.* Penguin Classics, London.

Ethridge, Robbie

2009 Introduction: Mapping the Mississippian Shatterzone. In *Mapping the Mississippian Shatterzone: The Colonial Indian Slave Trade and Regional Instability in the American South*, edited by Robbie Ethridge and Sheri M. Shuck-Hall, pp. 1–62. University of Nebraska Press, Lincoln.

2010 *From Chicaza to Chickasaw: The European Invasion and the Transformation of the Mississippian World, 1540–1715.* The University of North Carolina Press, Chapel Hill.

Etienne, Mona, and Eleanor Leacock, eds.

1980 *Women and Colonization: Anthropological Perspectives.* Praeger, New York.

Fine, Cordelia

2017 *Testosterone Rex: Myths of Sex, Science, and Society.* Icon Books Publishing, London.

Fowler, Melvin L., Jerome Rose, Barbara Vander Leest, and Steven Ahler
1999 *The Mound 72 Area: Dedicated and Sacred Space in Early Cahokia.* Illinois State Museum Reports of Investigations No 54. Illinois State Museum Society, Springfield.

Fritz, Gayle J.
2019 *Feeding Cahokia: Early Agriculture in the North American Heartland.* University of Alabama Press, Tuscaloosa.

Fritz, Gayle J., Virginia Drywater Whitekiller, and James W. McIntosh
2001 Ethnobotany of Ku-nu-che: Cherokee Hickory Nut Soup. *Journal of Ethnobiology* 21(2):1–27.

Fryer, Tiffany C., and Teresa P. Raczek
2020 Introduction: Toward an Engaged Feminist Heritage Praxis. *Archaeological Papers of the American Anthropological Association* 31: 7–25.

Fulkerson, Tiffany J., and Shannon Tushingham
2019 Who Dominates the Discourses of the Past? Gender, Occupational Affiliation, and Multivocality in North American Archaeology Publishing. *American Antiquity* 84(3): 379–399.

Galloway, Patricia K.
1998 Where Have All the Menstrual Huts Gone? The Invisibility of Menstrual Seclusion in the Late Prehistoric Southeast. In *Women in Prehistory: North American and Mesoamerica,* ed. by Cheryl Claassen and Rosemary A. Joyce, pp. 47–62. University of Pennsylvania Press, Philadelphia.

García-Del Moral, Paulina
2018 The Murders of Indigenous Women in Canada as Feminicides: Toward a Decolonial Intersectional Reconceptualization of Femicide. *Signs: Journal of Women in Culture and Society* 43(4): 929–954.

Gilchrist, Roberta
2009 The Archaeology of Sex and Gender. In *The Oxford Handbook of Archaeology,* ed. by Barry Cunliffe, Chris Gosden, and Rosemary Joyce, pp. 1929–1047. Oxford University Press, Oxford.

Goldstein, Lynne
2000 Mississippian Ritual as Viewed through the Practice of Secondary Disposal of the Dead. In *Mounds, Modoc, and Mesoamerica: Papers in Honor of Melvin L. Fowler,* edited by Steven R. Ahler, pp. 193–206. Illinois State Museum, Scientific Papers, Vol. XXVIII. Illinois State Museum, Springfield.

Gougeon, Ramie A.
2012 Activity Areas and Households in the Late Mississippian Southeast United States: Who Did What Where? In *Ancient Households of the Americas,* edited by J. Douglas and N. Gonlin, pp. 141–162. University Press of Colorado, Boulder.
2017 Considering Gender Analogies in Southeastern Prehistoric Archaeology. *Southeastern Archaeology* 36(3): 183–194.

Green, Joyce, ed.
2017 *Making Space for Indigenous Feminism, Second Edition.* Fernwood Publishing, Black Point, Nova Scotia.

Greenberg, David
1988 *The Construction of Homosexuality.* University of Chicago Press, Chicago.
Hally, David
2008 *King: The Social Archaeology of a Late Mississippian Town in Northwestern Georgia.* University of Alabama Press, Tuscaloosa.
Harle, Michaelyn S.
2003 A Bioarchaeological Analysis of Fains Island. Unpublished master's thesis, Department of Anthropology. University of Tennessee, Knoxville.
Hart, John P.
2021 The Effects of Charring on Common Bean (*Phaseolus vulgaris* L) Seed Morphology and Strength. *Journal of Archaeological Science: Reports* 37. DOI: 10.1016/j.jasrep.2021.102996.
Hatch, James W.
1975 Social Dimensions of Dallas Burials. *Southeastern Archaeological Conference Bulletin* 18: 132–138.
Hill, Erica
1998 Gender-informed Archaeology: The Priority of Definition, the Use of Analogy, and the Multivariate Approach. *Journal of Archaeological Method and Theory* 5(1): 99–128.
Hudson, Charles
1976 *The Southeastern Indians.* University of Tennessee Press, Knoxville.
2004 *Black Drink: A Native American Tea.* University of Georgia Press, Athens.
2005 *The Juan Pardo Expeditions: Explorations of the Carolinas and Tennessee, 1566–1568.* Revised Edition. University of Alabama Press, Tuscaloosa.
Joyce, Rosemary A. and Cheryl Claassen
1997 Women in the Ancient Americas: Archaeologists, Gender, and the Making of Prehistory. In *Women in Prehistory: North America and Mesoamerica,* edited by Cheryl Claassen and Rosemary A. Joyce, pp. 1–14. University of Pennsylvania Press, Philadelphia.
Kehoe, Alice B.
1983 The Shackles of Tradition. In *The Hidden Half: Studies of Plains Indian Women,* edited by P. Albers and B. Medicine, pp. 53–73. University Press of America, Lanham, Maryland.
Kelton, Paul
2015 *Cherokee Medicine, Colonial Germs: An Indigenous Nation's Fight Against Smallpox, 1518–1824.* University of Oklahoma Press, Norman.
King, Megan M., Roger Cain, and Shawna Morton Cain
2019 An Experimental Ethnoarchaeological Approach to Understanding Development Use Wear Associated with the Processing of River Cane for Split-cane Technology. *Southeastern Archaeology* 38(1): 38–53.
Knight, Vernon J.
1986 The Institutional Organization of Mississippian Religion. *American Antiquity* 51:675–687.

Lankford, George E.
2008 *Looking for Lost Lore: Studies in Folklore, Ethnology, and Iconography.* University of Alabama Press, Tuscaloosa.
Leighton, Mary
2020 Myths of Meritocracy, Friendship, and Fun Work: Class and Gender in North American Academic Communities. *American Anthropologist* 122(3): 433–458.
LeMaster, Michelle
2014 Pocahontas Doesn't Live Here Anymore: Women and Gender in the Native South before Removal. *Native South* 7: 1–32.
Levy, Janet E.
1999 Gender, Power, and Heterarchy in Middle-Level Societies. In *Manifesting Power: Gender, and the Interpretation of Power in Archaeology*, edited by T. L. Sweely, pp. 62–78. Routledge, London.
2014 What I Believe: Doing Archaeology as a Feminist. *Southeastern Archaeology* 33(2): 226–237.
Lightfoot, Kent
2005 *Indians, Missionaries, and Merchants: The Legacy of Colonial Encounters on the California Frontiers.* University of California Press, Berkeley.
Lowery, Malinda Maynor
2013 Kinship and Capitalism in the Chickasaw and Choctaw Nations. In *The Native South: New Histories and Enduring Legacies*, edited by Tim Alan Garrison and Greg O'Brien, pp. 200–219. University of Nebraska Press, Lincoln.
2018 *The Lumbee Indians: An American Struggle.* University of North Carolina Press, Chapel Hill.
Manion, Jen
2020 *Female Husbands: A Trans History.* Cambridge University Press, Cambridge.
Mankiller, Wilma
2001 *Every Day Is a Good Day: Reflections by Contemporary Indigenous Women.* Fulcrum Publishing, Golden, Colorado.
Marcoux, Jon
2010 *Pox, Empire, Shackle, and Hides: The Townsend Site, 1670–1715.* University of Alabama Press, Tuscaloosa.
Marx, Karl
2017 [1867] *Capital, Volume 1: A Critique of Political Economy.* Digireads.com Publishing.
Meyers, Maureen S., Elizabeth T. Horton, Edmond A. Boudreaux, Stephen B. Carmody, Alice P. Wright, and Victoria G. Deckle
2018 The Context and Consequences of Sexual Harassment in Southeastern Archaeology. *Advances in Archaeological Practice* 6(4): 275–287.
Miller, Bruce G.
1994 Contemporary Native Women: Role Flexibility and Politics. *Anthropologica* 36(1): 57–72.
Moi, Toril
1991 Appropriating Bourdieu: Feminist Theory and Pierre Bourdieu's Sociology of Culture. *New Literary History* 22(4): 1017–1049.

Moss, Madonna L.
1993 Shellfish, Gender, and Status on the Northwest Coast: Reconciling Archeological, Ethnographic, and Ethnohistorical Records of the Tlingit. *American Anthropologist* 95(3): 631–652.

Mueller, Natalie G., and Gayle J. Fritz
2016 Women as Symbols and Actors in the Mississippi Valley: Evidence from Female Flint-Clay Statues and Effigy Vessels. In *Native American Landscapes: An Engendered Perspective*, edited by Cheryl Claassen, pp. 109–150. University of Tennessee Press, Knoxville.

Mueller, Natalie G., Gayle Fritz, Paul Patton, Stephen Carmody, and Elizabeth T. Horton
2017 Growing the Lost Crops of the Eastern North America's Original Agricultural System. *Nature Plants* 3. DOI: 10.1038/nplants.2017.92.

Nelson, Erin Stevens, Ashley Peles, and Mallory A. Melton
2023 A Mississippian Example of Harvest Renewal Ceremonialism. In *Ancient Foodways: Integrative Approaches to Understanding Subsistence and Society*, edited by C. Margaret Scarry, Dale Hutchinson, and Benjamin Arbuckle, pp. 152–182. University of Florida Press, Gainesville.

Nelson, Sarah M.
2006 Introduction: Archaeological Perspectives on Gender. In *Handbook of Gender in Archaeology*, edited by Sarah M. Nelson, pp. 1–27. AltaMira Press, Berkeley.

Panich, Lee M., and Sarah L. Gonzalez, eds.
2020 *The Routledge Handbook of the Archaeology of Indigenous-Colonial Interaction in the Americas*. Routledge, London.

Pate, Laura
2004 The Use and Abuse of Ethnographic Analogies in Interpretation of Gender Systems at Cahokia. In *Ungendering Civilization*, edited by J. A. Pyburn, pp. 71–93. Routledge, New York.

Pauketat, Timothy, Susan Alt, and Jeffery D. Kruchten
2017 The Emerald Acropolis: Elevating the Moon and Water in the Rise of Cahokia. *Antiquity* 91(355): 207–222.

Peasantubbee, Michelene E.
2005 *Choctaw Women in a Chaotic World: The Clash of Cultures in the Colonial Southeast*. University of New Mexico Press, Albuquerque.

Peebles, Christopher, and Susan M. Kus
1977 Some Archaeological Correlates of Ranked Societies. *American Antiquity* 42(3): 421–448.

Perdue, Theda
1980 Southern Indians and the Cult of True Womanhood. In *The Web of Southern Social Relations: Women, Family, and Education*, edited by Walter J. Fraser Jr., R. Frank Saunders, and Jon L. Wakelyn, pp. 35–51. University of Georgia Press, Athens.
1998 *Cherokee Women: Gender and Culture Change, 1700–1835*. University of Nebraska Press, Lincoln.

Peregrine, Peter N.
1996 Ethnology versus Ethnographic Analogy: A Common Confusion in Archaeological Interpretation. *Cross-Cultural Research* 30:316–329.

Purcell, Gabrielle
2023 Connecting the Present to the Past: How Collaborative Archaeology Can Inform Us about Ancient Foodways. In *Ancient Foodways: Integrative Approaches to Understanding Subsistence and Society*, edited by C. Margaret Scarry, Dale L. Hutchinson, and Benjamin S. Arbuckle, pp. 327–344. University Presses of Florida, Gainesville.

Reilly, F. Kent, III, James F. Garber, and George E. Lankford.
2011 Introduction. In *Visualizing the Sacred: Cosmic Visions, Regionalism, and the Art of the Mississippian World,* edited by George E. Lankford, F. Kent Reilly III, and James F. Garber, pp. xi–xviii. University of Texas Press, Austin.

Rodning, Christopher B.
1999 Archaeological Perspectives on Gender and Women in Traditional Cherokee Society. *Journal of Cherokee Studies* 20: 3–27.
2011 Mortuary Practices, Gender Ideology, and the Cherokee Town at the Coweeta Creek Site. *Journal of Anthropological Archaeology* 30(20):145–173.

Ross, Elizabeth
1938 "The Chief's Sausage Grinder." Indian Pioneer Oral History Project, Works Progress Association, accessed on November 4, 2022: https://digital.libraries.ou.edu/cdm/singleitem/collection/indianpp/id/6212/rec/1

Sattler, Richard A.
1995 The Southeast: Women's Status among the Muskogee and Cherokee. In *Women and Power in Native North America*, edited by Laura F. Klein, pp. 214–229. University of Oklahoma Press, Norman.

Saunders, Rebecca
2000 The Guale Indians of the Lower Atlantic Coast: Change and Continuity. In *Indians of the Greater Southeast*, edited by Bonnie G. McEwan, pp. 26–56. University Press of Florida, Gainesville.

Scarry, C. Margaret, and John F. Scarry
2005 Native American "Garden Agriculture" in Southeastern North America. *World Archaeology* 37: 259–274.

Schneider, Tsim D.
2021 "Dancing on the Brink of the World": Seeing Indigenous Dance and Resilience in the Archaeology of Colonial California. *American Anthropologist* 123(1): 50–66.

Schoeninger, Margaret J., and Mark R. Schurr
2007 Human Subsistence at Moundville: The Stable-Isotope Data. In *Archaeology of the Moundville Chiefdom*, edited by Vernon James Knight, Jr. and Vincas P. Steponaitis, pp. 120–132. University of Alabama Press, Tuscaloosa.

Sherwood, Sarah C., and Tristram R. Kidder
2011 The DaVincis of Dirt: Geoarchaeological Perspectives on Native American Mound Building in the Mississippi River Basin. *Journal of Anthropological Archaeology* 30: 69–87.

Shoemaker, Nancy

1995 Introduction. In *Negotiators of Change: Historical Perspectives on Native American Women*, edited by Nancy Shoemaker, pp. 1–25. Routledge, New York.

Smith, Bruce D.

1978 *Prehistoric Patterns of Human Behavior: A Case Study in the Mississippi Valley.* Academic Press, New York.

Smith, Claire, and H. Martin Wobst

2005 *Indigenous Archaeologies: Decolonizing Theory and Practice.* One World Archaeology, Volume 47. Routledge, London.

Smithers, Gregory D.

2014 Cherokee "Two Spirits": Gender, Ritual, and Spirituality in the Native South. *Early American Studies* 3: 626–651.

Smits, Daniel D.

1982 The "Squaw Drudge:" A Prime Index of Savagism. *Ethnohistory* 29(4): 281–306.

Snyder, Christina

2009 The Lady of Cofitachequi: Gender and Political Power among Native Southerners. In *South Carolina Women: Their Lives and Times—Volume 1*, edited by Marjorie Julian Spruill, Valinda W. Littlefield, and Joan Marie Johnson, pp. 11–25. University of Georgia Press, Athens.

Spector, Janet D.

1993 *What This Awl Means: Feminist Archaeology at a Wahpeton Dakota Village.* Minnesota Historical Society Press, Saint Paul.

Spradley, M. Katherine and Richard J. Jantz

2011 Sex estimation in Forensic Anthropology: Skull versus postcranial elements. *Journal of Forensic Sciences* 56(2): 289–296.

Spradley, M. Katherine, Richard J. Jantz, Richard Alan Robinson, and Fredy Peccerelli

2008 Demographic Change and Forensic Identification: Problems in Metric Identification of Hispanic Skeletons. *Journal of Forensic Sciences* 53: 21–28.

Sullivan, Lynne P.

1995 Mississippian Household and Community Organization in Eastern Tennessee. In *Mississippian Communities and Households*, edited by J. Daniel Rogers and Bruce D. Smith, pp. 99–123. University of Alabama Press, Tuscaloosa.

2001 Those Men in the Mounds: Gender, Politics, and Mortuary Practices in Eastern Tennessee. In *Archaeological Studies of Gender in the Southeastern United States*, edited by Jane M. Eastman and Christopher B. Rodning, pp. l0l–126, University Press of Florida, Gainesville.

2006 Gendered Contexts of Mississippian Leadership in Southern Appalachia. In *Borne on a Litter with Much Prestige: Leadership and Polity in Mississippian Society*, edited by Paul Welch and Brian Butler, pp. 264–285, Occasional Paper No. 33, Center for Archaeological Investigations, Southern Illinois University, Carbondale.

2014 What I Believe: Taking Up the Serpents of Social Theory and Southeastern Archaeology. *Southeastern Archaeology* 33(2): 238–245.

Sullivan, Lynne P., and Christopher B. Rodning

2001 Gender, Tradition, and the Negotiation of Power Relationships in Southern Appalachian Chiefdoms. In *The Archaeology of Traditions: Agency and History Before and After Columbus*, edited by Timothy R. Pauketat, pp. 107–120. University Press of Florida, Gainesville.

2011 Residential Burial, Gender Roles, and Political Development in Late Prehistoric and Early Cherokee Cultures of the Southern Appalachians. In *Residential Burial: A Multi-Regional Exploration*, edited by Ron Adams and Stacie King, pp. 79–97. AP3A Series, American Anthropological Association, Washington D.C.

Sullivan, Lynne P., and Michaelyn Harle

2010 Mortuary Practices and Cultural Identity at the Turn of the Sixteenth Century in Eastern Tennessee. In *Mississippian Mortuary Practices: Beyond Hierarchy and the Representationist Perspective*, edited by Lynne P. Sullivan and Robert C. Mainfort, Jr., pp. 234–249. University Press of Florida, Gainesville.

Swanton, John R.

1946 *Indians of the Southeastern United States.* Bureau of American Ethnology Bulletin 137. Smithsonian Institution, Washington, D.C.

Thomas, Larissa A.

1996 A Study of Shell Beads and Their Social Context in the Mississippian Period: A Case from the Carolina Piedmont and Mountains. *Southeastern Archaeology* 15: 29–46.

Thompson, Ian

2008 Chata Intikba Im Aiikhvna (Learning from the Choctaw Ancestors): Integrating Indigenous and Experimental Approaches in the Study of Mississippian Technology. Unpublished PhD dissertation, Department of Anthropology, University of New Mexico, Albuquerque.

Trocolli, Ruth

1999 Women Leaders in Native North American Societies: Invisible Women of Power. In *Manifesting Power: Gender and the Interpretation of Power in Archaeology*, edited by Tracy L. Sweely, pp. 49–61. Routledge, London.

2002 Mississippian Chiefs: Women and Men of Power. In *The Dynamics of Power*, edited by M. O'Donovan, pp. 168–187. Occasional Paper Np. 30. Center for Archaeological Investigations. Southern Illinois University, Carbondale.

Usner, Daniel

1992 *Indians, Settlers, and Slaves in a Frontier Exchange Economy: The Lower Mississippi Valley Before 1783.* University of North Carolina Press, Chapel Hill.

Voss, Barbara L.

2008 Gender, Race, and Labor in the Archaeology of the Spanish Colonial Americas. *Current Anthropology* 49(5): 861–893.

2021a Documenting Cultures of Harassment in Archaeology: A Review and Analysis of Quantitative and Qualitative Research Studies. *American Antiquity* 86(2): 244–260.

2021b Disrupting Cultures of Harassment in Archaeology: Social-Environmental and Trauma-Informed Approaches to Disciplinary Transformation. *American Antiquity* 86(2): 447–464.

Walker, Phillip L.

1995 Problems of Preservation and Sexism in Sexing: Some lessons from Historical

Collections for Paleodemographers. In *Grave Reflections: Portraying the Past Through Cemetery Studies*, edited by Shelly Saunders and Ann Herring, pp. 31–48. Canadian Scholar's Press, Toronto.

Weiss, Kenneth
1972 On the Systematic Bias in Skeletal Sexing. *American Journal of Physical Anthropology* 37:239–249.

White, Nancy Marie, Lynne P. Sullivan, and Rochelle A. Marrinan, eds.
1999 *Grit-Tempered: Early Women Archaeologists in the Southeastern United States.* University Press of Florida, Gainesville.

Whyte, Thomas R.
2019 An Experimental Study of Bean and Maize Burning to Interpret Evidence from Stillhouse Hollow Cave in Western North Carolina. *Southeastern Archaeology* 38(3). DOI: 10.1080/0734578X.2019.1616275.

Wilson, Waziyatawin Angela
2005 Introduction: Indigenous Knowledge Recovery is Indigenous Empowerment. *American Indian Quarterly* 28(3/4): 359–372.

Wobst, H. Martin
1978 The Archaeo-ethnology of Hunter-Gatherers, Or the Tyranny of the Ethnographic Record in Archaeology. *American Antiquity* 43: 303–309.

Worth, John
2000 The Lower Creeks: Origins and Early History. In *Indians of the Greater Southeast*, edited by Bonnie G. McEwan, pp. 265–298. University Press of Florida, Gainesville.

Zeder, Melinda
1997 *The American Archaeologist: A Profile.* AltaMira Press, Walnut Creek, California.

2

Recognizing Women at Cahokia

Farmers; Weavers; Agents of Polity Integration

Gayle J. Fritz

Archaeologists working in the Eastern Woodlands and Plains, including the Mississippi and Missouri river valleys, agree that pre-contact farming across this broad region was primarily the domain of Native American women. Historical and ethnographic sources all document a gender-based division of labor in which crops, at times excepting tobacco, were planted, tended, harvested, and processed either for immediate consumption or for storage by women and girls (Edwards 2018; Hudson 1976; Hunter 1985; Peters 1995; Scarry and Scarry 2005; Swanton 1979 [1946]; Thomas 2001; Watson and Kennedy 1991; Wilson 1987 [1917]). Individuals known today as two-spirit people probably joined their sisters in agricultural tasks (Edwards 2018: 19). Men contributed by clearing trees from heavily wooded fields and probably by helping to bring in harvests during situations such as weather-related emergencies. Iroquois and Hidatsa men helped women de-husk corn after it was harvested, enabling it to be put away for storage before the onset of inclement weather (Parker 1910; Wilson 1987 [1917]). Hidatsa women, however, dug their enormous storage pits by themselves (Wilson 1987 [1917]), an example of heavy labor not requiring male assistance.

In the American Bottom region of southwestern Illinois, considerable expanses of agricultural land in the Mississippi River floodplain and adjoining uplands had been cleared and converted to tilled fields centuries before Cahokia became an urban center at ca. A.D.1050 (Fritz 2019; Munoz et al. 2014). Family groups moving into the region at the time of Cahokia's consolidation into an aggregated, integrated polity may well have required additional field acreage, but old-growth or long-fallowed woods on well-drained soils in the floodplain were probably already scarce. Pollen cores analyzed by Munoz et al. (2014) indicate that significant clearance of trees took place during the Late Woodland period (A.D. 400–900), corresponding to archaeobotanical evidence for large-scale production of domesticated chenopod (*Chenopodium berlandieri* ssp. *jonesianum*), erect knotweed (*Polygonum erectum* ssp. *watsoniae*), maygrass (*Phalaris caroliniana*) and other members of the Eastern Agricultural Complex (or Eastern Complex) (Simon and Parker 2006). Maize (*Zea mays* ssp. *mays*) was incorporated into this group of native crops at ca. AD 900, resulting in the biologically diverse agricultural system that supported urban Cahokia for several centuries thereafter (Johannessen 1984, 1993; Lopinot 1994, 1997; Parker 2014; Simon 2014, 2017).

I return below to the importance of a diversified food production system in discussions of the roles and statuses of women at Cahokia. The key points here are that we can safely assume women were the farmers, and that their knowledge, labor, and strategic coordination and implementation of activities produced the food crops fueling the largest Mississippian center in North America. Women's roles, responsibilities, and influences extended beyond the foods they grew and cooked to broader economic, political, and ritual arenas, shaping the structure of neighborhoods, communities, and the Cahokian landscape.

I begin by critiquing constructions of sociopolitical organization at Cahokia that fail to recognize women as farmers or that relegate farmers to a bottom-tier class of commoners who worked the fields to provision authority-wielding elites. Next, I give examples of recent research elevating the statuses of women in Mississippian ideology and social structure. I move on to document the evidence for diversity, first within human populations moving into the American Bottom during the eleventh century AD, and second, in the mixture of maize and pre-maize Eastern Complex crops grown by Cahokia's farmers. I argue that women were essential agents in disseminating agronomic knowledge, managing access to field plots, and leading rituals that integrated newcomers into the expanding and increasingly complex social order.

The Status(es) of Farmers

Cahokia's massive scale, unmatched anywhere in the Mississippian world, makes it difficult to explain the structure of its hierarchy and the workings of its political and ritual economy. Archaeologists have not reached a consensus on Cahokia's sociopolitical organization, but a prominent school of thought holds that a demographic and social transformation occurred at AD 1050, with powerful leaders instituting a four-tiered settlement hierarchy with Cahokia and other large mound centers at the top and rural food-producing communities at the bottom. Emerson (1992: 201), for example, classifies farmsteads and hamlets as fourth-tier sites occupied by farmers producing food "for the populations of the larger communities." Emerson (1992: 201) continues: "A basic assumption of the model is that tight political, religious, and economic control emanated from a centralized Cahokian elite over the entire American Bottom."

Exhibits in the Interpretive Center at Cahokia Mounds State Historic Site reflect this four-tiered, centralized, top-down model, including murals and other visual props that clearly depict the ruling elites as men. The Cahokia Mounds State Historic Site Volunteer Handbook, revised in February of 2019, and given to all volunteers, places a "Paramount Chief" at the top of "Cahokia's system of social control" (29): "He may have claimed divine power. . . . He and his family led a life of privilege, possibly on Monk's Mound, with their needs provided for by others." According to this guide, the second "class" consisted of "The Elite," including priests, elders, and sub-chiefs, who were also privileged and who "ruled the satellite communities" (30). Below the elites was a class of "Leaders" described as "headmen of clans and communities" who "designed and supervised public construction projects and farming activities." These duties were seen as carried out "under the direction of the elite" (30). At the base of the system were "Commoners": "They grew the corn, built the mounds and stockade, and made their living as tradesmen, artisans, warriors, hunters, and fishermen." This lowest-ranking "class" toiled at the ground level of what is described in the volunteer manual as the "food chain of command": "Commoners produced abundant corn and other crops in their fields. The greater part of harvest was due in political and religious tribute to the elite" (30).

Gender-specific terms that give men and only men positions of authority are not universal in peer-reviewed publications, but interpreters at public sites, including Cahokia Mounds, take their cues from professional archaeologists. A new exhibit at Cahokia, "Wetlands and Waterways," does explicitly credit women as being the farmers, a fact that is not otherwise obvious from the museum's exhibits or from the volunteer manual. As welcome as this attribution is, it might unintentionally serve to undermine the status of women overall, since farmers are categorized elsewhere as commoners who labored first and foremost to provision those born into higher ranks than themselves, and who were said to be supervised by "headmen" rather than making their own decisions. An exhibit depicting aspects of hierarchy and succession, for example, includes no women in the top two levels of society, and places women in the third tier only on the bottom of three sub-levels constituting that societal segment (Figure 2.1).

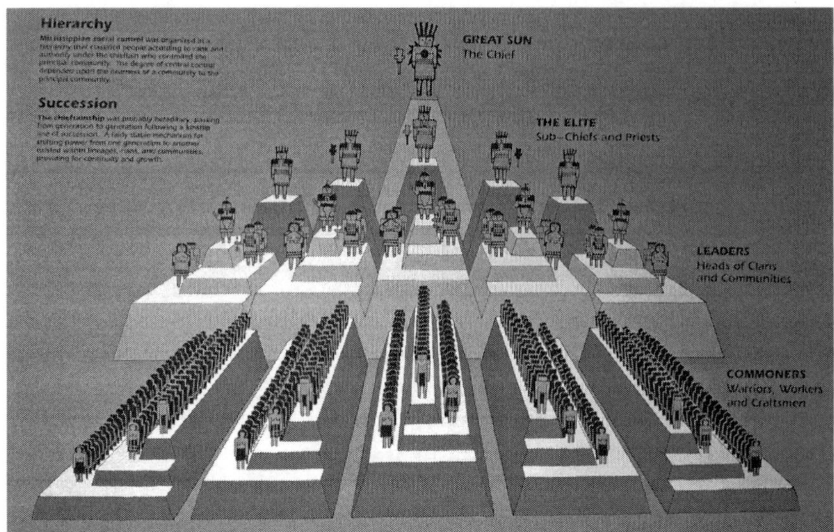

Figure 2.1. Social organization exhibit at Cahokia Mounds State Historic Site Interpretive Center. Note lack of women in top two tiers. Note presence of women in third tier, but only on lowest of that tier's three levels. Image courtesy of Cahokia Mounds State Historic Site.

Volunteers at Cahokia Mounds and other public archaeological museums are hard-working, competent individuals without whom the facilities could not function. Statements from their training manual that I criticize here were obviously written to depict a hierarchical social system that would make sense to members of the general public who visit this iconic site. It is easy for a professional archaeologist to fault these terms and statements for being at best simplistic, at worst blatantly sexist, and almost certainly incorrect. However, the written works and spoken words of academics and authors of cultural resource management (CRM) reports serve as the foundation for public exhibits and interpretive manuals, and women have rarely, until very recently, been given credit for leadership or agency of any kind, at any level.

Heightened Attention to Mississippian Women in the American Bottom Region

Two relatively recent research-related developments position women either directly or indirectly as influential players in the Cahokian world order and cosmic scheme. First is the importance of lunar cycle orientations, specifically at Emerald Mounds, an Early Mississippian ceremonial shrine complex containing 12 mounds, located 24 km east of Cahokia in the uplands above

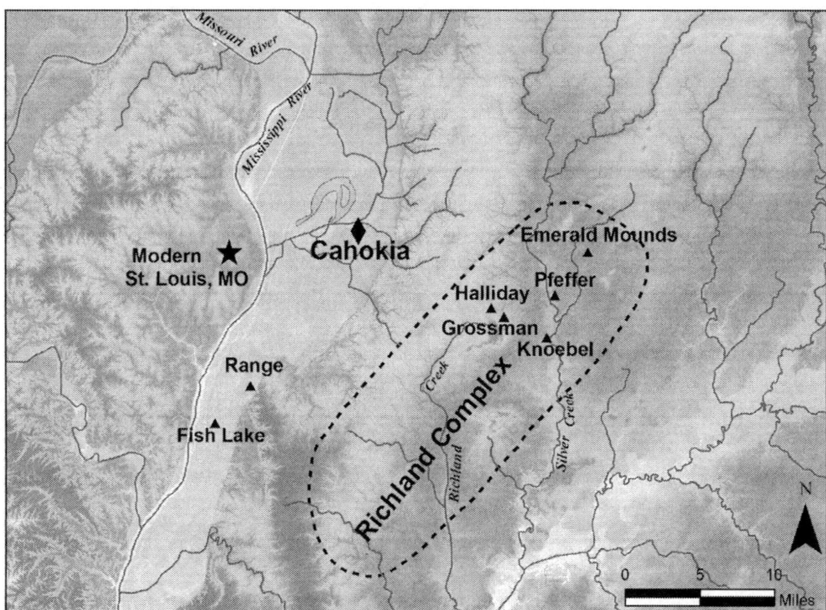

Figure 2.2. Map of the greater American Bottom region. The diamond symbol marks the location of Cahokia. Other mounds and non-mound sites are marked by triangles.

the American Bottom floodplain (Figure 2.2). Most of the hundreds of structures at this center date to the Lohmann phase (AD 1050–1100) and Stirling phase (AD 1100–1200), although the earliest shrine houses were built during the Emergent Mississippian Edelhart phase (AD 1000–1050) (Pauketat et al. 2017).

The Emerald Acropolis itself was built on a glacial ridge oriented along a northeast-southwest axis that corresponds to the maximum north moonrise, an astronomical phenomenon occurring once every 18.6 years. Numerous other alignments, both lunar and solar, have been recognized in the orientations of architectural complexes at Emerald. Pauketat et al. (2017: 218–219) discuss ethnographically recorded associations between the moon, femininity, fertility, and water central to Siouan and Caddoan ideology, which is relevant because central Siouan groups today (including Osage, Omaha, Quapaw, Kansa, Iowa, and Ho-Chunk) likely include descendants of ancient Cahokians. "Feminine powers" are seen by Pauketat et al. (2017:219) as holding fundamental and "causal significance" in the "founding and enlargement of Emerald and Cahokia" and in the religious movement that expanded from there.

Another recent research development—reanalysis of burials from Cahokia's Mound 72—sheds light directly on the status of women at early Cahokia (Emerson et al. 2016). Meticulous examination of osteological remains, maps, photographs, and excavation notes necessitated major reinterpretation of key burial groups, including Feature 101 ("the Beaded Burial Complex"), long interpreted as two high-status probable males, one (Burial 13) laid on top and the second (Burial 14) positioned underneath a deposit of more than 20,000 marine shell beads. Four individuals buried near the central burials in Feature 101 were seen as retainers. Feature 101 was arguably the most spectacular burial group in one of Mound 72's three sub-mound mortuary clusters (72 Sub 1), but seven partially articulated burials (Feature 102), laid in a row to the southwest of Feature 101, were accompanied by bundles of arrows, stone discoidals, sheets of mica, copper tubes, and deposits of shell beads including some that were strung together. Three individuals in a group labeled Feature 104 were later placed at the base of a shaft situated on top of Feature 102.

Previous interpretations by Fowler et al. (1999) held that Burial 13, the individual interpreted as lying on top of the shell beads in Feature 101, was a very high-status chief, or that the two central individuals (Burials 13 and 14) represented chiefs of the Sky World and Earth World, respectively, along with four retainers (Emerson et al. 2016: 411). After close reexamination, however, six previously unreported individuals were recognized. Most striking was the realization that Burials 13 and 14 were not both males as previously inferred, but rather a male and a female. Burial 14, which had been thought to be probably male and buried beneath the layer of shell beads on top of which Burial 13 was lain, is now described as a young adult female, 20–25 years old, whose upper torso was not separated by beads from Burial 13 (a young adult male), and whose lower body had a layer of beads below it (Emerson et al. 2016: 413). In other words, Burials 13 and 14 were both laid on shell beads, although beads also covered the legs of Burial 14, and Burial 13 was partially positioned to overlie Burial 14. More beads extended "beneath and along the right side of Burial 13" (Emerson et al. 2016: 413). Emerson et al. (2016: 420) question the interpretation that these beads represent a cape or blanket, instead describing them as "a structured deposit laid down as part of this event."

Feature 101 also included a secondary bundled burial of a male and a female (Emerson et al. 2016: 413). Instead of the originally reported 17 individuals in the 72 Sub 1 area, there are now 23 individuals, 10 of which could be sexed as females and seven as males. Very poor preservation prevents many of the burials recovered from Mound 72 from being classified as either male or female.

Remains of the seven individuals in Feature 102 (associated with the projectile points, discoidals, copper, etc.) were poorly preserved and were not originally assigned a sex. The new study, using dental discriminant function analysis, gives five—all young adults—the status of possible females. Sex of the other two is indeterminate (Emerson et al. 2016: 415). Females are now seen as "dominant" in the Beaded Burial group, corresponding to "the well known importance of female depictions in early Cahokia figurines," emphasizing "the role of fertility and life renewal motifs" (Emerson et al. 2016: 421). Rather than a direct reflection of one or more paramount chiefs accompanied by retainers, or a staged tableau featuring a mythological male warrior hero, the central burials in Mound 72 showcase women along with men, and the women appear anything but subordinate. Women were not a background chorus, but central members of the cast in whatever ritualized performance was being acted out.

These archaeological revelations are roughly contemporaneous with the publication of Tai S. Edwards's (2018) book, *Osage Women and Empire: Gender and Power.* Edwards emphasizes the positions of respect and authority held by Osage women throughout the challenging colonial period and the indispensability of the contributions they made as producers of children and plant foods, house builders and house owners, and core participants, along with men, in ritual and social activities, many of which embodied the fundamental cosmological complementarity of male and female powers.

In-Migration and Diversity at Early Cahokia

Strontium isotope analyses indicate that people who spent their earlier years in other regions moved into and died at Cahokia and the East St. Louis mound center during the eleventh and twelfth centuries AD (Nash et al. 2018; Slater et al. 2014). This evidence highlights the attraction of Cahokia for outsiders, along with the successful implementation of mechanisms to integrate newcomers into the expanding social order as individuals, as families, and probably as larger social groups. Isotopic data are, as yet, unable to pinpoint source areas, but regions suggested on the basis of material culture include southeastern Missouri, northeastern and east-central Arkansas, and the Yankeetown cultural area of southern Indiana and northern Kentucky (Alt 2002, 2006; Pauketat 2009). Production of Eastern Complex crops had been practiced for centuries across the proposed midcontinental homelands. Maize had likely been grown in many parts of the Midwest before AD 1000 as well, although its antiquity in each local region needs to be verified by directly dated archaeobotanical remains, as demonstrated by Simon (2017) for the greater American Bottom area.

Some archaeologists are reluctant to use the words "farmers" or "agriculturists" when writing about pre-maize Eastern Complex food producers, assuming that the terms "gardeners" and "horticulturalists" are more appropriate for Late Woodland societies in eastern North America. I disagree (Fritz 2019), drawing upon voluminous flotation-derived data for great abundance and high ubiquity of domesticated and cultivated indigenous starchy seeds in refuse pits and other archaeological contexts, dominating Late Woodland assemblages not only in the American Bottom, but across the central Mississippi River valley, the lower Illinois, Arkansas, and Ohio river valleys, and into the Ozark Highlands and upland South (Johannessen 1993). Although it is not possible to estimate the proportion of dietary contribution made by pre-maize crops, it is clear that Patrick phase (AD 650–900) settlements such as Fish Lake and Range were fueled by the combination of starchy and oily seeds, nuts and fruits, fish, waterfowl, and the large and small mammals that were available in both floodplain and nearby upland settings (Parker 2014; Simon and Parker 2006). As mentioned earlier, the pollen record from Horseshoe Lake reflects a significant reduction of arboreal species before AD 900, almost certainly due to clearance for fields (Munoz et al. 2014, 2015).

Pre-maize Native American food production is usually envisioned as low-level, shifting, slash-and-burn horticulture (e.g., Koldehoff and Galloy 2006), but this is difficult to reconcile with the density and strategic locations of settlements and the size and contents of features. I suggest that Late Woodland farmers such as those at Fish Lake tilled sizable fields that were open for many years, with any short-term shifting that occurred taking place among plots inside the boundaries of these semi-permanent fields rather than among fields planted for only a few years and then left to fallow for long stretches. Cahokia was quite different from Moundville and other southern Mississippian centers in that there was no direct and relatively rapid transition from foraging to a heavily maize-based agricultural economy. For centuries prior to the intensification of maize and rapid growth of urban Cahokia, the local economy included a significant segment based on Eastern Complex crops, and this is reflected by the material culture as well as the sizes, distribution, and contents of features (Johannessen 1993). Notable changes in ceramic technology—thinner walls and the manufacture of more globular jars—coincided with increasing dependence on native starchy seeds during the Late Woodland period, before the incorporation of maize into midcontinental cuisines (Braun 1983, 1987).

Agrobiodiversity

Like Mississippian farmers elsewhere, women across the greater American Bottom region grew maize, sunflowers (*Helianthus annuus* var. *macrocarpus*), bottle gourds (*Lagenaria siceraria*), and pepo and cushaw squashes (*Cucurbita pepo* ssp. *ovifera* and *Cucurbita argyrosperma* ssp. *argyrosperma*). Common beans (*Phaseolus vulgaris*) are absent from the record until the late thirteenth century, and are uncommon even then, which is not surprising given our current understanding of how long it took for midcontinental North American farmers to embrace this crop notwithstanding its nutritional advantages and nitrogen-fixing properties (Monaghan et al. 2014; Simon and Parker 2006). By the time beans earned their status as the third sister in the triad of squash, corn, and beans, Cahokia was well on its way to being depopulated. The native wild bean *Strophostyles helvola,* however, is present in many American Bottom assemblages, and may have been quasi-cultivated in the fields of the region.

Even without domestic beans, the Early Mississippian cropping system here was diversified by the inclusion of all members of the Eastern Complex. Mexican pepo pumpkins (*C. pepo* ssp. *pepo*) may also have spread into the North American heartland by AD 1050 or soon thereafter, but it will probably take ancient DNA research to distinguish the seeds or rind of that species from those of the cushaw and the ovifera squash cultivars.

The long history of massive flotation recovery and the heavy investment in analysis of archaeobotanical remains by regional experts situate the American Bottom at the forefront of places where subsistence systems are well known through time (Johannessen 1984, 1993; Lopinot 1991, 1994, 1997; Parker 1989, 2003, 2014; Simon and Parker 2006, to cite only a few of the many relevant reports by these and other authors). As soon as the earliest monographs were published summarizing the results of CRM work done for the highway project designated FAI-270, it was clear that Eastern Complex crops contributed heavily to the diets of Late Woodland, Emergent Mississippian, and Mississippian period Cahokians. Maize was incorporated into the cuisine at ca. AD 900 (Simon 2014, 2017), and while it obviously became a crucial staple food and a necessary element in Cahokia's rapid rise, it did not supplant the older, previously grown crops. The success of urban Cahokia must be credited to farmers who understood the needs and qualities of this entire suite of foods.

Evidence for a mixed and diversified system on both sides of the Emergent Mississippian/Mississippian boundary comes from several sources. Various

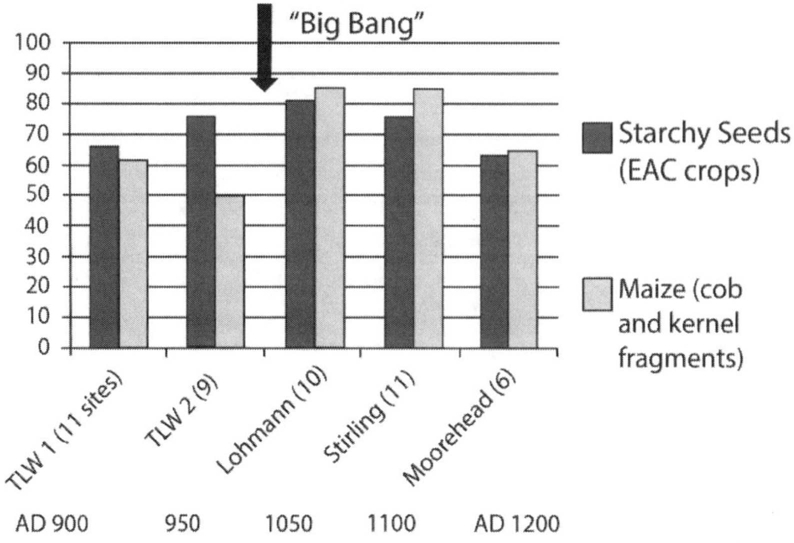

Figure 2.3. Average ubiquity values (percentage of flotation samples containing either starchy seeds or maize) for American Bottom sites, by time period. Data from Simon and Parker (2006).

archaeobotanical indexes show no decline in abundance of Eastern Complex crops from AD 900 to AD 1200 (Figures 2.3 and 2.4). The percentage of features in which a seed type occurs—known as ubiquity—for the starchy seeds (chenopod, maygrass, erect knotweed, and little barley), for example, rises from approximately 60% at AD 900–1000 and 50% at AD 1000–1050 to over 80% at AD 1050–1100, and it holds steady at AD 1100–1200. Maize was already relatively common before AD 1050, but less ubiquitous than starchy seeds as a group. The ubiquity of maize during the Early Mississippian Lohmann and Stirling phases (AD 1050–1200) was only slightly higher than starchy seed crops even though inedible cob fragments are included in this statistic along with kernel fragments. Ubiquity values of both maize and starchy seeds fell slightly but remained between 60 and 65% during Moorehead phase times (AD 1200–1275).

Density values (number of fragments per 10 liters of soil floated) for both maize and starchy seed crops are similarly at their highest during the Lohmann phase, Cahokia's period of most rapid population growth. Both crop categories rose significantly in density from their Emergent Mississippian (also

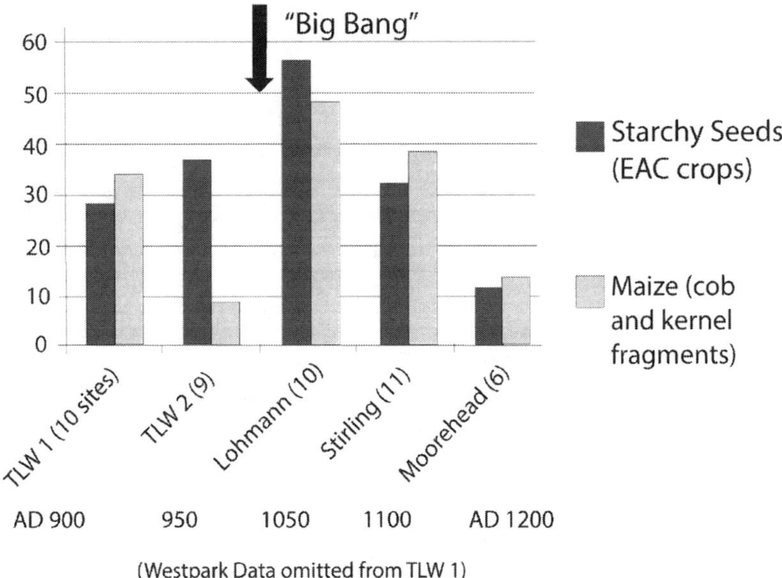

Figure 2.4. Average density values (number of fragments of maize or starchy seeds per 10 liters of soil floated) for American Bottom sites, by time period. Data from Simon and Parker (2006).

known as Terminal Late Woodland [or TLW from here on]) levels (Figure 2.4). Stirling phase density values for maize, again including cob as well as kernel fragments, are only slightly higher than those for starchy seeds, and both fall dramatically after AD 1200. I suspect many of the features excavated at Moorehead phase sites were less rich in organic remains overall than those at earlier components, because other types of evidence document the increased importance, rather than decline, of maize in the late Mississippian diet.

The presence of starchy seed masses at three Lohmann phase components, down from six for early Emergent Mississippian (TLW1), but the same number as reported for later Emergent Mississippian (TLW2) sites, again shows continuity of agrobiodiversity rather than decline in production of Eastern Complex crops when Cahokia boomed. Maize does, however, display increasing dominance by replacing the native seed crops in masses during the Stirling and Moorehead phases. Although Eastern Complex crops appear to have been processed and stored in lower volumes after AD 1200, they do not fall off completely until after the entire population moved away. Sunflowers and ovifera squashes persisted, but the high oil content of their seeds makes them far less likely to be preserved than their starchy-seeded counterparts; therefore, charting their frequencies through time is difficult.

Successful incorporation of maize into the previously existing agricultural system enabled far more mouths to be fed, and it complicated the tilling, planting, and harvesting schedules, but total transformation of field locations and layouts would have been unnecessary. Late Woodland occupants of the American Bottom were already serious food producers who had cleared fields that probably remained open for decades rather than being left fallow after a few years of cultivation. Sunflowers, squashes, and bottle gourds were already planted by burying one or a few seeds by hand, using a digging stick or hoe, the way maize was also planted. Archaeologists often speculate that the smaller-seeded native crops were hand-broadcast and allowed to grow in dense stands, but their optimal productivity also depends on spacing between individual plants (Mueller et al. 2017). The strategy of planting maize in evenly spaced, low mounds or hills may not have been much different from long-practiced methods of crop production.

Large, monocropped fields of maize probably did not exist in the American Bottom. An infield/outfield system described for Mississippians elsewhere in the Southeast may not apply in the American Bottom, with its extensive ridges, swales, point bars, old terraces, and alluvial/colluvial fans. Fields of various sizes and shapes probably occupied most prime agricultural soil outside the boundaries of densely occupied residential and ceremonial precincts, with maize, sunflower, sumpweed, squashes, gourds, chenopod, erect knotweed, and the two early-season grasses planted according to season and moisture level of specific soils (Fritz 2019). Intercropping or polycropping of older and newer crops was probably common, but exact patterning is unknown.

Polity Integration

Food Security for Newcomers

Wherever the non-local Early Mississippians came from, and to whatever degree they were already expert gardeners or farmers, they needed access to sufficient land to grow crops in order to feed the expanded population of Greater Cahokia. This process seems to have involved people from far enough away that they probably spoke multiple languages and self-identified in manners we would see today as ethnically distinct. Alt (2018: 6) discusses this phenomenon as an example of hybridity and a case study where "a profound effect" is evident: "the mixing of local and non-local people at and around Cahokia would have necessitated large-scale negotiations of difference in people's ways of being in and relating to the world." At Cahokia, locals and non-locals "created new cultural forms under novel situations of cultural contact" (Alt 2018: 14).

Fortuitously but not by accident, Alt's research rests heavily on her work in the Richland Complex, a cluster of sites in the uplands east of Cahokia, including the shrine complexes and mound centers of Emerald, with its 12 mounds, and Pfeffer with 10 mounds, along with well-studied settlements such as Halliday, Grossman, and Knoebel. The existence of a diverse agricultural system in which maize was grown along with the full suite of Eastern Complex crops is amply documented by the archaeobotanical remains (Simon and Parker 2006). Stone hoes and Mill Creek chert hoe flakes are abundant, as are spindle whorls attesting to the manufacture of twine and textiles. The presence of women as farmers and weavers is highly visible at these sites.

Access to suitable land for fields would have been one of the most important negotiating points for new and old residents. Women were the experts in soil qualities and crop attributes, motivated to observe and learn from other women the nuances of moisture and texture variation across the floodplain with its ridges, swales, meander scars, and swampy wetlands and the uplands with tillable alluvial bands near waterways such as Richland and Silver Creek. I argue that newly arriving families included prominent members of the communities from which the immigrants came. Some new arrivals, perhaps many, may have shared clan affiliations with those already living in the American Bottom area, and others may have been adopted or offered membership in sodalities (organizations that crosscut kinship). I agree with Beck (2006) that early Cahokia (prior to AD 1200) appears to conform to a constituent hierarchy rather than an apical one, meaning that aggregation was achieved by persuasion rather than coercion, and centralization was limited. Whether or not the force that drew so many people to Cahokia during the eleventh century was primarily ideological—a new religious movement in the view of Pauketat et al. (2017)—recruitment of immigrants probably involved retention of their previously held statuses—some higher and some lower—rather than subjugation of non-natives into a putative commoner class. Women belonged to many different social groups, and as farmers, they must have participated in, if not controlled, the process of land-use rights distribution. Not only was their agronomic expertise essential, but their added labor was needed to increase agricultural productivity and to support the aggregation, expansion, and construction of a ritual landscape dwarfing in scale all others in North America. Supplying tribute in the form of surplus produce was, however, not necessarily the task that Cahokian farmers perceived as their primary responsibility.

Divine and Worldly Integrative Mechanisms

An outcome of decades-long research efforts focusing on the iconography and symbolism manifested by Cahokia-style female flint-clay figurines is the interpretation that they represent a supernatural earthmother personage (Colvin 2012; Emerson 2022; Emerson et al. 2016; Duncan and Diaz-Granados 2004; Fritz 2019; Mueller and Fritz 2016), ancient enough to predate the adoption of maize but with strong enough influence to persist into the later, maize-dominated era. Modern Siouan speakers, including the Mandan and Hidatsa, recognize a mythic figure with regenerative powers called Grandmother or Old Woman Who Never Dies. She protects children and guides the souls of those who die young into the afterlife. She receives offerings from farmers seeking successful crop yields, and many sacred bundles contain objects in her repertoire (Bowers 1992 [1963]; Peters 1995). Hidatsa women of childbearing age whose statuses by birth and whose achievements as productive members of society (including as farmers) enabled them to buy into the sodality known as the Goose Society focused many of their activities around her, such as the blessing of seeds prior to planting and participation in other ceremonies to ensure bountiful harvests.

Cahokia-style figurines manufactured from red flint clay that was quarried from sinkholes located near the Missouri River west of St. Louis (Emerson and Hughes 2000; Emerson et al. 2002) were made in the twelfth century (Stirling phase, AD 1100–1200) rather than during the earliest days of urban Cahokia. They do, however, likely serve as dramatic images of a deeply rooted female power to whom farmers were devoted. Emerson (2022: 204) stresses the association of the female stone figures found at Greater Cahokia with temple structures and feature complexes that "indicate the existence of male and female religious practitioners who likely performed seasonal rites of intensification as part of established cults or religious activities associated with agricultural fertility, world renewal, and cycles of life and death." Other connections are possible, including an hypothesized role played by the statues in gender-specific sodalities (Colvin 2012; Mueller and Fritz 2016).

If a sodality such as the Goose Society existed at early Cahokia, it could have helped to integrate farmers across the American Bottom. Mandan and Hidatsa women did not make all of the decisions related to food production independently from male chiefs in their earth-lodge villages, and Cahokian farmers probably likewise worked together with kinsmen in efforts to allocate plots and to redistribute seed stock and surplus. To discount women's roles in determining land-use rights, field distribution, crop patterning, and intra-regional provisioning, however, seems certain to result in failure to accurately comprehend the past. For women not to have been central agents of agricultural administration at Cahokia would have been a recipe for frequent and widespread hunger.

Cahokia's Spinners and Weavers

Mississippian women living at Richland Complex sites not only grew crops on the prime agricultural soils of this upland zone (see Mt. Pleasant 2015 for relevant soils data), but at least some engaged in textile production. An unusually large number of spindle whorls—perforated pottery discs—ranging from 2.95 cm to 12.74 cm in diameter came from the Halliday site, and they were concentrated in a limited number of features rather than being distributed randomly across the site. Spindle whorls (76 disks, 66 of which were centrally drilled) were found in 25 features out of the total 163 features at this large Lohmann phase village, with 36 disks being found in only four features. The nearby Grossman and Knoebel sites also yielded high densities of drilled ceramic disks. Alt (1999, 2015) excavated, measured, and reported on this distinctive artifact type, and her insightful analysis brings to life the hidden industry of yarn and textile manufacture, an important aspect of material culture that is often neglected or even forgotten due to the extreme unlikelihood of organic preservation. Relying on historic and ethnographic accounts, we can infer that Mississippian women did the weaving (Alt 1999: 129; Hunter 1985; Swanton 1979 [1946]). Unlike farming, however, the production of at least some types of textiles was probably restricted to a subset of specialists or experts. Alt emphasizes the crucial function of clothing and other textiles for signaling social rank and identity, suggesting persuasively that it is no coincidence that spindle whorls increase in visibility across the American Bottom during Cahokia's growth spurt: "It seems likely that political consolidation at Cahokia was accompanied by a corresponding requirement for markers of status and position" (Alt 1999: 131).

Some species of plants yielding useful fibers, such as dogbane (*Apocynum cannabinum*) and rattlesnake master (*Eryngium yuccifolium*), were probably cultivated in the fields and gardens of both upland and lowland Greater Cahokia. Dogbane, also known as Indian hemp, is easily cultivated and grows as a weedy plant in agricultural fields in the American Bottom region today. I know of no archaeobotanical record from the American Bottom of carbonized seeds or stems of dogbane or any other major fiber plant, but this is not surprising given the low likelihood of their deposition and preservation. Regardless, access to dependable sources of fiber would require management, and Mississippian farmers could easily have augmented the natural populations within their domesticated landscape, possibly by encouraging them in the same fields where they grew food crops.

Floods, Droughts, Maize, and the "Collapse" of Cahokia

Studies by Benson et al. (2009), Munoz et al. (2014, 2015), and Bird et al. (2017) have directed professional and popular attention to climate change and its possible role in the decline of Cahokia as a city, a magnet for pilgrims and immigrants, and a hub of influence and power. Various types of environmental data show that climatic conditions were favorable during the decades of Cahokia's rise and maximum population density, but that a series of major droughts began as early as AD 1100, causing unfavorable, unpredictable environmental conditions. Hypotheses that a major flood occurred at approximately AD 1200 or that floods and detrimental rises in water table were caused by overuse of wood on the part of urban Cahokians have recently been challenged by Rankin et al. (2021), who found a stable ground surface beneath Mound 5, a Mississippian earthwork in the floodplain of Cahokia Creek, north of Monks Mound. Geomorphological evidence for deforestation severe enough to result in frequent flooding corresponded to nineteenth-century Euro-American activities, not Native American ones.

Maize is typically highlighted as *the* key food crop that people depended upon so heavily that its poor harvests would have triggered societal collapse across the American Bottom region and beyond. A journalistic coverage of the article by Bird et al. (2017) begins with the headline: "1,000 Years Ago, Corn Made This Society Big. Then a Changing Climate Destroyed It" (Chen, NPR, February 10, 2017). Science writer Angus Chen summarizes sedimentary core stratigraphy from a lake in northeastern Indiana, approximately 570 km from Cahokia, to support the authors' (Bird et al. 2017) conclusions that a switch from several centuries of adequate moisture to a prolonged dry spell began around AD 1200, at which time (as phrased by Chen): "the weather became poor for growing corn."

Deteriorating climatic conditions are correlated with increased signs of political instability and violence. Cahokia's wooden palisade, formerly interpreted as having been initially constructed during the middle of the twelfth century, has been re-dated using Bayesian modeling to AD 1250 (Krus 2016), a time of clear evidence for systemic conflict to the north, in the Central Illinois River Valley (Milner 1991; VanDerwarker and Wilson 2016). In the words of Bird et al. (2017: 9), "Shorter and drier growing seasons during the time would have significantly reduced agricultural yields, thereby contributing to intensified resource-related conflict that ultimately undermined the sociopolitical fabric and population dynamics of midcontinental Mississippian societies."

By AD 1200, maize had become the dominant crop in the American Bottom and across the midcontinent, but it was still augmented at Cahokia by Eastern Complex species with their diverse tolerances to high and low moisture levels, and with different seasonal life cycles that potentially moderated risks caused by unpredictable rainfall patterns. Mt. Pleasant (2015) argues convincingly that historical maize yield estimates projected back to ancient Cahokia are unreasonably low. This challenges the notion that agricultural productivity was inadequate to feed bottomland settlements either before or after AD 1200, when droughts evidently became severe across large parts of the American Midwest. Furthermore, population levels had dropped considerably by and after AD 1200. Out-migration probably began during the Late Stirling phase (AD 1150–1200) and accelerated during the thirteenth-century Moorehead phase, both in the floodplain proper and the upland Richland Complex region (Benson et al. 2009; Pauketat and Lopinot 1997). Although Cahokia was still a major center and was well connected to powerful Mississippian polities to the south and southeast, far fewer mouths in the American Bottom needed to be fed after AD 1200. A kin- and sodality-based system of field scattering across higher and lower elevation soils, together with social mechanisms of distributing food to those who lost most of their crops in a bad season, might have provided food sufficiency except during years of catastrophic failure.

Mississippian women were the farmers whose agronomic expertise and managerial skills were as essential as their labor, and whose responsibilities to the prosperity of their families and of the larger community dominated their actions. When and if security was compromised by regional conflicts, these farmers, together with their male kin, were called upon to make decisions such as pulling in the fields close to palisaded or otherwise protected settlements, even moving considerable distances to less violence-prone regions. Maize was a dependable and productive crop that could be intensified on smaller, more easily defended plots when constriction was necessary. Agrobiodiversity might have been sacrificed by no longer planting the full suite of Eastern Complex crops across the broad, undulating, and poorly defensible floodplain. This was also the time when common beans were incorporated into the system, although few have been recovered from Moorehead and Sand Prairie phase sites within the American Bottom. In the Central Illinois River Valley to the north, beans first became abundant in the Larsen phase occupation (AD 1250–1300) at the Meyer-Dickson site during a time of "heightened warfare and violence" (VanDerwarker and Wilson 2016: 85). As an intercropped companion plant that climbs up maize stalks and adds protein to the diet, beans could have offset the decline in nutritious Eastern Complex plants including chenopod, sumpweed, and maygrass, while taking up little space.

Interestingly, no reduction in levels of maize production through time are detectable by comparison of standardized counts of plant remains from four well-studied Early and Middle Mississippian sites (AD 1100–1300) in the Central Illinois River Valley. Even as abundance of starchy and oily-seeded native crops ebbed, and as frequencies of foraged foods got lower, maize held steady: "The continuity in maize abundance and the decline in wild plant foods together suggest that villages reduced their subsistence-related mobility" (VanDerwarker and Wilson 2016: 93). Maize was not a casualty of climatic deterioration and rising conflict in the midcontinent or Southeast. Rather, farmers appear to have depended on maize to an even greater degree than before, as other options became untenable.

Concluding Discussion

Women at Cahokia played important roles as the primary producers and gatherers of plant food, as weavers, and as performers of rituals conducted to ensure harvests, among many other activities. They are likely to have been among the administrators of land and surplus food distribution policies. As managers of fields (perhaps as owners, as was the case for historical Osage women) and overseers of subsistence-related tasks, women can be envisioned as key players in the socialization of newly arrived families at Cahokia. Depending on where they came from and when they arrived, new women were likely to have been accomplished growers of Eastern Complex crops, and they probably brought distinct landraces with them, both of the pre-maize native species and of maize itself. Growing all types and varieties of crops in the varied geomorphological settings of the American Bottom region was complicated. Hours each day spent by groups of women preparing for planting, sowing seeds, thinning plants, weeding, harvesting, and processing produce would have forged relationships and allowed multiple opportunities for immigrants to learn about American Bottom soils, foodways, and other social customs, especially if family plots were located next to each other in large, open fields as they were in historic Hidatsa territory (Wilson 1987 [1917]). Later, their responses to adverse climatic conditions and accelerated levels of conflict in the region made the difference between life and death, even if moving out of Cahokia was the final solution.

Although I doubt the existence of a centralized agricultural authority system managed by and for the primary benefit of a restricted elite class, it does seem likely that respected and knowledgeable women in highly ranked families were positioned to make decisions concerning land-use rights and to influence the hosting of events such as feasts at which food was redistributed. In other words, these farmers held prominent statuses and assumed consequential roles. Successful food production, moreover, offered an avenue for wealth acquisition and elevation of rank by farmers whose status by birth may have been less privileged.

Francis La Flesche (1930) recorded a traditional Osage practice involving a weaver that exemplifies how highly regarded a skilled Dhegiha Siouan woman could be and how essential her contributions were to tribal rituals. Kehoe (2007) vividly summarizes the relevant narrative of "The Weaver," part of the Osage rite of the *Wa-xo'-be*. Central to the *Wa-xo'-be A-wa-tho* ritual, which was attended by priests from the 24 Osage clans, is a hawkskin symbolizing a warrior's valor, kept rolled up in a rush mat woven by a woman "who has purchased the right to perform this ritual act" (Kehoe 2007: 251). A new mat was ceremoniously woven when a man came forward to be inducted into the priesthood, with the weaver first approached and formally beseeched by a caller (*Sho'-ka*) bearing a buffalo robe, bearskin, and other items brought by the initiate to compensate the weaver and provide materials she needs to perform this task. After accepting the mission and the gifts, the weaver spent four days secluded in a separate house or behind a partition in her house, rubbing mud on her face each morning and fasting. The male initiate to the priesthood also spent those four days keeping vigil, fasting, and wailing. At the end, the weaver and the initiate shared a meal cooked by one of the women's relatives, with the weaver reciting verses "giving symbols of reaching old age" (Kehoe 2007: 251).

This ritual illustrates the principle of complementary gender roles that Edwards (2018) emphasizes is foundational to Osage cosmology and which permeated their traditional village layout, art, and behavior. It is tempting to interpret the Beaded Burial in Mound 72, now seen as including two male-female pairs, as manifesting this principle.

> Osage cosmology embodied the union of masculine and feminine forces in the universe, which translated into a system of gender complementarity that dominated their lives. Women had innate power as the creators of human life, while men earned power through protecting and providing for women and children. The ability to dominate others did not determine gender status or power. Both genders constituted necessary pairs, and all of their work ensured, with *Wa-kon'-da's* aid, Osage perpetuation and prosperity. (Edwards 2018: 36)

The weaver memorialized by La Flesche may or may not have been born into a highly ranked kin group, but her indispensable role in the *Wa-xo'-be* ceremony clearly reflects her weaving skills as well as her knowledge of sacred verses. If she worked as a farmer or had done so earlier in her life, she may have actually cultivated fiber plants, although in this case, the green cattail and linden used for the warp and weft of the rush mat were probably gathered from wild stands.

It is not necessary to downplay the degree of complexity of sociopolitical organization at ancient Cahokia in order to recognize the presence and significance of women at all levels of economic and ritual operations. That Cahokia was designed and built according to a plan reflecting the cosmos has long been appreciated (Kelly 2006). Betzenhauser and Pauketat (2019) have recently made a strong case for what they, following Emerson (1997), call "architecture of power," the tight orientation and arrangement of both domestic and specialized structures "in socially and cosmologically meaningful ways" at both the East St. Louis and Cahokia Mounds precincts and across rural stretches of Greater Cahokia. Women who walked out daily from their houses to their fields understood this order, and their innate powers, skills, and material contributions were essential to its formation and maintenance for generations.

Acknowledgments

I am grateful to Bill Iseminger for sharing the image used in Figure 2.1 and to Kelly Ervin for drafting Figure 2.2. My sincere appreciation goes out to all the archaeologists who excavated, floated, and analyzed plant remains from tens of thousands of features at sites across the greater American Bottom region, especially to Sissel Johannessen, Neal Lopinot, Katie Parker, and Mary Simon. In recognizing the legacies of Indigenous farmers who supported ancient Cahokia, I hope to see a revival of crop diversity and agricultural sustainability in the Mississippi River valley.

References Cited

Alt, Susan M.

1999 Spindle Whorls and Fiber Production at Early Cahokian Settlements. *Southeastern Archaeology* 18: 124–133.

2002 Identities, Traditions, and Diversity in Cahokia's Uplands. *Midcontinental Journal of Archaeology* 27: 217–236.

2006 The Power of Diversity: Settlement in the Cahokian Uplands. In *Leadership and Polity in Mississippian Society*, edited by Brian M. Butler and Paul D. Welch, pp. 289–308. Occasional Paper No. 33. Center for Archaeological Investigations, Southern Illinois University, Carbondale.

2015 The Fabric of Mississippian Society. In *Medieval Mississippians: The Cahokian World*, edited by Timothy R. Pauketat and Susan M. Alt, pp. 75–80. School for Advanced Research Press, Santa Fe.

2018 *Cahokia's Complexities: Ceremonies and Politics of the First Mississippian Farmers*. University of Alabama Press, Tuscaloosa.

Beck, Robin A.

2006 Persuasive Politics and Domination at Cahokia and Moundville. In *Leadership and Polity in Mississippian Society*, edited by Brian M. Butler and Paul D. Welch, pp. 19–42. Center for Archaeological Investigations, Occasional Paper No. 33. Southern Illinois University Carbondale.

Benson, Larry V., Timothy R. Pauketat, and Edward R. Cook

2009 Cahokia's Boom and Bust in the Context of Climate Change. *American Antiquity* 74: 467–483.

Betzenhauser, Alleen, and Timothy R. Pauketat

2019 Elements of Cahokian Neighborhoods. In *Excavating Neighborhoods, A Cross-Cultural Exploration*, edited by David Pacifico and Lise Truex, pp. 133–147. Archaeological Papers of the American Anthropological Association No. 30.

Bird, Broxton W., Jeremy J. Wilson, William P. Gilhooly III, Bryon A. Steinman, and Lucas Stamps

2017 Midcontinental Native American Population Dynamics and Late Holocene Hydroclimate Extremes. *Nature Scientific Reports* 7: 41628. DOI:10.1039/srep41628.

Bowers, Alfred W.

1992 [1963] *Hidatsa Social and Ceremonial Organization*. University of Nebraska Press, Lincoln.

Braun, David P.

1983 Pots as Tools. In *Archaeological Hammers and Theories*, edited by James A. Moore and Arthur S. Keene, pp. 107–134. Academic Press, New York.

1987 Coevolution of Sedentism, Pottery Technology, and Horticulture in the Central Midwest, 200 B.C.–A.D.600. In *Emergent Horticultural Economies in the Eastern Woodlands*, edited by William F. Keegan, pp. 153–181. Center for Archaeological Investigations, Occasional Paper No. 7. Southern University Illinois, Carbondale.

Cahokia Mounds State Historic Site

2019 Volunteer Handbook. Revised February 2019.

Chen, Angus
2017 "1,000 Years Ago, Corn Made This Society Big. Then, A Changing Climate Destroyed It." The Salt: National Public Radio, February 10, 2017.
Colvin, Matthew H.
2012 Old-Woman-Who-Never-Dies: A Mississippian Survival in the Hidatsa World. Master's thesis, Anthropology Department, Texas State University, San Marcos.
Duncan, James R., and Carol Diaz-Granados
2004 Empowering the SECC: The "Old Woman" and Oral Tradition. In *The Rock-Art of Eastern North America: Capturing Images and Insights*, edited by Carol Diaz-Granados and James R. Duncan, pp. 190–215. University of Alabama Press, Tuscaloosa.
Edwards, Tai S.
2018 *Osage Women and Empire: Gender and Power.* University Press of Kansas, Lawrence.
Emerson, Thomas E.
1992 The Mississippian Dispersed Village as a Social and Environmental Strategy. In *Late Prehistoric Agriculture: Observations from the Midwest*, edited by William I. Woods, pp. 198–216. Illinois Historic Preservation Agency, Studies in Illinois Archaeology, No. 8. Springfield.
1997 *Cahokia and the Archaeology of Power.* University of Alabama Press, Tuscaloosa.
2022 Interpreting Context and Chronology of Cahokia-Caddo Mythic Female Stone Figures. *Southeastern Archaeology* 41(4): 203–215.
Emerson, Thomas E., and Randall E. Hughes
2000 Figurines, Flint Clay Sourcing, the Ozark Highlands, and Cahokian Acquisition. *American Antiquity* 65(1): 79–101
Emerson, Thomas E., Kristin M. Hedman, Eve A. Hargrave, Dawn E. Cobb, and Andrew R. Thompson
2016 Paradigms Lost: Reconfiguring Cahokia's Mound 72 Beaded Burial. *American Antiquity* 81: 405–425.
Emerson, Thomas E., Randall E. Hughes, Mary R. Hynes, and Sarah U. Wisseman
2002 Implications of Sourcing Cahokia-Style Flint Clay Figurines in the American Bottom and the Upper Mississippi River Valley. *Midcontinental Journal of Archaeology* 27: 309–338.
Fowler, Melvin L., Jerome Rose, Barbara Vander Leest, and Steven Ahler
1999 *The Mound 72 Area: Dedicated and Sacred Space in Early Cahokia.* Illinois State Museum Reports of Investigations No 54. Illinois State Museum Society, Springfield.
Fritz, Gayle J.
2019 *Feeding Cahokia: Early Agriculture in the North American Heartland.* University of Alabama Press, Tuscaloosa.
Hudson, Charles
1976 *The Southeastern Indians.* University of Tennessee Press, Knoxville.
Hunter, Andrea A.
1985 An Ethnoarchaeological Analysis of the Women's Role in Osage Society. Master's thesis, University of Missouri-Columbia.

Johannessen, Sissel

1984 Paleoethnobotany. In *American Bottom Archaeology*, edited by Charles J. Bareis and James B. Porter, pp. 197–214. University of Illinois Press, Urbana.

1993 Food, Dishes, and Society in the Mississippi Valley. In *Foraging and Farming in the Eastern Woodlands*, edited by C. Margaret Scarry, pp. 182–205. University Press of Florida, Gainesville.

Kehoe, Alice B.

2007 Osage Texts and Cahokia Data. In *Ancient Objects and Sacred Realms: Interpretations of Mississippian Iconography*, edited by F. Kent Reilly III and James Garber, pp. 256–261. University of Texas Press, Austin.

Kelly, John E.

2006 The Ritualization of Cahokia: The Structure and Organization of Early Cahokia Crafts. In *Leadership and Polity in Mississippian Society*, edited by Brian M. Butler and Paul D. Welch, pp. 236–263. Center for Archaeological Investigations, Occasional Paper No. 33. Southern Illinois University Carbondale.

Koldehoff, Brad, and Joseph M. Galloy

2006 Late Woodland Frontiers in the American Bottom Region. *Southeastern Archaeology* 25: 275–300.

Krus, Anthony M.

2016 The Timing of Precolumbian Militarization in the U.S. Midwest and Southeast. *American Antiquity* 81: 375–388.

La Flesche, Francis

1930 The Osage Tribe: Rite of the Wa-xo-be. Annual Report of the Bureau of American Ethnology 43: 23–164.

Lopinot, Neal H.

1991 Archaeobotanical Remains. In *The Archaeology of the Cahokia Mounds ICT-II: Biological Remains, Part 1*, edited by Neal H. Lopinot, Lucretia S. Kelly, George R. Miller, and R. Paine, pp. 1–268. Illinois Historic Preservation Agency, Illinois Cultural Resources Study No. 13. Springfield.

1994 A New Crop of Data on the Cahokian Polity. In *Agricultural Origins and Development in the American Midcontinent*, edited by William Green, pp. 127–154. Office of the State Archaeologist Report 19. University of Iowa, Iowa City.

1997 Cahokian Food Production Reconsidered. In *Cahokia: Domination and Ideology in the Mississippian World*, edited by Timothy R. Pauketat and Thomas E. Emerson, pp. 52–68. University of Nebraska Press, Lincoln.

Milner, George R.

1991 Health and Cultural Change in the Late Prehistoric American Bottom. In *What Mean These Bones? Studies in Southeastern Bioarchaeology*, edited by Mary Lucas Powell, Patricia S. Bridges, and Ann Marie Wagner Mires, pp. 52–69. University of Alabama Press, Tuscaloosa.

Monaghan, G. William, Timothy M. Schilling, and Kathryn E. Parker

2014 The Age and Distribution of Domesticated Beans (*Phaseolus vulgaris*) in Eastern North America: Implications for Agricultural Practices and Group Interactions. In *Reassessing the Timing, Rate, and Adoption Trajectories of Domesticate Use in the Midwest and Great Lakes*, edited by Maria E. Raviele and William A. Lovis, pp. 33–52. Midwest Archeological Conference Occasional Papers 1.

Mt. Pleasant, Jane
2015 A New Paradigm for Pre-Columbian Agriculture in North America. *Early American Studies* 13(2): 374–412.
Mueller, Natalie G., and Gayle J. Fritz
2016 Women as Symbols and Actors in the Mississippi Valley: Evidence from Female Flint-Clay Statues and Effigy Vessels. In *Native American Landscapes: An Engendered Perspective*, edited by Cheryl Claassen, pp. 109–150. University of Tennessee Press, Knoxville.
Mueller, Natalie G., Gayle J. Fritz, Paul Patton, Stephen Carmody, and Elizabeth T. Horton.
2017 Growing Lost Crops: New Directions in the Study of Eastern North America's Original Agricultural System. *Nature Plants* 3. DOI:10.1038/nplants.2017.92.
Munoz, Samuel E., Kristine E. Gruley, Ashtin Massie, David A. Fike, Sissel Schroeder, and John W. Williams
2015 Cahokia's Emergence and Decline Coincided with Shifts of Flood Frequency on the Mississippi River. *Proceedings of the National Academy of Science* 112(20): 6319–6324.
Munoz, Samuel E., Sissel Schroeder, David A. Fike, and John W. Williams
2014 A Record of Sustained Prehistoric and Historic Land Use from the Cahokia Region, Illinois, USA. *Geology* 42: 499–502.
Nash, Lenna M., Kristen M. Hedman, and Matthew A. Fort
2018 The People of East St. Louis. In *Revealing Greater Cahokia, North America's First Native City*, edited by Thomas E. Emerson, Brad H. Koldehoff, and Tamira K. Brennan, pp. 219–262. Illinois State Archaeological Survey, Studies in Archaeology No. 12, University of Illinois, Urbana-Champaign.
Parker, Arthur C.
1910 *Iroquois Uses of Maize and Other Food Plants.* New York State Museum Bulletin 144. Albany, NY.
Parker, Kathryn E.
1989 Archaeobotanical Assemblage. In *The Holding Site: A Hopewell Community in the American Bottom*, edited by Andrew C. Fortier, Thomas O. Maher, Joyce A. Williams, Michael C. Meinkoth, Kathryn E. Parker, and Lucretia S. Kelly, pp. 429–464. American Bottom Archaeology FAI-270 Site Reports Vol. 19. University of Illinois Press, Urbana.
2003 Stirling Phase Archaeobotany. In *The Range Site 3: Mississippian and Oneota Occupations*, edited by Ned H. Hanenberger, pp. 409–416. Illinois Transportation Archaeological Research Program, Transportation Archaeological Research Report No. 17. Illinois Department of Transportation and University of Illinois Urbana-Champaign.
2014 Archaeobotany. In *Late Woodland Communities in the American Bottom: The Fish Lake Site*, edited by Andrew C. Fortier, pp. 227–248. Illinois State Archaeological Survey Research Report 28. University of Illinois Urbana-Champaign.
Pauketat, Timothy R.
2009 *Cahokia: Ancient America's Great City on the Mississippi.* Penguin, New York.
Pauketat, Timothy R., and Neal H. Lopinot
1997 Cahokian Population Dynamics. In *Cahokia: Domination and Ideology in the*

Mississippian World, edited by Timothy R. Pauketat and Thomas E. Emerson, pp. 103–123. University of Nebraska Press, Lincoln.

Pauketat, Timothy R., Susan M. Alt, and Jeffery D. Kruchten

2017 The Emerald Acropolis: elevating the moon and water in the rise of Cahokia. *Antiquity* 91(355): 207–222.

Peters, Virginia B.

1995 *Women of the Earth Lodges*. University of Oklahoma Press, Norman.

Rankin, Caitlin G., Casey R. Barrier, and Timothy J. Horsley

2021 Evaluating Narratives of Ecocide with the Stratigraphic Record at Cahokia Mounds States Historic Site, Illinois, USA. *Geoarchaeology* 36: 369–387.

Scarry, C. Margaret, and John F. Scarry

2005 Native American "Garden Agriculture" in Southeastern North America. *World Archaeology* 37: 259–274.

Simon, Mary L.

2014 Reevaluating the Introduction of Maize into the American Bottom and Western Illinois. In *Reassessing the Timing, Rate, and Adoption Trajectories of Domesticate Use in the Midwest and Great Lakes*, edited by Maria E. Raviele and William A. Lovis, pp. 73–96. Midwest Archaeological Conference Occasional Paper 1.

2017 Reevaluating the Evidence for Middle Woodland Maize from the Holding Site. *American Antiquity* 82: 140–150.

Simon, Mary L., and Kathryn E. Parker

2006 Prehistoric Plant Use in the American Bottom: New Thoughts and Interpretations. *Southeastern Archaeology* 25: 212–257.

Slater, Philip A., Kristin M. Hedman, and Thomas E. Emerson

2014 Immigrants at the Mississippian Polity of Cahokia: Strontium Isotope Evidence for Population Movement. *Journal of Archaeological Science* 44: 117–127.

Swanton, John R.

1979 [1946] *The Indians of the Southeastern United States*. Smithsonian Institution Press, Washington DC.

Thomas, Larissa

2001 The Gender Division of Labor in Mississippian Households. In *Archaeological Studies of Gender in the Southeastern United States*, edited by Jane H. Eastman and Christopher B. Rodning, pp. 27–56. University Press of Florida, Gainesville.

VanDerwarker, Amber M., and Gregory D. Wilson

2016 War, Food, and Structural Violence in the Mississippian Central Illinois Valley. In *The Archaeology of Food and Warfare*, edited by A. M. VanDerwarker and G. D. Wilson, pp. 75–105. Springer International Publishing, Switzerland.

Watson, Patty Jo, and Mary C. Kennedy

1991 The Development of Horticulture in the Eastern Woodlands of North America: Women's Role. In *Engendering Archaeology: Women and Prehistory*, edited by Joan M. Gero and Margaret W. Conkey, pp. 255–275. Blackwell Publishers, Oxford, United Kingdom.

Wilson, Gilbert L.

1987 [1917] *Buffalo Bird Woman's Garden*. Minnesota Historical Society Press, St. Paul.

3

Cooks, Cooking, and Cooking Pots

A Landscape of Culinary Practice and the Origins of Moundville, AD 1070–1200

Rachel V. Briggs

This chapter is about the generative social power of cooking and cooking pots. Cooking pots are a class of culinary tool generally designed to boil food in water (Linton 1944). As tools central to the cultural act of cooking, which is a process by which raw, or natural, materials are transformed into cultural products like dishes and meals, their shape, size, and composition is informed by the intended purpose of and attendant practices associated with the pot. There is nothing obvious about cooking—it takes time, skill, and patience to not only learn how to transform raw products into "eatable" dishes (like those processes that remove cyanogens from manioc and bamboo shoots, or help remove harmful microbes from dairy products [McGee 2004: 259–261]), but also to master the transformation of raw and eatable products into "edible" dishes, or those dishes that meet our cultural and social expectations for how they should taste, smell, look, feel in our mouths, and even sound (Borthwick 2000; Hamilakis 1999; Joyce and Henderson 2008; Outram 2007; Sutton 2010). Cooking knowledge is not implicit, but experiential—learning to cook requires apprenticing with experts from whom a person can learn, among other things, about the chemical and gustatory relationships between ingredients; how to acquire, make, and prepare core ingredients; how to employ central culinary technologies; how various processes like freezing, heating, and even passive fermenting treatments affect dishes; how to use and craft culinary tools; and how to properly maintain cooking spaces (*sensu* Sutton 2010; Weiss 1996). Historically, those core experiences were not confined to "kitchens" alone—before cooking, raw ingredients had to be cultivated, gathered, and prepared, and culinary tools had to be crafted, with most all this knowledge, again, acquired through experience.

Cooking is incontestably important to humanity, but is cooking also powerful? Is the act of cooking simply a way to sustain life, and thus a key technology of subsistence, or can cooking generate more than new dishes and meals? Can cooking create new lifeways and new social realities? *Is cooking socially generative?* In this chapter, I argue that it is, and I argue that within Native communities in the pre-contact Late Woodland and Early Mississippian periods (AD 1070–1250) in the Black Warrior River valley of west-central Alabama, cooks, cooking, and cooking pots were the catalysts for the emergence of a new social, political, religious, and economic identity at what became the powerful Mississippian center of Moundville. Importantly, because cooking was intimately tied to femininity throughout post-contact Native communities in the US Southeast, and because archaeological evidence supports that feminine roles were similar in the late pre-contact period, I propose that Mississippian women were the key actors who created a new, emergent social identity through cooking. Here, I use tools and ingredients central to the cuisine of the post-contact Native US Southeast (specifically, cooking pots and maize) as proxies for a larger landscape of culinary practice and interpret changes in these resources as indicators of larger changes in culinary and social practices (*sensu* Deagan 1983). Doing so recasts the period from AD 1070–1250 as a time characterized by a dynamic and inclusive social landscape of culinary practice, providing a network for immigrant Mississippian women to introduce the hominy foodway to other women in the valley (Figure 3.1).

Beginning with the ethnohistoric record for the Native US Southeast, I demonstrate that three core and overlapping domains of cooking were and are strongly correlated with Native femininity: agricultural activities, cooking hominy, and producing ceramic cooking pots. Based on the relationship between culinary practices and femininity as well as evidence from the archaeological record that suggests these relationships were also active during the late pre-contact period, I argue that constituent resources, like maize and ceramic cooking pots, can be used as proxies for the social concept of womanhood, and thus as proxies for feminine actors (*sensu* Deagan 1983). Next, I re-create the landscape of culinary practice of the Black Warrior River valley between AD 1070 and 1250, or the Late Woodland West Jefferson phase (AD 1070–1120) and the Early Mississippian Moundville I phase (AD 1120–1250), and argue that taste and practice should be prioritized over political ambitions when considering the social forces that fostered Moundville's emergence. This model is strongly supported by the staggered arrival of gendered "Mis-

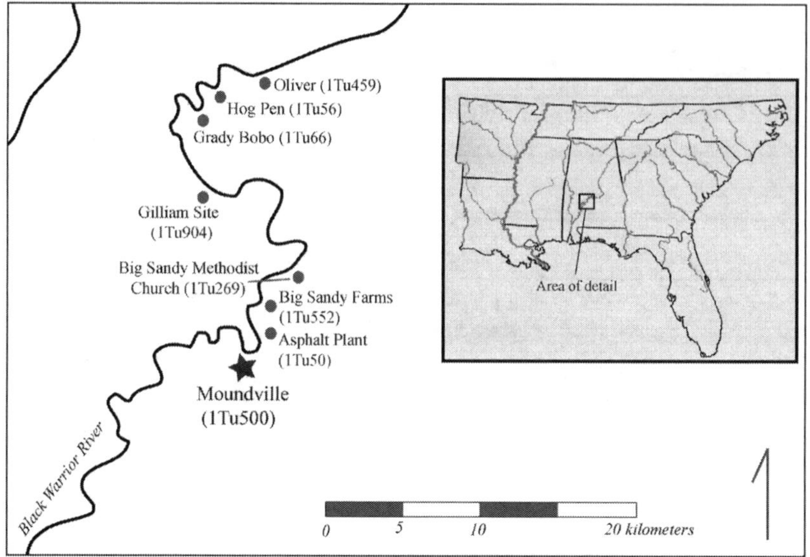

Figure 3.1. Map of the subject area, including Moundville I phase sites discussed in this chapter.

sissippian" material signatures from AD 1070–1250 (both maize and shell-tempered pottery appear nearly seventy years in the Black Warrior River valley before any other Mississippian material signatures, including rectangular wall-trench domestic buildings) as well as a recreation of the social landscape of the area. The chapter concludes with a consideration of the spatial organization of the culinary landscape of the Black Warrior River valley, proposing that everyday cooking and culinary activities, and the women who practiced them, are far more powerful social forces than previously credited.

Women and Cooking

Gender roles are social institutions, or structures, that prescribe practices, ideas, and even behaviors onto social actors through a complex combination of variables such as biological sex assigned at birth, age, status, religious affiliation, and social membership. While gender roles are structures, gender identities refer to how individuals relate to and negotiate gender within society. Unlike gender identities, gender roles are patterned, and are often used to ensure that essential social functions, like food procurement and preparation, are carried out in regular, predictable ways (Claassen 1992; Joyce and Claassen 1997). Gender roles ensure key knowledge and practices are passed down from generation to generation, maintaining both the biological and social life of a group.

Most Native societies in the post-contact (previously referred to as the historic period, ~AD 1500) US Southeast had at least three gender identities widely available to adult members: man, woman, and an identity available specifically for males who chose to live as women. While many females identified as women, and many males identified as men, there were virtually no social, political, or economic structures prior to Western colonialism that actively encouraged gender conformity. Females, for example, had the choice to engage in masculine activities: well-known examples of this include "war woman" Nanye'hi (Nancy Ward), a late eighteenth-century beloved Cherokee woman who fought alongside her community in various military campaigns (Peasantubbee 2014). And males, as mentioned, could choose to live as women. For those males who chose to live as women, European accounts indicate they did so openly, and their ranks included socially powerful individuals, like the sibling of the male *mico* (head chief) of Cauchi, a mid-sixteenth-century town in the Appalachian Summit (Bandera 1990: 267). That males could openly live as women, and further that that choice was not rendered socially invisible even to European observers (unlike female husbands in Western society; see Manion 2020), suggests that the social value of femininity and feminine actors within many Native societies was equal to that of masculinity (Mankiller 2011: 95–96).

Interestingly, there is little evidence suggesting third-gender identities were true gender roles in the post-contact Native US Southeastern societies. Presently, there is no evidence to suggest either males living as women or females enacting aspects of masculinity were granted exclusive social practices that were separate from the domains of femininity or masculinity (see White, this volume, for a possible exception). This suggests that there were only two gendered roles used to structure Native groups. While it is tempting to conceptualize this as a gender binary based on the Western philosophical tradition, masculine and feminine gender roles within Native societies in the US Southeast more accurately functioned as dyads, or two parts of a whole, both of which were essential for maintaining world order, regardless of the biological sex of individual actors (Perdue 2001: 4; Richardson 2013: 197–199). To this point, Perdue (2001: 4) suggests that within Native societies, masculinity and femininity were two basic categories used to divide all social responsibilities (see also Hudson 1976: 269).

The ethnohistoric record indicates that central to womanhood were several overlapping domains tied to cooking: food preparation, agricultural activities, and ceramic production (Hudson 1976; Swanton 1946). Cooking, narrowly defined, was considered a feminine activity, with women the primary culinary agents within their communities who transformed raw hunted, gathered, and cultivated materials into important cultural food products (Bauer 2022; Hudson 1976; Thompson 2008). Prior to the incorporation of European ingredients (like watermelon, peaches, pork, and cowpeas), technologies (like frying), and culinary concepts (like salads), American Indian cuisines were largely "one-pot" meals, with the one pot being an earthenware jar used to boil starchy carbohydrates like maize or acorns (Briggs and Lapham 2022). Arguably, the most important dish in late pre-contact and post-contact American Indian cuisines in the US Southeast, and the one essential to the enactment of a meal, was hominy (Briggs 2015). Hominy is a generic term used to refer to a variety of boiled maize dishes made from whole or ground maize kernels that are nixtamalized. Many hominy dishes are still prepared within Native US Southeastern communities today. Descriptions of hominy and hominy-like dishes were recorded by Western observers throughout the post-contact period for various groups, including the Choctaw, Chickasaw, and Yuchi (as well as other Muskogean language-speaking groups) whose ancestors lived in the Black Warrior River valley (Galloway 1995: 316–320; Green 2008: 122; Scarry and Steponaitis 2016: 222). As Bernard Romans (1962[1775]: 92) noted from his time among the eighteenth-century Choctaw,

> their women . . . are very hospitable and never fail of making a stranger heartily welcome, offering him the pipe as soon as he arrives, while the good women are employed to prepare a dish of venison and hominy [*tafula*], with some bread made of maize and flour, and being wrapped in maize leaves, baked under the ashes; when it is served up they accompany it with bears fat purified to a perfect chrystalline [oil].

To cook a pot of nixtamalized hominy, women first soaked dried maize kernels overnight in an alkaline solution made from woodash or woodash lye (which are chemically the same). Next, the kernels were drained, frequently ground, and the pericarps removed, then boiled from several hours to upward of a day (Briggs 2015). Common items added to hominy included proteins, fats, and seasonings like deer or bear meat and eventually pork; bear oil, pig fat, or hickory nut meat; beans; bone marrow; and even handfuls of ash or a spoonful of lye, the latter two used as condiments (Briggs and Lapham 2022). Among the Yuchi, *tsoci* (hominy) was believed to be a divine gift from the sun, one that was discovered when, importantly, ". . . *a woman* in the mythical ages cut a rent in the sky through which a peculiar liquid flowed which was found to be good to eat. The Sun then explained its preparation and use, from which fact it was called *tsoci,* inferably 'sun fluid'" (Frank Speck in Swanton 1946: 354; emphasis added).

Very few masculine domains overlapped with cooking, the most notable of those that did being hunting deer, bear, and other medium- to large-sized animals; however, women were not only involved in articulating animal carcasses and preparing hides, but also in roasting and drying meat, removing marrow, and rendering fat. Women exclusively prepared the dishes consumed by their households, communities, and even those central to ritual activities. Women were even responsible for brewing the Black Drink (a very hot tea prepared from the leaves and stems of yaupon holly, or *Ilex vomitoria*), whether consumed recreationally or ritually, despite social rules that prohibited women from consuming it (Hudson 2004).

In Native US Southeastern societies, women grew, cultivated, and cared for maize, squash, beans, and all Eastern agricultural products grown in fields and gardens (Fritz 2019; Fritz, this volume; Perdue 2001: 4; Scarry and Scarry 2005). Women owned and controlled agricultural fields and gardens, an ownership vested through matrilineal descent, which was practiced throughout much of the US Southeast during the early post-contact period. By the mid- to late nineteenth century, agricultural responsibilities and ownership shifted within many Native communities from the domain and control of women to that of men, in response to Western settler colonial pressures and the exertion of androcentric, European values, which believed it was the responsibility of masculine individuals to control and make decisions about valuable economic resources (Lowery 2013). However, previously, and to the dismay of many European and Euro-American observers, Native women were the agriculturalists. This division of labor was so striking that the only agricultural tasks men were repudiated to perform were periodic field clearing, some planting, and some assistance during harvesting (Scarry and Scarry 2005).

Unlike gardens and fields which were largely under feminine, domestic ownership, groves and orchards were communally owned, belonging not to a household but to a village or town. Women, children, and the elderly were largely responsible for collecting fruits and nuts, such as acorns, hickory, peaches, and persimmons, and were also primarily involved in collecting fallen limbs for firewood (Graham 2020). Men, conversely, were charged with clearing and thinning groves to help reduce vegetative competition and maintain clear lines of sight.

It was feminine to care for a pot of food, and it was feminine to care for plants; it was also feminine to make ceramic pots. Native women were responsible for making domestic ceramics, like cooking pots and serving ware, used within their homes and communities (Bauer 2022; Cushman 1899; Hudson

1976: 264; Swanton 1946; Thompson 2008: 136). Like cooking, ceramic production involves the acquisition of experiential knowledge through apprenticeship. The close social relationships fostered through learning and working in both realms help explain why both are heavily associated with storytelling and history making; the process, apprenticeship, and space designated for pottery making served and continues to serve within many Native communities as a school for social, cultural, and historical transmission (Bauer 2022; Perdue 2001). Native women were adept craftspeople, and building on this skillset, some were trained in specialized, ritual craft production, producing the fineware ritual ceramics archaeologists recover from mound tops, townhouses, and elite burials, a connection that further strengthened the relationship between femininity and social knowledge transmission.

To be feminine was to be powerful; Native women were equal to, and in certain respects, more powerful than Native men (*sensu* Briggs et al., 2023). One important source of feminine power was the practice of matrilineal kinship in many early post-contact US Southeastern Native communities, in which descent is traced through the mother's line, and male children are expected to marry and move away from their natal communities (a practice known as matrilocal residence). Many groups not only traced descent through the mother's line, but corporate ownership also passed through the matrilineage, meaning sacra, knowledge, and agricultural lands were bestowed to daughters, sisters, mothers, and feminine cousins (Hudson 1976). Control over both the home and agricultural resources and fields vested Native women with social power and privileges alien to Western, Euro-American women throughout the post-contact period, including the right to a voice (even a vote) in various town matters and the option to attain and hold political office (Bauer 2022; Briggs et al., 2023; Kidwell 1992; Peasantubbee 2005; see Rodning et al., this volume; Trocolli 2002, 2006). Native women routinely attained special, ritual statuses, like that of beloved women, in which their experience, social clout, and political power were revered and respected (Peasantubbee 2005, 2014). Appreciation and acknowledgment of this social power are echoed in the prolific origin myths for maize, in which a divine figure, generally considered Corn Mother, bestows the gift of maize through the self-sacrifice of her body to Native communities (Briggs 2023; Lankford 2008; Peasantubbee 2005; Thompson 2008: 90).

Feminine Workspaces

These overlapping culinary domains linked to femininity not only sketch the knowledge and practices central to cooking, but also provide a window into the spaces and communities of practice through which women learned feminine, culinary behaviors. Europeans and Euro-Americans commented on the stark social separation between Native men and women; men frequently socialized with other men, while women frequently socialized with other women, creating distinct gendered locations within Native villages and towns (Hudson 1976: 260, 309, 319). For men, socializing occurred in square grounds, public men's houses, the woods surrounding towns, and public spaces like plazas and gaming courts where they smoked tobacco, drank yaupon tea, and played games like chunkey; for women, socializing occurred in and near the home, in maize and agricultural fields, gardens, town edges, immovable workstations like the large wooden mortar and pestles used to grind maize, ceramic production areas, and outdoor cooking areas (Bauer 2022; Hudson 1976; Perrelli 1994, 2001; Thompson 2008). Outside of the domestic structure, public feminine structures, like "menstrual huts" and women's houses, became important spaces for the training and transmission of femininity and cooking practices (see Bengtson and Alexander, this volume).

The Archaeological Evidence for Mississippian Cooking

So far, Native cooking and femininity in the US Southeast has been defined by the ethnohistoric record, which was primarily informed by Europeans and Euro-Americans. Though biased, and though Native groups underwent profound social reorganization after contact (Ethridge 2009, 2010), currently, there is little reason to suspect the gender roles, and their respective relationships to culinary practices, were significantly different during the late precontact, Mississippian period (beginning AD 900–1000 through European contact). Indeed, the archaeological record corroborates much of the picture presented above. For example, males and females in agricultural groups from northern Alabama, when compared to earlier Archaic period (hunter-gatherer) groups from the same region, demonstrate significant changes in muscle attachment. Bridges (1989) suggests Mississippian females generally displayed patterns in their upper bodies that corresponded to the practices of using a large, wooden mortar and pestle like those used in grinding maize kernels to make hominy (Figure 3.2). Conversely, Mississippian males exhibited muscle attachment patterns similar to those seen in Archaic period males. To Bridges, this suggested that with the adoption of maize agriculture, the subsistence (and subsequent culinary) practices of males (men) changed very little, whereas those of females (women) changed considerably (Bridges 1989).

Further, isotopic evidence drawn from Moundville suggests they were eating nixtamalized maize. Schoeninger and Schurr (2007) demonstrated that the population of Moundville was generally healthy and ate a well-balanced

Figure 3.2. Cherokee woman grinding and sifting maize. (Photograph taken by John Hemmer, 1945. North Carolina Digital Collections.)

diet centered on maize, and one for which maize served as a true dietary staple. Alone and untreated, maize is an incomplete dietary staple. We lack the appropriate digestive system to extract key nutrients from maize kernels. As such, a diet for which maize is a true dietary staple that is not properly supplemented will result in pellagra, a chronic wasting disorder, the symptoms for which include dermatitis (a painful, terrible rash), diarrhea, dementia, and, ultimately, death (Chacko 2005; Hegyi et al. 2003). The two most common ways to counter the effects of a protein-deficient maize-based diet are to either (1) nixtamalize maize, which is an alkaline cooking technique that helps to predigest as well as chemically alter the bioavailability of maize, or (2) supplement a maize-based diet with high quantities of complementary proteins, such as beans or animal meat. For the latter, a ratio of one-to-one is required, maize-to-protein, placing a high demand on the production and acquisition of the protein source, a challenging and almost impossible feat if the protein source is wild (such as white-tailed deer or marine resources). Beans are the easiest, most efficient complementary protein. However, and important to this point, beans were not disseminated with maize in the US Southeast. Instead, while the presence of maize steadily increased beginning around AD 900, and by AD 1100, is a dietary staple in the Black Warrior River valley, beans *did not* make an appearance in the Eastern Woodlands until AD 1300 (Baumann and Crites 2016; Hart and Scarry 1999). What this suggests is that Early Mississippian populations were consuming high quantities of nixtamalized hominy, an alkaline cooked product that is a complete, nutritious dietary staple.

The combined archaeological and ethnohistoric evidence thus suggests that similar to post-contact Native femininity, approximately 1000 years ago, late pre-contact femininity in the Late Woodland/Early Mississippian world of west-central Alabama involved several overlapping domains of culinary practice that included gathered plants and other resources, food preparation (including hominy), ceramic production, the care for children and other family members, and, eventually, maize agriculture. Thus, the basic activities seem to have been the same, but were the social and physical spaces for learning and experiencing these activities the same? Based on village layouts and the recovery proveniences for the material correlates of these domains, these concepts were firmly tied to the home, establishing domestic structures and home villages and towns as key locations for acquiring feminine culinary experiences.

The Black Warrior River Valley Social Landscape, AD 1070–1250

Late Woodland West Jefferson phase people (AD 1070–1120) lived in small, relatively egalitarian hunter-gatherer communities. They spent much of the warm season living in floodplain villages, while the cold season was spent away from the village in extractive camps (Jenkins 2003; Jenkins and Nielsen 1974; Knight and Steponaitis 2007: 7; Scarry 1986; Welch 1981). Beginning around AD 1120, life in the valley changed. In contrast to the Late Woodland West Jefferson lifeway, people living in what would become Mississippian settlements fostered dependencies on maize agriculture, began practicing year-round sedentism, and ultimately congregated in comparatively large villages and town settings. Additionally, these societies were socially hierarchical. While most Mississippian settlements in the Black Warrior River valley were small, by around AD 1200, Moundville's population was close to a thousand people (Knight and Steponaitis 2007: 12–17). Researchers speculate about the historical relationship between these lifeways—did West Jefferson communities evolve into Mississippian communities, or were the West Jefferson peoples pushed out of the area, displaced by Mississippian immigrants? Did these groups exist coterminously, and if so, were social relations harmonious or acrimonious?

Though this picture is still developing, most agree that both non-local Mississippian and non-Mississippian immigrants (such as Coles Creek peoples) moved into the Black Warrior River, settling within West Jefferson phase communities (Briggs 2017; Jenkins and Krause 2009; Jenkins and Seckinger 2000; Steponaitis 2009). What researchers disagree on is the demography of immigrants and the nature of social interactions between local and non-local individuals. Jenkins and Krause (2009) proposed that in addition to smaller groups, entire Mississippian communities (men, women, and children, including families and the elderly) also immigrated to the area, establishing separate and exclusive "Mississippian" villages. As more and more Mississippian immigrants joined these newly established villages, West Jefferson populations were pushed east, suggesting a distant and acrimonious relationship. Alternatively, Steponaitis (2009; see also Thompson 2011) suggests Mississippian immigrants interacted with and settled among local West Jefferson communities, and the interaction between these traditions resulted in the Mississippian manifestation at Moundville identified by archaeologists today. Here, a more harmonious and socially fluid interaction is implied. However, despite their differences, both views share one basic assumption: that Mississippian peoples moved as "family units," or units comprised of men, women, children, and elderly members.

What if there's a third option, one congruent with the material culture: that Mississippian *women* were the first Mississippian immigrants in the Black Warrior River valley and settled within West Jefferson communities, followed close to fifty years later by Mississippian men and potentially Mississippian families, creating the staggered Mississippian community identity manifest at Moundville? During the West Jefferson phase (AD 1070–1120), the two earliest (and only) traces of the Mississippian expression in the area are maize remains and shell-tempered pottery sherds (Scarry 1986). Both comprise small, but ubiquitous quantities of the paleoethnobotanical and ceramic assemblages, which are dominated by the remains of wild plants (acorns being the most abundant) and grog-tempered pottery. Within fifty years, or by the beginning of the Moundville I phase (AD 1120), maize dominates the paleoethnobotanical assemblage, replacing acorns as the primary dietary carbohydrate and even being elevated to a dietary staple in the process (representing 40% or more of a person's daily caloric intake). Similarly, shell-tempered pottery dominates the pottery assemblage, displacing grog-tempered pottery in ubiquity (Hawsey 2015; Scarry 1986).

While the dietary shift from acorns to maize is fascinating, the corresponding change in cooking pot technology is telling. During the West Jefferson phase, women made and used grog-tempered vessels, including

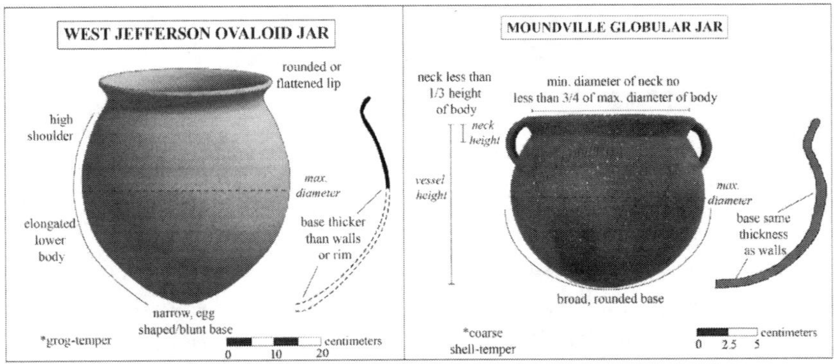

Figure 3.3. Functional comparison of two of the most common cooking pots during the Late Woodland West Jefferson phase and Early Mississippian Moundville I phase in the Black Warrior River valley.

grog-tempered cooking jars. West Jefferson cooking jars, which were tall-shouldered, ovaloid vessels with constricted necks and no handles, are pots designed to boil foods in water when placed in an open fire. Mississippian standard jars, which are squat-bodied globular jars with constricted openings, rims that flare out, and handles, are also adapted for boiling in water, but should not be used in open fires (where the flames lap up over the opening); instead, they should be suspended over or placed in a bed of hot coals (Briggs 2016, Figure 3.3). Hot coal cooking is an extraordinarily labor- and energy-efficient cooking method compared to open-fire cooking, making it possible to boil or simmer foods for extended periods using less labor and fuel (Briggs 2017), an invaluable quality when preparing dishes like hominy that require six or more hours of simmering. That West Jefferson jars were used in direct fires and Mississippian standard jars at Moundville were suspended over hot coals is not only demonstrated through functional analysis but is also supported by use wear analyses (Briggs 2016, 2017; Hawsey 2015).

Together, the presence of maize and shell-tempered, globular jars signals that between AD 1070–1120 within the Black Warrior valley, the hominy foodway was practiced in the area, and not two separate, unrelated domains. Further, it suggests that ingredients, technologies, skillsets, and even cooking setups changed considerably. Could the foodway spread without the subsequent immigration of Mississippian women? Perhaps, but consider what that would require: a woman had to learn how to cultivate and care for maize, how to nixtamalize maize, what a pot of "done" hominy smelled and tasted like, how to effectively cook using hot coals, where to source the materials to craft shell-tempered jars, and then how to craft a shell-tempered globular jar, as well as seasonal and specific culinary knowledge, like how to store maize, how to add water to a simmering pot of hominy without the pot exploding, which pots to use for soaking versus cooking, how to set up a tripod for hot coal cooking, how to keep cordage from burning, when a pot is too fragile to survive the thermal shock of cooking, as well as so much more. All of this is experience-based culinary knowledge that would require at least three months from roughly late spring through the fall to learn, a conservative timeframe based solely on the life cycle of the maize plant. The simplest solution is not that the knowledge, ingredients, and technology central to the hominy foodway spread independent of the movement of people, but instead, that hominy practitioners moved. And those practitioners were Mississippian women, raised in a culinary tradition that taught women, likely at a very early age in their own homes, how to cook hominy and craft shell-tempered cooking jars.

But why only Mississippian women? Is it possible Mississippian men, children, and elderly people moved as well? Despite the growing evidence for Mississippian women present in West Jefferson communities, and their ubiquitous presence in Moundville I phase communities, the material signatures for non-West Jefferson masculinity, including a Mississippian masculinity, do not appear until the Moundville I phase, after maize and shell-tempered pottery dominate the culinary landscape.

Mississippian Masculinity

An ethnohistoric review of Native masculine activities suggests that material correlates for some masculine behaviors are hunting implements, materials for hunting adjacent activities like the game of chunkey, and architecture (Briggs and Harle, this volume; Hudson 1976). While participants in the execution of these activities may include women, children, and both elderly men and women (such as structure construction and hide processing [Hudson 1976]), certain knowledge domains, like hunting and warfare, are central to these activities and are firmly associated with masculine actors and domains. The manifestation of some knowledge domains, like architectural understandings of earthen mound construction, likely represent communities more broadly, while the specialized knowledge for their design and execution may have been confined to specific lineages (Knight 2010; Sherwood and Kidder 2011).

In the Black Warrior River valley, signatures of a Late Woodland West Jefferson masculinity likely include projectile points and circular domestic architecture (Ensor 1993: 16–24); similarly, signatures for Mississippian masculinity likely include rectangular wall-trench architecture, Mississippian triangular projectile points, and the game of chunkey, all behaviors and activities associated with the Mississippian expression more broadly. From AD 1070–1120, all the signatures for masculinity suggest a Late Woodland West Jefferson masculinity. During the early Moundville I phase (AD 1120–1190), the first signs of a non-local masculinity appear in the form of at least four distinct domestic architectural styles: small basin-floor structures with single-set posts; large, rectangular single-set post structures; rectangular, basin-floor structures with a combination of single-set post walls at the narrow sides of the building and wall trenches along the longer sides; and square, open-corner wall-trench structures (Briggs 2017: 102–104). This heterogeneous architectural landscape was transformed into a homogeneous one by AD 1250 when Mississippian-style wall-trench rectangular structures became the only domestic architectural style (Davis 2014; Lacquement 2007; Wilson 2008). This staggered appearance suggests that Mississippian masculinity arrived in the Black Warrior River valley later than Mississippian femininity, approximately 50 to 100 years later, and following the same logic laid out above, it is far simpler that Mississippian men immigrated than that these domains were learned and mastered by local West Jefferson men over months of apprenticeships with Mississippian men.

Unlike Mississippian men, it is impossible to rule out the movement of Mississippian children, elderly men and women, or other individuals; however, if these groups did immigrate with Mississippian women, they either left no unique material signature for their presence or they intentionally did not enact certain elements of their Mississippian identities, assimilating instead to gendered and social expectations within the Late Woodland West Jefferson Black Warrior River valley.

What is clear is that Mississippian women, and Mississippian feminine actors, immigrated to the Black Warrior River valley beginning around AD 1070. While immigration is the product of complex factors, including environmental, political, and social, and while many models of immigration have been proposed to explore the dissemination of Mississippian peoples and ideas (see Cook and Comstock 2022), most models either imply or assert the movement of communities or families, and not cross-cutting social segments. Few models focus exclusively on women, and in those rare cases, slavery, imprisonment, or Western colonialism are cited as driving forces (see Deagan 1983; Rodning et al., this volume). Yet, the ethnohistoric record indicates a clear form of movement that removes group members from their natal communities based on gender: marriage. As noted, though, during the post-contact period, matrilineal marriage networks removed *men* from their natal communities through matrilocal residence, not women. Were matrilineal marriage networks, and resulting matrilocal residence patterns, also active during the Late Woodland and Early Mississippian periods, or instead, it is possible they were products of other social factors during the Mississippian period? Though kinship and marriage networks are produced by intersecting social and historical factors, Eggan (1937) demonstrated that kinship systems among many US Southeastern groups were particularly sensitive to social factors like economic organization, and could, and did, change in response to agricultural labor changes (Eggan 1937: 51). Prior to maize, the important subsistence resource in Late Woodland West Jefferson communities were groves of nut trees where acorns, the essential dietary resource, were harvested. Similar to the post-contact period, such groves may have been under the control of the group, and not under the domain of a particular gender. However, maize products and maize agriculture, through culinary domains, may have firmly been aligned with women beginning as early as AD 900 (*sensu* Fritz 2019; Fritz, this volume). Perhaps as the importance of maize grew in culinary and economic terms, marriage networks shifted, emphasizing the necessity for matrilineal, corporate ownership over maize resources. And perhaps prior to maize, other social domains impacted marriage networks resulting in women, and not men, moving from their natal communities.

Regardless of what drew Mississippian women to the area, it is important to ask if their prescient arrival challenges previously held models for the origins of Moundville. And if so, how?

The Social Power of Taste

If Mississippian women brought maize, hominy, and attendant culinary domains to the valley, as I propose they did, it should not be assumed a priori that maize was destined to be adopted. The spread and adoption of foodways is not inevitable; it is contingent. This is why previous models for Moundville's origins are wrong: they focus heavily on the economic potential of maize as a resource that could easily be extensified and then the surplus mobilized by aggrandizing elites to host political feasting events (Cobb 2003: 76; Knight 2001). However, these models do not consider that before maize can be used as a political or economic resource that feeds, supports, and mobilizes people, it must be understood as *edible*. People needed to eat it, and they needed to like it. Thus, the initial spread of maize from Mississippian women to their families and new communities had to be predicated on preference. And for West Jefferson women, as well as other women unaccustomed to maize, to begin practicing the culinary domains central to hominy, they had to taste it and like it. This suggests that the first reason why West Jefferson women and their communities adopted hominy is because they liked the way it tasted, and they understood its relationship to a meal (*sensu* Bourdieu 1984; Douglas 1971; Hastorf 2016).

Hominy and acorn porridge dishes are remarkably similar, and both, within post-contact Eastern Woodland Native cuisines, fulfilled a similar culinary category as primary dietary carbohydrates. Nixtamalizing maize gives hominy a slightly bitter taste and a porridge-like consistency resulting from grinding and extended boiling (Briggs 2015). Acorn porridge also has a slightly bitter flavor (from tannins, which remain in small doses even after leaching) and a mush-like consistency from grinding and boiling (Briggs 2017). Both were also central to the cultural idea of a meal in the minds of those living in the Black Warrior River valley. Finally, both held similar metaphoric and symbolic qualities—they were attached to ideas of hospitality and the home (Briggs 2023). Based on taste and meal preparation, it is very likely hominy was enjoyed and understood as edible by West Jefferson populations.

Were residents of the valley introduced to hominy in large feasting events? Likely not, based on the dearth of archaeological evidence for large-scale feasting from AD 1070–1200. Instead, the home seems the most probable locus for experiencing, learning, and preparing hominy—in domestic environments, not only could people try hominy, but they could also begin experiencing the hominy foodway, and thus begin acquiring the experiential knowledge central to making it. This suggests that top-down models for Moundville's origins may be inaccurate. If Moundville did not begin as the nascent dream of aspiring Mississippian elites, and if the planning for the center only came later after the settlement was established and the population present, then, at its very beginning, what was it?

Positioning Women's Work Within the Social Landscape: Culinary Practice Communities and Site Catchment Analysis

Perhaps Moundville began as an inclusive landscape of culinary practice.

To cook, a person not only needs specific ingredients, tools, and resources, but experiential knowledge of the process as well. This is no less true for crafting the tools central to making hominy: cooking jars. Indeed, changes in ceramic technology, style, and morphology signal deviations in the *chaine operatoire*, or those steps and choices inherent within a practice, and while these changes have long been studied by archaeologists as relative chronological markers, they also signal important cultural changes as well. To this point, Worth (2017) proposed that archaeological phases, long based on counts and differences in ceramic stylistic choices, should not be assumed representative of political, ethnic, or linguistic groups (after Eckert's [2008] communities of identity), but instead as representative of landscapes of ceramic practice (or communities of ceramic practice, after Eckert [2008] and Wegner [1998]). While communities of identity signal shared group identities founded in explicit knowledge (or knowledge that can be written down or verbally shared), practice communities signal membership through shared experiential knowledge. Importantly, while explicit knowledge is transmitted verbally, experiential knowledge is composed of practice-based skills, meaning that membership within practice communities is predicated on sustained shared practices that are learned by practice taking place in the same place at the same time. Further, practice communities are not inherently restricted by political, linguistic, or even ethnic membership because they are not founded on explicit or language-based knowledge.

Conceptualizing the Black Warrior valley between AD 1070–1120 as a landscape of culinary practice, for which cooking pots are a signature material feature, serves several purposes. First, it reduces the noise caused by what Moundville becomes; by AD 1250, Moundville is a prominent political-economic ritual center serviced by the surrounding region, but a century earlier, it is still a small (but growing, *sensu* Davis 2014) settlement within a valley that hosts several other small, burgeoning Mississippian settlements. Second, it remakes what has been conceptualized as a political landscape filled with aspiring elites using maize as a resource to acquire power into one where local and non-local women, practicing their gender roles and identities, are interacting and engaging with each other through shared locations and resources critical to their work. Finally, it eliminates the need for verbal interactions based on shared language; culinary practices can be understood and transmitted without verbal exchanges. Ultimately, this reconceptualization allows us to position the culinary domains of the acorn and hominy foodways within a landscape dominated by experiential knowledge, a model that fits well within the socially dynamic landscape of the Late Woodland and Early Mississippian Black Warrior River valley.

Using cooking jars to spatially explore the landscape of culinary practice within the valley makes it possible to highlight the social networks through which these practices were learned while providing a window into the social lives of practitioners. Through a comprehensive analysis of ceramic stylistic features of Mississippian standard jars, I (2017) demonstrated that throughout the Black Warrior River valley between AD 1120–1250, there were overlapping and intersecting communities of culinary practice, represented by both high- and low-visibility stylistic choices within and be-

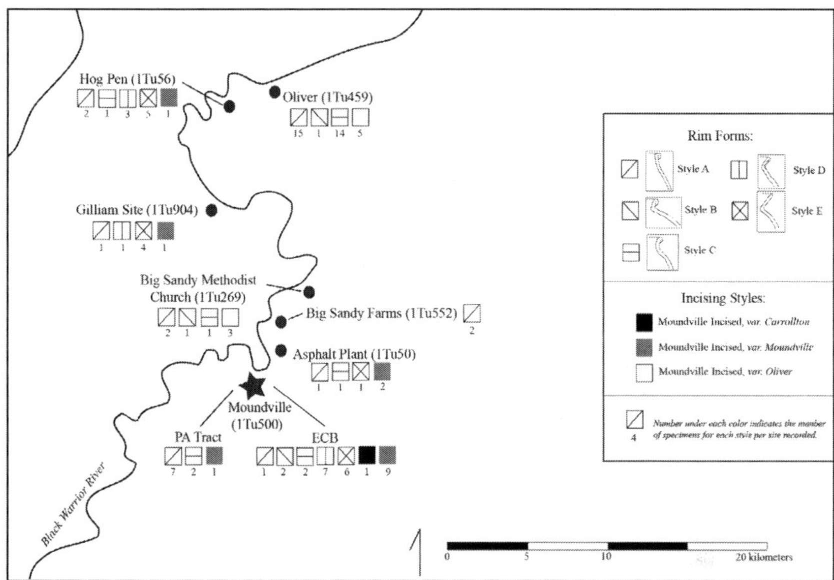

Figure 3.4. Mississippian standard jar rim treatments throughout Moundville I phase sites, demonstrating overlapping communities of practice of the hominy foodway.

tween Moundville I phase communities (Figure 3.4). In other words, there were not separate, exclusive schools of culinary practice confined either to villages or to enclaves within communities, which would be defined by exclusive, non-overlapping stylistic choices. Instead, high-visibility choices (styles that everyone can see) were mixed-and-matched with low-visibility choices (choices that are not visible to the naked eye). This suggests that practitioners may learn to fold lips (pottery rims) from one person, and to engrave arches and eyelashes on the shoulder of globular jars from another person. Because there is no discernable pattern to the dispersal of these choices, meaning practitioners freely combined various stylistic choices both consciously (with high-visibility choices) and unconsciously (with low-visibility choices), suggests there were no social pressures to signal membership to one group versus another within the larger community of culinary practice.

To continue following this line of reasoning: if women throughout the valley were making Mississippian standard jars, they were making them to prepare hominy in. And likely, the same networks through which they apprenticed and learned to make globular pots are the networks through which they learned to eat and cook hominy, and grow maize.

If the culinary landscape beginning around AD 1120 was one of inclusivity, then what about the culinary landscape fifty years earlier, during the Late Woodland West Jefferson phase? Though the ceramic assemblages from this time are too small for a comprehensive stylistic analysis of cooking jars like that discussed above, it is very likely that the social atmosphere that fostered an inclusive and overlapping landscape of culinary practice beginning around AD 1120 was present and active during the West Jefferson phase fifty years earlier, suggesting that during the Late Woodland West Jefferson phase, Mississippian women joined existing, active networks of culinary practices and did not create their own exclusive networks for Mississippian practitioners. Doing so not only brought them social acceptance, but also provided Mississippian women the opportunity to share their experiences with others, establishing and maintaining the high level of social inclusivity that defined the culinary landscape during the Early Mississippian Moundville I phase.

In addition to the stylistic ceramic analysis, it is also possible to chart the culinary landscape by considering the culinary taskscapes (or workstations, *sensu* Gruppuso and Whitehouse 2020; Ingold 1993; see Gougeon, this volume) during the Moundville I phase through a consideration of those spaces important to the domains of cooking. Perrelli (1994, 2001) noted among the post-contact Iroquois, that the places most significant for women and their work were agricultural fields and their villages, while the primary spatial domain for men was outside of the village in the forest. Claassen (2001: 20) translated this work into site catchment radii and suggested that the areas important for feminine work were located within a radius of one, two, or five kilometers from their homes, in contrast to a radius of five kilometers or more for those daily and yearly activities central to masculinity. By applying Perrelli's (2001) gendered parameters for a site catchment analysis to the Black Warrior River valley during the Moundville I phase demonstrates that work and social areas for women living at these early settlements overlapped, drawing women into a larger culinary landscape that crosscut settlements (Figure 3.5). (Contrast this to the site catchment analysis for masculine activities, which places those areas of interaction for men largely outside of the valley [Figure 3.6].) Did the greater landscape of culinary practice, including important locations for growing, cooking, and pottery making, influence, even dictate, where Moundville I phase settlements were located? While various factors influence settlement, it is worth wondering whether important culinary social and material resources are strong forces influencing settlement: what if Moundville I phase settlements, in addition to land and resource requirements, also needed to be close enough so that women could continue participating in everyday social networks?

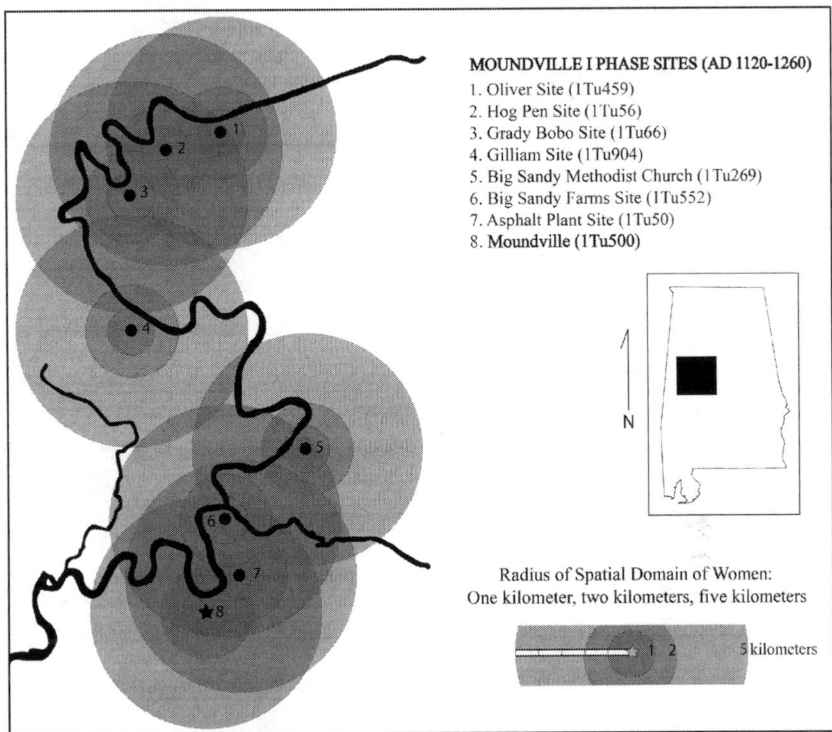

Figure 3.5. Feminine site catchment analysis for Moundville I phase Black Warrior River valley.

Regardless of the influence on settlement patterns, what is clear is that this overlapping culinary landscape of practice produced ample opportunities for local and non-local women, those who made hominy and those who made acorn porridge, those who produced grog-tempered ovaloid jars and those who made shell-tempered globular jars, to interact and engage with one another at important, common culinary places that provided spaces for practice and learning, side by side. Some of those shared culinary spaces included clay harvesting locations; shell harvesting locations; areas for mixing and producing ceramic pastes as well as burning and treating shell for tempering; areas for drying and firing pots; dependable stands for gathering wild foods, river cane, fibers, and materials; household gardens for growing semi-domesticated and domesticated plants; and public feminine structures and spaces like menstrual "huts" or women's houses (Galloway 1997; see Bengtson and Alexander, this volume), all becoming important spaces to socialize, to teach, to learn, and to experience.

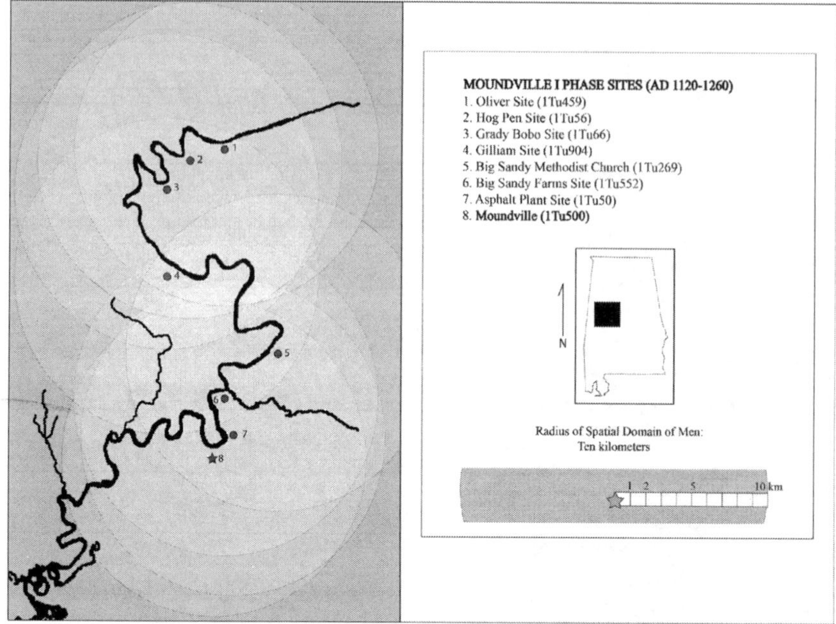

Figure 3.6. Masculine site catchment analysis for Moundville I phase Black Warrior River valley.

The Culinary Genesis of Moundville

To revisit the question posed at the beginning of the chapter—is cooking socially generative?—I would like to reiterate that I believe that it is, and more importantly, that it is the social practice behind the genesis of Moundville. Beginning around AD 1070, Mississippian women immigrated to the Black Warrior River valley, where they grew, processed, and cooked the dishes and meals they were familiar with, thus continuing a culinary Mississippian identity. Social domains central to this identity included those of maize agriculture, crafting and cooking with shell-tempered globular jars, and the hominy foodway. By practicing their culinary traditions within the larger, shared culinary landscape of the area, they introduced, taught, and shared elements of their practice with other women, including the knowledge, materials, and skills central to preparing and cooking hominy. Ultimately, their recipes and dishes were adopted and shared throughout the valley, and over fifty years, or by the Early Mississippian Moundville I phase (AD 1120), women across the area began growing maize, making shell-tempered globular jars, and cooking hominy. Through cooking, eating, and pottery making, women created Moundville—they created a shared, common culinary tradition that established the menu for everyday meals as well as those for special occasions; they crafted a common, shared set of tools and practices that standardized culinary spaces; they made similar looking cooking pots; they shared workstations and spaces central to their femininity. They created an *us*, an emergent social group that sponsored and united communities throughout the valley in culinary practice, providing a platform for everything to come. Before there can be public needs, and monumental projects built to manifest and commemorate, there needs to be a community, a group of people who recognize each other as those to whom they are obligated. While feasting is certainly one way to foster those obligations, so too are daily, everyday practices that bring people into contact with one another. The power of sharing a meal need not only be understood by aspiring elites and those with political aspirations, and mound construction need not be the only way to bring people together; cooking and sharing a pot of food is an equally powerful social activity that can actively transform a landscape and build new worlds in the process.

Acknowledgments

I am forever grateful to a number of cooks/academics who have informed my understanding of hominy, Moundville, acorns, and cooking pots. First, thank you to Jim Knight and Ian Brown, two excellent mentors. Bill Dressler and Jo Weaver provided comments on this research several years ago, and Margie Scarry continues to share a lifetime of incomparable knowledge about food and cooking; all have challenged me to think more broadly about food. The ceramic analysis referenced within was only possible with the support and help of Bill Allen at the Office of Archaeological Research at Moundville. Thank you to Chris Rodning, Rob Beck, and David Moore, who decided they needed one more cook in the kitchen. I am forever grateful to Michaelyn Harle and Lynne Sullivan—their insights, support, and experience are invaluable, and it has truly been a privilege to work with both. Thank you to Mary Puckett, Romi Gutierrez, and two anonymous reviewers—your thoughtful, insightful comments elevated this chapter, as well as this manuscript more generally. And finally, thank you Andrew, Charlie, and Ernie for joining me on this long, strange, gustatory journey.

References Cited

Bandera, Juan de la

1990 The "Long" Bandera Relation. Translated by Paul Hoffman. In *The Juan Pardo Expeditions: Exploration of the Carolinas and Tennessee, 1566-1568,* by Charles Hudson, pp. 205-296. Smithsonian Institution Press, Washington, D.C.

Bauer, Brooke Michele

2022 *Being Catawba: Catawba Indian Women and Nation-Building.* University of Alabama Press, Tuscaloosa.

Baumann, Timothy, and Gary Crites

2016 The Age and Distribution of the Common Bean (*Phaseolus vulgaris*) in Tennessee and the Southeastern U.S. Presented at the 81st Annual Meeting of the Society for American Archaeology, Orlando, Florida.

Borthwick, F.

2000 Olfaction and Taste: Invasive Odors and Disappearing Objects. *Australian Journal of Anthropology* 11: 127–140.

Bourdieu, Pierre

1984 *Distinction: A Social Critique of the Judgment of Taste.* Harvard University Press, Cambridge.

Bridges, Patricia S.

1989 Changes in Activities with the Shift to Agriculture in the Southeastern United States. *Current Anthropology* 30: 385–394.

Briggs, Rachel V.

2015 The Hominy Foodway of the Historic Native Eastern Woodlands. *Native South* 8(1): 112–146.

2016 The Civil Cooking Pot: Hominy and the Mississippian Standard Jar in the Black Warrior River Valley, Alabama. *American Antiquity* 81(2): 316–332.

2017 From Bitter Seeds: A Historical Anthropological Approach to Moundville's Origins, A.D. 1050–1120. PhD dissertation, Department of Anthropology, University of Alabama, Tuscaloosa.

2023 Edible Metaphors and the Mississippian Phenomenon: A Case Study from the Black Warrior River Valley, Alabama, AD 1070–1250. In *Ancient Foodways: Integrative Approaches to Understanding Subsistence and Society*, edited by C. Margaret Scarry, Dale L. Hutchinson, and Benjamin Arbuckle, pp. 183–207. University of Florida Press, Gainesville.

Briggs, Rachel V., and Heather Lapham

2022 Chewing the Fat: Native Eastern Woodland Edible Metaphors of Pig and Bear. Presented at the 78th Annual Southeastern Archaeology Conference, November 9, 2022, Little Rock, Arkansas.

Briggs, Rachel V., Christopher Rodning, Robin A. Beck, and David G. Moore

2023 Fear the Native Woman: Femininity, Food, and Power in the Sixteenth-Century North Carolina Piedmont. *American Anthropology,*1-15. DOI:10.1111/aman.13918

Chacko, Elizabeth

2005 Understanding the Geography of Pellagra in the United States: The Role of Social and Place-Based Identities. *Gender, Place, and Culture* 2: 197–212.

Claassen, Cheryl

1992 Questioning Gender: An Introduction. In *Exploring Gender through Archaeology,* ed. Cheryle Claassen, 1–10. Prehistory Press, Monographs in World Archaeology 11, Madison.

2001 Challenges for Regendering Southeastern Prehistory. In *Archaeological Studies of Gender in the Southeastern United States*, edited by by Jane Eastman and Christopher Rodning, pp. 10–26. University Press of Florida, Tallahassee

Cobb, Charles

2003 Mississippian Chiefdoms: How Complex? *Annual Review of Anthropology* 32: 63–84.

Cook, Robert A., and Aaron R. Comstock, eds.

2022 *Following Mississippian Spread: Climate Change and Migration in the Eastern US (ca. AD 1000–1600).* Springer Press. DOI: 10.1007/978-3-030-89082-7_2.

Cushman, H. B.

1899 *History of the Choctaw, Chickasaw, and Natchez Indians.* Russell and Russell, New York.

Davis, Jera R.

2014 On Common Ground: Social Memory and the Plaza at Early Moundville. PhD dissertation, Department of Anthropology, University of Alabama, Tuscaloosa.

Deagan, Kathleen A.

1983 *Spanish St. Augustine: The Archaeology of a Colonial Creole Community.* New York, Academic Press.

Douglas, Mary

1971 Deciphering a Meal. In *Myth, Symbol, and Culture*, edited by Clifford Geertz, pp. 61–82. W. Norton Press, New York.

Eckert, Suzanne

2008 *Pottery and Practice: The Expression of Identity at Pottery Mound and Hummingbird Pueblo.* University of New Mexico Press, Albuquerque.

Eggan, Fred

1937 Historical Changes in the Choctaw Kinship System. *American Anthropologist* 39(1): 34–52.

Ensor, H. Blaine

1993 *Big Sandy Farms: A Prehistoric Agricultural Community near Moundville, Black Warrior River Floodplain, Tuscaloosa County, Alabama.* Report of Investigations 68. Office of Archaeological Research, University of Alabama, Tuscaloosa.

Ethridge, Robbie

2009 Introduction: Mapping the Mississippian Shatterzone. In *Mapping the Mississippian Shatterzone: The Colonial Indian Slave Trade and Regional Instability in the American South*, edited by Robbie Ethridge and Sheri M. Shuck-Hall, pp. 1–62. University of Nebraska Press, Lincoln.

2010 *From Chicaza to Chickasaw: The European Invasion and the Transformation of the Mississippian World, 1540–1715.* The University of North Carolina Press, Chapel Hill.

Fritz, Gayle J.
2019 *Feeding Cahokia: Early Agriculture in the North American Heartland.* University of Alabama Press, Tuscaloosa.

Galloway, Patricia K.
1995 *Choctaw Genesis 1500–1700.* University of Nebraska Press, Lincoln.
1997 Where Have All the Menstrual Huts Gone? The Invisibility of Menstrual Seclusion in the Late Prehistoric Southeast. In *Women in Prehistory: North American and Mesoamerica*, edited by Cheryl Claassen and Rosemary A. Joyce, pp. 47–62. University of Pennsylvania Press, Philadelphia.

Graham, Anna F.
2020 Fuelwood Collection as Daily Practice: A Wood Charcoal Study for the Colonial Period North Carolina Piedmont. *Southeastern Archaeology* 39(3): 166–182.

Green, Rayna
2008 Mother Corn and the Dixie Pig: Native Food in the Native South. *Southern Cultures* 14(4): 114–126.

Gruppuso, Paulo, and Andrew Whitehouse
2020 Exploring Taskscapes: An Introduction. *Social Anthropology* 28(3): 588–597.

Hamilakis, Yannis
1999 Food Technologies/Technologies of the Body: The Social Context of Wine and Oil Production and Consumption in Bronze Age Crete. *World Archaeology* 31: 38–54.

Hart, John P., and C. Margaret Scarry
1999 The Age of Common Beans (*Phaseolus vulgaris*) in the Northeastern United States. *American Antiquity* 64(4): 653–658.

Hastorf, Christine
2016 *The Social Archaeology of Food: Thinking about Eating from Prehistory to the Present.* Cambridge University Press, Cambridge.

Hawsey, Kareen L.
2015 Vessel Morphology and Function in the West Jefferson Phase of the Black Warrior Valley, Alabama. Unpublished master's thesis, Department of Anthropology, University of Alabama, Tuscaloosa.

Hegyi, Jurai, Robert A. Schwartz, and Vladimir Hegyi
2003 Pellagra: Dermatitis, Dementia, and Diarrhea. *International Journal of Dermatology* 43: 1–5.

Hudson, Charles
1976 *The Southeastern Indians.* University of Tennessee Press, Knoxville.
2004 *Black Drink: A Native American Tea.* University of Georgia Press, Athens.

Ingold, Timothy
1993 The Temporality of the Landscape. *World Archaeology* 25: 152–174.

Jenkins, Ned J.
2003 The Terminal Woodland/Mississippian Transition in West Central Alabama. *Journal of Alabama Archaeology* 49(1–2): 1–62.

Jenkins, Ned J., and Ernest W. Seckinger
2000 A Plural Society in Prehistoric Alabama. *Journal of Alabama Archaeology* 46: 43–57.

Jenkins, Ned J., and Jerry Nielsen

1974 Archaeological Salvage Investigations at the West Jefferson Steam Plant Site, Jefferson County, Alabama. Report on File at the Office of Archaeological Research, Moundville.

Jenkins, Ned J., and Richard Krause

2009 The Woodland-Mississippian Interface in Alabama, ca. A.D. 1075–1200: An Adaptive Radiation? *Southeastern Archaeology* 28(2): 202–219.

Joyce, Rosemary A. and Cheryl Claassen

1997 Women in the Ancient Americas: Archaeologists, Gender, and the Making of Prehistory. In *Women in Prehistory: North America and Mesoamerica,* edited by Cheryl Claassen and Rosemary A. Joyce, pp. 1–14. University of Pennsylvania Press, Philadelphia.

Joyce, Rosemary, and J. Henderson

2008 From Feasting to Cuisine: Implications of Archaeological Research in an Early Honduran Village. *American Anthropologist* 109: 642–653.

Kidwell, Clara Sue

1992 Indian Women as Cultural Mediators. *Ethnohistory* 39(2): 97–107.

Knight, Vernon J.

2001 Feasting and the Emergence of Platform Mound Ceremonialism in Eastern North America. In *Feasts: Archaeological and Ethnographic Perspectives on Food, Politics, and Power,* edited by Michael Dietler and Brian Hayden, pp. 239–254. Smithsonian Institution Press, Washington, D.C.

2010 *Mound Excavations at Moundville: Architecture, Elites, and Social Order.* University of Alabama Press, Tuscaloosa.

Knight, Vernon J., Jr., and Vincas P. Steponaitis

2007 A New History of Moundville. In *Archaeology of the Moundville Chiefdom,* edited by Vernon J. Knight, Jr., and Vincas P. Steponaitis, pp. 1–26. University of Alabama Press, Tuscaloosa.

Lacquement, Cameron H.

2007 Typology, Chronology, and Technology of Mississippian Domestic Architecture in West-Central Alabama. In *Architectural Variability in the Southeast,* edited by Cameron H. Lacquement, pp. 49–72. University of Alabama Press, Tuscaloosa.

Lankford, George

2008 *Looking for Lost Lore: Studies in Folklore, Ethnology, and Iconography.* University of Alabama Press, Tuscaloosa.

Linton, Ralph

1944 North American Cooking Pots. *American Antiquity* 9(4): 369–380.

Lowery, Malinda Maynor

2013 Kinship and Capitalism in the Chickasaw and Choctaw Nations. In *The Native South: New Histories and Enduring Legacies*, edited by Tim Alan Garrison and Greg O'Brien, pp. 200–219. University of Nebraska Press, Lincoln.

Manion, Jen

2020 *Female Husbands: A Trans History.* Cambridge University Press, Cambridge.

Mankiller, Wilma

2011 *Every Day Is a Good Day: Reflections by Contemporary Indigenous Women.* Fulcrum Publishing, Golden, Colorado.

McGee, Harold

2004 *On Food and Cooking: The Science and Lore of the Kitchen.* Scribner, New York.

Outram, Alan

2007 Hunter-Gatherers and the First Farmers: The Evolution of Taste in Prehistory. In *Food: The History of Taste*, edited by Paul Freedman, pp. 35–61. University of California Press, Berkely.

Peasantubbee, Michelene E.

2005 *Choctaw Women in a Chaotic World: The Clash of Cultures in the Colonial Southeast.* University of New Mexico Press, Albuquerque.

2014 Nancy Ward: American Patriot or Cherokee Nationalist? *The American Indian Quarterly* 38(2): 177–206.

Perdue, Theda

2001 *Sifters: Native American Women's Lives.* Oxford University Press, Oxford.

Perrelli, Douglas

1994 Gender, Mobility and Subsistence in Iroquoian Prehistory: An Ethnohistorical Approach to Archaeological Interpretation. Master's thesis, Department of Anthropology, State University of New York, Buffalo.

2001 Gender Roles and Seasonal Site Use in Western New York, c. AD 1500: Iroquoian Domestic and Ceremonial Production at the Piestrak and Spaulding Lake Sites. PhD dissertation, Department of Anthropology, State University of New York, Buffalo.

Richardson, Sarah S.

2013 *Sex Itself: The Search for Male and Female in the Human Genome.* University of Chicago Press, Chicago.

Romans, Bernard

1962 [1775] *A Concise Natural History of East and West Florida.* University of Florida Press, Gainesville.

Scarry, C. Margaret

1986 Change in Plant Procurement and Production During the Emergence of the Moundville Chiefdom. Unpublished PhD dissertation, Department of Anthropology, University of Michigan, Ann Arbor.

Scarry, C. Margaret, and John F. Scarry

2005 Native American "Garden Agriculture" in Southeastern North America. *World Archaeology* 37:259–274.

Scarry, C. Margaret, and Vincas Steponaitis

2016 Moundville as a Ceremonial Ground. In *Rethinking Moundville and Its Hinterlands*, edited by Vincas P. Steponaits and C. Margaret Scarry, pp. 255–268. University of Florida Press, Gainesville.

Schoeninger, Margaret J., and Mark R. Schurr

2007 Human Subsistence at Moundville: The Stable-Isotope Data. In *Archaeology of the Moundville Chiefdom*, edited by Vernon James Knight, Jr., and Vincas P. Steponaitis, pp. 120–132. University of Alabama Press, Tuscaloosa.

Sherwood, Sarah C., and Tristam R. Kidder
2011 The DaVincis of Dirt: Geoarchaeological Perspectives on Native American Mound Building in the Mississippi River Basin. *Journal of Anthropological Archaeology* 30: 69–87.

Steponaitis, Vincas
2009 *Ceramics, Chronology, and Community Patterns: An Archaeological Study of Moundville.* Academic Press, New York.

Sutton, David E.
2010 Food and the Senses. *Annual Review of Anthropology* 39: 209–223.

Swanton, John R.
1946 *Indians of the Southeastern United States.* Bureau of American Ethnology Bulletin 137. Smithsonian Institution, Washington, D.C.

Trocolli, Ruth
2002 Mississippian Chiefs: Women and Men of Power. In *The Dynamics of Power*, edited by M. O'Donovan, pp. 168–187. Occasional Paper Np. 30. Center for Archaeological Investigations. Southern Illinois University, Carbondale.
2006 Elite Status and Gender: Women Leaders in Chiefdom Societies of the Southeastern U.S. PhD dissertation, Department of Anthropology, University of Florida, Gainesville.

Thompson, Claire E.
2011 Ritual and Power: Examining the Economy of Moundville's Residential Population. Unpublished PhD dissertation, Department of Anthropology, University of Alabama, Tuscaloosa.

Thompson, Ian
2008 Chata Intikba Im Aiikhvna (Learning from the Choctaw Ancestors): Integrating Indigenous and Experimental Approaches in the Study of Mississippian Technology. PhD dissertation, Department of Anthropology, The University of New Mexico, Albuquerque.

Wegner, Etienne
1998 *Communities of Practice: Learning, Meaning, and Identity.* Cambridge University Press, Cambridge.

Weiss, Brad
1996 *The Making and Unmaking of the Haya Lived World: Consumption, Commoditization, and Everyday Practice.* Duke University Press, Durham, North Carolina.

Welch, Paul D.
1981 The West Jefferson Phase: Terminal Woodland Tribal Society in West Central Alabama. *Southeastern Archaeological Conference Bulletin* 24: 81–83.

Wilson, Gregory
2008 *The Archaeology of Everyday Life at Early Moundville.* University of Alabama Press, Tuscaloosa.

Worth, John E.
2017 What in a Phase? Disentangling Communities of Practice from Communities of Identity in Southeastern North America. In *Forging Southeastern Identities*, edited by Gregory A. Waselkov and Marvin T. Smith, pp. 117–156. University of Alabama Press, Tuscaloosa.

4

The Life Course of Women in Upper Tennessee Valley, Dallas Phase Communities

Michaelyn S. Harle, Tracy K. Betsinger, and Lynne P. Sullivan

This volume highlights a continuing trend in research on the Mississippian period, a movement from the male-centric chiefdom model to one that incorporates a wider range of actors, especially women, in the construction and maintenance of Mississippian societies (Alt and Pauketat 2007; Boudreaux 2010; Fritz 2019; Pauketat 2007; Sullivan 2001, 2006; Sullivan and Rodning 2011). Levy (2014: 234) called for Southeastern archaeologists "to examine women's lives more closely," not just to better understand women's roles, but as a means to explore the "implications of different activities being practiced by different categories of people." To gain a more holistic understanding of women in the precolumbian Southeast, we must not view their roles as simply static, but as a continuous process. In this discussion, we use bioarchaeological and mortuary data, while also drawing upon regional ethnographic and ethnohistorical sources, to explore the life courses and intergenerational relationships of Late Mississippian women within Dallas phase communities of the Upper Tennessee Valley. This study enables us to better understand the life experiences of these women at different intersections in their lives, especially pertaining to identity, morbidity, labor, and prestige. In doing so, we answer Levy's call by focusing on a particular salient, if often ignored, activity - the act of mothering and caregiving. We examine how this concept of "mothering" evolves throughout women's life cycle and extends far beyond the care of a biological mother for her offspring.

While archaeological research has expanded to include the roles of women and children in shaping past societies (e.g., Baxter 2005; Conkey and Gero

1991; Derevenski 2000; Gilchrist 1999; Moore and Scott 1997; Nelson 1997), the role of women as mothers has received less exploration in both biological anthropological and archaeological literature. In fact, as Wilkie (2003) notes, the term mother or motherhood is rarely mentioned even in archaeological volumes dedicated specifically to these subjects. While there has been some research that has focused specifically on archaeological material correlates of birthing (Beausang 2000; Bengtson 2017) and bioarchaeological evidence of breastfeeding and weaning (e.g., Fogel et al. 1989; Katzenberg et al. 1996; Wright and Schwarcz 1998), very little archaeological research has focused on the act of mothering outside the early stages of birth and infant rearing, nor has research explored the various types of care work in which women were engaged.

This omission leads to an underappreciation of the act of mothering and caregiving as undoubtedly playing vital roles in the maintenance and reproduction of past societies. Perhaps the lack of exploration is because unlike, for instance, faunal remains and stone tool technologies that have a direct correlate to food procurement, as Bolen (1992: 54) points out, "little material culture evidence seems to 'get at' prehistoric mothers directly." From a biological standpoint, skeletal indicators of pregnancy and parturition can be highly unreliable (Ubelaker and De La Paz 2012). Moreover, caregiving in the past, especially childcare, was more than just giving birth. What types of evidence can provide insight into the complexities of caregiving and how might it change through one's lifespan?

Some of the reticence to focus on or include studies of mothers is perhaps because the concept of motherhood is embedded in the perception of biological determinism (Beauvoir 1989 [1952]; Firestone 2003 [1970]; Friedan 2001 [1963]; Ortner 1974). The conceptualization of motherhood all too often is placed within the Western industrial-era, patriarchal framework that separates women from public life and views motherhood as a basis for subjugation (e.g., Beauvoir 1989 [1952]; Mill 1984; Vogel 1995). Additionally, this viewpoint assumes that all women are biologically mothers, which, of course, is not the case. In contrast to the Western view of motherhood, many cross-cultural ethnographic studies demonstrate there is a remarkable amount of variation in the social role of mothering (e.g., Collins 2000; Ragoné and Twine 2000; Scheper-Hughes 1992; Stearney 1994).

To move away from the problematic terminology of "motherhood," Rich (1986) makes the distinction between the *institution of motherhood,* viewed through the lens of a source of oppression of women, and the act of *mothering* as the experience of raising, feeding, and caring for children. She suggests that viewed from this perspective, the act of mothering can be a source of women's empowerment rather than their oppression. In other words, the experience of mothering is culturally mediated and not universal. This perspective guides our discussion of mothering within Dallas phase communities of the Upper Tennessee Valley. While not all women are mothers in the traditional (i.e., biological) sense of the word, women from the Mississippian period were caregivers on several levels and in a variety of roles. In our discussion, we extend the mothering concept to go beyond the care of children to the *raising, feeding, and caring* of the entire community, or "community care." We assert that it is the act of mothering in the Late Mississippian communities of East Tennessee that served, "as a basis of their [women's] power . . . not as a basis of oppression," an interpretation that is similar to Johnston's (2003) discussion of Cherokee women.

Life Course Perspective in Archaeology

Important to this discussion is the distinction between gender and biological sex. Gender, as opposed to biological sex, focuses on the social norms a society places on its members (Butler 1993). Gender is performative by nature, can be actively resisted and engaged, and is neither necessarily equitable to a person's sex nor binary. These gender roles are often taught early in life and continually reinforced throughout one's life, but are culturally mediated and can vary by geography, time, and age (Halim et al. 2011; Joyce 2008; Geller 2009; Gilchrist 1999, 2014; Meskell 1999). The limitation of bioarchaeological analysis is the dependency on biological sex and its assignment based on skeletal markers (Buikstra and Ubelaker 1994). This limit is further complicated by the decrease in accuracy of sex assignment among females with increasing age (see Walker 1995). Further, there is the additional issue that gender does not necessarily equate to binary sex characteristics. This circumstance is especially the case among Southeastern tribes that recognized third- and fourth-gender peoples (Aimers and Rutecki 2016; Smithers 2014). The exploration of multiple genders among pre-contact Southeastern groups has remained largely unexplored with a few exceptions (Emerson 2003; Hally 2008). As a result, there is an inherent tension between the biological body that is visible to archaeologists and bioarchaeologists and the social interactions and material culture that shape gender. Nevertheless, we agree with Sofaer (2006) that biological sex based on skeletal data is crucial to understanding gender roles among past populations. Sofaer (2006) suggests, and it is the approach we take in this chapter, that we should view the body as another form of material culture for which gender can be expressed by human action. As Joyce (2008) points out, gender expectations are continuously contested, embraced, or reframed over one's lifetime. Teasing out gender norms and personal gender identity on the basis of osteological sex is especially difficult when these norms can be fluid throughout one's life. In this respect, integrating age with gender highlights "the dynamism of identity—the processes and performances of socializations from cradle to grave" (Geller 2009: 70).

The life course perspective is a particularly useful tool to examine the intersection of age and gender. Devised in the 1960s, the life course perspective is a multidisciplinary approach that views individual development through the lens of not only the passage of time, but also social, biological, cultural, and structural contexts (Alwin 2012; Elder 1995). Just as gender is culturally mediated, the life course perspective encourages the identification of "age roles and thresholds that are culturally specific" (Gilchrist 2009: 18). Not only can perceptions of age vary culturally, but they can also vary internally depending on other organizing factors such as social class and gender.

Born out of sociology, the life course perspective tends to focus on longitudinal studies. Like gender analysis, bioarchaeological analysis of age roles comes with limitations as bioarchaeologists must rely on biological age cohorts based on the level of skeletal maturation or degeneration, which does not always correlate with chronological age. Identifying early gendered processes in childhood is especially difficult given the inaccuracies of osteological methods in determining sex in nonadults (Mays 2013), as well as the aforementioned problem of decreasing the accuracy of sex determination in older females. Despite these limitations, the life course analysis has been increasingly used in both archaeological and bioarchaeological contexts to examine how notions of identity are dynamic and are changed and created by experiences over one's life, and how this fluidity can be manifested in both material culture and the body itself (Agarwal 2016; Gilchrist 2009).

Archaeological and Ethnohistorical Context

Our data originate from multiple fourteenth- through sixteenth-century Late Mississippian, Dallas phase communities in the Upper Tennessee River Valley (Figure 4.1). The Dallas phase is characterized by intensive maize agriculturalists, who resided in towns that included public structures associated with large, earthen platform mounds, a central plaza, and domestic dwellings consisting of paired summer and winter structures. These domestic dwellings are often marked by multiple building episodes, suggesting continuity over generations by what has been interpreted as corporate kin groups (Schroedl 1998; Sullivan 1995, 2001, 2006, 2018). As a result of the intensification of agriculture, population size and density increased significantly, making the

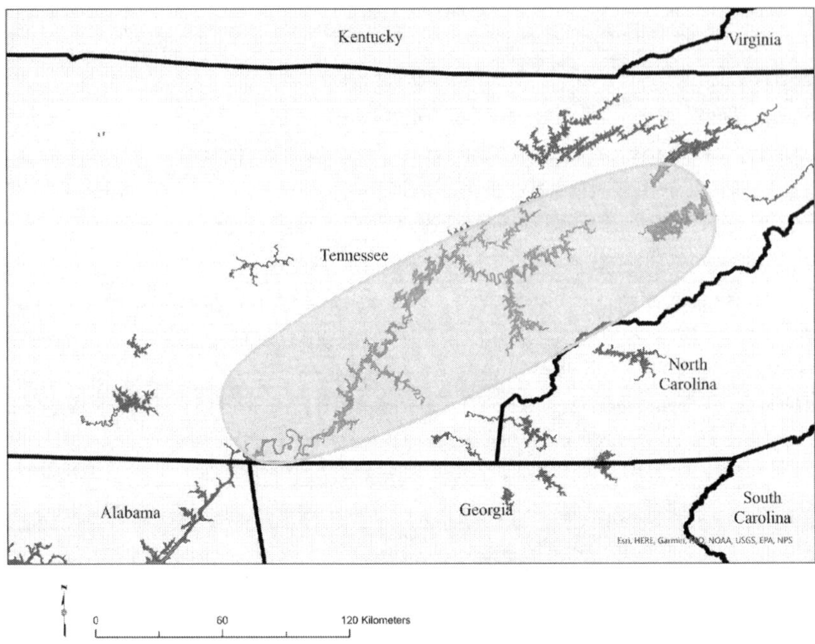

Figure 4.1. Map depicting the study area.

people of the Dallas phase distinct from earlier, incipient farmers. The deceased are buried in both public and residential locations, often reflecting age- and sex-based differences. Burials within platform mounds and associated with public buildings typically are males. In contrast, most female burials are associated with residences (Hatch 1974; Schroedl 1998; Sullivan 1995, 2001). Likewise, males are more likely interred with artifacts associated with hunting and warfare activities (e.g., triangular points, ceremonial blades, cores, flakes, bone awls, and utilitarian celts) while females were more likely associated with shell, pottery, and other "culinary" and domestic implements (Hatch 1974; Sullivan 1995, 2001).

A considerable amount of previous attention has been devoted to these Dallas phase communities as chiefdom-level societies, and consequently sought evidence of hierarchical divisions both internally within communities and externally between populations (Hally et al. 1990; Hatch 1974; Hudson et al. 1985; Scott and Polhemus 1987). Only recently have researchers moved beyond this chiefdom construction to explore alternate, more heterarchical notions of power and how others, in addition to chiefs, actively constructed these communities (Harle 2010; Sullivan and Harle 2010; Sullivan 2001, 2006, 2018).

Our discussion focuses heavily on Cherokee ethnographic and ethnohistorical sources. In doing so, we do not suggest that there is necessarily continuity between these late precolumbian communities and the post-contact Cherokee towns. We also recognize that early ethnohistorical sources can be fraught with Eurocentric biases (Ethridge 2010; Galloway 1995). We instead use this literature as a starting point to identify archaeological and biological correlates of women's work, including mothering as it relates to age and gender identity.

Based on ethnographic and ethnohistorical sources, the Cherokees were divided into regional clusters of towns with a central so-called mother town (or beloved town) linking various communities in the southern Appalachian region (Reid 1970). Within these towns, centralized public structures called townhouses marked the focus of public life (Rodning 2015). Cherokee mothers figure prominently in Cherokee cosmology and still play important roles in the reproduction of society, and in fact, their role as mothers/caregivers was instrumental in their source of power (Cooper 2022; Johnston 2003). A quote from the Cherokee leader Attakullakulla highlights this point. After the shock of seeing no white women present during trade negotiations with the governor of South Carolina, he states, "Since the white man as well as the red was born of woman, did not the white man admit women to their councils?" (Corkran 1962: 110).

Cherokee kinship was, and still is, determined by matrilineal clan membership. Within each clan, the Cherokee household generally included several families, all related through the matriarch who was the highest authority within the household (Cooper 2022; Reid 1970). Women in these matrilineal/matrilocal societies were in charge of the households and agricultural production, which were sources of considerable power and influence. In other words, the role of women and mothers involved not only physical care of children, but also care of the household and care of their agricultural activities, which sustained the entire population. Their political clout was especially strong for the most senior women, often referred to as "beloved" women, who had authority over their kin groups as clan officers (Perdue 1998: 46; Sattler 1995: 222), again demonstrating that their scope of care expanded beyond their own children to include their wider kin. These "grandmothers," so to speak, were highly regarded and consulted regarding herbal medicine, sacred matters, and tribal history, reflecting how their role involved care of community traditions and history as well as community health. These senior women also spoke in the council[1] where they could veto a declaration of war (Niethammer 1977). They actively participated in multigenerational care through their assistance in physical caring for grandchildren as well as through teaching these children tribal traditions, emphasizing their role in caring for the continuity of tradition for the community (Niethammer 1977: 249–250). In fact, Gilbert (1955: 300) noted that the literal translation for *gilisis*, the Eastern Cherokee's generalized term for both maternal and paternal grandmothers, is "she bears on her back," likely referring to grandmothers' roles in relieving young mothers of the care of the young (Gilbert 1955: 300) and reflecting the expansive nature of their caregiving. In Cherokee society, the act of mothering and caregiving thus continues throughout a woman's life, both within the literal sense of her maternal kin and within the clan system as a whole. Mothering, then, for the Cherokee, is not simply defined as raising your children; it is a lifelong process of providing care for the larger kin group and for the overall community as well, both in terms of maintaining tradition and passing on history, but also through the essential task of caring for food resources, which sustains the entire population (Fritz 2019).

Early Childhood through Adolescence

The locations where communities choose to place their dead and the funerary objects associated with those graves have social meanings that relate to cultural constructs of identity, including age, gender, rank, and kinship (Carr 1995; Goldstein 1980; Parker Pearson 1982; Rakita 2008; Sullivan and Mainfort 2010). The examination of the mortuary patterning of nonadult burials has a long history in Mississippian period archaeological research in general and among Dallas phase research in particular (e.g., Brown 1981; Hatch 1974; Scott and Polhemus 1987; Wilson et al. 2010). Researchers have often framed these analyses within the context of identifying the social structure (specifically vertical rank) of the entire community. Children in southeastern archaeological research, if considered at all, are often viewed in terms of passive recipients. The presence of so-called preeminent nonadult burials (in other words, nonadults buried within a mound, sometimes with elaborate funerary objects) was considered suggestive of some level of ascribed status within a society (Hatch 1974; Brown 1981).

As Gilchrist (2004: 13) states, "perhaps because contemporary western society regards children as socially passive, economically non-productive and culturally peripheral, children were largely disregarded in archaeological interpretations." A growing body of archaeological research challenges this assumption when it pertains to past societies (Beauchesne and Agarwal 2018; Derevenski 2000; Moore and Scott 1997). Beyond providing indicators of a parent's social rank, mortuary treatment can provide important clues regarding parent-child relationships, the role of children as active agents within their society, the personhood or identity of children at various ages, and incipient gender roles.

To examine this assertion more closely, we studied the mortuary treatments of subadults at the Toqua (40MR6), Dallas (40HA1) and the Dallas phase village component at Hiwassee Island (40MG31)[2]. When examining the location of burials, nonadult burials occur in conjunction with adults in both the domestic sphere (within residences) and public spaces (platform mounds), although they are more likely to occur within domestic spaces. The exception to this patterning is perinates (i.e., newborns 0–1 month) who are exclusively buried within the residential sphere. We have argued elsewhere that perinates' association with the maternal body may have led to their preferential burial in residential spaces (Han et al. 2018), which is where women were also preferentially interred.

The most common types of funerary object inclusions for all subadult age categories are shell ornamentations (beads, pins, shell face masks, and gorgets) and pottery (Figures 4.2 and 4.3). In fact, for perinates and infants (0 to 2 years), other types of funerary associations are rare. Shell gorgets, pendants made of the outer whorl of whelk shells and engraved with images often depicting mythical beings or other supernatural symbols, have been interpreted as markers of social status through the female line (Hatch 1974; King 2004), but the demographic distribution of these objects is skewed by age, to the very young and the elderly, not by sex (Sullivan 2019). While shell ornaments and pottery as funerary objects crosscut age and gender categories, these materials occur more frequently with women and children in the Dallas communities in our study. Hally (2008) previously argued that the presence of shell ornamentation may reflect personal and household wealth. Thomas (1996: 46) came to the same conclusion, but she also argues "they seem to have been an optional element of costume, available to a diverse array of people through various mechanisms." Given the occurrence of shell ornaments in perinatal and newborn graves, it is unlikely this was necessarily a "costume" worn by the recipient. If Dallas women, like Cherokee women, controlled the household economy, then it would make sense that the "signaling" would pass through women to their kin. A similar pattern has been identified by Sullivan (Chapter 6, this volume), indicating a strong connection between pottery motifs and styles linking both infants with each other and with adult females.

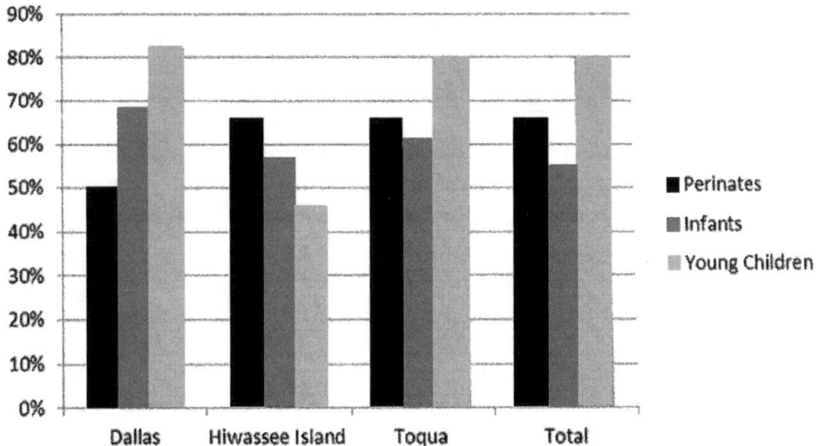

Figure 4.2. Percentage of subadults interred with funerary objects containing shell ornaments.

Similar to burial placement, the material accompaniments suggest that early reflections of personhood directly tied to the infant/mother bond and within the larger kinship network.

It is noteworthy that while shell ornaments and pottery continue to be the most common type of funerary inclusion for older children, a wider variety of funerary object types was placed with older than with younger children (starting around 8–9 years of age). Because of the unreliability of determining sex of nonadults, it is difficult to discern what the variety of artifact types interred with children indicates about early gender roles. We suggest that this increase may point to the beginning of the acculturation of children within the larger socioeconomic system.

We see this pattern mentioned in Cherokee ethnohistorical literature. Childcare involved the child's active participation in day-to-day economic activities. Starting early in childhood, children learned through doing. Mothers and their extended kin taught older girls "women's work," which included housework, tending the gardens, keeping the fire going, and making pottery and basketry. Boys learned to hunt by spending most of their time practicing using their weapons on small animals and practicing the ballgame often under the tutelage of their mothers' brothers (Hudson 1976). Claassen (2002) suggests that the contribution of children's labor may have extended to the Woodland period and was born out of women's "time management crises" resulting from increased economic demands associated with the transition to horticulture.

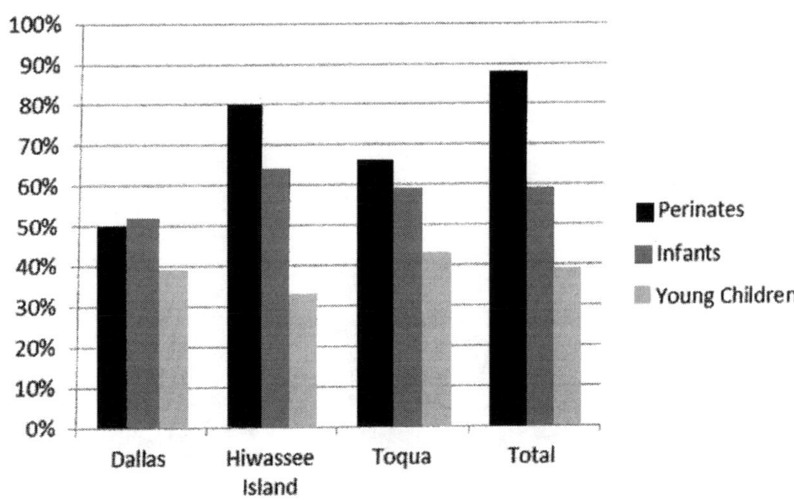

Figure 4.3. Percentage of subadults interred with funerary objects containing pottery.

Also of interest is the appearance of possible ritual/ceremonial items (a pipe, minerals, and of particular interest turtle shell rattles, including pebbles and turtle carapaces suggestive of rattles) found occurring around later childhood and extending into adolescence. For a better understanding of this pattern, we considered all instances of rattles recorded in Late Mississippian burials in East Tennessee and found a marked increase in their occurrence starting at age eight, continuing through adolescence, and peaking in the 20–30 age range (Figures 4.4 and 4.5). Because of the difficulties in determining sex in children, we cannot say if these children are males or females, but there are some clues. Of the adolescents (post-pubertal) who could be assessed for sex, all are females, and the majority (80%) of rattles found with adults of identifiable sex are also interred with females.

Rattles continue to play a central role in ceremonies such as Stomp Dances among contemporary Southeastern native tribes (Figure 4.6). These rattles, most often worn by women, "shell-shakers," provide the "driving pulse" of the ceremony (Heth 1975: 146–50). Turtles, who hibernate underwater in lake and pond sediments, but walk on land, also are associated with portals between this world and the lower world (Heth 1975). The occurrence of rattles among older children and adolescent females suggests that girls, starting around late childhood, begin to take their place within ceremonial ritual life.

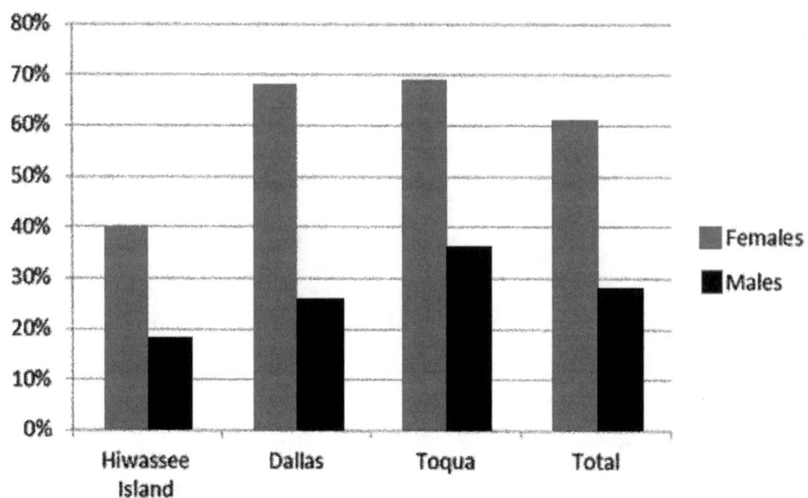

Figure 4.4. Percentage of males and females interred with funerary objects containing shell ornaments.

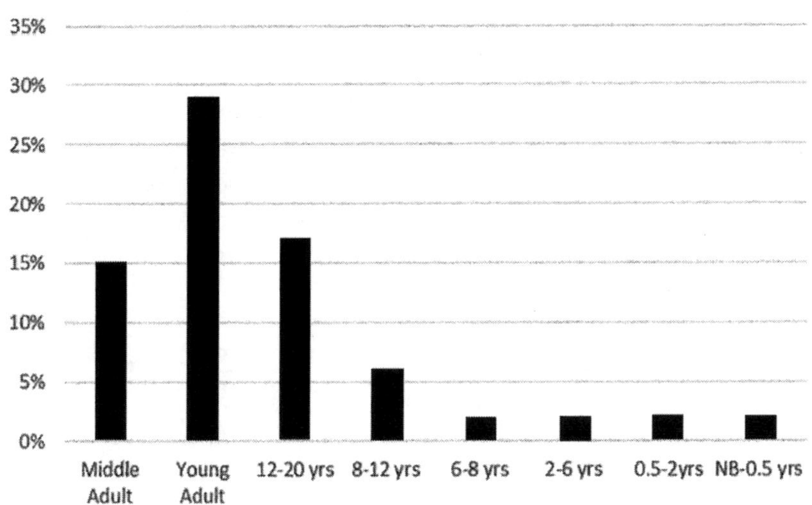

Figure 4.5. Percentage of turtle shell buried with individuals who could be osteologically aged (sites 40AN19, 40AN15, 40BY13, 40HA1, 40KN14, 40RE12, 40RH41).

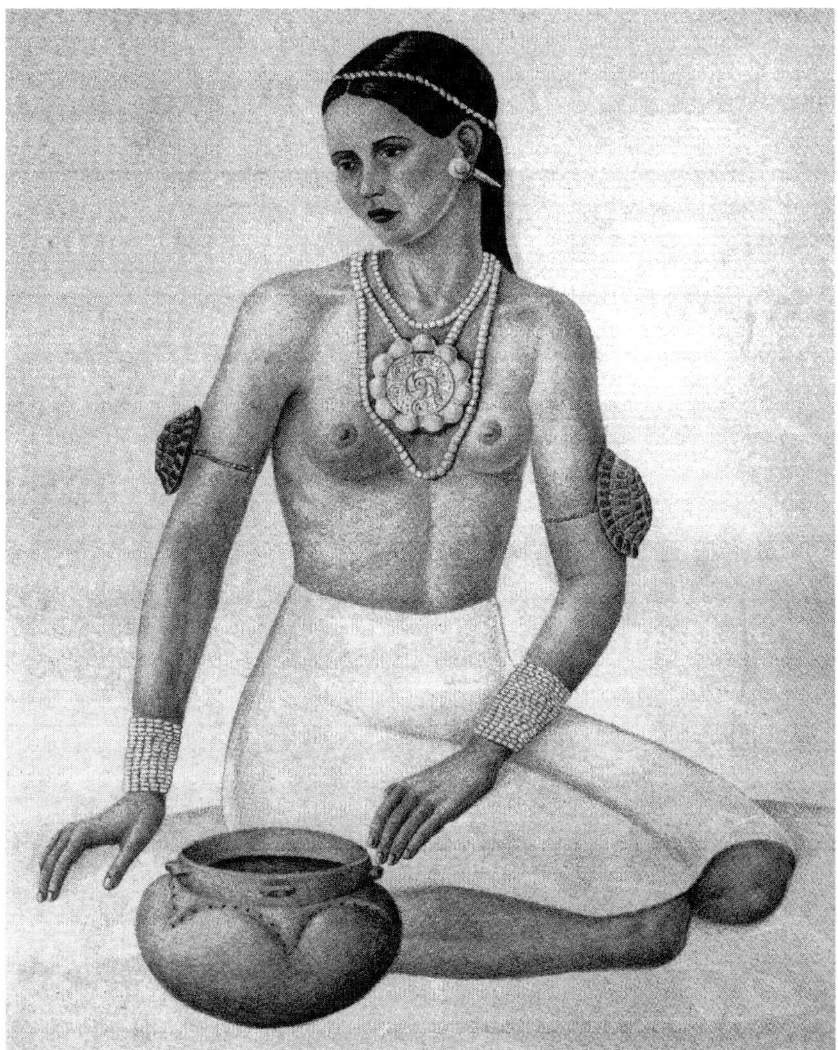

Figure 4.6. Representation of Dallas Phase woman wearing turtle shell rattles (Lewis and Kneberg 1970: Plate 103).

Early Adult: Mothers, Caregivers, and Economic Producers

In early Cherokee societies, females were subject to ritual taboos during mensuration, pregnancy, and at birth. At the same time, fathers-to-be were also subject to their own set of taboos. Breakage of such taboos by either sex was seen as being detrimental to the child's health. Johnston (2003: 459) argues that this points to "the Cherokees' sense of interconnectedness and the necessity for both of them to ensure the child's health." While this may be the case, women, of course, bore the biological consequences of birthing. While the act of mothering may have been a source of power, it also may have come at a biological cost. Many studies have pointed to high maternal mortality rates in preindustrial societies (Stone 2000). Within precolumbian societies, the biological cost of childbearing can be difficult to ascertain. Often, mortality profiles are used as a proxy for risk of maternal mortality. High rates of female mortality during childbearing years could suggest that maternal mortality was an issue for the population. Earlier paleodemographic studies relied heavily on the life table approach in order to make inferences regarding morbidity and mortality of past populations (Wood et al. 2002). As a result of subsequent criticisms on the limitations of such an approach, researchers proposed using computer simulations and maximum likelihood estimations to model population structures (Herrmann and Konigsberg 2002; Milner et al. 2000; Wood et al. 2002). This maximum likelihood estimation could then be used to compute a hazard rate (i.e., the risk that an event will occur at a specific time [or age] that has not previously occurred, or age specific hazard at death).

As a starting point to explore the effects of the childbearing years on a woman's life, we assessed the differences in risks of mortality between adult males and females by pooling age-at-death data from three Dallas phase sites (Toqua [40MR6], Dallas [40HA1], and Fains Island [40JE1]) to create a hazard model for samples from the three sites.[3] Chi-square and likelihood ratio tests were used to test the significance of differences. The likelihood ratio test showed no statistical difference between the sexes, but comparisons of the survivorship curves indicate a decreased survivorship for females during childbearing years (Figure 4.7). While decreased survivorship may be suggestive of mortality associated with the risk of childbirth, Stone (2000) warns against using maternal mortality as the sole factor of higher rates of mortality in young females without considering other factors. These early deaths may attest to the "cost" of care for the physical body beyond just the risk of pregnancy and birth. For example, breastfeeding is energetically expensive. If there is insufficient caloric intake, the risk of contracting infections, for example, would increase, which would, in turn, raise the risk of dying. Economic labor, as we argue in the subsequent section, also was a significant source of women's power, and may have led to further stressors on an already taxed body. It is noteworthy that around thirty years of age, survivorship of men and women are virtually equal, and, in fact, women surpass men in later years of life, suggesting that women experienced greater longevity. This

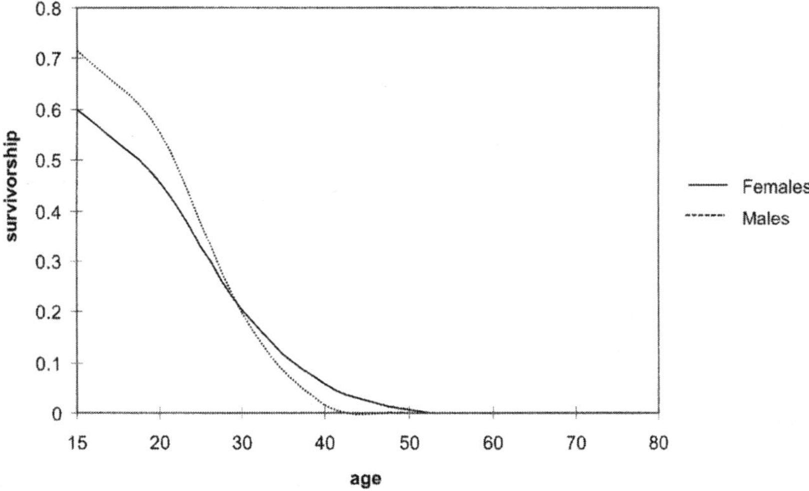

Figure 4.7. Survivorship by age.

greater longevity is of particular interest when we consider the importance of elder women or "grandmothers" in Cherokee society and, as we will argue, Dallas phase societies as well. Thus, the paleodemographic data suggest that women during the earlier childbearing years bear the biological cost of being a caregiver both to children and to the community at large.

Paleodemography may be a good indicator of the biological consequences of pregnancy, birthing, and breastfeeding, but how do we examine early infant care in the past? Early Cherokee accounts suggest that women frequently used cradleboarding, which may have served to lighten the burden of childcare. The use of such implements may explain, to the surprise of many European males who recorded early ethnohistorical accounts, the rapid return of many Cherokee women to the agricultural fields after giving birth. This return to work is significant because, as stated previously, these fields were a source of women's economic power. Although we cannot assume that the sexual division of labor described in ethnohistorical accounts, including women's control of the agricultural fields and food production, extended into the past, certain biological data can provide an opportunity to test this hypothesis. Harle and King (2004) and Lloyd (2017) both examined musculoskeletal stress markers (MSM) to examine possible evidence of a sexual division of labor at the Toqua site. MSMs are the result of repetitive loading on particular muscles that lead to osseous changes at muscular origin or insertion sites. The results of both studies point to interesting parallels regarding gendered roles, even though they used different analytical techniques. Harle and King (2004) focused primarily on robusticity scores of muscle attachment sites between males and females. The study found significantly higher robusticity scores in males in the upper limb, especially in the forearm, involving muscles associated with extension and supination. This pattern is interpreted as related to hunting activities, specifically bow and arrow use. Conversely, women had significantly higher scores in the lower limb adductors and flexors that are associated with squatting activities, which may be related to planting and harvesting. In a study solely focusing on the upper extremities, Lloyd (2017) found that age was a significant factor in the expression of skeletal attachment entheseal changes for both males and females, as robusticity scores peak between 30 and 45 years of age and then decrease throughout the older age group. This shift may suggest a change in labor patterns during older adulthood (45+ years).

Cradleboarding may have enabled women to return to their vital economic activities while simultaneously caring for their infants. As Claassen (2002) has argued, domestication created an additional labor burden, especially for women. One way to manage this increased workload, is through the use of cradleboarding, as is noted in ethnohistorical accounts. These carriers typically were fashioned from organic materials and were unlikely to preserve, explaining why such implements are rarely mentioned in the archaeological literature. No artifactual evidence has been identified in Dallas communities that indicates the use of cradleboards, but their use may be identified through other means–namely the presence of cranial deformation. Previous research by Langdon (1989) reports a high percentage of artificial cranial deformation among Dallas phase communities (frequencies range from 84 to 96 percent of Dallas phase samples in his study). The most predominant type of cranial deformation is occipital deformation (42%) in which the external occipital protuberance and superior nuchal lines on the back of the skull become flattened and the parietal bosses on the sides are slightly exaggerated. This type of cranial deformation is often considered unintentional and a possible artifact of the practice of infant cradleboarding (Langdon 1989; Parham 1982; Kamp 2002). Langdon found that incidences of intentional cranial deformation (33%) occur less frequently than unintentional types (67%). His analysis also showed no statistically significant difference between males and females in the occurrence of unintentional cranial deformation. The high percentage of unintentional cranial deformation among Dallas samples suggests that cultural innovations to lighten some of the burden of childcare were well established during the Mississippian period.

Late Adult: From Mothers of Children to Community Mothers

Appleby (2010) argues that while senescence was undoubtedly an important constructed identity in the past, the concept is rarely reflected in bioarchaeological and archaeological literature. Old age generally is perceived in Western societies as a time of decreased social status, but this perspective is not the case for Cherokee, or most Native American, societies. Elderly males and females occupied places of prestige albeit via different avenues.

As Lloyd's (2017) study suggests, physical labor in Dallas phase communities decreased for both males and females later in life, but the pattern is less marked in females than in males. The exception to this pattern is entheseal changes associated with the deltoid muscle (arm abductor) that continue to increase in females throughout their lifespan. He suggests that the increase may indicate a transition from more generalized activities to more specialized activities. Though speculative this could be related to greater emphasis on food preparation (c.f., Eshed et al. 2004). When past childbearing years and when their ability to work the agricultural fields decreased, the caretaker work of older females may have transitioned beyond the family to care for the community, as heads of households and conservators and transmitters of cultural traditions for new generations.

Mortuary treatment is an area of research that can give us some insight to this potential transition. As previously mentioned, there is strong spatial patterning of male and female burials, but these patterns are also reflective of age. The youngest and oldest males tend to be the most likely to be buried in public spaces. Although some females are buried within mounds, it is interesting that these females tend to be of younger, childbearing years, not older females. Previous research by Sullivan and Rodning (Sullivan 2001, 2006; Sullivan and Rodning 2001) demonstrated that females in the oldest age categories are exclusively buried within the residential contexts at the Dallas and Toqua sites. These older females also tend to have a wider variety of funerary objects than their younger counterparts. They argue that the correlations of male burials with public spaces and females with domestic spaces do not necessarily indicate political marginality of women. Instead, the spatial dimensions of this mortuary patterning reflect "gender duality" rather than "gender hierarchy." (Sullivan 2001, 2006). The high concentrations of female graves (especially older females, or "grandmothers") in village spaces may reflect their access to alternate sources of power anchored in the context of heads of households and kin groups. This patterning is suggestive of what we see in Cherokee societies, where adult males brokered their power in more public realms of warfare, trade, and other inter-community relationships, whereas women's leadership was centered on their positions as heads of (matrilineal) clans and kinship groups (Rodning 1999; Sullivan 2001, 2006; Sullivan and Rodning 2011). While paleodemographic analysis indicates that the childbearing years were risky for females, older females seemed to enjoy greater longevity than males, perhaps reflecting their increased social standing later in life.

The Power of Motherhood

The lives of women in Dallas phase communities are complicated, complex, and much more nuanced than either early ethnohistorical or archaeological information suggest. Women were involved in mothering in the traditional sense of the word, and they were also caring for the community as a whole. Assumptions about women having lower social standing than men are not borne out in the bioarchaeological, archaeological, and ethnohistorical records. Instead, Mississippian societies were likely heterarchical, with women possessing their own economic power and social status that was distinct from that of men. In particular, mortuary treatment and changes to the physical bodies of women indicate that their economic labor and mothering played significant roles in shaping their own identities and the identities of their communities. The use of cradleboards for infants reflects the inclusion of children in household and agricultural duties that simultaneously enabled mothers to have greater visibility in the economic sphere and the ability to continue to be engaged in agricultural production while caring for young children. The physical toll of pregnancy, birth, breastfeeding, and ongoing care of children is reflected in the decreased survivorship of women during childbearing years. But, if females survived the earlier risk, they enjoyed greater longevity and, based on mortuary treatment, more prestige in later life.

This chapter outlines a broad array of bioarchaeological and mortuary evidence reflecting the life course of women among Late Mississippian populations in the Upper Tennessee Valley. This preliminary synthesis of disparate research outlines the benefits of coalescing and comparing various data to create a better understanding of women throughout their lives. We have previously argued that there is significant variation within Dallas phase communities that might indicate differences in cultural or ethnic identities (Sullivan and Harle 2010). Much of our analysis for this chapter relies on data from Tennessee Valley Authority's Tellico and Chickamauga Basin reservoir projects. Elsewhere in the region, spatial patterning of age and sex categories of burials within public and private spheres is less demarcated and funerary object inclusions with sex and age groups, especially shell ornamentation, is somewhat different. Detailed analyses across this regional spectrum could provide insight as to how varying "identities" within a larger cultural system affected perceived gender roles and differences in the ways these roles were enacted with material culture.

Bioarchaeologists are in a unique position to be able to challenge narratives that gender roles are universal and timeless. We certainly are not the first to make this observation, but this opportunity is particularly salient when the descendants of the communities we study were directly affected and are actively resisting gender and kinship systems imposed by colonizers. We hope this chapter can provide additional insight to this discussion.

Authors' Note

The sites for which this study was based are subject to the Native American Graves Protection and Repatriation Act. The data presented here has been collected based on previous data collected by the authors for prior research projects or published data.

Acknowledgments

The idea for this chapter was born out of many conversations with women both in academic circles and Indigenous women. As mothers ourselves, we would be remiss to not acknowledge our children for their inspiration.

Notes

1 The basic political unit of Cherokee society centered on clans and towns. Each town contained its own council composed of the chief or "beloved" man, a council of elders, ceremonial leaders, council of clans, and council of women. This latter council would advise on aspects of war and domestic matters.

2 Age and sex determinations used in this chapter are based on an inventory conducted by Maria O. Smith as part of a National Science Foundation grant.

3 For this study, the maximum likelihood analysis was generated using the computer program *mle* version 2.1 (Holman 2000). The results then were used to compute a 2-parameter Gompertz model, to create a survivorship curve mortality index: where α = the overall level of adult mortality and β = acceleration of risk of death by age (Wood et al. 2002).

References Cited

Agarwal, Sabrina

2016 Bone Morphologies and Histories: Life Course Approaches in Bioarchaeology. *Yearbook of Physical Anthropology, American Journal of Physical Anthropology* 159: S130–S149.

Aimers, James, and Dawn M. Rutecki

2016 Brave New World: Interpreting Sex, Gender, and Sexuality in the Past. *The SAA Archaeological Record* 16.1: 12–17.

Alt, Susan M., and Timothy R. Pauketat

2007 Sex and the Southern Cult. In *Southeastern Ceremonial Complex: Chronology, Content, Context*, edited by Adam King, pp. 232–250. University of Alabama Press, Tuscaloosa.

Alwin Duane F.

2012 Integrating Varieties of Life Course Concepts. *The Journals of Gerontology* 67B(2): 206–220.

Appleby, Joanna E.

2010 Why We Need an Archaeology of Old Age, and a Suggested Approach. *Norwegian Archaeological Review* 43(2): 145–168.

Baxter, Jane Eva

2005 *The Archaeology of Childhood: Children, Gender, and Material Culture*. AltaMira Press, Walnut Creek, CA.

Beauchesne, Patrick, and Sabrina C. Agarwal, eds.

2018 *Children and Childhood in Bioarchaeology*. University Press of Florida, Gainesville.

Beausang, Elisabeth

2000 Childbirth in Prehistory: An Introduction. *European Journal of Archaeology* 3(1): 69–87.

Beauvoir, Simone de

1989 [1952] *The Second Sex*. Vintage Books, New York, NY.

Bengtson, Jennifer D

2017 Infants, Mothers, and Gendered Space in a Mississippian Village: Revisiting Wilkie's House 1 at the Hunze-Evans Site. *Childhood in the Past* 10(2): 102–121.

Bolen, Kathleen M.

1992 Prehistoric Construction of Mothering. In *Exploring Gender through Archaeology: Selected Papers from the 1991 Boone Conference*, edited by Cheryl Claassen, pp. 49–62. Prehistory Press, Monographs in World Archaeology, No 11. Madison, WI.

Boudreaux, Edmond A., III

2010 Mound Construction and Community Changes within the Mississippian Town at Town Creek. In *Mississippian Mortuary Practices: Beyond Hierarchy and the Representationist Perspective*, edited by Lynne P. Sullivan and Robert C. Mainfort, Jr., pp. 195–233. University Press of Florida, Gainesville.

Brown, James A.

1981 The Search for Rank in Prehistoric Burials. In *The Archaeology of Death*, edited by Robert Chapman, Ian Kinnes, and Klavs Randsborg, pp. 25–37. Cambridge University Press, UK.

Buikstra, Jane E., and Douglas H. Ubelaker, eds.

1994 *Standards for Data Collection from Human Skeletal Remains: Proceedings of a Seminar at the Field Museum of Natural History*. Arkansas Archaeology Research Series 44, Fayetteville.

Butler, Judith

1993 *Bodies that Matter: On the Discursive Limits of "Sex."* Routledge, New York.

Carr, Christopher

1995 Mortuary Practices: Their Social, Philosophical-Religious, Circumstantial, and Physical Determinants. *Journal of Archaeological Method and Theory* 2(2): 105–200.

Claassen, Cheryl

2002 Mother's Workload and Children's Labor during the Woodland Period. In *Pursuit of Gender: Worldwide Archaeological Approaches*, edited by Sarah Nelson and Myriam Rosen-Ayalon, pp. 225–234. AltaMira Press, Walnut Creek. CA.

Collins, Patricia

2000 *Black Feminist Thought: Knowledge, Consciousness and the Politics of Empowerment*, Routledge, London, UK.

Conkey, Margaret, and Joan M. Gero

1991 *Engendering Archaeology Women and Prehistory*. Blackwell, Oxford, UK.

Cooper, Karen Coody

2022 Cherokee Women in Charge: Female Power and Leadership in American Indian Nations of Eastern North America. McFarland and Company, Jefferson, North Carolina.

Corkran, David

1962 *The Cherokee Frontier: Conflict and Survival 1740–1760*. University of Oklahoma Press, Norman.

Derevenski, Joanna Sofaer, ed.

2000 *Children and Material Culture*. Routledge, London UK.

Elder, Glen H., Jr.

1995 The Life Course Paradigm: Social Change and Individual Development. In *Examining Lives in Context: Perspectives on the Ecology of Human Development*, edited by Phyllis Moen, Glen H. Elder, Jr., and Kurt Lüscher, pp. 101–139. American Psychological Association, Washington, DC.

Emerson, Thomas E.

2003 Materializing Cahokia Shaman. *Southeastern Archaeology* 22(2): 135–154.

Eshed, Vered, Avi Gopher, Ehud Galili, and Israel Hershkovitz

2004 Musculoskeletal Stress Markers in Natufian hunter-gatherers and Neolithic Farmers in the Levant: The Upper Limb. American Journal of Physical Anthropology 123: 303–315.

Firestone, Shulamith

2003 [1970] *The Dialectic of Sex: The Case for Feminist Revolution*. Farrar, Straus and Giroux, New York.

Fogel, Marilyn L., Noreen Tuross, and Douglas W. Owsley

1989 Nitrogen Isotope Tracers of Human lactation in Modern and Archaeological Populations. In *Annual Report of the Director, Geophysical Laboratory, Carnegie Institution of Washington, 1988–1989*, pp. 111–117. Washington, DC.

Friedan, Betty

2001 [1963] *The Feminine Mystique.* Norton, New York.

Fritz, Gayle

2019 *Feeding Cahokia: Early Agriculture in the North American Heartland.* University of Alabama Press, Tuscaloosa.

Galloway, Patricia

1995 *Choctaw Genesis 1500–1700.* University of Nebraska Press, Lincoln.

Geller, Pamela

2009 Identity and Difference: Complicating Gender in Archaeology. *Annual Review of Anthropology* 38: 65–81.

Gilbert, William H., Jr.

1955 Eastern Cherokee Social Organization. In *Social Anthropology of North American Indian Tribes*, edited by Fred Eggan, pp. 285–338, University of Chicago Press.

Gilchrist, Roberta

1999 *Gender and Archaeology: Contesting the Past.* Routledge, London, UK.

2004 Archaeology and the Life Course: A Time and Place for Gender. In *A Companion to Social Archaeology*, edited by Lynn Meskell and Robert W. Preucel, pp. 142–60. John Wiley and Sons, Hoboken, NJ.

2009 The Archaeology of Sex and Gender. In *The Oxford Handbook of Archaeology*, edited by Barry W. Cunliffe, Chris Gosden, and Rosemary A. Joyce, pp. 1029–47. Oxford University Press, UK.

Goldstein, Lynne G.

1980 *Mississippian Mortuary Practices: A Case Study of Two Cemeteries in the Lower Illinois Valley.* Northwestern University Archaeology Program Scientific Papers #4, Evanston, Illinois.

Johnston, Carolyn

2003 *Cherokee Women in Crisis.* University of Alabama Press, Tuscaloosa.

Joyce, Rosemary A.

2008 *Ancient Bodies, Ancient Lives: Sex, Gender, and Archaeology.* Thames and Hudson, London, UK.

Kamp, Kathryn A., ed.

2002 *Children in the Prehistoric Puebloan Southwest.* University of Utah Press, Salt Lake City.

Katzenberg, M. Anne, D. Ann Herring, and Shelley R. Saunders

1996 Weaning and Infant Mortality: Evaluating the Skeletal Evidence. *American Journal of Physical Anthropology* 101.S23: 177–199.

King, Adam

2004 Deciphering Etowah's Mound C: The Construction History and Mortuary Record of a Mississippian Burial Mound. *Southeastern Archaeology* 23(2): 153–165.

Halim, May Ling, Diane N. Ruble, and David M. Amodio
2011 From Pink Frilly Dresses to 'One of the Boys': A Social-Cognitive Analysis of Gender Identity Development and Gender Bias. *Social and Personality Psychology Compass* 5(11): 933–949.

Hally, David J
2008 *King: The Social Archaeology of a Late Mississippian Town in Northwestern Georgia.* University of Alabama Press, Tuscaloosa.

Hally, David J., Marvin T. Smith, and James B. Langford
1990 The Archaeological Reality of DeSoto's Coosa. In *Columbian Consequences, vol. 2: Archaeological and Historical Perspectives on the Spanish Borderlands East*, edited by David H. Thomas, pp. 121–138. Smithsonian Institution Press, Washington, D.C.

Han, Sallie, Tracy Betsinger, Michaelyn Harle, and Amy Scott
2018 Reconceiving the Human Fetus in Reproductive Bioethics: Perspectives from Cultural Anthropology and Bioarchaeology: New Ideas and Innovations. In *Reproductive Ethics II: New Ideas and Innovations*, edited by Lisa Campo-Engelstein and Paul Burcher, pp. 139–150. Springer Press, New York.

Harle, Michaelyn
2010 Biological Affinities and the Construction of Cultural Identity for the Proposed Coosa Chiefdom. Unpublished PhD dissertation, Department of Anthropology, University of Tennessee, Knoxville.

Harle, Michaelyn, and Kathryn King
2004 Skeletal Markers of Occupational Stress: Gender and Rank Based Division of Labor in a Late Mississippian Population. Paper presented at the Sixty-First Annual Meeting of Southeastern Archaeological Conference. St. Louis, MO.

Hatch, James W.
1974 Social Dimensions of Dallas Mortuary Practices. Unpublished master's thesis, Department of Anthropology, The Pennsylvania State University, State College.

Herrmann, Nicholas P., and Lyle W. Konigsberg
2002 A Re-Examination of the Age-at-Death Distribution of lndian Knoll. In *Paleodemography: Age Distributions from Skeletal Samples*, edited by Robert D. Hoppa and James W. Vaupel, pp. 243–257. Cambridge University Press, UK.

Heth, Charlotte
1975 The Stomp Dance Music of the Oklahoma Cherokee: A Study of Contemporary Practice with Special Reference to the Illinois District Council Ground. Unpublished PhD dissertation, Department of Music, University of California, Los Angeles.

Holman, Darryl J.
2000 Mle: A Programming Language for Building Likelihood Models. Version 2.1. Software and Manual. http://faculty.washington.edul-djholman/mle/.

Hudson, Charles
1976 *The Southeastern Indians.* University of Tennessee Press, Knoxville.

Hudson, Charles, Marvin Smith, David Hally, Richard Polhemus, and Chester DePratter
1985 Coosa: A Chiefdom in the Sixteenth-Century Southeastern United States. *American Antiquity* 50(4): 723–737.

Langdon, Stephen P.

1989 Porotic Hyperostosis and Artificial Cranial Deformation in Dallas Society. Unpublished master's thesis, Department of Anthropology, University of Tennessee, Knoxville.

Lewis, Thomas M. N., and Madeline Kneberg

1946 *Hiwassee Island: An Archaeological Account of Four Tennessee Indian Peoples.* University of Tennessee Press, Knoxville.

Levy, Janet E.

2014 What I Believe: Doing Archaeology as a Feminist. *Southeastern Archaeology* 33(2): 226–237.

Lloyd, Dustin

2017 Activity Patterns of Division of Labor at a Southeastern Tennessee Late Mississippian Site. Unpublished master's thesis, Anthropology Department, Illinois State University, Normal.

Mays, Simon

2013 A Discussion of Some Recent Methodological Developments in the Osteoarchaeology of Childhood. *Childhood in the Past* 6(1): 4–21.

Meskell, Lynne

1999 *Archaeologies of Social Life: Age, Sex, Class et cetera in Ancient Egypt.* Blackwell, Oxford, UK.

Mill, John S.

1984 The Subjection of Women. In *The Collected Works of John Stuart Mill, Vol. 21: Essays on Equality, Law and Education*, edited by John M. Robson, pp. 259–340. University of Toronto Press, Canada.

Milner, George R, James W. Wood, and Jesper L. Boldsen

2000 Paleodemography. In *Biological Anthropology of the Human Skeleton*, edited by M. Anne Katzenberg and Shelley R. Saunders, pp.467–498. Wiley-Liss, New York, NY.

Moore, Jenny, and Eleanor Scott, eds.

1997 *Invisible People and Processes: Writing Gender and Childhood into European Archaeology.* Leicester University Press, London, UK.

Nelson, Sarah M.

1997 *Gender in Archaeology: Analyzing Power and Prestige.* AltaMira Press, Walnut Creek, CA.

Niethammer, Carolyn

1977 *Daughters of the Earth: The Lives and Legends of American Indian Women,* Collier Books. New York, NY.

Ortner, Sherry B.

1974 Is Female to Male as Nature is to Culture? In *Woman, Culture, and Society*, edited by Michelle Zimbalist Rosaldo and Louise Lamphere, pp. 68–87. Stanford University Press, CA.

Parham, Kenneth R.

1982 A Biocultural Approach to the Skeletal Biology of the Dallas People from Toqua. Unpublished master's thesis, Department of Anthropology, University of Tennessee, Knoxville.

Parker Pearson, Michael

1982 Mortuary Practices, Society and Ideology: An Ethnoarchaeological Study. In *Symbolic and Structural Archaeology*, edited by Ian A. Hodder, pp. 99–113, Cambridge University Press, UK.

Pauketat, Timothy

2007 *Chiefdoms and Other Archaeological Delusions.* AltaMira Press, Walnut Creek, CA.

Perdue, Theda

1998 *Cherokee Women: Gender and Culture Change, 1700–1835.* University of Nebraska Press, Lincoln.

Ragoné, Helena, and Frances Winddance Twine, eds.

2000 *Ideologies and Technologies of Motherhood: Race, Class, Sexuality, Nationalism.* Routledge, New York.

Rakita, Gordon F.M.

2008 Mortuary and Non-Mortuary Ritual Practices at the Pre-Hispanic Site of Paquimé (Casas Grandes), Chihuahua, Mexico. In *Reanalysis and Reinterpretation in Southwestern Bioarchaeology*, edited by Ann L. W. Stodder, pp. 55–79, Arizona State Museum, Anthropological Monograph Series volume 59, Arizona State University Press.

Reid, John P.

1970 *A Law of Blood: The Primitive Law of the Cherokee Nation.* New York University Press, New York.

Rich, Adrienne

1986 *Of Woman Born: Motherhood as Experience and Institution.* 2nd ed. W.W. Norton, New York, NY.

Rodning, Christopher B.

1999 Archaeological Perspectives on Gender and Women in Traditional Cherokee Society. *Journal of Cherokee Studies* 20:3–27

1999 Archaeological Perspectives on Gender and Women in Traditional Cherokee Society. Journal of Cherokee Studies 20: 3–27.

2015 *Center Places and Cherokee Towns: Archaeological Perspectives on Native American Architecture and Landscape in the Southern Appalachians.* University of Alabama Press, Tuscaloosa.

Sattler, Richard A.

1995 Women's Status among the Muskogee and Cherokee. In *Women and Power in Native North America,* edited by Laura F. Klein and Lillian A. Ackerman, pp. 214–229. University of Oklahoma Press, Norman.

Scheper-Hughes, Nancy

1992 *Death Without Weeping: The Violence of Everyday Life in Brazil.* University of California Press, Berkeley.

Schroedl, Gerald F.

1998 Mississippian Towns in the Eastern Tennessee Valley. In *Mississippian Towns and Sacred Spaces: Searching for an Architectural Grammar,* edited by R. Barry Lewis and Charles Stout, pp. 64–92. University of Alabama Press, Tuscaloosa.

Scott, Gary T., and Richard R. Polhemus

1987 Mortuary Patterns. In *The Toqua Site: A Late Mississippian Dallas Phase Town*. 2 vols. Department of Anthropology, University of Tennessee, Report of Investigations, no.41, and Tennessee Valley Authority, Publications in Anthropology no. 44, Knoxville.

Smithers, Gregory D.

2014 Beyond the Binaries: Critical Approaches to Sex and Gender in Early America. *Early American Studies* 12(3): 626–651.

Sofaer, Joanna R.

2006 *The Body as Material Culture: A Theoretical Osteoarchaeology.* Cambridge University Press, UK.

Stearney, Lynn M.

1994 Feminism, Ecofeminism, and the Maternal Archetype: Motherhood as a Feminine Universal. *Communication Quarterly* 42(2): 145–159.

Stone, Pamela Kendall

2000 Paleoobstetrics: Reproduction, Workload and Mortality for Ancestral Pueblo Women. Unpublished PhD dissertation, Department of Anthropology, University of Massachusetts, Amherst.

Sullivan, Lynne P.

1995 Mississippian Household and Community Organization in Eastern Tennessee. In *Mississippian Communities and Households*, edited by J. Daniel. Rogers and Bruce D. Smith, pp. 99–123, University of Alabama Press, Tuscaloosa.

2001 Those Men in the Mounds: Gender, Politics, and Mortuary Practices in Eastern Tennessee. In *Archaeological Studies of Gender in the Southeastern United States*, edited by Jane M. Eastman and Christopher B. Rodning, pp. 101–126, University Press of Florida, Gainesville.

2006 Gendered Contexts of Mississippian Leadership in Southern Appalachia. In *Borne on a Litter with Much Prestige: Leadership and Polity in Mississippian Society*, edited by Paul Welch and Brian Butler, pp. 264–285, Occasional Paper No. 33, Center for Archaeological Investigations, Southern Illinois University, Carbondale.

2018 The Path to the Council House: The Development of Mississippian Communities in Southeast Tennessee. In *The Archaeology of Villages in Eastern North America*, edited by Jennifer Birch and Victor Thompson, pp. 106–123. University of Florida Press, Gainesville.

2019 Medicine for the Dead: Shell Gorgets as Accompaniments for Rites of Passage. In *Mississippian Culture Heroes, Ritual Regalia, and Sacred Bundles*, edited by David Dye and Kent Reilly, pp. 271–290. Lexington Books, Lanham, MD. In press.

Sullivan, Lynne P., and Christopher B. Rodning

2001 Gender, Tradition, and Social Negotiation in Southern Appalachian Chiefdoms. In *The Archaeological of Historical Processes, Agency and Tradition Before and After Columbus*, edited by Timothy Pauketat, pp. 107–120. University Press of Florida, Gainesville

2011 Residential Burial, Gender Roles, and Political Development in Late Prehistoric and Early Cherokee Cultures of the Southern Appalachians. In *Residential*

Burial: A Multi-Regional Exploration, edited by Ron Adams and Stacie King, pp. 79–97. AP3A Series, American Anthropological Association. Washington D.C.

Sullivan, Lynne P., and Michaelyn S. Harle

2010 Mortuary Practices and Cultural Identity at the Turn of the Sixteenth Century in Eastern Tennessee. In *Mississippian Mortuary Practices: Beyond Hierarchy and the Representationist Perspective*, edited by Lynne P. Sullivan and Robert C. Mainfort, Jr., pp. 234–249. University Press of Florida, Gainesville

Sullivan, Lynne P, and Robert C. Mainfort, Jr., eds.

2010 *Mississippian Mortuary Practices: Beyond Hierarchy and the Representationist Perspective,* University Press of Florida, Gainesville.

Thomas, Larissa A.

1996 The Study of Shell Beads and Their Social Context in the Mississippian Period: A Case from the Carolina Piedmont and Mountains. *Southeastern Archaeology* 15(1): 29–46.

Ubelaker, Douglas H., and J. S. De La Paz

2012 Skeletal Indicators of Pregnancy and Parturition: A Historical Review. *Journal of Forensic Science* 57(4): 866–872.

Vogel, Lise

1995 *Woman Questions: Essays for a Materialist Feminism.* Psychology Press, Routledge, New York, NY.

Walker, Phillip L.

1995 Problems of Preservation and Sexism in Sexing: Some Lessons from Historical Collections for Paleo- demographers. In *Grave Reflections: Portraying the Past through Skeletal Studies*, edited by Anne Herring and Shelley Saunders, pp. 31–47. Canadian Scholars' Press, Toronto, Canada.

Wilkie, Laurie A.

2003 *The Archaeology of Mothering: An African-American Midwife's Tale.* Routledge, New York.

Wilson, Gregory D., Vincas P. Steponaitis, and Keith Jacobi

2010 Social and Spatial Dimensions of Moundville Mortuary Practices. In *Mississippian Mortuary Practices*, edited by Lynne P. Sullivan and Robert C. Mainfort, Jr., pp. 74–89. University Press of Florida, Gainesville.

Wood, James, Darryl J. Holman, Kathleen A. O'Conner, and Rebecca J. Ferrell

2002 Mortality Models for Paleodeomography. In *Paleodemography: Age Distributions from Skeletal Samples*, edited by Robert D. Hoppa and James W. Vaupel, pp. 129–168. Cambridge University Press, UK.

Wright, Lori E., and Schwarcz, Henry P.

1998 Stable Carbon and Oxygen Isotopes in Human Tooth Enamel: Identifying Breastfeeding and Weaning in Prehistory. *American Journal of Physical Anthropology* 106: 1–18.

5

Mississippian Geographies of Fertility

A Multiscalar View from Southeast Missouri

Jennifer Bengtson and Toni Alexander

Human experiences occur within and link together places at multiple spatial scales, and this chapter considers the mutual benefit of geographic and archaeological perspectives for exploring these linkages in the context of Mississippian women's reproductive experiences. Inspired by archaeologies of embodiment and engendered landscapes, we delve into the cultural geography literature for further theoretical guidance in our consideration of how Mississippian women's use of place and space in their biological, emotional, cosmological, and ritual experiences of fertility emerged from their relationships with (and within) the landscape and was woven into the construction of communities and cosmologies. We highlight the ways that structures, villages, and outlying natural and cultural places are linked by the theme of fertility, particularly via the practiced and idealized experience of fertility as a force obscuring the boundary between women's biologically circumscribed bodies and their external, surrounding spaces. This disruption is material and physical as well as emotional and spiritual—women physically moved among places of fertility, engaging with and linking themselves to these places through their bodily practices as well as through their bodily products, such as spatially situated parturition and menstruation.

We also explore the ways that Mississippian women's experiences of fertility were actively *structured* and were *structured by* experiences of space and place at multiple scales. Fertility and childbirth were central features of not only the lived experience of Mississippian women, but also the households, communities, and socio-spiritual worlds of which they were part. As such, ideas about fertility conditioned not only how the landscape was understood, but also how Mississippian people positioned themselves within it and moved through it. The Hunze-Evans site in Southeastern Missouri serves as a case study for situating a small Mississippian village within a multiscalar and embodied geography of fertility.

Fertility, Body, and Place in Archaeological and Geographic Perspective

Fertility is a prominent theme in Mississippian cosmologies (Emerson 1989, 2003; Knight 1986). Womanhood, in particular, is closely linked to fertility in terms of both human reproduction and agriculture, and a large body of literature addresses the iconographic and symbolic expression of this association in Mississippian archaeological materials. Dye (2013) provides a detailed overview of the importance of Mississippian women in religious, cosmological, and ritual celebrations of fertility, regeneration, and renewal through metaphors of childbirth. Much of the interpretive strength of these associations comes from linkages to the ethnohistoric literature on Siouan (including Osage, Quapaw, and others), Iroquoian (Cherokee), and Muskogean (Creek, Chickasaw, and Choctaw) groups (King 2007). One of the most prominent deities in many of these cosmologies is a female earth deity—referred to as *Our Grandmother, Earthmother,* or *Old-Woman-Who-Never-Dies* (Brown 2011; Diaz-Granados 2004; Reilly 2004)—who is symbolically associated with the moon, water, renewal, and regeneration (Mueller and Fritz 2016; Reilly 2004). Among the materially expressed symbols often linked with women and fertility based on these associations are water, the moon, and the underworld (Dye 2013; Edwards 2018; Krutak 2013; Pauketat et al. 2017). Linkages between women, the moon, water, and both reproductive and agricultural fertility are prominently featured in Dhegihan narratives as well as Mississippian iconography and are related to socio-physiological processes such as menstruation and childbirth (Bailey and La Flesche 2010: 65–67; Lankford et al. 2011; Reilly and Garber 2007; Townsend 2004). It is important to note that fertility associations are exclusive to neither human reproduction nor to women. Even those places commonly utilized by men within Indigenous communities were often imbued with fertility-related symbolism (e.g., sweat-lodges representing wombs from which one emerges renewed [Hall 1997]). Nevertheless, this is a volume on women, and we choose to focus this chapter on the concept of fertility as it relates specifically to feminine biocultural aspects of human reproduction—particularly to themes of menstruation, pregnancy, and childbirth.

Because the body is a fundamental space of reproductive fertility, the literature on embodiment serves as a theoretical backdrop for our case study. Themes of agency, structure, and practice—inspired by Pierre Bourdieu's and

Anthony Gidden's work—provide a materialist foundation from which much consideration of the body in archaeology (Boric and Robb 2008) and geography (Cresswell 2013) has been rooted, bodies being the media by which culture is practiced in spatial context. Fowler (2011) recognizes bodily engagement as key to enacting and participating in cosmological order, and he notes the attention to bodily boundaries—the nature, circumstances, and careful consideration of what crosses those boundaries and when—as an important element of spiritual practice in many cultures. In addition to recognizing the body as a geographic space in and of itself, Fowler also notes that the "limits of the person extend beyond the skin," as is made particularly clear in the movement of bodies through space as with religious pilgrimage, forming a "bodily and personal connection between the person, the sacred place, and the divine" (2001: 144–145).

Joyce's (2005) overview of archaeological considerations of the body emphasizes how associations between biological bodies and the symbols referencing them can illuminate the gendered dimensions of the landscape at multiple scales. She critiques the separate consideration traditionally given to *physical bodies* versus *representations of bodies,* stating that, "body practices and representations of bodies [work] together to produce experiences of embodied personhood differentiated along lines of sex, age, power, etc." (Joyce 2005: 149). Elsewhere, Joyce (2003) has explored the concept of bodily materiality as linking together ideas about physical bodies, artifactual representations of bodies, and adornments of bodies. She emphasizes the dialectical relationships between what we *put on* our bodies, what we *do* with our bodies, and the *biological condition* of our bodies. In doing so, she alludes to the spatiality of the body and bodily practice—not only in the sense of the body as a bounded unit, but also in the ways people use spaces and spatial context to manipulate and transform their own experiences of personhood.

These spatial references invite an explicit incorporation of the cultural geography literature to help bridge the gap between the intimate space of the individual body and the larger scale of regional landscapes and more distant places. Both cultural geographers and anthropologists alike have been concerned with embodiment issues with respect to Indigeneity; however, much of this scholarly effort focuses on contemporary outcomes associated with colonialism (Radcliffe 2018). The integration of socio-spatial relationships within precontact archaeological studies of Indigenous populations offers a new avenue for geographic inquiry.

General trends in the historical and theoretical development of cultural geography are likely to sound familiar to those versed in the histories of archaeology and anthropology. As have archaeologists, cultural geographers have long sought to better understand the ways in which humans interact with the environments they inhabit through cultural landscape studies (Sauer 1925). In contrast to previous deterministic approaches, which assumed humans to have little agency with respect to their interactions with the natural environment, cultural landscape studies in geography recognized humans as modifiers of the earth. Drawing heavily upon the work of cultural anthropologists, Sauer (1925) proposed that a society's culture could be revealed through empirical studies of the cultural landscape created by that society (Cresswell 2013; Jackson 1989).

In the latter decades of the twentieth century, the influence of historical materialist approaches came to the forefront of cultural geography and sought to better understand the economic and political structures that shaped the spatial patterns and cultural landscapes (Cloke et al. 1991). As a counterpoint to the overtly structural emphasis of Marxist geographers but also in response to positivist approaches, humanistic cultural geographers at the time like Tuan (1977) sought to place humans back at the center of cultural geography. For humanistic geographers, the cultural landscape was a consequence of human agency and, therefore, subject to individual and group values and attachments. The abstract territorial characteristics of "space" were to be distinguished from those of "places," which were imbued with a wide range of human emotions and values.

Both Marxist and humanistic geographers sought to understand the development and existence of cultural landscapes; however, each approach was critiqued as being either overly global or local with respect to geographic scales of analysis. While Marxism focused on global capitalist geopolitical structures at play in shaping the landscape, humanism emphasized individual perception and experience. As with other social sciences, the structure-agency dichotomy in geography was initially bridged by drawing upon structuration theory as proposed by Anthony Giddens (Castree 2009; Cloke et al. 1991; Cresswell 2013; Giddens 1984). Gidden's efforts to integrate larger social systems with individual and group action offered a means by which geographic research could highlight the ways in which "social structure and social agency come together differently *in different places* [emphasis added] such that they mutually determine one another" (Castree 2009: 159). Moreover, place is not immutable, but rather dynamic. The cultural landscape does not simply reflect the structural aspects of society but rather is created and re-created through practice. Drawing upon Pierre Bourdieu, Cresswell (1996) notes, "Places are neither totally material nor completely mental . . . Places are duplicitous in that they cannot be reduced to the concrete or the 'merely ideological'; rather they display an uneasy and fluid tension between them" (13).

This dynamic relationship between place and time has informed geographic research at a variety of spatial scales, including the most intimate of all, the body (Davidson and Milligan 2004; Mountz 2018; Simonsen 2000). Drawing on geographic scholarship, philosopher Casey (2001) explains that the body is not only the means by which humans directly interact with the world in a physical, sensory experience, but becomes the medium through which place and the cultural landscape are recorded, noting, "a body is shaped by the places it has come to know and that have come to it–come to take up residence in it, by a special kind of placial incorporation" (414). Not only are our lives written into the landscape of places, but those places are written into our bodies on an ongoing basis. Contemporary geographic scholarship and its focus on embodiment further highlights the way in which emotions, including those of fertility and birth, are experienced as internal and external processes (Bondi 2005; Mountz 2018). Furthermore, the work of McKinnon (2014) explores how the birth experience of a mother and child is intertwined with larger geopolitical landscapes. By combining a feminist geography and geopolitical approach, she offers a perspective which includes territorial and material concerns, ranging from the micro- to macroscales of human experience and provides an alternative to much feminist birth literature which draws upon a binary approach to contemporary birth experiences as either at home or in a clinical setting. Thus, the birth experience can be felt in myriad ways and in multiple places, even by the individual (Robinson 2018).

These geographical perspectives inform our consideration of the archaeological case study presented here, although we are certainly not the first to center an archaeological study of fertility on spatial context. Claassen (2013, 2016), for example, writes about gendered Native landscapes in North America and specifically writes of "fertility as a place-based gift to groups" (2013: 198). She connects fertility themes to archaeological perspectives on landscapes, linking places near and far to women's use of and symbolic gaze upon the world around them (Claassen 2016). Building on classic critiques of the dual 'woman-at-home/dangerous landscape' trope (*sensu* Gero 1985), Claassen emphasizes the mobility of Native American women in the sense of their knowledge of a landscape symbolically imbued with fertility symbolism, but also in their actual movement through it. She points out that the movement of women through a gendered landscape is a critical component of origin narratives of many eastern tribes who trace their histories to well-traveled female deities.

Biocultural and Spatial Correlates of Fertility in the Indigenous Southeast

A significant body of literature indicates that fertility, menarche, menstruation, pregnancy, and childbirth are cross-culturally and diachronically meaningful experiences not only in the lives of women, but also in the lives of the broader families, communities, and cultures of which they are part (Beausang 2000; Gottlieb and DeLoache 2017; Buckley and Gottlieb 1988; Finlay 2013; Tremayne 2001; McCourt 2009). The literature on such issues from Midwestern and Southeastern perspectives is an undeniable testament to the fact that the Indigenous peoples of this region recognized these widespread tendencies in culturally specific ways. A young woman's first menses was announced and recognized by both men and women among the Oglala (Powers 1980) and Santee (Landes 1968: 129). Powers (1980) notes that, upon her first menses, an Oglala woman began to wear her hair differently, painted the part of her hair red, and even changed the way she positioned her body when sitting, aligning her bodily practice with her new role as a woman and potential mother. She also painted the part of her hair red, which Edwards (2018) notes Osage women also did when clearing fields and planting. Sundstrom (2004) suggests that the supernatural power of menstruating Dakota women is on par with that of vision-questing men, while Pesantubbee (2004) equated Choctaw women's loss of menstrual blood with men's shedding of blood in warfare—each of these instances required spatially situated ritual treatment before reintegration into the community. Pesantubbee (2004: 24) further cites Adair (1930 [1775]) in her discussion of Choctaw women who secluded themselves within special structures during menstruation and childbirth. This seclusion provided a dedicated time and place for reflection upon and celebration of fertility, which was solemnly recognized by men and women alike as a central community concern (Galloway 1997; Pesantubbee 2004). Loubser (2013) also reviews ethnohistoric literature referencing direct symbolic connections between menstruation and fertility, with several Southeastern tribes relaying narratives of babies resulting from the admixture of river water and the menstrual blood of powerful women.

While the ideological marginalization of menstruation—and spatial marginalization of the places of menstruation—are noted in some North American ethnohistoric accounts, Buckley and Gottlieb (1988) lament the Western, androcentric bent of traditional interpretations of menstrual symbolism, arguing against uncritical acceptance of the universality of menstrual taboos centered on negative notions of pollution and danger. They argue that such perspectives have contributed to a perpetuation of negative bias surrounding menstruation among scholars and the lay public alike. In speaking of cross-cultural diversity of rules, roles, and characteristics of menstruating women, they state:

> Many menstrual taboos, rather than protecting society from a universally ascribed female evil, explicitly protect the perceived creative spirituality of menstruous women from the influence of others in a more neutral state, as well as protecting the latter in turn from the potent, positive spiritual forces ascribed to such women . . . [menstrual customs] provide women with a means of ensuring their own autonomy, influence, and social control. (Buckley and Gottlieb 1988: 7)

More specific to peoples of concern in this chapter, Powers (1980) blames the perceived negative connotation of menstruation on a failure among anthropologists to recognize that menstrual ritual is inextricable from its broader cultural context, which included a range of practices and beliefs much more likely to be considered in a positive light, from puberty rituals to the maintenance of cosmological order. She suggests that menstruation is bound to be viewed more negatively if it is solely considered in isolation from such central ritual practices.

These criticisms remain prescient today for both ethnographic and archaeological studies of women, fertility, and ritual practice. Claassen (2011) points out that, among several ethnohistorically documented tribes of the Southeast, the places of menstruation were also the sites of a range of rituals related to associated concerns such as fertility, childbirth, medicinal practices, and post-natal seclusion of infants and mothers, and that we should expect this to be reflected in the archaeological record. She cites Swanton's (1946: 360) observation that, among many Southeastern tribes, childbirth traditionally did not take place in domestic structures; rather, new mothers gave birth and recovered in the same places as menstruating women. They did not return to their domestic houses for up to forty days after their babies were born (Claassen 2011; Miller 1991; Herman 1950). Powers (1980) reports that the Oglala women also traditionally gave birth in the same structures used by menstruating women. Childbirth was seen as the feminine equivalent of warfare-related bravery among some Siouan groups (Landes 1959: 46; Landes 1968: 206), and Hudson (1976: 321) notes that, among many Southeastern tribes, women observed many rituals and restrictions to ensure a successful pregnancy and delivery of a healthy infant. Childbirth was a cooperative effort between mother, infant, broader kin group, and medicine people, with many rituals, herbal concoctions, songs, and sayings employed to coax or startle the infant into 'jumping down' when necessary to facilitate an expedient and uncomplicated birth (Olbrechts 1931). In several tribes, older women were involved as midwives, medicine people, and as spiritual consultants for pregnant or menstruating women, adding generational depth to the practices within these structures (Powers 1980; Pesantubbee 2004 citing Swanton 1931: 118). Names were conferred to Osage infants soon after birth, involving community-based ritual and often invoking themes of fertility, procreation, and the continuity of life (La Flesche 1928).

While several authors have taken up the cause of locating these kinds of places in the North American archaeological record (Galloway 1997, Claassen 2011, Stelle 2006, Carney et al. 2019, Bengtson 2017), we might take care to heed Powers' (1980) advice to not focus on menstruation in isolation from related biocultural phenomena, nor should we necessarily assume the wholesale spatial segregation of these places from the community proper. This is especially true given Claassen's (2011) observation that places of menstruation are often also the places of broader practice of feminine-focused ritual. Though not specifically concerned with menstruation, Alt (2018) explores women's roles in temples dedicated to feminine ideologies of fertility, water, and the moon at the Emerald site, which she and colleagues (Pauketat et al. 2017) argue represented a powerful catalyst for the material and symbolic construction of Mississippian community. There is no reason to assume a priori that other kinds of feminine structures in other places were not equally important in the spatial construction and interpretation of the village within the broader landscape.

Further, childbirth and the neonatal period for both mother and infant remind us of the mortal perils of fertility, and we should thus not be surprised to find references to death where we also see reference to life and the life-giving power of women—in fact, such dualities abound in native cosmologies. Some sources link the Beneath World to conceptions of the female body. Duncan (2011: 29) recounts an Osage narrative in which First Woman births the sun and her children anew every morning and receives them back into her vulva—their graves—at night, only to give birth to them again the next day. Edwards (2018) notes cosmological associations between women, fertility, and the night—night being the "mother of the day." Fertility, death, the night sky, the Beneath World are entangled with feminine symbolism and female bodies, and it is not a leap of the imagination to consider women's pregnancy and birth experiences as both a source of *and* a perpetual retelling of this cultural narrative, both symbolically and physically. With this, we turn to a case study from a Mississippian village in southeast Missouri to explore the place of one particular structure within a broader landscape of fertility.

The Hunze-Evans Site (23CG8)

The Hunze-Evans site, sometimes referred to as the South Cape site or Hunze Mound, is a Mississippian site just south of the city of Cape Girardeau, in Cape Girardeau County, Missouri (Figure 5.1). It is located less than one kilometer west of the Mississippi River, atop an elevated erosional remnant of a natural sand levee that protects it from even the most severe seasonal flooding. Radiocarbon dating suggests an occupation in the early fourteenth century AD (Christensen 2010). It is unlikely that occupation lasted beyond the mid-fifteenth century, as the site is located within a region known as the Vacant Quarter that was largely abandoned by that time (Williams 1990; Cobb and Butler 2002). Professional archaeological excavations at Hunze-Evans date back to the late 1970s, with Duncan Wilkie's tenure at Southeast Missouri State University. Since then, several archaeologists have excavated, published, and presented research on the site (Bengtson 2017; Christensen 2010; Brennan et al. 2019; Helton 2017; Stephens 2010).

The context and significance of the Hunze-Evans site within the broader region is the subject of ongoing research (Brennan et al. 2019). Williams (1954), O'Brien (2001), and O'Brien and Wood (1998) provide general overviews of the cultural history and Mississippian expression in southeast Missouri. The presence of non-local raw materials at the site suggests interactions with communities in distant lands, which is not surprising given well-established Mississippian propensities for long-distance contacts. Furthermore, the Hunze-Evans site is transitional in terms of both its cultural and natural geography—it is located at an ecotone between the wooded uplands of the Ozark Escarpment and the vast lowlands of the Mississippi Valley Alluvial Plain and is situated between distinct regional material Mississippian expressions to the north and south. Preliminary analyses of domestic ceramic assemblages from previously excavated features suggest an affinity with Mississippian sites to the south and east more so than those of the north (Brennan and Stephens 2009; Stephens 2010).

Little is known about overall village organization, but ongoing work seeks to ameliorate this through geophysical exploration and targeted excavations (Brennan et al. 2019). To date, significant research at the site has focused on a structure known as House One, a building central to the ideas we present here (Figure 5.2). House One was excavated by Wilkie in the late 1970s, and although we are unsure of its exact location, significant work is being dedicated to relocating those excavation units. Wilkie indicates in several places (Wilkie 1982, 1983) and in field notes that House One was located near the northern extent of the erosional remnant, and a former student who partici-

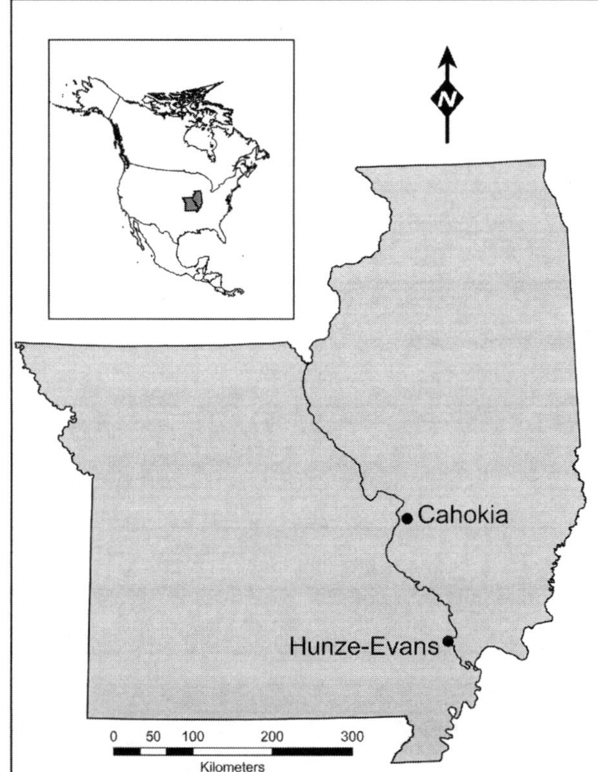

Figure 5.1. Map showing location of Hunze-Evans site in relation to Cahokia.

pated in these excavations has shown us their likely location on the ground (Figure 5.3). Although we are confident in this general assessment, planned work incorporates more precise relocation as an express goal.

Wilkie immediately recognized the feminine significance of House One and was particularly struck by a triskele-style shell gorget found on the structure floor (Figure 5.4). Triskele-style shell gorgets are generally found in infant and female burial contexts (Kneberg 1959) at late Mississippian sites—their connotation of gender and age ideologies are particularly intriguing when considered in this non-burial context. Wilkie's excavations also uncovered at least four infant interments in the floor around the perimeter of House One, a unique nursing mother effigy bottle, large ceramic vessels within a subfloor pit, and a cache of mica, strengthening his initial impressions of this structure as a women's structure.

The first author of this chapter has preliminarily explored House One through the lens of infancy and fertility symbolism (Bengtson 2017), augmenting Wilkie's interpretation of House One as feminine-focused, suggest-

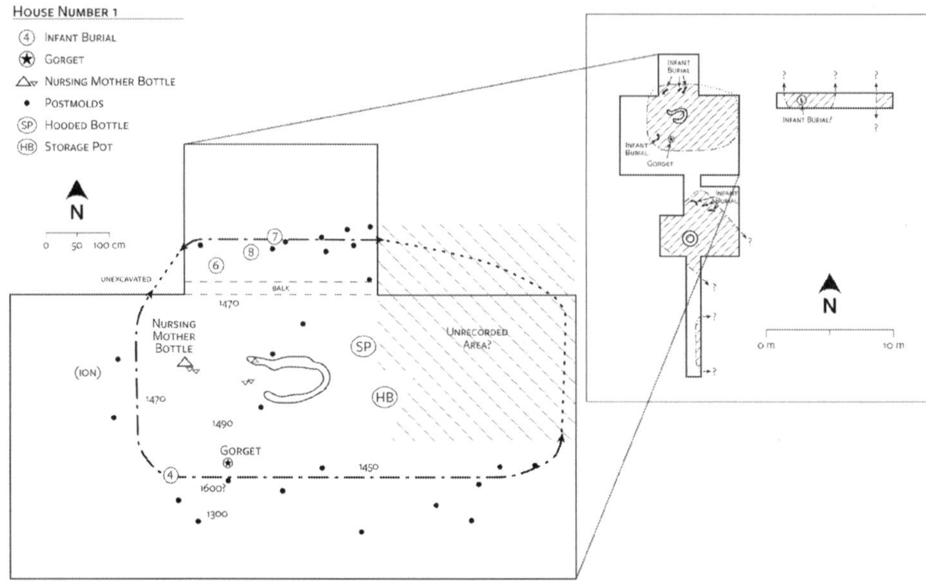

Figure 5.2. Digital reproduction of House 1 based on field notes and Wilkie (1983). Dashed lines indicate Wilkie's original interpretations of the boundaries of the structure.

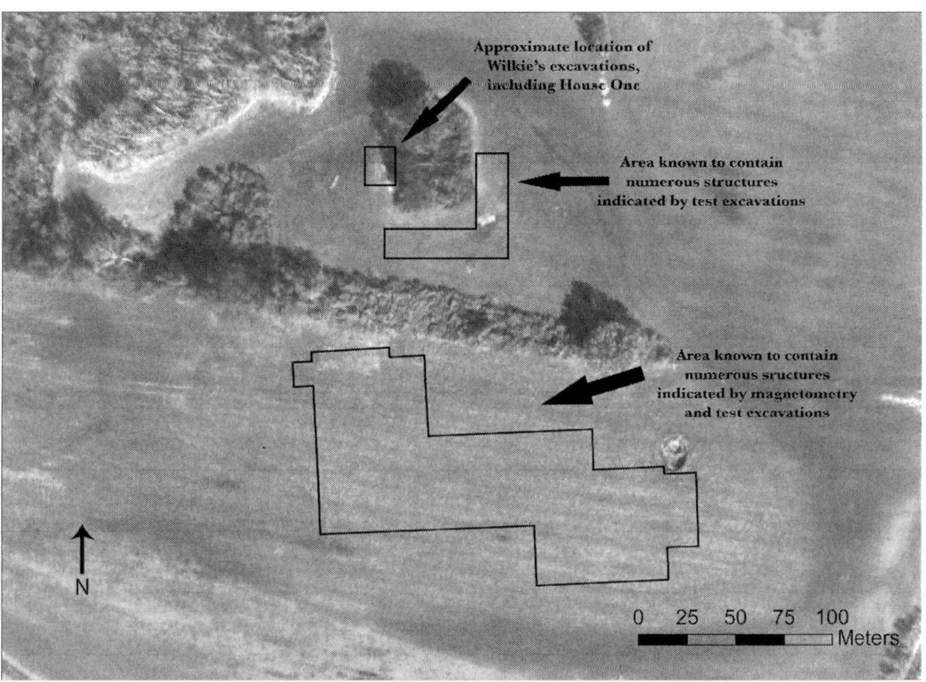

Figure 5.3. Aerial view of the Hunze-Evans site. House 1 is located approximately in the area indicated near the grove of trees to the north (*top*). Figure created by Brendan McGraw.

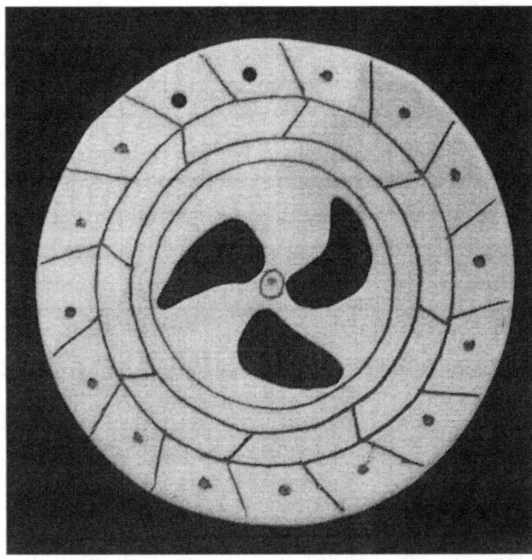

Figure 5.4. Triskele shell gorget from House 1. Modern artist reconstruction based on sketch from Wilkie (1983).

ing that it may have served as a place of birth, menstruation, or other ritually charged, female-centered ceremony and seclusion. However, that work did little to place this structure within the broader context of a symbol-laden geography. Our goal in this chapter is to do just that—to contextualize House One at the Hunze-Evans site within a broader geography of fertility.

Fertility and the Mississippian Landscape

A brief comment on geographic scale is warranted here. While we employ a three-tiered (local/regional/distant) spatial perspective in this chapter, we recognize that the experience of landscape—in terms of physical mobility through it, engagement with it, and symbolic and ideological connections to it—can collapse what we might conceive of as great distances, rendering a *near:far* dichotomy somewhat false (Merriman 2011; Warf 2011). In fact, Mississippian cosmologies often reference portals (Lankford 2004; Reilly 2004) as well as humans, animals, and earth divers crossing back and forth through boundaries between worlds (Emerson 2003; Hall 1997), representing a dynamic, complex, and spiritually charged conflation of time and space. We use a local/regional/distant approach not to argue that this is necessarily how Hunze-Evans women conceived of geographic space, but instead to serve as a simple heuristic that ultimately emphasizes the proximity and connectedness of places separated by significant geographic distances. We refer to the space of House One and the village itself as *local,* the immediate surrounding area and up to a roughly 80-kilometer radius as *regional,* and more outlying areas as *distant.*

Local: House One and the Hunze-Evans Village

Among the clearest fertility associations in House One are the infants interred in shallow basins in the structure floor. Intramural infant burials are documented at several other Mississippian sites in the region (Wilkie 1983). Wilkie assessed the infants as "less than 4 months old" (Wilkie 1982: 40), and we suggest that these remains may represent stillbirths or neonatal deaths occurring before the ritually prescribed time when new mothers would have rejoined the community. The incorporation of recently born and deceased infants into a structure charged with ideas of womanhood, fertility, and feminine power blurs boundaries between the geographic spaces of body and building, and this practice may have represented a symbolic reinvestment into the ritual cycle of life, death, kinship, and social reproduction (Brereton 2013; Pluckhahn 2010). The association of at least some of these infants with turtle carapaces furthers the connection—many sources link turtles to fertility and femininity (Claassen 2013; Duncan 2011; Dye 2013; Krutak 2013; Reilly 2004; see also Bengtson 2017: 116), while Hudson (1976) points to turtles as transitional, transformational, and boundary-crossing beings. That these infants (who had themselves recently crossed a boundary from inside to outside their mothers' bodies) were associated with an animal known for breaching boundaries melds well with a geographic perspective on fertility.

Wilkie also recovered a distinctive ceramic bottle depicting a mother nursing an infant (Figure 5.5). The negative-painted design on this bottle is reminiscent of designs on female effigy bottles from the Middle Cumberland River Basin over 200 kilometers to the east (Sharp et al. 2011). Female effigy bottles from Mississippian sites have been shown to represent women whose various life stages are evident through age-related physical traits. Among these, older women are commonly depicted and are thought to represent *Our Grandmother* or *Old-Woman-Who-Never-Dies,* a feminine deity who is presumably past her childbearing years but who is nonetheless imbued with regenerative powers (Diaz-Granados 2004; Reilly 2004). However, the House One bottle is unique in its depiction of a presumably younger mother in the act of nursing an infant. We are aware of only one other Mississippian bottle depicting a nursing mother; this bottle is in the Whepley collection, and its specific provenience is unknown, although it was recovered from St. Clair County, Illinois, located approximately 140 kilometers north of the Hunze-Evans site (see Diaz-Granados 2004: 141).

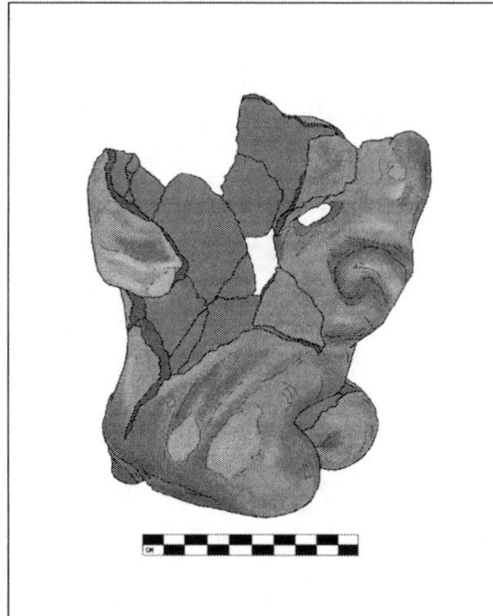
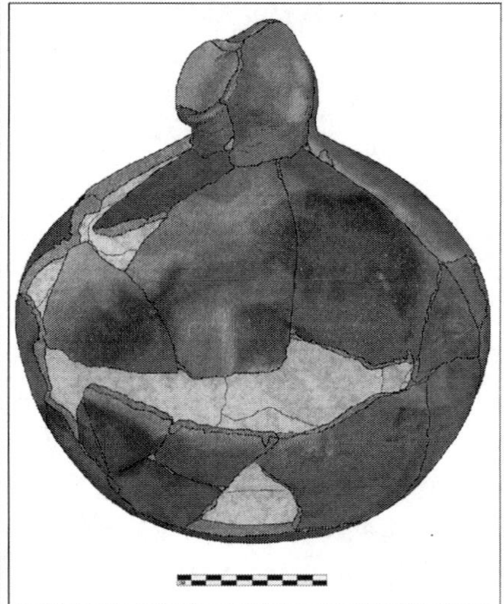

Figure 5.5. Drawings of nursing mother effigy bottle (*left*) and hooded bottle (*right*) from House 1. Drawings generated by Erin Lowe.

Additionally, a large hooded bottle (Figure 5.5) was also recovered from House One and may represent a less explicit reference to fertility. Mueller and Fritz (2016) suggest that such hooded bottles represent gourd effigies linked to ideas of regeneration. Wilkie indicates that the hooded bottle was recovered from within a central recessed basin within the broader structural basin within which House One was built. Pauketat et al. (2017) note that structures that they characterize as lunar shrines at the Early Mississippian Emerald site in the uplands just east of Cahokia also featured similar recessed basins and may have been the sites of water-related rituals. Together with the unambiguous material representation of female reproductive capacity as depicted in the nursing mother bottle, the presence and placement of the hooded bottle within House One further suggest fertility as an organizing theme within this special place.

Another artifact recovered from House One and central to our geographic perspective is the shell gorget (Figure 5.4). Although it is now missing, Wilkie (1982, 1983) wrote extensively about it, and his detailed notes and sketches provided the basis for the reproduction pictured here (Figure 5.4). This gorget was carved in the triskele style, and Wilkie cites Kneberg (1959) in relating this style to the circle-in-cross motif. Loubser (2013), following Mooney (1900) and Bartram (1955), links the circle-in-cross with menstruation and fertility, while Lankford (2011) recognizes the triskele-style as a variant of the swirl-cross cosmogram motif representing the underworld and fertility. Such gorgets are most often found in the burials of women and infants (Kneberg 1959; Brain and Phillips 1996), and as such, their recovery in a place imbued with feminine and infant-centered symbolism is central for our exploration of Hunze-Evans women and their experiences of fertility. Perhaps it was made and worn by women who occupied the structure as part of fertility rites, or perhaps it was used to decorate the bodies of newly born infants. Regardless, an association with women and infants—and hence the unifying theme of fertility—seems probable, especially in this atypical, non-burial context.

A final consideration of the local scale is the selection of the specific location for the Hunze-Evans village, which is atop a notable natural rise on the landscape and may represent a significant part of the Hunze-Evans geography of fertility. Although no cultural mound has yet been definitively identified at the site, the entire erosional remnant is reminiscent of a very large platform mound—so much so that locals have referred to the entire site as "Hunze Mound" for decades. The village's elevated location is brought into dramatic focus during times of moderate to severe seasonal flooding, when the site becomes an island surrounded by flood waters. Hall (1997) has related mound-building to Earth Diver narratives prominent among a number of Eastern and Plains tribes, in which a creature dives into a watery world to bring up mud to build land for humans to live upon. A mound (or in our case a natural rise on the landscape) surrounded by floodwaters may conjure memories of earth islands and creation narratives, which are ideologically linked to ideas of fertility and renewal (Emerson 1997). Thus, the entire Hunze-Evans site, located on an elevated spot in the floodplain, might have served as a geo-metaphor for fertility and related concepts, and represented a communal endeavor to geographically center this community within their own narratives of creation. Within such a setting, the significance of House One might be further spatially distinguished by its askew placement relative to surrounding structures (Figure 5.2) and its single post construction as opposed to the wall-trench style more typical structures at this site, including nearby structures excavated by Wilkie.

Regional: Rock Art and the Ethnobotanical Landscape Surrounding Hunze-Evans

Concerned with Hunze-Evans women's engagement with and ideas about areas outside their village, we look to the surrounding region for further hints of their fertility as marked upon the broader landscape. Mississippian rock art has been well documented throughout Missouri and across the Mississippi

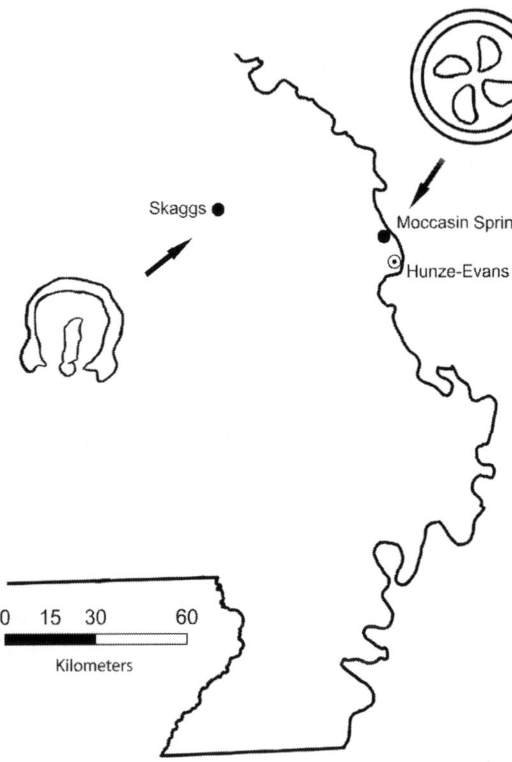

Figure 5.6. Feminine rock art motifs in the region of Hunze-Evans, as described in Diaz-Granados and Duncan (2000). Vulvar motifs at the Scaggs site, and a "spinning cross" from Moccasin Spring. Motif sketches are approximations based on descriptions and depictions in Diaz-Granados and Duncan (2000) and reproduced with permission of the University of Alabama Press. Figure created by Brendan McGraw.

River into Illinois, and its representation of gendered cosmological themes in the region of the Hunze-Evans site is described in detail by Diaz-Granados and Duncan (2000) and Duncan and Diaz-Granados (2004, 2016). Imagery most explicitly linked with women and fertility—vulvar imprints and birthing (or puerperal) figures—are not particularly plentiful in the region immediately surrounding Hunze-Evans, but vulvar-themed rock art is documented at the Scaggs site about 70 kilometers to the northwest in Bollinger County, Missouri (Figure 5.6). In fact, Duncan and Diaz-Granados (2004) note that vulvar rock art is particularly plentiful in Eastern Missouri. Vulvae have a self-evident relationship to reproduction and childbirth and are considered by some tribes as portals between worlds (Hall 1997). Diaz-Granados and Duncan (2004) cite Bowers (1950, 1992) and Ronda (1984) in their review of Siouan recognition of the vulva as an important site of female power, particularly in its propensity for acquiring, storing, and transferring power from men. Sundstrom (2004) describes vulvar petroglyphs in the Black Hills as commonly coupled with deer track motifs, noting that these motifs are so similar to one another they are virtually indistinguishable in some cases and suggesting that this symbolic link has roots in the Siouan Southeast. Southeastern tribes recount narratives of traveling women leaving a trail of vulvar prints upon the mythic landscape (Loubser 2013), just as a traveling deer leaves a trail of footprints behind it. In his review of Osage child-naming ceremonies, La Flesche (1928) states that names given to female infants sometimes specifically reference deer tracks (e.g., "Here are the Footprints," "Footprints in the Woods").

Closer to the Hunze-Evans Site is the Moccasin Spring rock art site in northern Cape Girardeau County, Missouri, described briefly by Diaz-Granados and Duncan (2000). Among other motifs depicted here is a "spinning cross." This spinning cross is similar to and may reference the same ideas as the swirl-cross or triskele motif on the House One gorget, linking the disparate places of the Moccasin Spring and House One. In Mississippian iconography, spiral motifs relate to water themes, especially whirlpools, representing portals to the Beneath World (Lankford 2007; Reilly 2004). The objects and places on the landscape that bear these motifs might therefore be viewed as conflating and connecting places and people in the Hunze-Evans region of this world to distant places within the Mississippian cosmos. In this case, the association between the triskele-style gorget and House One and the swirl-cross symbol at Moccasin Spring may demonstrate how related themes of femininity, fertility, and the Beneath World are expressed on the landscape at multiple scales, linking the village to the broader landscape as well as to the Beneath World.

Although it is difficult to say for sure who created the Scaggs site vulvar motifs and the Moccasin Spring swirl-cross, Sundstrom (2004) builds a strong case for women as the creators of similar rock art in other places. Noting that no direct Siouan ethnohistoric references are available specifically relating to vulvar/deer track rock art, feminine art in other parts of native North America was created by women as part of pilgrimages and puberty rites (Sundstrom 2004: 88–89). She also points out that some Siouan tribes identify the creator of rock art as Double Woman, a powerful spirit consisting of two women—linked together via a cord to which is attached a lifeless infant—who could sometimes be heard laughing in the night as she engraved the motifs (Sundstrom 2004: 96). Double Woman appears to women in visions obtained during puberty or menstruation, particularly to those who go on to become artists (Berlo 1993; Sundstrom 2004). Whether or not Hunze-Evans women themselves created this art or visited these sites specifically, the power of their reproductive potential and their spiritual role in its creation was celebrated in stories and inscribed widely and visibly through their landscape, from the engraving of these symbols and to the tracks of the deer who inhabited the surrounding woodlands. Women engaged with these places by creating and contemplating these powerful motifs. The vulva motif itself may actually be inscribed within House One through the shape of the hearth. Wilkie mapped his hearth as shaped somewhat like the Mississippian vulvar motif (although he did not note it as such) with a westward-facing orifice (see Figure 5.2), distinctive in form from the circular hearth in the structure located to the south. If this hearth is indeed intended to reflect the vulvar motif, this is a further link between the people and activities within this structure to the broader cultural landscape throughout which this motif was distributed.

The location of the Moccasin Spring petroglyphs at an *actual spring* may have further gendered meaning. Pauketat et al. (2017) link certain Mississippian ideologies of water to themes of femininity and fertility through Siouan cosmologies. They cite what Dorsey (1894: 538) refers to as "water under the hills" or "subterranean streams" (which we believe are references to springs) as being occupied by feminine spirits. While we cannot definitively state that Hunze-Evans women visited these regional sites, their existence nearby certainly speaks to the regional landscape as charged with fertility symbolism, often with explicit references to the female body, which reflected and incorporated their experiences of fertility with their views on the landscape outside of their village. Claassen (2016) points out that Native American origin narratives and ethnographies abound with adventurous and well-traveled women. It seems likely that Hunze-Evans women were at least aware of and perhaps also traveled far and wide through a gendered, meaningful landscape, visiting places associated with fertility, puberty, the underworld and femininity in general.

Finally, while paleoethnobotanical data from House One is currently unavailable, themes of fertility and its biocultural correlates most certainly flourished within the botanical landscape of the region, serving as a another means of linking places within the villages to places in the surrounding landscape. Ethnohistoric sources provide some insight into the medicinal plants used by women to ease the physical pains and consequent symptoms of their fertility. Mooney (1891) mentions a Cherokee medicine, "Yellow Root," which purportedly sped up the labor process. Although he does not identify the Western name for this particular plant, he notes that it was to be either consumed by the mother or rubbed on her head, breast, or the palm of each hand. Mooney also mentions women using milkweed to treat skin eruptions, including sore nipples, and skullcap for labor and menstrual-related symptoms. Olbrechts (1931) provides details of medicinal plants that were traditionally used for

Table 5.1. Examples of medicinal plants related to women's reproduction

Scientific name	Common Western name	Function	Present in SE Missouri?
Ulmus fulva	Slippery Elm	Labor aid (prenatal)	Yes (Foster and Duke 1990)
Impatiens biflora	Spotted Touch-Me-Not	"Startle" infant from womb (prenatal and during problematic labor)	Yes (Foster and Duke 1990)
Prunus serotina	Black Cherry	Labor aid	Yes (Foster and Duke 1990)
Geastrum spp.	Earth Star mushroom	Umbilical treatment	Yes (Phillps 1991)
Scutellaria lateriflora	Blue Skull-Cap	Placental delivery aid, menstrual aid	Yes (Foster and Duke 1990)

treating labor, delivery, menstruation, and infants' umbilical stumps, while Bailey and La Flesche (2010: 66) and La Flesche (1928) report that yellow lotus was particularly important for infants. Further, Lewis and Elvins-Lewis (1977: 316–324) identify a number of plants available to pre-contact women that would have been useful in alleviating menstrual cramps and reducing hemorrhaging in birthing mothers.

The region surrounding the Hunze-Evans site was an open pine-oak woodland prior to modern development (Nelson 2005), and many of the aforementioned plants would have flourished in the immediate area (Foster and Duke 1990; Table 5.1). Not only might Hunze-Evans women have been linked by fertility to these surrounding regions through their journeys to acquire these medicines and bringing them back to the village, but the act of ingestion constitutes a physical incorporation of the broader region *into* their bodies—a boundary-crossing act that distorts the margin between the fertility of the internal body and the fertility of the outside world. We know such acts of ingesting plants have deep spiritual meaning among southeastern peoples in other contexts (e.g., Black Drink ceremonialism), so the power of plants in ritual is clear. For Mississippian women, such practices may have linked pregnancy, birth, and menstrual ritual to the natural regional landscape in both physical and symbolic ways.

Distant: The Greater Mississippian World and Beyond

Although we currently lack ceramic and lithic provenance data to explore the histories and movements of the majority of the artifacts recovered from House One, two items in particular are so obviously non-local (at least in their raw material origins) that they warrant consideration in light of our geographic focus. Located near the hooded ceramic bottle in House One was a cache of mica, the nearest natural source of which is located roughly 650 kilometers away in the Blue Ridge Mountains of North Carolina. The mica was recovered in the form of several palm-sized sheets and smaller flakes totaling about 250 grams, and it is not modified in any obvious way. Although mica may not be directly connected to ideas about femininity and fertility, its presence in Mississippian ritual contexts has been widely documented. Baltus and Baries (2012: 177) in particular note that mica is often part of a suite of substances and items gathered together by ritual practitioners who operated within these special structures, which became "empowered and animated" through their use.

To extend the Hunze-Evans geography of fertility even further, we return once again to the shell gorget. We have already situated it as a link between the village and broader regional constructs of fertility, but here we focus not on the motif, but on the raw material from which it was made. Claassen's (2008) study of the link between shell and fertility among diverse Indigenous traditions in North and Mesoamerica informs this perspective, as does Emerson's (2003) work connecting whelk shells and themes of the underworld, water, fertility, and renewal in the Mississippian American Bottom. Strezewski's (2009) study of the prevalence of shell in Mississippian children's graves is also relevant—children, after all, are the ultimate products of reproductive fertility. Quoting Miller and Hammell (1986: 318), Stezewski suggests that shell beads are involved in "rituals of creation and re-creation, resuscitation, and the continuity of life" among Eastern Woodlands peoples (Miller and Hamell 1986: 318). While the House One shell gorget's triskele motif encapsulated a *metaphoric* distance in its symbolic reference to portals, fertility, and the underworld, the marine shell from which it was made draws power from *geographic* distance as it likely originated in the Gulf of Mexico, over 800 kilometers away. As Lankford (2004) eloquently stated in his overview of Mississippian iconography, "Whatever the precise meaning and function of these images, the reality was that human beings wore *upon their bodies* symbols of the cosmos, a practice that surely linked them to the larger reality in which they understood themselves to be participants" (217). We appreciate not only to the *cosmological* but also to the *geospatial* connotations of Lankford's interpretation—that the symbols Mississippians used, wore, and recognized also linked their bodies to an array of otherworldly places as well as to geographically identifiable places in *this* physical world—as nearby as the village itself and as distant as the Blue Ridge Mountains or the Gulf of Mexico—representing a broader geography of fertility. Taken together, House One and its contents are key to exploring how women created and moved through a Mississippian landscape of fertility, within and around the Hunze-Evans site and the broader Mississippian world.

Geographies of Fertility: Linking Bodies to the Cosmos

In their introduction to a volume on emotional geographies, Bondi et al. (2007) describe the ways that emotional experiences disrupt the boundaries of the body—from the decidedly unpleasant experience of agoraphobia where the sufferer is confronted with the fragility of the boundary between the body and the outside world, to the more positive emotional experience of feeling so affected by a beautiful landscape that the boundary between it and your body are pleasantly permeated. "Emotions," they state, "help to construct, maintain as well as sometimes to disrupt the very distinction between bodily interiors and exteriors" (Bondi et al. 2007: 7). Menstruation, childbirth, and infancy—all encapsulated in the theme of fertility—were emotionally and corporeally experienced episodes in the lives of Mississippian women, and women inscribed those emotions and experiences onto their cultural landscape at various spatial scales via daily and ritual practice. For Mississippian women, fertility was not only a biologically embodied experience, but also a spiritual and emotional experience transcending boundaries between themselves, their villages, their landscapes, and their cosmos.

In this chapter, we have highlighted the ways that House One, the Hunze-Evans village, and the outlying natural and cultural landscapes surrounding the site were linked within a larger geography of fertility that ultimately drew on greater Mississippian styles, symbols, and themes. This geography of fertility structured—and was structured by—women's practiced and idealized experience of fertility as a force that blurs the boundary between women's biologically circumscribed bodies and their external, surrounding spaces. This disruption was material and physical as well as emotional and spiritual. Mississippian women physically moved among places of fertility to which they linked themselves through their bodily products, their journeys to acquire and ingest medicines, or their pilgrimages to visit/create places marked in stone with powerful symbols. It is only through the action and agency of women that this landscape could have been created and maintained. We cannot attempt to understand the Mississippian cultural landscape at Hunze-Evans (or anywhere) without attempting to understand women's engagement with it.

Further lines of inquiry arise from these musings, not the least of which are empirical and systematic analyses of botanical and faunal remains to augment our understanding of activities—ritual and mundane alike—that occurred within House One and linked it to other places. Beyond the quantifiable, we are also drawn to consider the more emotive and less tangible aspects of women's interactions with one another within this space. For example, Buckley and Gottlieb (1988) emphasize the communal nature of "menstrual seclusion" and consider the opportunities for female solidarity and cohesion that were ripe to develop in such places. Their entrance into, stay within, and eventual emergence from such structures or journeys to and back from the other places mentioned in this chapter are apt to be explored as ritual cycles and opportunities for the experience of what Victor and Edith Turner refer to as *communitas* (E. Turner 2011; V. Turner 1969). House One may be an appropriate place for considering these phenomena at Hunze-Evans.

From the new ways that a woman may have decorated and even postured her body upon her first menses, to her old age in which she may have transitioned to the role of midwife or spiritual guide, a Mississippian woman's entry into the world of fertility and potential motherhood was the beginning of a physical and figurative journey that connected her to particular structures, to her village, and to people and places both near and far. While it may be difficult to determine which came first—the Hunze-Evans village or the geography of fertility in which it was situated—what is clear is that the lived experiences of Mississippian women at this site were not afterthoughts in the construction of the Mississippian world. Instead, women's bodies and experiences were central to understanding the powerful forces of the Mississippian worldview. That vulvae were symbols for portals between worlds, just as they served as portals for bringing new human life into this world, and that women's biological acts of fertility were not confined to invisible, unobtrusive huts outside of communal space—but rather were writ large across the landscape at multiple scales—speaks to the importance given to women's lived experiences in constructing and understanding the Mississippian world.

Note

All human remains referenced in this chapter were excavated in the late 1970s and early 1980s. They are reported in Native American Graves Protection and Repatriation Act (NAGPRA) inventories and are curated at the University of Missouri Museum of Anthropology. No new data were collected specifically for this chapter.

References Cited

Adair, James
1930 [1775] *History of the American Indians.* Promontory Press, New York.

Alt, Susan
2018 The Emerald Site, Mississippian Women, and the Moon. In *Archaeology of the Night: Life after Dark in the Ancient World*, edited by Nancy Gonlin and April Nowell, pp. 323–348. University Press of Colorado, Boulder.

Bailey, Garrick A., and Francis La Flesche
2010 *Traditions of the Osage: Stories Collected and Translated by Francis La Flesche.* University of New Mexico Press, Albuquerque.

Baltus, Melissa. R., and Sarah E. Baires
2012 Elements of Ancient Power in the Cahokian World. *Journal of Social Archaeology* 12(2): 167–192.

Bartram, William
1955 *Travels of William Bartram.* Dover Publications, New York.

Beausang, Elizabeth
2000 Childbirth in Prehistory: An Introduction. *European Journal of Archaeology* 3(1): 69–87.

Bengtson, Jennifer D.
2017 Infants, Mothers, and Gendered Space in a Mississippian Village: Revisiting Wilkie's House 1 at the Hunze-Evans Site. *Childhood in the Past* 10(2): 102–121.

Berlo, Janet
1993 Dreaming of Double Woman: The Ambivalent Role of the Female Artist in North American Indian Myth. *American Indian Quarterly* 17(1): 31–43.

Bondi, Liz
2005 Making Connections and Thinking Through Emotions: Between Geography and Psychotherapy. *Transactions of the Institute of British Geographers* 30(4): 433–448.

Bondi, Liz, Joyce Davidson, and Mick Smith
2007 Introduction: Geography's Emotional Turn. In *Emotional Geographies*, edited by Joyce Davidson, Liz Bondi, Mick Smith, pp. 1–8. Routledge, London.

Boric, Dusan, and John Robb
2008 Body Theory in Archaeology. In *Past Bodies: Body Centered Research in Archaeology*, edited by Dusan Boric and John Robb, pp. 1–8. Oxbow Books, Oxford.

Bowers, Alfred W.
1950 *Mandan Social and Ceremonial Organization*. University of Chicago Press, Chicago.
1992 *Hidatsa Social and Ceremonial Organization*. University of Nebraska Press, Lincoln.
Brain, Jeffrey, and Phillip Phillips
1996 *Shell Gorgets: Styles of the Late Prehistoric and Protohistoric Southeast*. Peabody Museum Press: Cambridge.
Brennan, Tamira, and Sarah Stephens
2009 Old Collections and New Finds at the South Cape Site, Missouri. Paper Presented at the Kincaid Field Conference, Metropolis, IL.
Brennan, Tamira, Jennifer Bengtson, and Robert McCullough
2019 "Geophysical Survey of a Late Mississippian Site in Southeast Missouri (23Cg8)." Poster presented at 2019 Mississippian Conference, Lewiston, Illinois.
Brereton, Gareth
2013 Cultures of Infancy and Capital Accumulation in Pre-Urban Mesopotamia. *World Archaeology* 45(2): 232–251.
Brown, James
2011 The Regional Culture Signature of the Braden Art Style. In *Visualizing the Sacred: Cosmic Visions, Regionalism, and the Art of the Mississippian World*, edited by George Lankford, F. Kent Reilly and James Garber, pp. 37–63. University of Texas Press, Austin.
Buckley, Thomas, and Alma Gottlieb, eds.
1988 A Critical Appraisal of Theories of Menstrual Symbolism. In *Blood Magic: The Anthropology of Menstruation*, edited by Thomas Buckley and Alma Gottlieb, pp. 1–54. University of California Press, Berkeley.
Carney, Molly, Jade D'Alpoim Guedes, Kevin Lyons, and Melissa Elgar
2019 Gendered Places and Depositional Histories: Reconstructing a Menstrual Lodge in the Interior Northwest. *American Antiquity* 84(3): 400–419.
Casey, Edward S.
2001 Body, Self, and Landscape: A Geophilosophical Inquiry into the Place-World. In *Textures of Place: Exploring Humanist Geographies*, edited by Paul C. Adams, Steven Hoelscher, and Karen E. Till, pp. 403–425. University of Minnesota Press, Minneapolis.
Castree, Noel
2009 Place: Connections and Boundaries in an Interdependent World. In *Key Concepts in Geography*, 2nd edition, edited by Nicholas J. Clifford, Sarah L. Holloway, Stephen P. Rice, and Gill Valentine, pp. 153–172. Sage, Los Angeles.
Christensen, Tamira Brennan
2010 The South Cape Site: A Fortified Mississippian Village in Southeast Missouri. *Missouri Archaeological Society Quarterly* 27: 12–19.
Claassen, Cheryl
2008 Shell Symbolism in Pre-Columbian North America. In *Early Human Impact on Megamolluscs*, edited by Andrzej Antczak and Roberto Cipriani, pp. 231–236. British Archaeological Reports 21865. Oxford.

2011 Rock Shelters as Women's Retreats: Understanding Newt Kash. *American Antiquity* 76(4): 628–641.

2013 Fertility: A Place-Based Gift to Groups. In *Género y Arqueología en Mesoamérica. Homenaje a Rosemary Joyce*, edited by María Rodríguez-Shadow and Susan Kellogg, pp. 198–215. Centro de Estudios de Antropología de la Mujer, Las Cruces, New Mexico.

2016 Native Women, Men, and American Landscape: The Gendered Gaze. In *Native American Landscapes: An Engendered Perspective*, edited by Cheryl Claassen, pp. xiii–xxxv. University of Tennessee Press, Knoxville

Cloke, Paul, Chris Philo, and David Sadler

1991 *Approaching Human Geography: An Introduction to Contemporary Theoretical Debates*. Guilford Press, New York

Cobb, Charles, and Brian Butler

2002 The Vacant Quarter Revisited: Late Mississippian Abandonment of the Lower Ohio Valley. *American Antiquity* 67(4): 625–641.

Cresswell, Tim

1996 *In Place/Out of Place: Geography, Ideology, and Transgression*. University of Minnesota Press, Minneapolis and London.

2013 *Geographic Thought: A Critical Introduction*. Wiley Blackwell: Chichester, UK.

Davidson, Joyce, and Christine Milligan

2004 Embodying Emotion, Sensing Space: Introducing Emotional Geographies. *Social & Cultural Geography* 5(4): 523–532.

Diaz-Granados, Carol

2004 Marking Stone, Land, Body, and Spirit. In *Hero, Hawk, and Open Hand American Indian Art of the Ancient Midwest and South*, edited by Richard F. Townsend, pp. 138–149. Yale University Press, New Haven.

Diaz-Granados, Carol, and James Duncan

2000 *The Petroglyphs and Pictographs of Missouri*. University of Alabama Press, Tuscaloosa.

2004 Reflections of Power, Wealth, and Sex in Missouri Rock-Art Motifs. In *The Rock-Art of Eastern North America: Capturing Images and Insight*, edited by Carol Diaz-Granados and James R. Duncan, pp. 145–158. University Alabama Press, Tuscaloosa.

Dorsey, James Owen

1894 *A Study of Siouan Cults*. Smithsonian Institution, Washington.

Duncan, James

2011 The Cosmology of the Osage: The Star People and their Universe. In *Visualizing the Sacred: Cosmic Visions, Regionalism, and the Art of the Mississippian World*, edited by George Lankford, F. Kent Reilly III, and James Garber, pp. 18–36. University of Texas Press, Austin.

Duncan, James R., and Carol Diaz-Granados

2004 Empowering the SECC: The "Old Woman" and Oral Tradition. In *The Rock-Art of Eastern North America: Capturing Images and Insight*, edited by Carol Diaz-Granados and James R. Duncan, pp. 190–216. University Alabama Press, Tuscaloosa.

2016 Rock art, gender, and the Dhegihan landscape. In *Native American Landscapes: An Engendered Perspective,* edited by Claassen, Cheryl. University of Tennessee Press, Knoxville.

Dye, David

2013 Snaring Life from the Stars and the Sun: Mississippian Tattooing and the Enduring Cycle of Life and Death. In *Drawing with Great Needles: Ancient Tattoo Traditions of North America*, edited by Aaron Deter-Wolf and Carol Diaz-Granados, pp. 215–252. University of Texas Press, Austin.

Edwards, Tai

2018 *Osage Women and Empire: Women and Power.* University Press of Kansas, Lawrence.

Emerson, Thomas

1989 Water, Serpents, and the Underworld: An Exploration into Cahokian Symbolism. In *The Southeastern Ceremonial Complex: Artifacts and Analysis*, edited by Patricia Galloway, pp. 45–92. University of Nebraska Press, Lincoln.

1997 Cahokia Elite Ideology and the Mississippian Cosmos. In *Cahokia: Ideology and Domination in the Mississippian World*, edited by Timothy Pauketat and Thomas Emerson, pp. 190–228. University of Nebraska Press, Lincoln

2003 Crossing Boundaries between Worlds: Changing Beliefs and Mortuary Practices at Cahokia. *The Wisconsin Archaeologist* 84(1&2): 73–80.

Finlay, Nyree

2013 Archaeologies of the Beginning of Life. *World Archaeology* 45(2): 207–214.

Foster, Steven, and James A. Duke

1990 *Field Guide to Medicinal Plants.* Houghton Mifflin, New York.

Fowler, Chris

2011 Personhood and the Body. In *The Archaeology of Ritual and Religion*, edited by Timothy Insoll, pp. 133–150. Oxford University Press, Oxford.

Galloway, Patricia

1997 Where Have All the Menstrual Huts Gone? The Invisibility of Menstrual Seclusion in the Late Prehistoric Southeast. In *Women in Prehistory: North America and Mesoamerica*, edited by Cheryl Claassen and Rosemary Joyce, pp. 47–62. University of Pennsylvania Press, Philadelphia.

Gero, Joan

1985 Socio-politics and the Woman-at-Home Ideology. *American Antiquity* 50(2): 342–350.

Giddens, Anthony

1984 *The Constitution of Society: Outline of the Theory of Structuration.* Polity Press, Cambridge.

Gottlieb, Alma, and Judy DeLoache

2017 *A World of Babies: Imagined Childcare Guides for Eight Societies.* Cambridge University Press: Cambridge.

Hall, Robert

1997 *An Archaeology of the Soul: North American Indian Belief and Ritual.* University of Illinois Press, Urbana.

Helton, Deseray L.
2017 Household Chipped Stone Technology at South Cape (23CG8), a Mississippian Hinterland Site in Southeast Missouri. Unpublished master's thesis, Department of Sociology and Anthropology, Missouri State University, Springfield.
Herman, Mary
1950 A Reconstruction of Aboriginal Delaware Culture from Contemporary Sources. *Kroeber Anthropological Society Papers* 1: 45–77.
Hudson, Charles
1976 *The Southeastern Indians.* University of Tennessee Press, Knoxville.
Jackson, Peter
1989 *Maps of Meaning.* Routledge, London.
Joyce, Rosemary
2003 Making Something of Herself: Embodiment in Life and Death at Playa de los Muertos, Honduras. *Cambridge Archaeological Journal* 13: 48–261.
2005 Archaeology of the Body. *Annual Review of Anthropology* 34: 139–158.
King, Adam
2007 The Southeastern Ceremonial Complex: From Cult to Complex. In *Southeastern Ceremonial Complex: Chronology, Content, Contest,* edited by Adam King, pp. 1–14. The University of Alabama Press, Tuscaloosa.
Kneberg, Madeline
1959 Engraved Shell Gorgets and Their Associations. *Tennessee Archaeologist* 5:1–3.
Knight, Vernon J.
1986 The Institutional Organization of Mississippian Religion. *American Antiquity* 51(4): 675–687.
Krutak, Lars
2013 The Art of Enchantment: Corporeal Marking and Tattooing Bundles of the Great Plains. In *Drawing with Great Needles: Ancient Tattoo Traditions of North America,* edited by Aaron Deter-Wolf and Carol Diaz-Granados, pp. 131–174. University of Texas Press, Austin.
La Flesche, Francis
1928 *The Osage Tribe: Two Versions of the Child-Naming Rite.* Forty-third Annual Report of the Bureau of American Ethnology to the Secretary of the Smithsonian Institution, 1925–1926. Printing Office, Washington.
Landes, Ruth
1959 Dakota warfare. *Southwestern Journal of Anthropology* 15(1): 43–52.
1968 *The Mystic Lake Sioux: Sociology of the Mdewakantonwan Santee.* University of Wisconsin Press, Madison.
Lankford, George
2004 World on a String: Some Cosmological Components of the Southeastern Ceremonial Complex. In *Hero, Hawk, and Open Hand: American Indian Art of the Ancient Midwest and South,* edited by Richard Townsend, pp. 207–218. Art Institute of Chicago, Chicago.
2007 Some Cosmological Motifs in the Southeastern Ceremonial Complex. In *Ancient Objects and Sacred Realms,* edited by V. Steponaitis, F. Reilly, and J. Garber, pp. 8–38. University of Texas Press.

2011 The Swirl-Cross and the Center. In *Visualizing the Sacred: Cosmic Visions, Regionalism, and the Art of the Mississippian World*, edited by George E. Lankford, F. Kent Reilly III, and James F. Garber, pp. 251–275. University of Texas Press, Austin.

Lankford, George, F. Kent Reilly, and James Garber

2011 Introduction. In *Visualizing the Sacred: Cosmic Visions, Regionalism, and the Art of the Mississippian World*, edited by George E. Lankford, F. Kent Reilly III, and James F. Garber, pp. 12–19. University of Texas Press, Austin.

Lewis, Walter, and Memory P.F. Elvin-Lewis

1977 *Medical Botany: Plants Affecting Man's Health.* Wiley, New York.

Loubser, Johannes

2013 The Ritual and Socio-Economic Contexts of Petroglyph Boulders in the Southeastern United States. In *Art as a Source of History*, edited by E. Anati, pp. 83–93. Centro Camuno di Studi Preistorici, Capo di Ponte.

McCourt, Christine, ed.

2009 *Childbirth, Midwifery, and Concepts of Time.* Berghahn Books, New York.

McKinnon, Katherine

2014 The Geopolitics of Birth. *Area* 48(3): 285–291.

Merriman, Peter

2011 Human Geography without Time-Space. *Transactions of the Institute of British Geographers* 37(1): 13–27.

Miller, Jay

1991 Delaware Personhood. *Man in the Northeast* 42: 17–27.

Miller, Christopher L., and George R. Hamell

1986 A New Perspective on Indian-White Contact: Cultural Symbols and Colonial Trade. *Journal of American History* 73(2): 311–328

Mooney, James

1891 *Sacred Formulas of the Cherokees.* Seventh Annual Report of the Bureau of Ethnology to the Secretary of the Smithsonian Institution, 1885–1886. Government Printing Office, Washington.

1900 *Myths of the Cherokee.* Nineteenth Annual Report of the Bureau of American Ethnology, 1885–86. Washington DC: Government Printing Office.

Mountz, Alison

2018 Political geography III: Bodies. *Progress in Human Geography* 42(5): 759–769.

Mueller, Natalie, and Gayle Fritz

2016 Women as Symbols and Actors in the Mississippi Valley: Evidence from Female Flint-Clay Statues and Effigy Vessels. In *Native American Landscapes: An Engendered Perspective*, edited by Cheryl Claassen, pp. 109–148. University of Tennessee Press, Knoxville.

Nelson, Paul W.

2005 *The Terrestrial Communities of Missouri.* 2nd ed. Missouri Natural Areas Committee.

O'Brien, Michael

2001 *Mississippian Community Organization: The Powers Phase in Southeastern Missouri.* Kluwer Academic/Plenum, New York.

O'Brien, Michael, and Raymond Wood
1998 *The Prehistory of Missouri.* University of Missouri Press, Columbia.
Olbrechts, Frans
1931 Cherokee Belief and Practice with Regard to Childbirth. *Anthropos* 26 (1/2): 17–33.
Pauketat, Timothy, Susan Alt, and Jeffery D. Kruchten
2017 The Emerald Acropolis: Elevating the Moon and Water in the Rise of Cahokia. *Antiquity* 91(355): 207–222.
Pesantubbee, Michelene
2004 *Choctaw Women in a Chaotic World.* University of New Mexico Press, Albuquerque.
Pluckhahn, Thomas
2010 Household Archaeology in the Southeastern United States: History, Trends, and Challenges. *Journal of Archaeological Research* 18(4): 331–385.
Powers, Marla
1980 Menstruation and Reproduction: An Oglala Case. *Signs: Journal of Women in Culture and Society* 6(1): 54–65.
Radcliffe, Sarah A.
2018 Geography and Indigeneity II: Critical Geographies of Indigenous Bodily Politics. *Progress in Human Geography* 42(3): 436–445.
Reilly, F. Kent.
2004 People of Earth, People of Sky: Visualizing the Sacred in Native American Art of the Mississippian Period. In *Hero, Hawk, and Open Hand American Indian Art of the Ancient Midwest and South*, edited by Richard F. Townsend, pp. 125–138. Yale University Press, New Haven.
Reilly, F. Kent, and James Garber
2007 *Ancient Objects and Sacred Realms: Interpretations of Mississippian Iconography.* University of Texas Press, Austin.
Robinson, Catherine
2018 Maternal Geographies. *Emotion, Space and Society* 26: 31–32.
Ronda, James P.
1984 *Lewis and Clark among the Indians.* University of Nebraska Press, Lincoln.
Sauer, Carl Ortwin
1925 The Morphology of Landscape. In *Land and life: A Selection from the Writings of Carl Ortwin Sauer*, edited by John Leighly, pp. 315–350. University of California Press, Berkeley.
Sharp, Robert, Vernon Knight, and George Lankford
2011 Woman in the Patterned Shawl: Female Effigy Vessels and Figurines from the Middle Cumberland Basin. In *Visualizing the Sacred: Cosmic Visions, Regionalism, and the Art of the Mississippian World*, edited by George Lankford, F. Kent Reilly III, and James F. Garber, pp. 177–200. University of Texas Press, Austin.
Simonsen, Kirsten
2000 The Body as Battlefield. *Transactions of the Institute of British Geographers* 25(1): 7–9.
Stelle, Linville
2006 The Rock Art of the Blood of the Ancestors Grotto: Methodology: Imaging the

Pictographs. Center for Social Research, Parkland College, Champaign, Illinois. Electronic document accessed August 1, 2019. http://virtual.parkland.edu/lstellel/len/center_for_social_research/BAG/BAG_main.html

Stephens, Sarah A.

2010 The South Cape Site (23CG8) of Cape Girardeau, Missouri. Master's thesis, Department of Anthropology, University of Mississippi, Oxford.

Strezewski, Michael

2009 The Concept of Personhood in Mississippian Society. *Illinois Archaeology* 21: 166–190.

Sundstrom, Linea

2004 *Storied Stone: Indian Rock Art of the Black Hills Country.* University of Oklahoma Press, Norman.

Swanton, John

1946 *The Indians of the Southeastern United States.* Bureau of American Ethnology Bulletin, No. 137. Government Printing Office, Washington.

Townsend, R., ed.

2004 *Hero, Hawk, and Open Hand: American Indian Art of the Ancient Midwest and South.* Art Institute of Chicago, Chicago.

Tremayne, Soraya, ed.

2001 *Managing Reproductive Life: Cross-Cultural Themes in Fertility and Sexuality.* Berghahn Books, New York.

Tuan, Yi-Fu

1977 *Space and Place: The Perspective of Experience.* University of Minnesota Press, Minneapolis.

Turner, Edith

2011 *Communitas: The Anthropology of Collective Joy.* Palgrave Macmillan, New York.

Turner, Victor

1969 *The Ritual Process: Structure and Anti-Structure.* Aldine Transaction, Brunswick and London.

Warf, Barney

2011 Excavating the Prehistory of Time-space Compression. *Geographical Review* 101(3): 435–446.

Wilkie, Duncan

1982 Preliminary Findings of Mississippian Occupation on the Ozark Escarpment, Missouri. Paper presented at the 39th annual meeting of the Southeastern Archaeological Conference, Memphis.

1983 Shell Gorget in a Small Village Context. Paper presented at the 48th annual meeting of the Society for American Archaeology, Pittsburgh.

Williams, Stephen

1954 An Archaeological Study of the Mississippian Culture in Southeast Missouri. PhD dissertation, Department of Anthropology, Yale University, New Haven.

1990 The Vacant Quarter and Other Late Events in the Lower Valley. In *Towns and Temples Along the Mississippi*, edited by D.H. Dye and C.A. Cox, pp. 170–180. University of Alabama Press, Tuscaloosa.

6

Matrilineal Kinship Networks and Late Mississippian Politics in the Upper Tennessee Valley

LYNNE P. SULLIVAN

Relations of kin, both biological and adoptive, are powerful organizational determinants among Indigenous communities across the world. In the Southeast, concepts of kinship were intimately tied to everyday matters such as household ownership and corporate labor groups, both of which were controlled by women. Ethnohistoric accounts and comparative sociopolitics worldwide demonstrate that kinship ties, especially when these are matrilineal, often formed the basis of Indigenous women's political power and influence. Cherokee women served as leaders of extended-family households and kinship organizations, including matrilineal clans (Cooper 2022; Perdue 1999; Sattler 1995), and archaeological evidence, as discussed in several articles by this author and Rodning (2001, 2011; Rodning 1999, 2011; Rodning and Sullivan 2020; Sullivan 2001, 2006), suggests that Late Mississippian women across Southern Appalachia did so as well. These female roles as Clan Mothers and family leaders likely served to generate balance with community leadership positions commonly held by men, as is well documented in Cherokee society (Cooper 2022; Perdue 1999), but less so in Creek society to the south (Sattler 1995).

In societal roles that included tradition-keeping and teaching, women also served as the social and cultural connections between generations, passing down information through communities of practice and kin groups within which processes of teaching and learning took place. Mississippian women surely practiced many traditional crafts, but pottery making has arguably the most visible (and most abundant) archaeological signature. Pottery-making knowledge likely was more often than not passed from skilled potters to students along the lines of kinship, co-residence, or some other intimate rela-

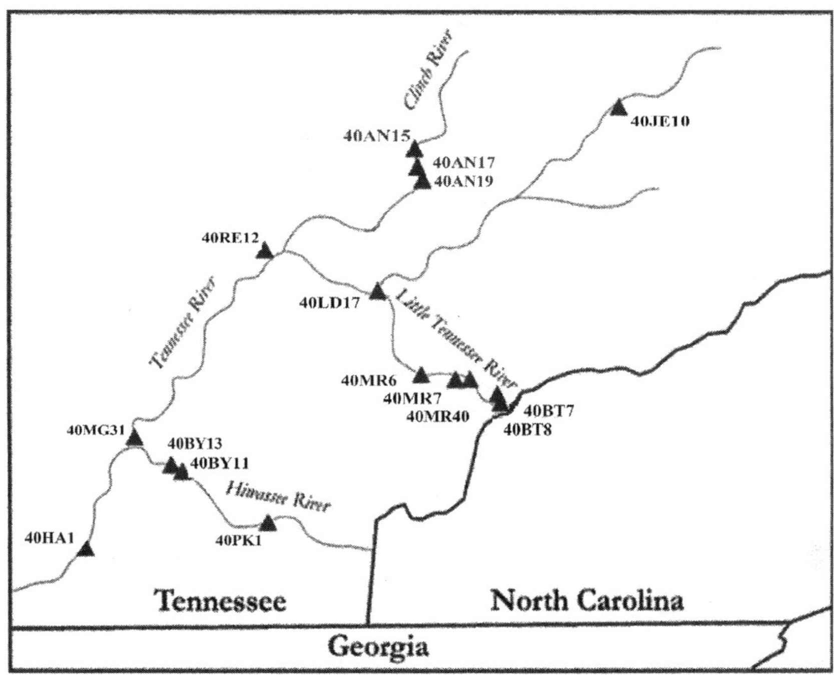

Figure 6.1. Map of the study area showing sites from which vessel data were collected. 40AN15 Johnson Farm; 40AN17 Lea Farm; 40AN19 Cox Mound; 40BT7 Chilhowee; 40BT8 Tallassee; 40BY11 Rymer; 40BY13 Ledford Island; 40HA1 Dallas; 40JE10 Loy; 40LD17 Bussell Island; 40MG31 Hiwassee Island; 40MR6 Toqua; 40MR7 Citico; 40MR40 Patrick; 40PK1 Ocoee; 40RE12 Dearmond.

tionships. Such relationships required continued, face-to-face interactions, as older women in matrilineal households and extended-family groupings taught the skills of pottery making to their daughters, sisters' daughters, or even granddaughters and grandnieces (Briggs, this volume; see Worth 2017).

These relational concepts can be explored within a network perspective to investigate the organization of regional kinship relations during the Late Mississippian period among communities in one region of Southern Appalachia—the Upper Tennessee Valley (Figure 6.1). Pottery attributes can be viewed as an indicator for communities of practice connecting women to one another, and used to trace associated kin relations through which Mississippian political endeavors were carried out.

This study employs formal network analyses based on Late Mississippian pottery attributes to investigate the potential relational structures of regional kin-ties and communities of practice within the Upper Tennessee Valley. The results of this analysis of networks based on pottery attributes can be used to observe gendered networks and political dynamics across the Late Mississippian Upper Tennessee Valley and may offer interpretations relevant to the southern Appalachian region.

A bottom-up, inductive approach is used to evaluate gendered domains of practice with data derived from whole pottery vessels from individual burials. This analysis allows for an exploration of the relationships through which Mississippian societies and communities were intertwined, highlighting gendered dimensions of regional relationships. In doing so, the study also illustrates the fundamental stability that kinship politics likely provided to balance the competition and impermanence that may have characterized changes related to individual personalities and dynamics among male leaders. These masculine-oriented processes are more often the focus of discussions of Mississippian politics. Children are usually associated with the domain of women and kinship, and this study additionally demonstrates the integral role of children in tying communities together.

Gender from the Bottom-Up

"General models [for gender in the archaeological record] often project a modern preoccupation with differences between men and women on the past" (Joyce 2008: 9). When a study begins with top-down frameworks of gender identity, the resulting analysis often tends to predetermine the significance of characteristics. That is, the focus is on what is shared and to propose such shared characteristics as evidence for gender identity (Joyce 2008: 56). These predetermined values also often tend to be placed on gendered characteristics derived from modern-day cultural referents, as traditionally has been the case for studies of Southern Appalachian Mississippian gender and politics, as I have previously discussed (Sullivan 2001: 102):

> Many studies of Mississippian mortuary programs interpret as elite those burials associated with prestige goods and interred in public places, such as mounds or public buildings. The majority of such individuals are adult males . . . a circumstance typically interpreted as implying that men were the political leaders and wielded more political power than women in these societies. Such interpretations are reinforced by accounts of early [male] chroniclers, especially those of the Mississippi Valley (e.g., Tregle 1975), who detail the political activity of, and offices held by, men . . .

I also have argued that unique domains of political expression do not imply a priori different degrees of power, influence, authority, or dominance of one group over another. When gendered domains of power and politics are investigated from the top down, the understanding tends to be lost that there may exist multiple venues for political expression, and the possibility that different groups may have had different degrees of power that were dependent on circumstance and context (Sullivan 2001: 103). This contextual perspective of political and social power has been discussed under the classification "heterarchy" (as opposed to hierarchy) by Crumley (1995) and Levy (1999).

From a bottom-up perspective, based on the empirical exploration of mortuary contexts and critical readings of ethnohistoric documentation, I previously argued that gender-related differences observed in Mississippian mortuary programs across eastern Tennessee correlate with gender-specific differences in political leadership and in how men and women acquired prestige (Sullivan 2001: 102–103). My argument contrasts with approaches that use differences in mortuary characteristics that correlate with biological sex to argue for differences in prestige. Those analyses typically use maleness as the basis for measuring prestige and wealth among individuals of all biological sexes. While traditional top-down approaches have tended to begin with what people *are*, bottom-up approaches begin with what people *do*, and such a perspective fundamentally changes how we look at the archaeological record as clues to gendered lives (Joyce 2008: 61).

A major factor in why top-down approaches ineffectively characterize gendered participation in Mississippian politics has been the dichotomization of the "public" and the "private." While women's political influence in one realm (e.g., "public") of a society may be low, it may dominate, relative to males, in another (e.g., "private") (Friedl 1967; Miller 1993: 7). The valuation of "public" over "domestic" or "private" also tends to be derived from Western patriarchal ideologies and traditions that may have little relevance in, or similarity to, traditions across non-Western societies (Briggs and Harle, this volume; MacCormack 1980; Mathews 1985; Rosaldo 1980; Rothstein 1982; Sudarkasa 1981). Because Late Mississippian women of Southern Appalachia primarily were interred in domestic spaces (e.g., within and adjacent to houses), their affiliation with domestic spheres of life have been used to undervalue, underrepresent, and wholly mischaracterize their political participation. As Hendon (1996: 46–47) highlights, "the household is, in effect, politicized in that its internal relations are inextricable from the large economic and political structure of society."

This chapter specifically explores how the relationships forged across "domestic" domains not only articulated with broader "public" politics, but in fact gave structure to this male-dominated domain. The traditional focus on the public political arena of Mississippian-era sociopolitics has heavily undermined an understanding of women's political roles. As I have pointed out (Sullivan 2001: 105), the invisibility of women in the public, male-dominated sphere does not mean that they lacked prestige or power (Mukhopadhyay and Higgins 1988). The fact is well documented that women's political participation will often take place "behind the scenes" (although the "public," "male scenes," may well have taken place behind the "female scenes" in particular circumstances and contexts) (Sullivan 2001: 105). For example, in Cherokee culture, "clan authority supported female rights in superseding a chief's orders," women "were essential participants in political deliberations," and also "determined a captive's entitlement to adoption and tribal citizenship" (Cooper 2022: 8; see also Rodning 2011: 152). Women additionally owned "the households, furnishings, and gardens" (Cooper 2022: 8).

From the bottom-up then, it is wholly appropriate for women to be interred in household contexts, because their prestige and power in the matrilineal societies of Southern Appalachia were derived from, and rooted in, the social contexts of households and kinship groups (Sullivan 2001: 124). Similarly, it is appropriate for men to have been buried in mounds (or near townhouses), as their political power was likely rooted in such affairs as foreign relations and town-centric decision-making. Unfortunately, given the continued archaeological preoccupation with earthen mounds and their significance among the Indigenous societies of the Southeast, the correlation of men with earthen mounds has resulted in an unbalanced and incomplete understanding of Mississippian sociopolitics (Sullivan 2001: 110). My work (Sullivan 2001, 2006) in eastern Tennessee, Rodning's work (1999, 2011) in western North Carolina, and jointly (Rodning and Sullivan 2020; Sullivan and Rodning 2011), has demonstrated that the perceived "inferiority" of women can be accounted for by gendered life cycles (see Harle et al., this volume), gendered divisions of labor, and gendered burial programs rather than differences of wealth and prestige between the biological sexes. I have summarized the pattern as follows (Sullivan 2001: 124):

> Mounds, with their public political connotations, symbolize the male [masculine] sphere of community leadership and foreign relations. In contrast, the houses represent the female [feminine] sphere of everyday life, family, and kin. These complementary spheres of men and women involve different social institutions: individual settlements or localities (towns), on one hand, and kinship groups that crosscut communities, on the other.

The remaining sections of this chapter explore how this gendered political balance was enacted within and across communities, what institutional forms these gendered differences produced, and how these political domains were intertwined through social networks that cut across political spheres, gendered contexts, formal kinship groups, and community membership.

Southern Appalachian Sociopolitics

The focus of this section is the central role of kinship (the political domain of Mississippian women) in structuring Mississippian sociopolitics. Previous and recent research demonstrates the central and enduring role of kinship politics as the foundation of Mississippian societies, both counterpoised and complementary to the masculine-dominated political practices often characterized by instability (Lulewicz 2019; Sullivan 2018; Sullivan and Rodning 2011). In contrast, kinship relations, both within villages and across the region, were the most stable features of Late Mississippian societies in Southern Appalachia, providing consistency and structure even in the midst of social, economic, and political uncertainty associated with the fluctuating politics of "the men on the mounds." The Late Mississippian societies (ca. fourteenth-sixteenth centuries) discussed in this chapter are part of a long history of kinship dynamics and sociopolitical transformation. A synopsis is useful here of how the form of Late Mississippian societies in Southern Appalachia came into being and the sociopolitical dynamics that are used to define the organizational structures that characterized this period.

The transition to the Late Mississippian period in East Tennessee (Dallas and Mouse Creek[1] phase societies) is characterized archaeologically by new styles of pottery, architecture, and symbolism, as well as significant changes in mortuary practices and new forms of community leadership from the preceding Hiwassee Island phase societies (Sullivan 2016, 2018: 111). Importantly, these new societal features were overlain upon a long-standing social base of kinship groupings, initially materialized in kin-based burial mounds (Cole 1975). These preceding mortuary patterns were almost exclusively defined by the use of communal burial mounds located away from dispersed villages, and that likely served multiple communities from across local regions (Schroedl et al. 1990). These Hamilton mounds, as they are known, were likely the product of use by discrete, egalitarian social groups such as lineages, clans, or sibs (Cole 1975). While the primary burial in each mound was typically an adult male, both women and children also were buried within the mounds, and little evidence exists for inequality based on wealth, prestige, gender, or age (Cole 1975; Schroedl et al. 1990).

Sometime just after the turn of the fourteenth century, villages across eastern Tennessee coalesced around earlier platform mounds, which became incorporated into new village layouts that, for the first time, were relatively formal in their arrangement and planning (Sullivan 2016, 2018). At this time, individuals began to be interred under and adjacent to houses, in platform mounds, or, in the absence of platform mounds, central plazas. Biologically sexed females began to be associated primarily with burials in domestic contexts, while males became associated with mound and plaza contexts. These new mortuary patterns were used to highlight kinship in the new, amalgamated settlements, as well as to reify gendered political domains. This shift in mortuary practices does not likely represent the beginning of gendered dynamics, but it certainly represents an explicit recognition and material categorization of gendered political domains.

Households, consisting of paired summer and winter structures, during this time are assumed to represent residences of matrilineal kinship groups and compare favorably with those of historically known groups such as the Cherokee in the southern Appalachians (Cooper 2022; Rodning 1999, 2007, 2011; Sullivan and Rodning 2001, 2011). The burials of female elders, the likely leaders of the matrilineal kin groups, are associated with household units (Sullivan 2001, 2018: 118). Village councils run by senior men would have facilitated a cohesive political structure and, at the same time, male leaders would have been representative of their mothers' and sisters' lineages, and potentially chosen for community leadership roles by the matriarchs of their kin groups (Sullivan 2018: 118). Senior women would have assumed leadership of matrilineal kin groups and, through these positions, managed and owned agricultural lands and the means of agricultural production, a pattern noted across various Indigenous groups of the Southeast (Ethridge 2003; Fritz 2019; Sullivan 2018). Additionally, by being the keepers of the traditional practices associated with their kin groups, women would balance the integrative councils of the men (Sullivan 2018: 118). As I have noted, "Gender duality, with men acting in community leadership roles in councils and women serving as kin-group leaders, was a strategy for social integration in a region with a long history of dispersal" (Sullivan 2018: 118).

Beyond village dynamics, women's networks also served to forge a durable political base across Southern Appalachia (Lulewicz 2019). Networks among women, forged through the distribution of kin and clan membership that crosscut related southern Appalachian communities via population movement, marriage, and communal gatherings produced the social capital upon which Mississippian politics were built. The "ability to wield political power, influence, and authority is entwined with an individual's social rank and prestige" (Sullivan 2001: 103). A look toward the sources of these characteristics can refine this argument to propose that the ability to wield power, influence, and authority (and to gain social rank and prestige) is through the accumulation and production of social capital by way of social networks.

Social capital describes relations of trust and reciprocity and, simply put, can be defined as a set of relations that enable actors to gain, maintain, or expand access to resources and directly references the resources embedded in one's social network that can be accessed or mobilized through network ties (whether material or immaterial) (Adger 2003; Crowe 2007; Granovetter 1985; Lin 1999; Ostrom and Ahn 2008; Putnam 2000; van Staveren and Knorringa 2007; Woolock and Narayan 2000). Lulewicz (2019) argues that the networks through which social capital was generated across Southern Appalachia were stable, enduring, and widespread, linking related communities in dense webs of interactions and obligation across the region. The result is that the relationships forged and maintained between communities and individuals provided specific access to bonding capital that emerges from strong social ties that are based on social identities such as family, kinship, gender, ethnicity, or organizational culture (van Staveren and Knorringa 2007).

In the case of eastern Tennessee, tight-knit networks that characterize the relationships between related communities likely were the result of dense kinship networks generated through the ties between Mississippian women (Lulewicz 2019). It was through these networks that community leaders and individuals could access critical pools of social capital. Such capital would have been leveraged to generate high levels of trust, cooperation, and organization, facilitating collective action and learning. Modes of production are often based on bonding ties (Repetti 2002). As such, the very social resources leveraged by men in the public domain would have been produced and supplied through the social capital generated, maintained, and made available through the relationships among women. Also significant, the structure of networks in East Tennessee is more densely connected and lacks the hierarchy that can be seen for contemporaneous Late Mississippian sites in northern Georgia (see Lulewicz 2018: Figure 6.1). These types of connections among communities compare favorably with the inter-community relationships discussed by Rodning (2011) for the eighteenth-century Cherokee.

Reconstructing Social Networks

To reconstruct the social networks of female individuals from across eastern Tennessee during the Late Mississippian period, pottery data derived from mortuary contexts is the only available data set that can be directly associated with women, has sufficient sample size, measurable attributes, and is derived from many sites across the region. Based on ethnohistoric accounts and ethnographic correlates, it is presumed here that women were producers of pottery in Mississippian societies (Briggs and Harle, this volume). Such traditions would have been passed down within contexts of teaching and learning, likely within communities of practice that corresponded to extended matrilineal kin groups, as mothers and grandmothers taught their daughters, granddaughters, or nieces and grandnieces (Briggs, this volume; Worth 2017). Because technological information and the production of pottery must be taught, it is reasonable to presume intimate relations of teaching and learning, as these would have been necessary for information to be passed between generations of women (e.g., Birch and Hart 2018; Bliege Bird and Smith 2005; Crown 2014; Gosselain 2000; Peeples 2018). An evaluation and comparison of the characteristics of pottery vessels from across the region, with attention to their geographic contexts, makes it possible to characterize particular features of women's networks. Although the complexity of this line of logic moves from pottery in burial contexts to practices and behaviors related to interaction, identity, and gender, the resulting stylistic and spatial analyses provide a broad scale perspective on the social networks that defined the Late Mississippian social landscape of the Upper Tennessee Valley. Rather than exploring gendered differences, this study uses attributes of whole pottery vessels to trace the interactions and networks of presumably female pottery makers across the region, through an inductive exploration of the similarities and differences in the forms and styles of the pots. The main focus of the analysis is to discover the connections of Mississippian women across communities and the landscape so as to discern the presumed interactions of related kin groups among geographically discrete communities.

The data for this study are derived from 196 whole vessels found in 87 burials and one domestic structure, which are contexts from sixteen Late Mississippian sites (Figure 6.1) that represent the Dallas and Mouse Creek phases, dating to between the fourteenth and mid-sixteenth centuries. Most of the collections from the sites included in this study are the result of University of Tennessee excavations before the construction of Tennessee Valley Authority reservoirs between the 1930s and 1970s. Data were collected by Tim Baumann from pots curated at the McClung Museum of Natural History and Culture as part of a National Science Foundation grant awarded to this author in 1998 for the study of Mississippian ceramic chronologies in the region. Qualitative and quantitative data were collected for vessel form, appendages, and stylistic attributes on whole pots from Late Mississippian mortuary contexts in which at least two pots were present. For the purposes of the network analysis, only data for the traditional Mississippian globular jar forms were included to make data comparable across vessels. The frequencies in age and sex representations in the dataset reflect the tendency for pots more often to be associated with females than males, the higher mortality rates of females because of childbirth, and a high mortality rate for infants: 24 percent adult females; 13 percent adult males; 5 percent adults unidentified as to sex; 18 percent children; and 40 percent infants. Individuals for which neither sex nor age data were available were omitted from these frequency calculations.

Because different ceramic attributes (e.g., decoration vs. temper) can be related to the different human relationships and networks within which potters do their craft, vessels were first categorized into three distinct domains. Principal coordinates analysis was used to statistically assign the vessels to clusters based on similar attributes in each domain. The first domain of variation for which vessels were analyzed was associated with vessel form (e.g., rim, neck, body measurements and proportions). The second domain was appendage attributes (e.g., lugs, handles, measurements of appendages), and the third domain was assignment to clusters based on variation in decorative styles. The result is that each of the 196 vessels was assigned to three different clusters: a vessel form cluster, where it would be grouped with vessels of similar form; an appendage cluster, grouped with vessels exhibiting similar appendages; and a style cluster, in which the vessel was grouped with stylistically similar vessels. To further approximate the signatures of individual potters, vessels were assigned to a fourth group: a combination of all three groupings based on form, appendage, and style characteristics. Thus, if two vessels were assigned to all three of the same clusters for form, appendage, and style, they were also assigned to the same composite cluster.

The resulting cluster assignments served as the basis upon which social networks were reconstructed between individual burials. In the network analyses performed here, each individual node in the network represents an individual burial. Clusters associated with each burial were the basis of network ties assigned between burials. That is, when two individuals were associated with a vessel assigned to the same formal, appendage, stylistic, or composite cluster, they received a tie. If two burials did not share this similarity in their associated vessel assemblages, a tie was not assigned. Four networks were analyzed, one for each of the four domains of ceramic variation outlined above. The resulting arrangements of ties and nodes were then assessed using formal network analyses and are the basis of interpretations of the interconnections of potters, and the inferred relationships to Mississippian kinship, gender, and personhood.

The Gendered Dimensions of Mississippian Social Networks

The cluster analyses identified 7 distinct form clusters, 5 distinct clusters of appendage characteristics, 5 distinct stylistic clusters, and 92 composite clusters. The networks constructed for each of these domains depict slightly varying relational dynamics. Networks are described in terms of their shape, the position of nodes of individuals of different ages and biological sexes,[2] and formally by the betweenness centrality for specific nodes. Betweenness centrality is based on the number of times a node falls along the shortest path between all other pairs of nodes in the network. A node's betweenness centrality reflects the potential for a node to connect nodes, or groups of nodes, that are otherwise not directly connected. In this way, nodes with high betweenness values are often considered brokers or gatekeepers within their network. Average centrality measures for nodes belonging to specific age/sex categories are presented in Table 6.1.

For the network based on vessel form similarities (Figure 6.2), two single individuals stand out as important structural features that connect many parts of the network. The pots with these individuals represent popular vessel form attributes from diverse potting communities across eastern Tennessee. Both are from the Citico (40MR7) site in the Tellico Reservoir; one is an adult female, while the other is an infant. Significantly, no other spatial correlates could be used to explain the structure of this network. Connections among pots are not centered upon specific sites, groups of sites, or even subregions or river drainages.

The network based on attributes related to style and decoration (Figure 6.3) paints a different picture. In this network, infants and children from a range of sites serve as the most central nodes, followed by an unidentified adult from the Citico site (40MR7) and several adult females. Infants and children from Toqua (40MR6) also seem to have especially high centrality values. Like the network based on vessel form attributes, no clear geographic spatial patterns emerge in the networks.

The same can be said for the third network based on appendage attributes (Figure 6.4). Women and children still have the highest centrality scores on average, but two adults with unidentified sexes have by far the highest centrality scores and, in fact, are almost identical to one another in terms of the appendage attributes of their associated jars. One is from the Loy site (40JE10) on the lower Holston River, and one from Citico (40MR7). A third signifi-

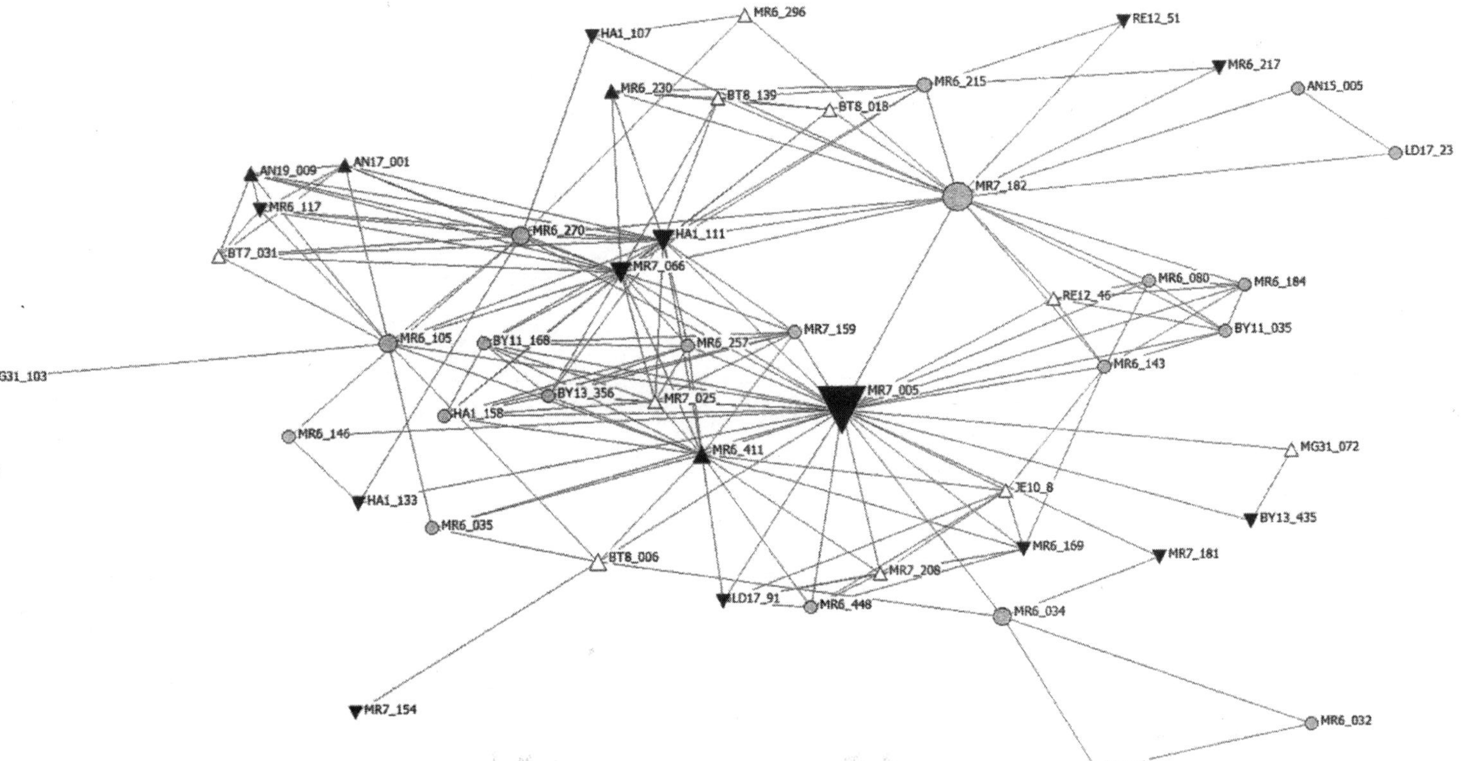

Figure 6.2. Network showing relationships between individual burials based on vessel form attributes. Each individual node represents an individual. A tie represents shared vessel form characteristics. Nodes are scaled to betweenness centrality. The larger the node, the more central it is to the network, connecting parts of the network that would not otherwise be connected. Legend: Females (inverted black triangles); Males (black triangles); Infants/Children (gray circles); UID Sex Adults (white triangles).

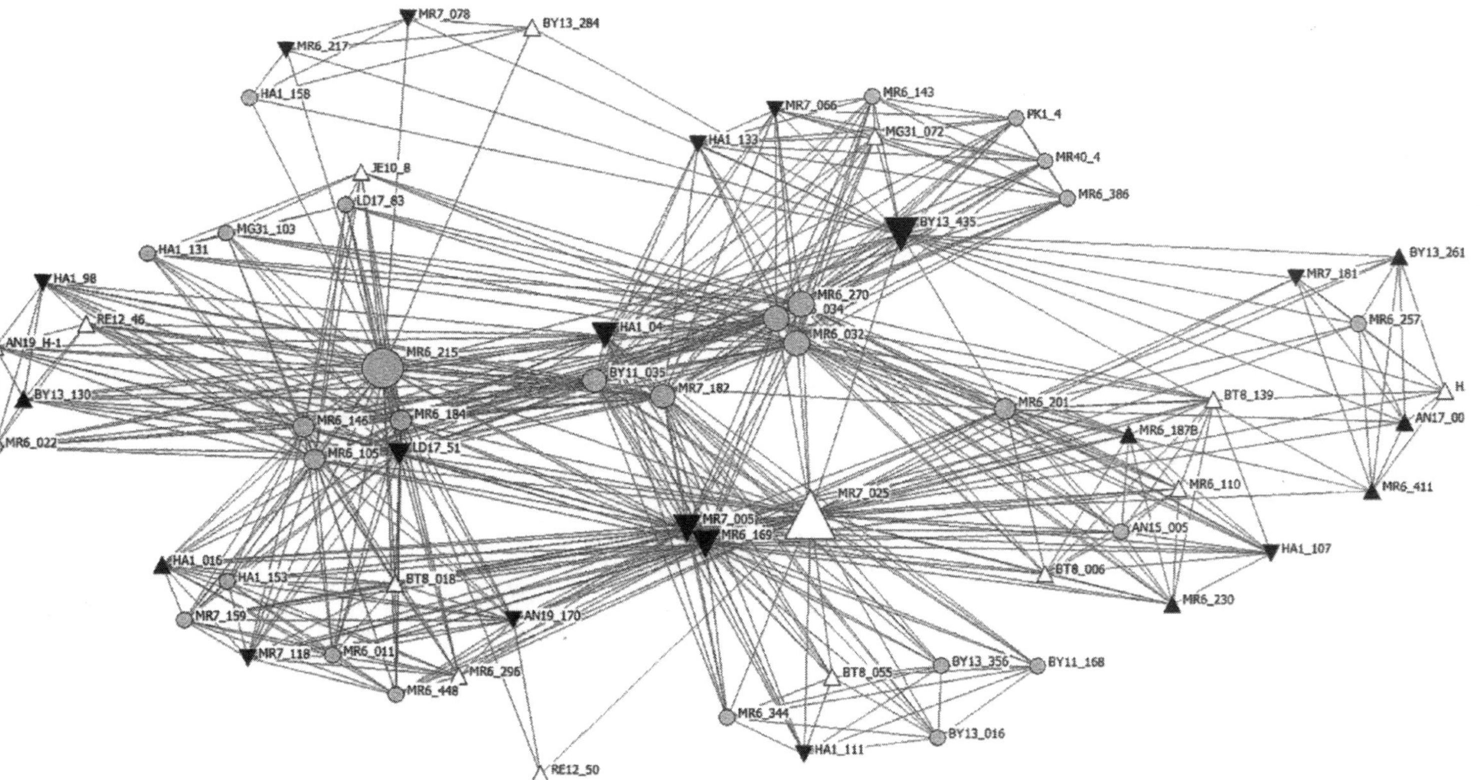

Figure 6.3. Network showing relationships between individual burials based on stylistic/decorative attributes. Each individual node represents an individual. A tie represents shared stylistic/decorative characteristics. Nodes are scaled to betweenness centrality. The larger the node, the more central it is to the network, connecting parts of the network that would not otherwise be connected. Legend: Females (inverted black triangles); Males (black triangles); Infants/Children (gray circles); UID Sex Adults (white triangles).

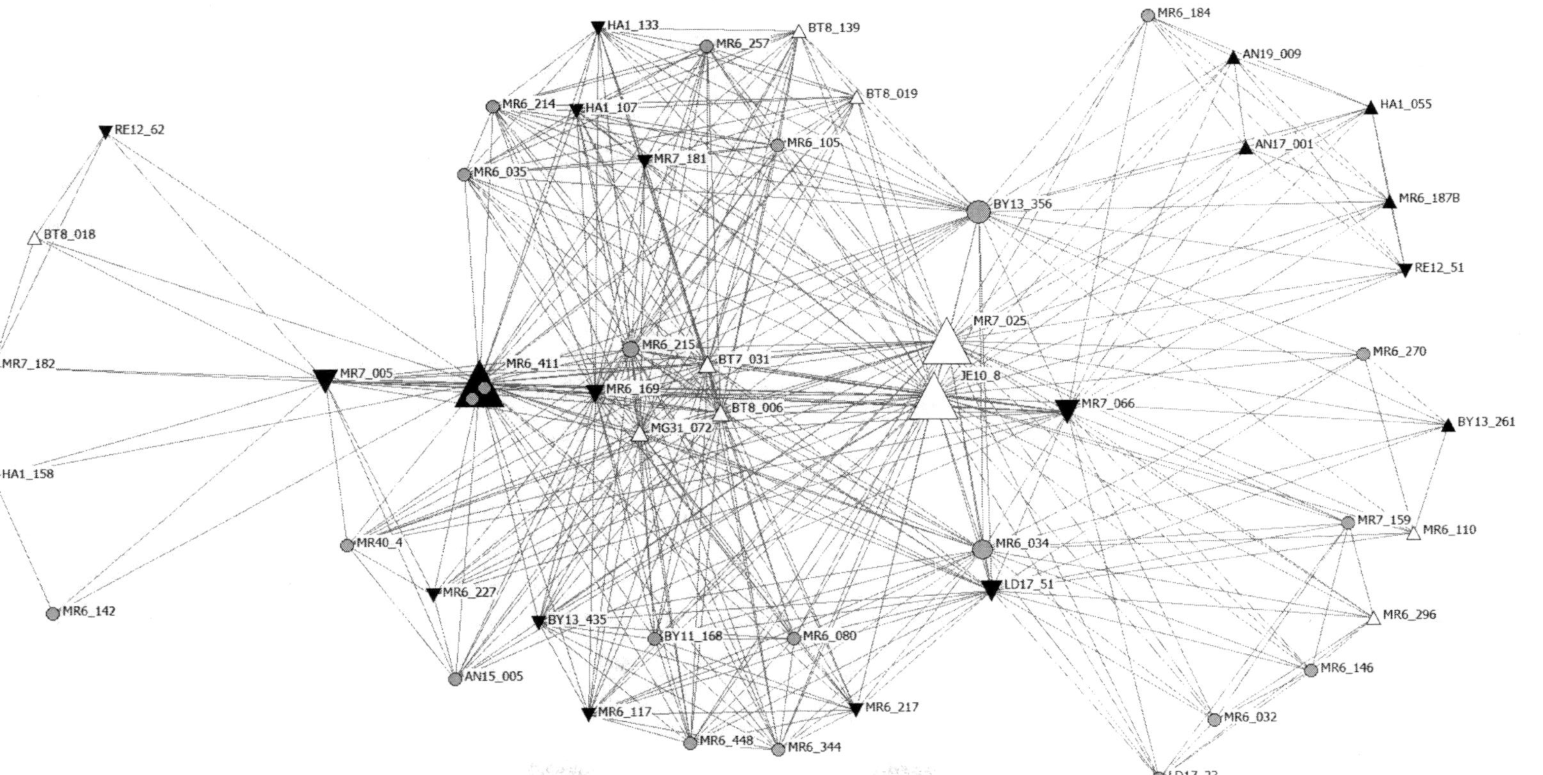

Figure 6.4. Network showing relationships between individual burials based on appendage attributes. Each individual node represents an individual. A tie represents shared appendage characteristics. Nodes are scaled to betweenness centrality. The larger the node, the more central it is to the network, connecting parts of the network that would not otherwise be connected. Legend: Females (inverted black triangles); Males (black triangles); Infants/Children (gray circles); UID Sex Adults (white triangles).

cantly connected burial, in which three individuals, an adult male and two infants, were interred together with five jars, is from the Toqua site (40MR6). Again, there is no clear patterning in the geographic connections of the sites.

The patterns identified in the networks associated with these three domains of ceramic variation can be summarized as follows. For vessel form attributes (Figure 6.2), women had, on average, the highest centrality scores, potentially indicating the diversity of relationships within which women would have been interconnected across this landscape. Women were closely followed by infants and children, with adult males having the lowest scores, indicating a more restricted network of local relationships. For networks based on stylistic attributes (Figure 6.3), women, children, and infants were almost identical in their average centrality scores, with men once again trailing behind. But for networks based on appendage attributes (Figure 6.4), the main difference seems to be between children and adults, with adults having higher average centrality scores, indicating an increased diversity in appendage attributes among jars with adults.

While the entangled patterns of connectedness of the recipients of the pots across the region do not seem to provide much information on localized communities of practice among potters, the connectedness undoubtedly is related to the complexities of kinship and women's political leadership in Late Mississippian society in the East Tennessee region. In the context of mortuary rites, it is likely that the distribution of the pots follows the larger kinship networks, most probably the matrilineal clans. In the Southeast, members of the same clan were family. For example, a Cherokee tribal town had each of the seven Cherokee clans represented. A clan member thus had relatives in almost all Cherokee towns. In a mortuary context, dispersal of pots from local potters to their kin-group/clan members in other towns likely would take place when someone in the clan passed. The dispersal of pots for funerary rites within regional kin groups would create highly interconnected, but varied patterns of pottery distribution because times and places of death have no consistent patterns.

On the other hand, when the ages are included of women who occupy the most central roles in each of the presented networks, that is, those women in the two highest tiers of betweenness centrality, a pattern does become apparent. These two tiers include eight women from just five sites. All eight women have been identified as being middle-aged (30 to 50 years of age) or old (over 50) [middle-aged (n=1), old (n=3), and middle-aged/old (n=4)]. The five sites are Bussell Island (40LD17), Citico (40MR7), and Toqua (40MR6) in the Little Tennessee Valley, and Dallas (40HA1) and Ledford Island (40BY13) in the Chickamauga Basin. These results may indicate two potential characteristics of women's political participation. The first is that older women have accumulated more social capital throughout their lives, compared to their younger kin, and can leverage these toward the maintenance of extensive social networks. The second characteristic is that it may be the case that not all women, however old, have the ability to access and generate such social and political resources. The eight most central women across the networks come from only five sites, indicating that there may be some social and political advantages to being part of particular communities. Among the Cherokee, there were larger important towns that had council houses and that sometimes offered support for smaller surrounding communities. All of the five sites with the "well-connected" older women had council houses. It is possible, for example, that during these women's lives, these larger towns were the sites of ceremonies and other gatherings of people from outlying towns. Through such events, these women may have become known to a large network of kin and others because of widely respected characteristics such as skills, or other personal qualities.

The frequency and density of interactions taking place across eastern Tennessee, especially in the context of matrilineal clan memberships that crosscut many communities, likely was a significant factor in the distributions of pottery used for death rites. Such wares from local potting communities would be dispersed throughout the region, according to personal relationships, as well as in conjunction with the personal renown of the deceased individuals. Although, in the case of the deaths of children, different factors perhaps influenced both the kind of pottery that was used and its distribution. These factors are discussed in the following sections.

To create a finer resolution of individual relationships and connections, each of the three attribute sets was combined to create composite clusters. The pots had to be assigned to the same cluster for all three attribute domains for a tie to be made between burials. This procedure raised the threshold for similarity, and identified vessel clusters that approach a rough proxy for individual potters, or at least, individual production events or restricted potting communities of only a few potters. Like the others, this network also depicts diverse relationships connecting many individuals with no clear sub-networks or discrete groupings, and no clear geographic groups can be identified in the network structure (Figure 6.5). The five sites in the composite analysis with the highest numbers of raw connections (ten or more) are: Citico (40MR7) and Toqua (40MR6) on the Little Tennessee River; Dallas (40HA1) and Ledford Island (40BY13) on the Tennessee and Hiwassee Rivers, respectively, in the Chickamauga Basin; and Johnson Farm (40AN15) on the Clinch River in the Norris Basin.

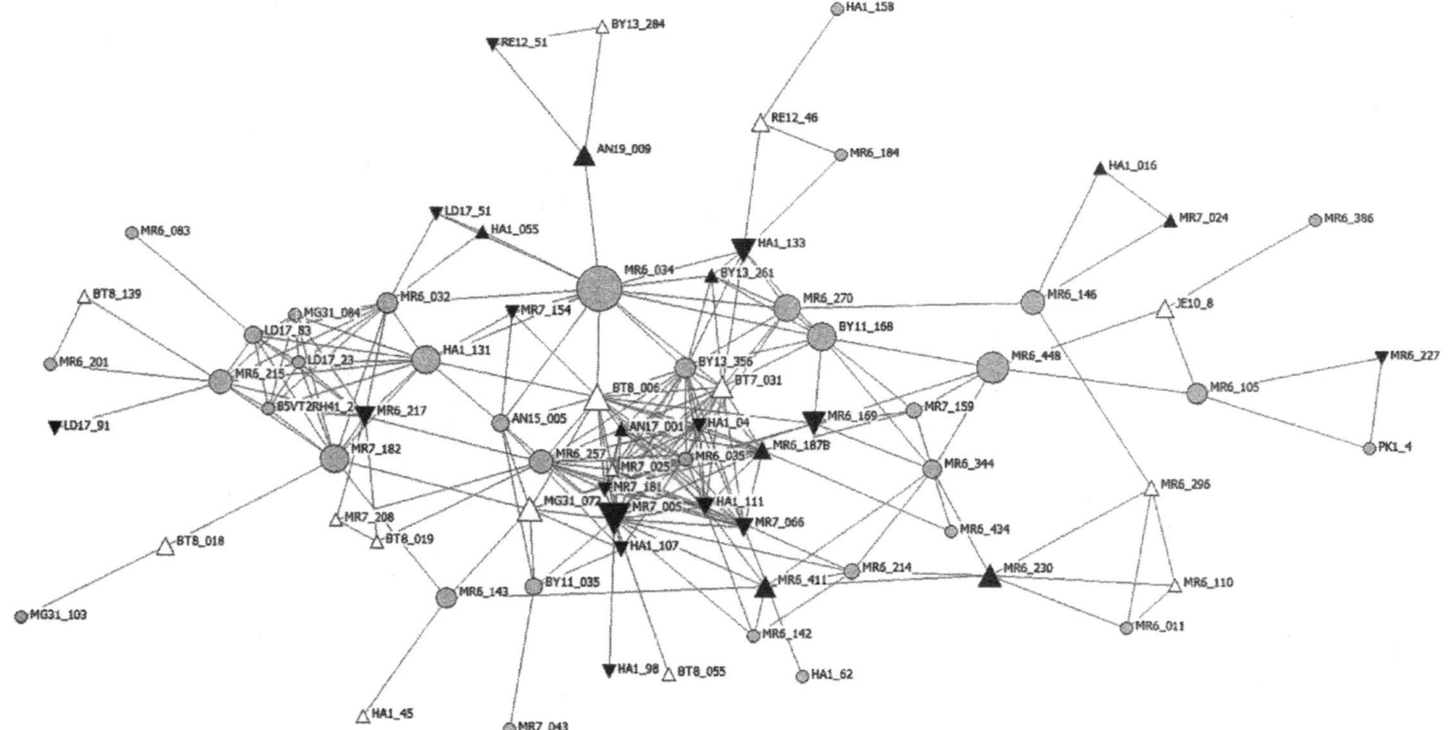

Figure 6.5. Network showing relationships between individual burials based on their composite cluster. Each individual node represents an individual. A tie represents the presence of a vessel in each burial belonging to the same composite cluster. Nodes are scaled to betweenness centrality. The larger the node, the more central it is to the network, connecting parts of the network that would not otherwise be connected. Legend: Females (inverted black triangles); Males (black triangles); Infants/Children (gray circles); UID Sex Adults (white triangles).

Table 6.1. Average betweenness centrality scores by sex/age for each network

	Form	Style	Appendage	Composite	n
Infant	22	18	11	89	30
Child	20	18	13	90	13
Male	16	9	17	55	10
Female	33	16	17	49	20
Infant/ Child	21	18	12	89	43
Adult	28	15	21	50	34

But, unlike the other networks, some surprising patterns do emerge. There seems to be a central core of individuals with similar vessel assemblages, and a second group of individuals associated with vessels that are less common. The most central nodes in this network, the nodes that link the dense inner core to the outlying individuals, are almost exclusively infants and children. The average centrality score for infants and children (i.e., newborns through eleven-year-olds) is twice as high as the average centrality scores for adults, both males and females (Table 6.1). If one looks at the infants and children with the highest centrality scores, five out of twelve can be classified as newborns up to six months old, while nine are classified between six months and three/four years old. Only three children with high centrality scores are classified as over five years of age. Infants are disproportionately connected to other infants, with over 46 percent of ties being to other infants, while over 60 percent of infant ties are to either another infant or a child. Likewise, over 60 percent of ties from women are connected to an infant or child, probably indicating social and cultural links between women and children that are defined by relations of kinship and concepts of motherhood and childhood—relationships that are reflected in the socio-material assemblages of mortuary rites.

An especially noteworthy pattern of the distribution of pottery with infants and children is the style and iconography of the associated vessels. These jars are decorated with composites of cross-and-circle and sun-circle motifs on the upper portions of the vessels, and frog effigy elements on the shoulders and lower vessel portions. I have conducted an ongoing exploration of the iconography of these jars (Sullivan n.d.), including informal conversations with Indigenous informants, that suggests the vessels may represent portals between the worlds, bridging the watery underworld, this world, and the upperworld, suggesting they are "cosmos pots." Age and sex demographics of the 23 individuals included in this study, and interred with these jars that seem to represent the cosmos, are: 11 infants, three children, three adult females, three adult males, and three adults unidentified as to sex.

Infants have the highest average centrality scores across all nodes (regardless of age and gender). Fifteen of the 23 individual burials with the highest centrality scores are also associated with the cosmos jars, and of the 14 individuals with the greatest raw number of ties, 13 are buried with cosmos jars. A similar pattern can be noted for the seven sites with average betweenness centrality scores above 100: Citico (40MR7), Toqua (40MR6), and Chilhowee (40BT7) on the Little Tennessee River, and Dallas (40HA1), Ledford Island (40BY13), Rymer (40BY11), and Hiwassee Island (40MG31) in the Chickamauga Basin. These sites also include 15 of the 23 burials in this study that were buried with cosmos pots. From these data, it is clear that the cosmos pots not only seem to have particular significance for infants, but the individuals associated with these pots also held central positions in their networks.

While the loss of infants and children is devastating to immediate families in most circumstances in human cultures, Cooper (2022: 84) notes that in Indigenous societies of the southern Appalachians, such a loss would also be significant to the larger kin group: "The goal most ingrained in Cherokee minds was to assure their own clan persisted . . . ." Recent work on post-contact Cherokee communities in eastern Tennessee that focuses on the mortuary distribution of European glass trade beads has found a similar pattern: infants and children occupy important positions within regional relations of mourning (Babin 2018). The central positions of infants and children in the networks likely are created by links beyond immediate kin relations to the larger clan networks, as young members are significant to the survival of the clan itself. This idea may be supported and related to the different burial practices for infants in Mouse Creek phase towns. Infant burials are more likely to be associated with winter houses, while adult burials are more often associated with summer houses (Sullivan 1987). In another example of differential mortuary treatments of the young, Rosemary Joyce (1999, 2001, 2002a, 2002b) has found that, at the Early Formative site of Tlatilco in Mexico, mortuary patterns were distinguished by age. The largest number of objects and most unusual things were placed in the burials of young adults (Joyce 2008: 50). She states, that "for survivors, young adults were social bridges, linking families together. If they had lived, young adults—through the children they would have raised—would have united different families and created enduring kinship relations between them" (Joyce 2008: 50).

Women, Children, Matrilineal Kinship, and Mississippian Society

A main goal in this chapter was to explore the structure and dynamics of women-dominated Mississippian kinship networks in Southern Appalachia, specifically across the Upper Tennessee Valley. The data and analyses may also be used to address broader issues of gender and personhood in Mississippian societies, but these themes can be addressed only briefly here as a starting point for future research. The network analyses provided more complex and nuanced perspectives on communities of practice focused on pottery making than was anticipated. The densely woven matrilineal kinship networks through which pottery was transported in the context of funerary rites were highlighted by the analyses. Evidence of variability, especially for women, possibly gained with age, experience, and respect for skills or personal qualities was also suggested by the centrality and connectedness of certain older women. The reflection in the pottery attribute networks of parallel recognition of the kin groups' youngest members was unexpected, but not surprising when viewed in ethnographic context.

The ceramic attributes studied here relate not only to local technological and stylistic variation, but to relationships of kinship and clan that crosscut community membership at a *regional* scale in a landscape of frequent interaction, movements of people, and inevitable end-of-life rites of passage. These networks were based on crafts made by women and highlight the interactions of women through relationships in the matrilineal clans that women headed. From a broader perspective, the social and political relationships among communities intertwined by kinship relations of matrilineal clans formed the fabric of Late Mississippian communities in the Upper Tennessee Valley. The local resources, relationships, and social capital necessary for these Mississippian communities to function would have been available to local leaders only through the networks generated and maintained through the relationships—social, political, and economic—between and among Mississippian women.

Finally, a significant aspect of the regional networks revealed by this study is the likelihood that the presence of highly connected kinship, and presumably clan-based, networks throughout the study region also implies that the communities themselves represent webs of related people. This implication is congruent with studies by Harle (2010) and McCarthy (2011) that found evidence of biological relationships among the people who had been residents of many of the communities investigated in this study. Harle's (2010) work also showed the lack of evidence for biological relationships of the Upper Tennessee Valley residents with contemporaneous people of the Barnett phase who lived farther south and had different pottery traditions. Although people originating from different societies or polities perhaps were resident in, and members of these communities, the cross-cutting kinship structure suggested by the networks likely required a context of one dominant societal and cultural setting. That is, during this period, these archaeological sites likely were the settlements of predominantly one ethnic group that resided in non-hierarchically ranked communities. This implication is congruent with processes of cultural coalescence reflected in the dramatic changes that define the beginnings of the Dallas and Mouse Creek phases after AD 1300 when in-migration from the west likely influenced social and political relationships and led to the use of council houses (Sullivan 2018; Sullivan et al. 2022).

Acknowledgments

Jacob Holland-Lulewicz provided technical assistance with the statistical analyses.

Notes

1 The Mouse Creek phase is the latter ca. two centuries of the Dallas phase in the Chickamauga and adjacent portion of the Watts Bar Basins. Elsewhere in the Upper Tennessee Valley, this time period continues to be termed the Dallas phase. The use of platform mounds was discontinued in the Mouse Creek phase (Sullivan 1987, 2016, 2018).

2 Age and sex determinations for the individuals included in this study are based on an inventory conducted by Maria O. Smith as part of a National Science Foundation grant.

References Cited

Adger, W. Neil

2003 Social Capital, Collective Action, and Adaptation to Climate Change. *Economic Geography* 79: 387–404.

Babin, Mark

2018 Glass Beads of Chota-Tanasee: An Historical and Archaeological Analysis of Overhill Cherokee Networks. Unpublished master's thesis, Department of Anthropology, University of Tennessee, Knoxville.

Birch, Jennifer, and John Hart

2018 Social Networks and Northern Iroquoian Confederacy Dynamics. *American Antiquity* 83: 13–33.

Bliege Bird, Rebecca, and Eric Smith

2005 Signaling Theory, Strategic Interaction, and Symbolic Capital. *Current Anthropology* 46: 221–248.

Cole, Patricia E.
1975 A Synthesis and Interpretation of the Hamilton Mortuary Pattern in East Tennessee. Unpublished master's thesis, Department of Anthropology, University of Tennessee, Knoxville.

Cooper, Karen Coody
2022 *Cherokee Women in Charge: Female Power and Leadership in American Indian Nations of Eastern North America.* McFarland & Company, Incorporated Publishers, Jefferson, North Carolina.

Crowe, Jessica A.
2007 In Search of a Happy Medium: How the Structure of Interorganizational Networks Influence Community Economic Development Strategies. *Social Networks* 29(4): 469– 488.

Crown, Patricia L.
2014 The Archaeology of Crafts Learning: Becoming a Potter in the Puebloan Southwest. *Annual Review of Anthropology* 43: 71–88.

Crumley, Carole L.
1995 Heterarchy and the Analysis of Complex Societies. In *Heterarchy and the Analysis of Complex Societies*, edited by Robert M. Ehrenreich, Carole L. Crumley, and Janet E. Levy, pp. 1–5. Archeological Papers 3. American Anthropological Association, Washington, D.C.

Ethridge, Robbie
2003 *Creek Country: The Creek Indians and Their World.* University of North Carolina Press, Chapel Hill.

Friedl, Ernestine
1967 The Position of Women: Appearance and Reality. *Anthropological Quarterly* 40: 97–198.

Fritz, Gayle
2019 *Feeding Cahokia: Early Agriculture in the North American Heartland.* University of Alabama Press, Tuscaloosa.

Gosselain, Oliver P.
2000 Materializing Identities: An African Perspective. *Journal of Archaeological Method and Theory* 7(3): 187–217.

Granovetter, M.
1985 Economic Action and Social Structure: The Problem of Embeddedness. *American Journal of Sociology* 91(3): 481–510.

Harle, Michaelyn S.
2010 Biological Affinities and the Construction of Cultural Identity within the Proposed Coosa Chiefdom. Unpublished PhD dissertation, Department of Anthropology, University of Tennessee, Knoxville.

Hendon, Julia
1996 Archaeological Approaches to the Organization of Domestic Labor: Household Practice and Domestic Relations. *Annual Review of Anthropology* 25: 45–61.

Joyce, Rosemary
1999 Social Dimension of Pre-Classic burials. In *Social Patterns in Pre-Classic Mesoamerica*, edited by David C. Grove and Rosemary A. Joyce, pp. 15–47. Dumbarton Oaks, Washington, D.C.

2001 Burying the Dead at Tlatilco: Social Memory and Social Identities. In *New Perspectives on Mortuary Analysis*, edited by Meredith Chesson, pp. 12–26. American Anthropological Association, Alexandria, VA.

2002a Beauty, Sexuality, Body Ornamentation, and Gender in Ancient Mesoamerica. In *In Pursuit of Gender*, edited by Sarah Nelson and Myriam Rosen-Ayalon, pp. 81–92. AltaMira Press, Walnut Creek, CA.

2002b *The Languages of Archaeology.* Blackwell Press, Oxford, UK.

2008 *Ancient Bodies, Ancient Lives: Sex, Gender, and Archaeology.* Thames and Hudson, London, UK.

Levy, Janet E.

1999 Gender, Power, and Heterarchy in Middle-Level Societies. In *Manifesting Power: Gender and the Interpretation of Power in Archaeology*, edited by Tracy L. Sweely, pp. 62–78. Routledge, London.

Lin, Nan

1999 Building a Network Theory of Social Capital. *Connections* 22: 28–51.

Lulewicz, Jacob

2018 Network Histories of Southern Appalachia AD 600–1600. Unpublished PhD dissertation, Department of Anthropology, University of Georgia, Athens.

2019 The Social Networks and Structural Variation of Mississippian Sociopolitics in the Southeastern United States. *Proceedings of the National Academy of Sciences* 116(14):6707–6712.

MacCormack, Carol P.

1980 Nature, Culture and Gender: A Critique. In *Nature, Culture and Gender*, edited by Marilyn Strathern and Carol P. MacCormack, pp. 1–24. Cambridge University Press, UK.

Mathews, Holly F.

1985 We are Mayordomo: A Reinterpretation of Women's Roles in the Mexican Cargo System. *American Ethnologist* 14: 210–25.

McCarthy, Donna M.

2011 Using Osteological Evidence to Assess Biological Affinity: A Re-Evaluation of Selected Sites in East Tennessee. Unpublished PhD dissertation, Department of Anthropology, University of Tennessee, Knoxville.

Miller, Barbara Diane

1993 The Anthropology of Sex and Gender Hierarchies. In *Sex and Gender Hierarchies*, edited by Barbara Diane Miller, pp. 3–31. Cambridge University Press, UK.

Mukhopadhyay, Carol C., and Patricia J. Higgins

1988 Anthropological Studies of Women's Status Revisited: 1977–1987. *Annual Review of Anthropology* 17: 461–95.

Ostrom, Elinor, and Toh-Kyeong Ahn

2008 The Meaning of Social Capital and its Link to Collective Action. In *Handbook on Social Capital*, edited by Gert Tinggaard Svendsen and Gunnar Lind Haase Svendsen, pp. 17–35. Edward Elgar, Cheltenham, PA.

Peeples, Matthew A.

2018 *Connected Communities: Networks, Identity, and Social Change in the Ancient Cibola World.* University of Arizona Press, Tucson.

Perdue, Theda
1999 *Cherokee Women: Gender and Culture Change, 1700–1835*. Bison Books, University of Nebraska Press, Lincoln.

Putnam, Robert D.
2000 Bowling Alone: America's Declining Social Capital. In *Culture and Politics*, edited by Lane Crothers and Charles Lockhart, pp. 223–234. Palgrave Macmillan, New York.

Repetti, Massimo
2002 Social Relations in Lieu of Capital. *Research in Economic Anthropology* 21: 43–59.

Rodning, Christopher B.
1999 The Archaeology of Gender and Women in Traditional Cherokee Society. *Journal of Cherokee Studies* 20: 3–27.
2007 Building and Rebuilding Cherokee Houses and Townhouses in Southwestern North Carolina. In *The Durable House: Architecture, Ancestors, and Origins*, edited by Robin A. Beck, pp. 464–484. Center for Archaeological Investigations, Carbondale, IL.
2011 Mortuary Practices, Gender Ideology, and the Cherokee Town at the Coweeta Creek Site. *Journal of Anthropological Archaeology* 30: 145–173.

Rodning, Christopher B., and Lynne P. Sullivan
2020 An Archaeology of Native American Placemaking in the Southern Appalachians. In *The Historical Turn in Southeastern Archaeology*, edited by Robbie Ethridge and Eric Bowne, pp. 101–121. University Press of Florida, Gainesville.

Rosaldo, Michelle Zimbalist
1980 The Use and Misuse of Anthropology: Reflections on Feminism and Cross-Cultural Understanding. *Signs* 5: 389–441.

Rothstein, Frances A.
1982 *Three Different Worlds: Women, Men, and Children in an Industrial Community.* Greenwood Press, Westport, CT.

Sattler, Richard A.
1995 Women's Status among the Muskogee and Cherokee. In *Women and Power in Native North America*, edited by Laura F. Klein and Lillian A. Ackerman, pp. 214–29. University of Oklahoma Press, Norman.

Schroedl, Gerald F., C. Clifford Boyd, Jr., and R.P. Stephen Davis, Jr.
1990 Explaining Mississippian Origins in East Tennessee. In *The Mississippian Emergence*, edited by Bruce D. Smith, pp. 175–96. Smithsonian Institution Press, Washington, D.C.

Sudarkasa, Niara
1981 Female Employment and Family Organization in West Africa. In *The Black Woman Cross-Culturally*, edited by Filomina Chioma Steady, pp. 49–63. Schenkman, Cambridge, MA.

Sullivan, Lynne P.
n.d. The Cosmos on Ceramics. Unpublished manuscript online. https://www.academia.edu/2653640/The_Cosmos_on_Ceramics.
1987 The Mouse Creek Phase Household. *Southeastern Archaeology* 6(1): 16–29.

2001 Those Men in Mounds: Gender, Politics, and Mortuary Practices in Late Prehistoric Tennessee. In *Archaeological Studies of Gender in the Southeastern United States*, edited by Jane Eastman and Christopher Rodning, pp. 101–126. University Press of Florida, Gainesville.

2006 Gendered Contexts of Mississippian Leadership in Southern Appalachia. In *Leadership and Polity in Mississippian Society*, edited by Paul Welch and Brian Butler, pp. 264–285. Southern Illinois University Press, Carbondale.

2016 Reconfiguring the Chickamauga Basin. In *New Deal Archaeology in the Tennessee Valley*, edited by David Dye, pp. 138–170. University of Alabama Press, Tuscaloosa.

2018 The Path to the Council House: The Development of Mississippian Communities in Southeast Tennessee. In *The Archaeology of Villages in Eastern North America*, edited by Jennifer Birch and Victor Thompson, pp. 106–123. University of Florida Press, Gainesville.

Sullivan, Lynne P., and Christopher B. Rodning

2001 Gender, Tradition, and Social Negotiation in Southern Appalachian Chiefdoms. In *The Archaeological of Historical Processes, Agency and Tradition Before and After Columbus*, edited by Timothy Pauketat, pp. 107–120. University Press of Florida, Gainesville.

2011 Residential Burial, Gender Roles, and Political Development in Late Prehistoric and Early Cherokee Culture of the Southern Appalachians. In *Residential Burial: A Multi- Regional Exploration*, edited by Ron Adams and Stacie King, pp. 89–97. American Anthropological Association, Washington, D.C.

Sullivan, Lynne P., Kevin E. Smith, Shawn Patch, Sarah Lowry, John Jacob Holland-Lulewicz, and Scott Meeks

2022 Heading for the Hills: New Evidence for Migrations to the Upper Tennessee Valley. In *Following the Mississippian Spread: Climate Change and Migration in the Eastern U.S. (ca. AD 1000–1600)*, edited by Robert A. Cook and Aaron R. Comstock, pp. 227–256. Springer Nature, Switzerland.

Tregle, Joseph G., Jr.

1975 *The History of Louisiana*. Louisiana State University Press, Baton Rouge.

Van Staveren, Irene, and Peter Knorringa

2007 Unpacking Social Capital in Economic Development: How Social Relations Matter. *Review of Social Economics* 65: 107–135.

Woolock, Michael, and Deepa Narayan

2000 Social Capital: Implications for Development Theory, Research, and Policy. *World Bank Research Observations* 15: 225–249.

Worth, John E.

2017 What is a Phase? Disentangling Communities of Practice from Communities of Identity in Southeastern North America. In *Forging Southeastern Identities*, edited by Gregory A. Waselkov and Marvin T. Smith, pp. 117–156. University of Alabama Press, Tuscaloosa.

7

Where Women Work

Taskscapes and Activity Area Analysis

Ramie A. Gougeon

Anthropological study of households has long been hampered by the absence of a clear definition of what the concept entails. This is due to the incredible diversity in their forms and functions. Households have a social dimension, in the form of varying relationships among members; a material dimension, in the form of built environments, activity areas, and possessions; and a behavioral dimension, in the form of the activities performed by individuals and groups, frequently on behalf of the household (Wilk and Rathje 1982: 618). Several decades ago, archaeologists interested in household research began to define the household as an activity or task-oriented group to move beyond the long-recognized limits that came with assumed cohabitation or kinship among household members (Ashmore and Wilk 1988; Bender 1967; Carter 1984; Netting et al. 1984; Wilk and Rathje 1982). Perhaps more fundamental to the practice of a discipline that is ontologically materialist and epistemologically realist (after Trigger 2006: xix, 30), focusing on the material and behavioral dimensions seems to be the only means for archaeologists to study the social aspects of groups and individuals through the archaeological record.

Wilk and Netting (1984) recognized five spheres of household activity: production, distribution, transmission, reproduction, and co-residence. Their intent was to cease treating households as "black boxes" or uniform units of a larger society, but this approach could and did result in simple considerations of each sphere without further examinations of where and how they overlap (Wilk 1990: 324–325; see also Moore 1988: 54–56). Wilk rightly noted households may look very similar in composition, numbers, and kinship structure but be very different in terms of decision-making (about resource allocation

Figure 7.1. A household of faceless blobs.

in his example). Whether the black boxes were opened or not, many of the earliest archaeological studies of households in general, but from the precolumbian Southeast in particular, rarely penetrated beyond the material, economical, and functional aspects of production and distribution (Pluckhahn 2010). Households were largely comprised of "faceless blobs" (Tringham 1991: 94) (Figure 7.1).

The rise of household archaeology coincided with efforts to "engender" archaeology, drawing attention to the need for interpretations of gender, power, and identity within human relationships and social interactions (Conkey and Gero 1991: 4–5; Moore 1991; Tomášková 2011: 128). To some, attempts to engender archaeological interpretations too often took on the now familiar damning adage, "add women and stir" (Tomášková 2011: 121, 125–126). Gender was (and still is) mistaken as a "thing" rather than a process (Conkey and Gero 1991: 8–11). Conkey and Gero (1997) posited that some theoretical approaches facilitate engendering archaeology because of their underlying assumptions, scales of analysis, or interpretive frameworks. However, because households have so often been associated with women's roles, lives, and status, theory-building about the domestic sphere has been stagnant (Spencer-Wood 2004). Others have argued that studies of the domestic sphere in the precolumbian Southeast were overshadowed by a focus on examinations of the political sphere (Sullivan 2001). Some progress has been made to apply postmodern and postprocessual theories to household studies in historical archaeology (e.g., contributors to Barlie and Brandon 2004), including examinations of power dynamics. "Power-to," "power-over," "power-with," as well as domination and resistance, heterarchy, and integration are just a few lenses through which to consider individual relationships within households as well as household-to-household interactions (Crumley 1995; Gero and Scattolin 2002; Spencer-Wood 2004: 247–252). To be sure, studies of precolumbian households in the Southeast since the 1990s have included examinations of power (Pluckhahn 2010). For example, Southeastern Native household matriarchs had "ties of obligation" over their offspring, and older and post-menopausal women likely had a lifetime to nurture social networks and "power bases" that would have put them on par with their male peers in terms of power, status, and prestige (Sullivan 2001: 106–107, 111–112). Economic roles have also been found to be closely tied to rank and status and might have been an arena where one's power determined access to wealth or prestige generated by economic activities, or where power-to, -over, or -with might come into conflict with other household members (Sullivan 2001: 108; Thomas 2001: 54; see also Nelson et al. 2002: 130–131). It is critical that studies of households and the many processes that take place within them do not become black-box affairs.

My own analyses have not aged well given the criticisms and considerations above. I undertook a study of three Late Mississippian housefloors from the Little Egypt site (9MU102) in northwest Georgia to discern discrete activity areas used by women and men as members of households (Gougeon 2002, 2012). Activity areas were identified by seeking patterns of spatially co-occurring artifact types associated with specific activities, activities frequently correlated strongly with a specific gender in cross-cultural ethnological studies. Women's activities dominated the assemblages and occupied the most space in all three houses. Many artifacts recovered from house floors at Little Egypt are associated primarily with activities performed by women, namely those involved with food production. Within domestic structures, women were the dominant forces behind production. This model of household activity areas mirrors findings from late precolumbian and early post-contact sites across the southern Appalachian region but does little to advance our understanding of the social aspects of production within multigenerational, matrilineal, and arguably matrifocal households (Hally 2008).

One means of further considering the gendered uses of space to interrogate the experiences of being a Mississippian woman in a household is through the lens of taskscapes. Taskscapes are, in their simplest sense, arrays of related activities performed by social actors (Ingold 1993). Where taskscapes are considerably more complex is when we consider how those activities include enculturation through engendered knowledge production, dissemination, transmission, and negotiation. Taskscapes are an analytical lens through which to consider lives lived as engendered people. In this chapter, I will review the Little Egypt samples and my process of identifying activity areas and assigning activities to specific genders. I will then reconsider these patterns by imagining the lived lives and experiences of the people–primarily those practicing and acquiring feminine knowledge–who constituted these "households with faces" (after Tringham 1991). To do so, I will revise my previous model of domestic spaces at the Little Egypt site with taskscapes in mind, demonstrating how this device can be employed to think critically about how gender is created and reinforced through social practices within the domestic spaces of Late Mississippian Barnett phase households.

Women's Activities, Women's Households

The Little Egypt site is situated in the Coosawattee River valley in northwest Georgia. A multicomponent site, the most intensive period of occupation occurred during the Late Mississippian Barnett phase (AD 1350–1575) (Hally and Langford 1988). At this time, Little Egypt was the capital village of the chiefdom and paramount chiefdom Coosa, as recorded in 1540 by chroniclers of the Hernando de Soto expedition (Hally 1994; Hudson et al. 1985; Hudson 1997). David Hally of the University of Georgia conducted archaeological field schools at the site between 1969 and 1974, prior to its inundation by the construction of a reregulation reservoir by the Corps of Engineers in 1976 (Hally 1979, 1980). Manually excavated test units and mechanical stripping were used to identify the remains of domestic structures, or houses. Three structures identified as "winter" houses[1] were then completely excavated by hand using a methodology designed to capture artifacts at a rather fine-grained spatial scale (Hally 1983a: 164–166). House floors were more easily observed in two structures that had burned at the time of occupation, capping floor deposits *in situ* under a thick layer of charred wall and roofing material (e.g., Hally 1980: 93–98). Each occupation surface uncovered within large block excavation units was divided into 2-ft squares (approximately 60 cm by 60 cm). Larger artifacts lying on the intact floors were piece-plotted. Soil samples from the two-foot squares of all three structures were later processed using flotation; half of these samples (from alternating squares) were analyzed.

Elsewhere, I have detailed the architectural pattern language evident in the construction and layout of these domestic structures (Gougeon 2007, 2012,

2015). Each was constructed in a shallowly excavated basin containing four roof support posts, which framed a central hearth and adjoining clay apron. The four exterior walls contained a nearly uniform number of single-set posts. Given the height differences of the low exterior walls and the rafters supported by the central posts, a condition of varying ceiling height under a pyramidal-shaped roof was created. Most critical to this study, partitions of the floor created by interior walls or barriers likely reflected different needs regarding spatial functionality and ideology.

Domestic structures were sometimes rebuilt or rejuvenated. Evidence for this includes superimposed floors, where new, clean-fill sediments were lain over the previous surface (Hally 2008: 67, 77). Hearths were also often refreshed or completely rebuilt, often near or overlapping the previous hearth. Exterior walls and interior roof support posts were sometimes reoriented rather than simply shifted in a cardinal direction. These slight changes in structure orientation created a palimpsest of postholes within the confines of the house basin. However, new alignments of exterior wall posts equidistant to and in parallel with the "grid" defined by the orientation of interior support posts make identifying individual structure stages possible. Subfloor burials were usually placed around the central hearth space or parallel to raised beds or benches placed against the back walls of rooms created by partition walls. Their locations do not appear to have been forgotten during structure rejuvenations or reconstructions, as posts and other burial pits do not often intrude upon earlier burial pits (Hally 2008: 216–217).

Given the symmetry of these Late Mississippian house forms, shifting the hearth and wall posts in any direction would likely have required expanding the house basin as well. This latter activity is more challenging to detect archaeologically as it presumably removed some or all of the previous transitions from intact subsoil and any redeposited materials piled against the exteriors of the house walls. Erasure would be nearly complete in cases where the square footage of the house was greatly increased.

This basic architectural pattern language was employed across much of the southern Appalachian in the late precolumbian era (Hally 2002, 2008; Polhemus 1987; Rodning 2009; Steere 2017; Sullivan 1987). What remains understudied are the *households* associated with domestic structures. After Wilk and Rathje (1982: 618), households have a social dimension and a behavioral dimension. The household also has a material dimension. Households who created these domestic structures and cultural deposits remain understudied due in part to this material dimension. Preservation issues can result in inadequate materials for sampling, and inadequate recovery strategies can hamper research on the material signatures of patterned behaviors. Systematic, fine-grained sampling of floor deposits is a must (Polhemus 1998: 329–330; Tringham 1994: 178). Where analyses have been undertaken, there is reason to assert that discrete and patterned activity areas within domestic structures are not unique to one site or culture.

For my previous model for household organization for the Barnett phase, activity areas were identified in a three-stage process (Gougeon 2002, 2012). First, ethnohistoric sources and ethnological analyses were used to develop lists of activities typically performed by women, men, and children. For each activity, material requirements, including tools and byproducts, were considered (Gougeon 2012: 149–150). There undoubtedly existed a division of labor by gender and age in the precolumbian Southeast, which has been examined in a few studies (e.g., Polhemus 1998; Smith 1978; Thomas 2001). These studies, like my own, have relied largely on ethnohistoric data compiled by Swanton (1946), Hudson (1976), and the oft-cited ethnological analysis of 185 societies published by Murdock and Provost (1973).

In my previous model, those tasks I identified as likely performed indoors by women which had the potential to leave a material trace included a wide variety of food preparation and cooking activities, but also spinning, weaving, making cordage, hide working, fire maintenance, and cleaning (e.g., Gougeon 2012: 148). Distributions of whole and partial ceramic vessels of various forms and functions comprise one important set of data about women's domestic tasks (Hally 1983a). Food remains, including nutshells, corncobs, seeds, and bone, comprise another (Hally 1981, 1984, 1986). Trace evidences like soot patterns on vessel exteriors or wear patterns on the interior surfaces of vessels also point to specific cooking techniques, competencies, and activities (Hally 1983b). Correlating material remains and artifacts to tasks requires consideration not only of co-occurring artifact classes, but also an understanding of the material requirements of specific activities. For example, preparing hominy using a Mississippian standard jar requires a cooking pot of particular form, a means of suspending the pot, a utensil to manipulate the contents of the pot, nixtamalized maize kernels, water, and heat (Briggs 2016).

A second step used a statistical measure to explore the data for relationships within the spatial distribution of artifacts across the house floors. Piece-plotted materials and features were examined in a third step in conjunction with data from the flotation samples displayed as isopleth maps. In brief, strongly correlated artifact classes were identified and then visually examined. These clusters of artifact classes were then compared to the supposed material correlations for different activities. The resultant activity areas were then assigned to one or more gender and age categories.

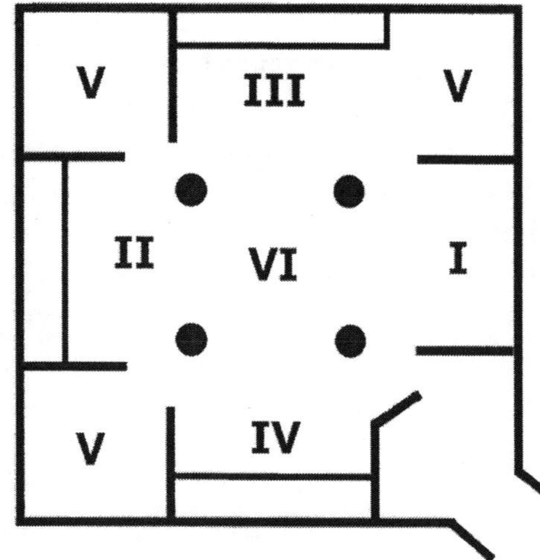

Figure 7.2. Models of winter house activities by gender for Barnett phase households.

A model of activities conducted in winter houses by gender for Barnett phase households is presented in Figure 7.2. I previously designated the area demarcated by the four central support posts and containing the hearth and hearth apron a "public" area, as opposed to those spaces against the walls created by the partition walls, which I supposed were "private" (Gougeon 2012: 156).

Immediately to the right of the entrance is a room that was used by men (and sometimes women) for processing bulk foodstuffs and lithic materials. The south half of this compartment in particular is frequently ringed in dense lithic debitage deposits. The lithic production area likely represents one of only two "male" areas of the house. I interpreted the compartment opposite the entrance as an "adult" area, perhaps the bed shared by the female and male heads of the family. Immediately to the left of the entrance and directly across from the presumed parents' area is one I assigned to subadults. The left side of the structure is an adult women's work area. Storage areas are found in the three other corners not used as an entrance.

Reflexivity as Reform

I have recently reconsidered my own rather uncritical use of problematic or at least under-justified ethnographic sources, particularly Murdock and

Provost (Gougeon 2017: 4–5). My primary concerns with these sources stem from a critique by Laura Pate (2004), who points to biases in source materials, problems with overly generalized or "universalized" models of Native American culture, and the unexamined overuse of lists of activities exclusively performed by one gender without identifying any shared or genderless tasks.[1]

I now see a number of problems with my previous model. First, it is rather two-dimensional, without providing a sense of whether some materials may have been hung from rafters or whether some activities were performed above the floor. A useful avenue of future research should include a careful study of where in three-dimensional space activities are performed and how different steps or stages of an activity may occur at different distances from the floor or across an activity area.

Second, the division of the floor into "public" and "private" areas are problematic categories (see Hendon 2006; Sullivan 2001: 104–105; Nelson 1997). Notions of "privacy" often read as inherently Western and would require careful consideration before being applied to the layout and uses of spaces in precolumbian Southeastern houses. As I ultimately assigned nearly the entirety of the floor space to the performance of women's activities, I must consider whether it was likely that related women involved in myriad spatially and temporally overlapping tasks would be cognizant of dichotomous private and public areas only potentially important when someone outside of the household was present. Some kind of functionally based distinction between the central area containing the hearth and the outer areas containing benches against the walls of the compartments would be useful, however. This distinction could probably be made on the amount of light and heat available from the central hearth (see also Hally 1983b: 173).

The third flaw with this model is its lack of temporality. The shape of each activity area and the absence of overlap between them gives the impression that activities occur independently, and that it may be possible to have household members performing their various tasks in their assigned areas simultaneously. A flat, static model cannot account for activities that may prevent others from occurring (either needing to be done in sequence, or perhaps just being hazardous. The prospect of getting flaked stone debris in foodstuffs seems an obvious reason to disallow knapping while someone else is preparing food.)

Perhaps the greatest flaw in this model of household activities is the absence of people. While I have proposed genders and ages for the likely users of each activity area, there is a distinct lack of dynamism in the delineated areas and coldly anonymous labels. Where are the lived lives and experiences of the people–primarily women–who constituted these households and created the patterned activity areas I modeled? Another perspective is necessary to populate the model with human beings in order to breathe life into a rather lifeless schematic diagram. Considering these activities from the perspective of the social actors who performed them may add the elements I have identified as missing above.

The Taskscape Concept

The concept of the *taskscape* emerged as an extension of the landscape methodological approach of the mid-1970s to early 2000s (Crumley and Marquardt 1990; Fleming 2006; Thomas 2012; Tilley 1997; Westerdahl 1992). In a very basic sense, a taskscape is an array of related activities (Ingold 1993: 158), or, more specifically, actions undertaken by people at particular points in time (Walker 2011: 277). In this latter sense, landscapes can be conceived as materials found at particular points in space. As I will discuss below, taskscapes are not separate from landscapes, but instead connect elements and features of landscapes to specific groups of people engaged in shared tasks (after Ingold 1993; see also Walker 2011: 277). A task is "any practical operation, carried out by a skilled agent in an environment, as part of his or her normal business of life" (Ingold 1993: 158).

Ingold (1993: 162–163) suggests taskscapes are defined by activities, movements, and sound, whereas landscapes are more visual. I am not so certain that such a clear distinction between landscapes and taskscapes can be made on these grounds. Rather, I think the distinction is partially one of scale. Taskscapes are much more intimate than landscapes and occur most frequently at the scale of human proximity and interaction. The largest taskscape I can think of might be an agricultural field, but I suspect taskscapes are more typically represented by the activities and space encompassed by a small group of people.[2] Landscapes, which might encompass regions, can involve what a person can immediately perceive as well as what they remember and imagine "out there."

Ingold (1993: 161–164) ultimately removes the distinction between landscape and taskscape by instead interlocking them via time, or temporality. Taskscapes reflect an interactivity of people and animate and inanimate objects at particular points in time (Ingold 1993: 161, 163). "Time" in this sense is far removed from Western notions of time or time as linked to labor and as a commodity (Logan and Cruz 2014: 206–207) and is operating at scales much finer grained than the temporal scales archaeologists are accustomed to. A challenge for archaeologists is teasing out the shorter temporal moments from deposits representing the superimposed and accumulated (and altered) deposits made over the lifespan of the house.

The temporal quality of the taskscape is inherently social because people enjoined by activities "also attend to one another" (Ingold 1993: 159–160). People engaged in shared tasks or performing tasks in close proximity, what Ingold refers to as activities of dwelling (see also Tilly 1997: 10), are constantly adjusting their behaviors while monitoring and considering the actions and behaviors of others. It is within these moments that engendered behavior is learned, both directly and tacitly. Roles are taught and reinforced, and identities are learned and performed (e.g., Hendon 2006; Krais 1993; Sørensen 2006). Feminist theorists would note that these situations are replete with expressions of different types of power (Spencer-Wood 2004: 249). A taskscape perspective can be a further means of examining power within households—between and among elders and juniors, mothers and daughters, wives and husbands.

Taskscapes also have a spatial element, even as they are defined more by temporal and social qualities. Taskscapes occur at the intersections of daily practice and the environment (Walker 2011: 277), with the qualification that the taskscapes under consideration here are within built environments. The deliberate, planned construction of specifically patterned architectural space creates places for human activities and experiences (Tilley 1997: 14–15). More than simply form following function (or vice versa), spaces structure and order social interactions and can reinforce social relations (Knapp and Ashmore 1999: 16; Nelson et al. 2002: 132; Rapoport 1969); this includes spaces within domestic structures. A new Mississippian house or one with a rejuvenated floor was not a blank slate. Each house was imbued by the builders and occupants with expectations about behaviors within planned spaces. Occupants of the house engaged in household activities manipulate and engage with both the material world and spaces they have built with each other as audience-observers. Taskscapes, with their qualities related to sociality and temporality, similarly retain elements and memories of past activities while shaping future activities by participants in these places (Ingold 1993: 157, 162). We can see that these expectations are met more often than not when we observe repeated patterns of artifacts across the excavated floors of multiple houses.

Late Mississippian Women's Taskscapes at Little Egypt

Women are nearly universally the most visible individuals in household contexts, and arguably "disproportionately represented" in household middens

(Gero 1991: 170). This appears to be the case at Little Egypt. In all three structures, artifacts related to women's activities dominate the assemblages and, interpreted as discrete activity areas, occupy the most space. This stands to reason. Ethnographic analogies suggest that many activities commonly performed by women, including those of native Southeastern societies, take place within or near domestic structures (Gougeon 2012: Table 5.2). Men's activities commonly occurred outside of domestic structures, or away from village settings entirely. A taskscape perspective puts people–mostly women–among the vessels, tools, and food remains found in these domestic structures.

Women's taskscapes were performed against a backdrop of matrilineality and matrilocality. Based on the observed structure of early post-contact native Southeastern groups, it is widely assumed that many were matrilineal (Hudson 1976). Rules of exogamy dictated that individuals marry outside of their lineage. Matrilocal postmarital residency was likely also followed (Hally 2008). Women, their unmarried and married daughters, mothers, grandmothers, and aunts were all closely related, consanguineal members of households who likely gave the household its very identity. Women did not marry out of their mother's household, but rather established a new house in immediate proximity to the founding household. Archaeological and bioarchaeological evidence strongly supports this interpretation (Hally 2008; Hally and Kelly 1998; Polhemus 1987). Because of this, apart from any young, unmarried sons, most adult men of a household would be "outsiders." This practice persisted far into the post-contact period, as noted ruefully by Indian agent Benjamin Hawkins to Thomas Jefferson: the Creek husband "is a tenant at will only so far as the occupancy of the premises of the women" (quoted in Frank 2005: 61; see also Saunt 2004: 39, 139).

Taskscapes also require that we consider the activities of gendered individuals who may not have left a material trace but were undoubtedly part of the performative process of living. Considering the list of activities performed indoors presented in the previous section, we should also add child rearing, implicit and tacit teaching and learning, storytelling, and the myriad ways people "attend" to one another. The nearly universal domestic activities of preparing and eating food with other people are "fundamental components of the human experience," where the places food is made and consumed become "hub(s) of human interaction" (Walls and Keith 2018: 137). An examination of only the material correlates of preparing hominy omits important but somewhat materially invisible "ingredients" like the cook, her expertise, her company, and her time. How likely was it that the head of the household was preparing food alongside other women and girls from her family? Who was tasting the hominy, assessing its quality, and commenting on the skills of the cook? Who could sense by smell that the hominy needed attention in the way of a stir or more water? Who could ask for another water run or for a few more sticks for the fire? Who responded to those requests? Considering these activities as taskscapes adds much-needed qualities of temporality and sociality to these interpretations.

As late precolumbian households were multigenerational, children should be considered as participants and subjects of many women's taskscapes. At times, children were undoubtedly co-laborers (Baxter 2008: 165; Claassen 1991; Kamp 2001: 14–18; Watson and Kennedy 1991: 258). Children were sometimes "tasks" themselves (Gero 1991; Kamp 2001: 10–14), although if the post-contact Creek can serve as a guide, it is likely that no boys were under the watch or tutelage of women by the age of six or seven (Saunt 2004: 141). Girls were co-laborers in their mother's households, but the degree to which they might be "visible" in archaeological deposits is unknown. Outside of repeated production tasks related to durable materials like pottery, where methods for examining different forms of apprenticeships, instruction, and learning may be applied (e.g., Wallaert-Pêtre 2001), I presume that many of the activities performed by girls will be indistinguishable from their mother's or aunt's. This seeming invisibility should not diminish the importance of understanding how people of different ages contributed to household production and other activities. In fact, it was during these critical early years when women were "made" within their households through their participation in gendered taskscapes.

I have previously speculated that the inability to account for variation introduced by children in the distributions of artifacts might be a shortcoming to my model of domestic activities (Gougeon 2002: 194–195). A rather commonsense approach to recognizing material assemblages created by children is to look for artifacts that appear "out of place." That is to say, children may combine materials, tools, and objects not normally used together in a typical domestic task. One problem with this approach is that children often "play" by imitating adults. This may include mimicking domestic activities, which can, as proposed for the cases of girls and young women, potentially create assemblages identical to those created by adults actually performing the tasks. Further complicating this commonsense approach is the notion that children are not immune to the social influences, expectations, and symbolic lives within which adults act (Baxter 2008: 169). A taskscape approach requires us to place children in these domestic settings and consider how their presence affected the actions of the other household members. Was the workspace altered by the presence of a child? For instance, were items shifted to be out of reach of a toddler, or were areas on the floor or on a bench no longer accessible due to the physical presence of a child? Were items or food given to children as playthings or distractions? A ball of dough or clay, a wooden spoon, large sherds, or smooth stones might end up "out of place" to an archaeologist while perfectly in place within the taskscape of a child and attendant family members.

Recent scholarship on the "archaeology of the night" calls us to consider how we "privilege descriptions of daytime doings" (Gonlin and Nowell 2018: 5). Of particular relevance to the study of household taskscapes, they note that most human beings spend their nighttime hours "at home" (Gonlin and Nowell 2018: 11). Because human beings are not so diurnal as to collapse into sleep instantaneously at dusk, this means that a considerable number of activities and social interactions occur in the period between twilight and dawn. How were women's tasks affected by, for example, putting children to bed? Or by men and boys returning home? How common was the practice of co-sleeping? The houses in the sample from Little Egypt are interpreted as "winter structures," sturdier and more insulated than the household's adjoining and simpler porticos or shed-like buildings used in warmer seasons. Given the absence of evidence for lamps, for example, the central hearth was the sole source of heat and nearly all light. At night, when only the brightest of moonlight might have entered through the smokehole at the roof's pyramidal peak, which activities were ceased or moved closer to the hearth to take advantage of the light it provided? Given that women were presumed to be the producers of ceramics and as some late precolumbian ceramic designs have been interpreted as representing celestial features like the Milky Way (Lankford 2017; Reilly 2007; Sommerkamp 2008), when did women make these observations? Were they alone when they did so? Did this occur during times of great ritual significance, or were these observations made while performing routine bodily functions out of doors?

Taskscapes were times and places of direct and indirect socialized learning. Every element of socialized learning, from the activities learned, to the materials and tools used in the activities, to the actions of instructing and learning, was inherently gendered (Kamp 2001: 12–14). Women's taskscapes included mothers instructing daughters in food preparation and crafting (e.g., Auguste 2009; Franklin et al. 2016). How instruction was delivered should also be considered. In addition to proposing a nearly universal role of grandmothers in child rearing, Schweitzer (1999: 11) posits that in many Southwestern Native societies, autonomy is a critical aspect of teaching and learning. Individuals have the right to make their own decisions, but this is coupled with the recognition that they are also responsible for the outcomes of their behavior. This degree of autonomy should be explored and not assumed for precolumbian native Southeastern societies, particularly in light of the implications of this quality on the transmission of ceramic styles and variability, for instance (e.g., Worth 2017).

Taskscapes were also the setting for learning one's gender identity, roles, and expectations. Learning one's specific engendered activities and gender identity was reinforced in at least some Southeastern native societies by the very words one spoke, as evidenced by distinct dialects for women and men in the Muscogee language (Bell 1990; Saunt 2004: 140–141).[3] Another aspect of identity and roles for women and men included fertility and sexuality.[4] These topics have been explored in the arena of symbolism, for example (Claassen 2011, 2016), but should also be considered as taskscapes in the domestic sphere. Was sexuality talked about, and how observable, audible, or even knowable were sexual acts by others in the household (Alexander et al. 1977: 676–680; Voss 2008)? How directly and indirectly were understandings of menstruation and any related social taboos conveyed (e.g., Bengtson and Alexander, this volume)? How were foodways and other domestic activities altered (or not) during the menstrual phase of women's cycles (Bell 1990; Galloway 1997)?

Women's Works and Lives

The excavated houses from Little Egypt, when interpreted as taskscapes, become households with faces (Figure 7.3). Taskscapes are the times and places of enculturation, and household taskscapes are when and where women become women. In her study of late precolumbian Siouan communities, Jane Eastman (2001: 58) proposes that women "experienced more profound changes in their gender roles and identities as they aged than did men." She argues that these changes were marked in many ways, including changes in expected behavior, specific dress, and in the division of labor. I suggest that these changes in gender roles and identities through a life cycle would also be seen in the places individuals occupied in domestic structures. Children occupied a shared area or sleeping bench while adults occupied another. However, as girls and boys matured and their responsibilities changed, the areas where they worked and lived also changed. For a woman, this might have culminated in the establishment of her own household.

Most importantly, Mississippian women lived their lives with other people, particularly other women. Through a taskscape perspective, domestic activities that left material traces, like cooking, crafting, and tool maintenance, were entangled with less archaeologically obvious but no less important activities like socializing, speaking, performing, resting, remembering, teaching, learn-

Figure 7.3. A household with faces.

ing, observing, interacting, cooperating, resisting, and assessing. A taskscape approach suggests that some of the most important aspects and qualities of Mississippian women's lives are not so easily captured in two-dimensional models of domestic activities and production. Theirs was undoubtedly a materially three-dimensional and socially dynamic world.

Acknowledgments

A serendipitous scheduling decision by the organizers of the 2018 Southeastern Archaeological Conference in Augusta, Georgia put my poster just outside the door of the symposium that led to this volume. Social media posts are evidence that I did not abandon my poster, even as I strained to hear what was happening in the nearby room. My thanks to Rachel Briggs, Michaelyn Harle, and Lynne P. Sullivan for extending an opportunity to contribute and for their editorial work. This chapter is dedicated to my mom, Teresa Gougeon, whose lifetime of diverse and evolving taskscapes inspire my thinking about the infinite possibilities of anthropological archaeology.

Notes

1 Late precolumbian households in the southern Appalachians created clusters of primary and ancillary structures around open areas, presumed to be outdoor activity areas (Gougeon 2015). The primary domestic structures had more substantial superstructures and were constructed in shallow basins with wattle walls, which would have provided a degree of insulation from the elements. Some studies of seasonality suggest the primary domestic structures were occupied in cooler months, hence "winter" houses. Ancillary structures likely were elevated granaries or storage facilities.

2 I suppose it is conceivable that someday, some anthropologist will discuss a "taskscape" of the coordinated efforts of people working at a similar task but on a global scale (perhaps a cyberattack or the machinations of online commerce).

3 Kehoe (2016) offers a vital reminder of the importance of distinguishing between context and syntax in Algonkian dialects, as well as recalling that the topic of gender may be more important to anthropologists and linguists than native speakers.

4 This current work is challenged at the outset by being heteronormative, discussing only the dual-gender categories of "women" and "men" without consideration of the presence of third genders or non-heterosexualities (see Ardren 2008; Geller 2009; Prine 2000).

References Cited

Alexander, Christopher, Sara Ishikawa, and Murray Silverstein

1977 *A Pattern Language.* With contributions from Max Jacobson, Ingrid Fiksdahl-King, and Shlomo Angel. Oxford University Press, New York.

Ardren, Traci

2008 Studies of Gender in the Prehispanic Americas. *Journal of Archaeological Research* 16: 1–35.

Ashmore, Wendy, and Richard R. Wilk

1988 Household and Community in the Mesoamerican Past. In *Household and Community in the Mesoamerican Past*, edited by Richard R. Wilk and Wendy Ashmore, pp. 1–27. University of New Mexico Press, Albuquerque.

Augusté, N. N.

2009 By Her Hands: Catawba Women and Survival, Civil War through Reconstruction. *Native South* 2: 148–162.

Barlie, Kerri S., and Jamie C. Brandon, eds.

2004 *Household Chores and Household Choices: Theorizing the Domestic Sphere in Historical Archaeology.* University of Alabama Press, Tuscaloosa.

Baxter, Jane Eva
2008 The Archaeology of Childhood. *Annual Review of Anthropology* 37: 159–175.

Bell, Amelia Rector
1990 Separate People: Speaking of Creek Men and Women. *American Anthropologist* 92(x): 332–345.

Bender, Donald R.
1967 A Refinement of the Concept of Household: Families, Co-residence, and Domestic Functions. *American Anthropologist* 69(5): 493–504.

Briggs, Rachel V.
2016 The Civil Cooking Pot: Hominy and the Mississippian Standard Jar in the Black Warrior River Valley, Alabama. *American Antiquity* 81(2): 316–332.

Carter, Anthony
1984 Household Histories. In *Households*, edited by Robert McC. Netting, Richard R. Wilk, and Eric J. Arnould, pp. 44–83. University of California Press, Berkeley.

Claassen, Cheryl P.
1991 Gender, Shellfishing, and the Shell Mound Archaic. In *Engendering Archaeology: Women and Prehistory*, edited by Joan M. Gero and Margaret W. Conkey, pp. 276–300. Basil Blackwell, Oxford.
2011 Rock Shelters as Women's Retreats: Understanding Newt Kash. *American Antiquity* 76(4): 628–641.
2016 Rock Shelters, Boulders, and Bleeding Rocks: Uncovering Elements of Women's Ritual Landscape in the Midcontinent. In *Native American Landscapes: An Engendered Perspective*, edited by Cheryl Claassen, pp. 3–34. University of Tennessee Press, Knoxville.

Conkey, Margaret W., and Joan M. Gero
1991 Tensions, Pluralities, and Engendering Archaeology: An Introduction to Women and Prehistory. In *Engendering Archaeology: Women and Prehistory*, edited by Joan M. Gero and Margaret W. Conkey, pp. 3–30. Basil Blackwell, Oxford.
1997 Programme to Practice: Gender and Feminism in Archaeology. *Annual Review of Anthropology* 26:411–437.

Crumley, Carole L.
1995 Heterarchy and the Analysis of Complex Societies. *Special Issue: Heterarchy and the Analysis of Complex Sciences.* Archaeological Papers of the American Anthropological Association 6, pp. 1–5. DOI: 10.1525/ap3a.1995.6.1.1.

Crumley, Carole L., and William H. Marquardt
1990 Landscape: A Unifying Concept in Regional Analysis. In *Interpreting Space: GIS and Archaeology*, edited by K. Allen, S. Green and E. Zubrow, pp. 73–79. Taylor and Francis, London.

Eastman, Jane M.
2001 Life Courses and Gender among Prehistoric Siouan Communities. In *Archaeological Studies of Gender* in *the Southeastern United States*, edited by Jane M. Eastman and Christopher B. Rodning, pp. 57–76. University Press of Florida, Gainesville.

Fleming, Andrew
2006 Post-processual Landscape Archaeology: A Critique. *Cambridge Archaeological Journal* 16(3): 267–280.

Frank, Andrew K.
2005 *Creeks and Southerners: Biculturalism on the Early American Frontier.* University of Nebraska Press, Lincoln.
Franklin, Jay, Lucinda Langston, and Meagan Dennison
2016 Bedrock Mortar Hole Sites as Artifacts of Women's Taskscapes. In *Native American Landscapes: An Engendered Perspective*, edited by Cheryl Claassen, pp. 35–84. University of Tennessee Press, Knoxville.
Galloway, Patricia
1997 Where Have All the Menstrual Huts Gone? The Invisibility of Menstrual Seclusion in the Late Prehistoric Southeast. In *Women in Prehistory: North America and Mesoamerica*, edited by Cheryl Claassen and Rosemary A. Joyce, pp. 47–62. University of Pennsylvania Press, Philadelphia.
Geller, Pamela L.
2009 Identity and Difference: Complicating Gender in Archaeology. *Annual Review of Anthropology* 38: 65–81.
Gero, Joan M.
1991 Genderlithics: Women's Roles in Stone Tool Production. In *Engendering Archaeology: Women and Prehistory*, edited by Joan M. Gero and Margaret W. Conkey, pp. 163–193. Blackwell, Oxford.
Gero, Joan M., and M. Cristina Scattolin
2002 Beyond Complementarity and Hierarchy: New Definitions for Archaeological Gender Relations. In *In Pursuit of Gender: Worldwide Archaeological Approaches*, edited by Sarah Milledge Nelson and Myriam Rosen-Ayalon, pp. 155–171. AltaMira Press, Walnut Creek, California.
Gonlin, Nancy, and April Nowell
2018 Introduction to Archaeology of the Night. In *Archaeology of the Night: Life after Dark in the Ancient World*, edited by Nancy Gonlin and April Nowell, pp. 5–24. University Press of Colorado, Boulder.
Gougeon, Ramie A.
2002 Household Research at the Late Mississippian Little Egypt Site (9MU102). Unpublished PhD dissertation, Department of Anthropology, University of Georgia, Athens.
2007 An Architectural Grammar of Late Mississippian Houses in Northwest Georgia. In *Architectural Variability in the Southeast*, edited by Cameron H. Lacquement, pp. 136–152. University Press of Alabama, Tuscaloosa.
2012 Activity Areas and Households in the Late Mississippian Southeast United States: Who Did What Where? In *Ancient Households of the Americas*, edited by John Douglass and Nancy Gonlin, pp. 141–162, University Press of Colorado.
2015 The King Site: Refining a Pattern Language Model for the Late Mississippian Period in Northwest Georgia. In *Archaeological Perspectives on the Southern Appalachians: A Multiscalar Approach*, edited by Ramie A. Gougeon and Maureen S. Meyers, pp. 85–103, University of Tennessee Press, Knoxville.
2017 Considering Gender Analogies in Prehistoric Southeastern Archaeology. *Southeastern Archaeology* 36(3): 183–194. DOI: 10.1080/0734578X.2017.1309517

Hally, David J.

1979 *Archaeological Investigation of the Little Egypt Site (9MU102) Murray County, Georgia, 1969 Season.* University of Georgia Laboratory of Archaeology Series, Report No. 18. Athens.

1980 *Archaeological Investigation of the Little Egypt Site (9MU102) Murray County, Georgia, 1970–1972 Seasons.* Report submitted to the National Park Service, United States Department of the Interior.

1981 Plant Preservation and the Context of Paleobotanical Samples: A Case Study. *American Antiquity* 46(4): 723–742.

1983a The Interpretive Potential of Pottery from Domestic Contexts. *Midcontinental Journal of Archaeology* 8(2): 163–196.

1983b Use Alteration of Pottery Vessel Surfaces: An Important Source of Evidence for the Identification of Vessel Function. *North American Archaeologist* 4(1): 3–26.

1984 Vessel Assemblages and Food Habits: A Comparison of Two Aboriginal Southeastern Vessel Assemblages. *Southeastern Archaeology* 3(1): 46–64.

1986 The Identification of Vessel Function: A Case Study from Northwest Georgia. *American Antiquity* 51(2): 267–295.

1994 The Chiefdom of Coosa. In *The Forgotten Centuries: Indians and Europeans in the American South 1521–1704*, edited by Charles Hudson and Carmen Chaves Tesser, pp. 227–253. University of Georgia Press, Athens.

2002 "As Caves Below the Ground": Making Sense of Aboriginal House Form in the Protohistoric and Historic Southeast. In *Between Contacts and Colonies: Archaeological Perspectives on the Protohistoric Southeast*, edited by Cameron B. Wesson and Mark A. Rees, pp. 90–109. University of Alabama Press, Tuscaloosa.

2008 *King: The Social Archaeology of a Late Mississippian Town in Northwestern Georgia.* University of Alabama Press, Tuscaloosa.

Hally, David J., and Hypatia Kelly

1998 The Nature of Mississippian Towns in Georgia. In *Mississippian Towns and Sacred Spaces: Searching for an Architectural Grammar*, edited by R. Barry Lewis and Charles Stout, pp. 49–63. University of Alabama Press, Tuscaloosa.

Hally, David J., and James B. Langford, Jr.

1988 *Mississippi Period Archaeology of the Georgia Valley and Ridge Province.* University of Georgia Laboratory of Archaeology Series, Report No. 25, Georgia Archaeological Research Design Papers No. 4. Athens.

Hendon, Julia A.

2006 The Engendered Household. In *Handbook of Gender in Archaeology*, edited by Sarah Milledge Nelson, pp. 171–198. AltaMira Press, Lanham, Maryland.

Hudson, Charles

1976 *The Southeastern Indians.* University of Tennessee Press, Knoxville.

1997 *Knights of Spain, Warriors of the Sun.* Georgia University Press, Athens.

Hudson, Charles, Marvin Smith, David Hally, Richard Polhemus, and Chester DePratter

1985 Coosa: A Chiefdom in the Sixteenth-Century Southeastern United States. *American Antiquity* 50: 723–737.

Ingold, Tim

1993 The Temporality of the Landscape. *World Archaeology* 25(2): 152–174.

Kamp, Kathryn A.

2001 Where Have All the Children Gone? The Archaeology of Childhood. *Journal of Archaeological Method and Theory* 8(1): 1–34.

Kehoe, Alice Beck

2016 Gendered Landscapes? If You Speak an Algonkian Language. In *Native American Landscapes: An Engendered Perspective*, edited by Cheryl Claassen, pp. 177–189. University of Tennessee Press, Knoxville.

Knapp, Bernard, and Wendy Ashmore

1999 Archaeological Landscape: Constructed, Conceptualized Ideational. In *Archaeologies of Landscape: Contemporary Perspectives*, edited by Wendy Ashmore and Bernard Knapp, pp. 1–32. Blackwell Publishers, Oxford.

Krais, Beate

1993 Gender and Symbolic Violence: Female Oppression in the Light of Pierre Bourdieu's Theory of Social Practice. In *Bourdieu: Critical Perspectives*, edited by Craig Calhoun, Edward LiPuma, and Moishe Postone, pp. 156–177. Polity Press, Cambridge.

Lankford, George E.

2017 The "Path of Souls": Some Death Imagery in the Southeastern Ceremonial Complex. In *Ancient Objects and Sacred Realms: Interpretations of Mississippian Iconography*, edited by F. Kent Reilly III and James F. Garber, pp. 174–212. University of Texas Press, Austin.

Logan, Amanda L., and M. Dores Cruz

2014 Gendered Taskscapes: Food, Farming, and Craft Production in Banda, Ghana in the Eighteenth to Twenty-first Centuries. *African Archaeological Review* 31: 203–231.

Moore, Henrietta L.

1988 *Feminism and Anthropology.* University of Minnesota Press, Minneapolis.

1991 Epilogue. In *Engendering Archaeology: Women and Prehistory*, edited by Joan M. Gero and Margaret W. Conkey, pp. 407–411. Basil Blackwell, Oxford.

Murdock, George P., and Caterina Provost

1973 Factors in the Division of Labor by Sex: A Cross-Cultural Analysis. *Ethnology* 12: 203–225.

Nelson, Sarah Milledge

1997 *Gender in Archaeology: Analyzing Power and Prestige.* AltaMira Press, Walnut Creek, California.

Nelson, Margaret, Donna Glowacki, and Annette Smith

2002 The Impact of Women on Household Economies: A Maya Case Study. In *In Pursuit of Gender: Worldwide Archaeological Approaches*, edited by Sarah Milledge Nelson and Myriam Rosen-Ayalon, pp. 125–154. AltaMira Press, Walnut Creek, California.

Netting, Robert McC., Richard R. Wilk, and Eric J. Arnould

1984 Introduction. In *Households*, edited by Robert McC. Netting, Richard R. Wilk, and Eric J. Arnould, pp. xiii-xxxviii. University of California Press, Berkeley.

Pate, Laura

2004 The Use and Abuse of Ethnographic Analogies in Interpretations of Gender Systems at Cahokia. In *Ungendering Civilization*, edited by J.A. Pyburn, pp. 71–93. Routledge, New York.

Pluckhahn, Thomas J.

2010 Household Archaeology in the Southeastern United States: History, Trends, and Challenges. *Journal of Archaeological Research* 18(4): 331–385.

Polhemus, Richard

1987 *The Toqua Site: A Late Mississippian Phase Town.* University of Tennessee, Department of Anthropology, Report of Investigations No. 41, Tennessee Valley Authority, Publications in Anthropology No. 44.

1998 Activity Organization in Mississippian Households: A Case Study from the Loy Site in East Tennessee. Unpublished PhD dissertation, Department of Anthropology, University of Tennessee, Knoxville.

Prine, Elizabeth

2000 Searching for Third Genders: Towards a Prehistory of Domestic Space in Middle Missouri Villages. In *Archaeologies of Sexuality*, edited by Robert A. Schmidt and Barbara L. Voss, pp. 197–235. Routledge, New York.

Rapoport, Amos

1969 *House Form and Culture.* Prentice-Hall, New Jersey.

Reilly, F. Kent, III.

2007 The Petaloid Motif: A Celestial Symbolic Locative in the Shell Art of Spiro. In *Ancient Objects and Sacred Realms: Interpretations of Mississippian Iconography*, edited by F. Kent Reilly III and James F. Garber, pp. 39–55. University of Texas Press, Austin.

Rodning, Christopher B.

2009 Domestic Houses at Coweta Creek. *Southeastern Archaeology* 28(1): 1–26.

Saunt, Claudio

2004 *A New Order of Things: Property, Power, and the Transformation of the Creek Indians, 1733–1816.* Cambridge University Press, Cambridge.

Schweitzer, Marjorie M.

1999 Introduction. *American Indian Grandmothers: Traditions and Transitions*, edited by Marjorie M. Schweitzer, pp. 3–24. University of New Mexico Press, Albuquerque.

Smith, Bruce D.

1978 *Prehistoric Patterns of Human Behavior: A Case Study in the Mississippi Valley.* Academic Press, New York.

Sommerkamp, Cindy Loretto

2008 Along the Pathway of Souls: An Iconographic Analysis of the Hickory Ridge Cemetery Site (8ES1280) in Pensacola, Florida. Unpublished master's thesis, Department of Anthropology, University of West Florida.

Sørensen, Marie Louise Stig

2006 Gender, Things, and Material Culture. In *Handbook of Gender in Archaeology*, edited by Sarah Milledge Nelson, pp. 105–135. AltaMira Press, Lanham, Maryland.

Spencer-Wood, Suzanne

2004 What Difference Does Feminist Theory Make in Researching Households? A

Commentary. In *Household Chores and Household Choice: Theorizing the Domestic Sphere in Historical Archaeology*, edited by Kerri S. Barile and Jamie C. Brandon, pp. 235–253. University of Alabama Press, Tuscaloosa.

Steere, Benjamin A.

2017 *The Archaeology of Houses and Households in the Native Southeast.* University of Alabama Press, Tuscaloosa.

Sullivan, Lynne P.

1987 The Mouse Creek Phase Household. *Southeastern Archaeology* 6(1): 16–29.

2001 "Those Men in the Mounds": Gender, Politics, and Mortuary Practices in Late Prehistoric Eastern Tennessee. In *Archaeological Studies of Gender in the Southeastern United States*, edited by Jane M. Eastman and Christopher B. Rodning, pp. 101–126. University Press of Florida, Gainesville.

Swanton, John R.

1946 *The Indians of the Southeastern United States.* Bulletin No. 137, Bureau of American Ethnology, Smithsonian Institution, Washington, D.C.

Thomas, Julian

2012 Archaeologies of Place and Landscape. In *Archaeological Theory Today,* 2nd ed., edited by Ian Hodder, pp. 167–187. Polity Press, Cambridge.

Thomas, Larissa

2001 The Gender Division of Labor in Mississippian Households. In *Archaeological Studies of Gender in the Southeastern United States*, edited by Jane M. Eastman and Christopher B. Rodning, pp. 27–56. University Press of Florida, Gainesville.

Tilley, Christopher

1997 Space, Place, Landscape, and Perception: Phenomenological Perspectives. In *A Phenomenology of Landscape: Places, Paths and Monuments*, edited by C. Tilley, pp. 7–34. Berg Publishers, Oxford.

Tomášková, Silvia

2011 Landscape for a Good Feminist: An Archaeological Review. *Archaeological Dialogues* 18(1): 109–136.

Trigger, Bruce G.

2006 *A History of Archaeological Thought,* 2nd ed. Cambridge University Press, New York.

Tringham, Ruth E.

1991 Households with Faces: The Challenge of Gender in Prehistoric Architectural Remains. In *Engendering Archaeology: Women and Prehistory*, edited by Joan M. Gero and Margaret W. Conkey, pp. 93–131. Basil Blackwell, Oxford.

1994 Engendering Places in Prehistory. *Gender, Place and Culture* 1(2): 169–203.

Voss, Barbara L.

2008 Sexuality Studies in Archaeology. *Annual Review of Anthropology* 37: 317–336.

Walker, John H.

2011 Social Implications from Agricultural Taskscapes in the Southwestern Amazon. *Latin American Antiquity* 22(3): 275–295.

Wallaert-Pêtre, Hélène

2001 Learning How to Make the Right Pots: Apprenticeship Strategies and Material

Culture, a Case Study in Handmade Pottery from Cameroon. *Journal of Archaeological Research* 57(4): 471–493.

Walls, Lauren A., and Scot Keith

2018 Cooking Connects Them: Earth Ovens as Persistent Places during the Woodland Period. In *Baking, Bourbon, and Black Drink: Foodways Archaeology in the American Southeast*, edited by Tanya M. Peres and Aaron Deter-Wolf, pp. 119–137. University of Alabama Press, Tuscaloosa.

Watson, Patty Jo, and Mary C. Kennedy

1991 The Development of Horticulture in the Eastern Woodlands of North America: Women's Role. In *Engendering Archaeology: Women and Prehistory*, edited by Joan M. Gero and Margaret W. Conkey, pp. 255–275. Blackwell Publishers, Oxford.

Westerdahl, Christer

1992 The Maritime Cultural Landscape. *International Journal of Nautical Archaeology* 21(1): 5–14.

Wilk, Richard R.

1990 Household Ecology: Decision Making and Resource Flows. In *The Ecosystem Approach in Anthropology: From Concept to Practice*, edited by Emilio F. Moran, pp. 323–356. University of Michigan Press, Ann Arbor.

Wilk, Richard R., and Robert McC. Netting

1984 Households: Changing Forms and Functions. In *Households*, edited by Robert McC. Netting, Richard R. Wilk, and E. J. Arnould, pp. 1–28. University of California Press, Berkeley.

Wilk, Richard R., and William L. Rathje

1982 Household Archaeology. *American Behavioral Scientist* 25(6): 617–639.

Worth, John E.

2017 What's in a Phase? Disentangling Communities of Practice from Communities of Identity in Southeastern North America. In *Forging Southeastern Identities: Social Archaeology, Ethnohistory, and Folklore of the Mississippian to Early Historic South*, edited by Gregory A. Waselkov and Marvin T. Smith, pp. 117–156. University of Alabama Press, Tuscaloosa.

8

Earth Mother and Her Children

The Role of Mississippian Women in Shaping Beliefs and Material Culture in the Middle Cumberland Region

Robert V. Sharp

Recognizing both the opportunity and responsibility that attended our efforts to conduct the first study dedicated solely to the representation of female figures in the Middle Cumberland region during the Mississippian period, I, along with Vernon James Knight Jr. and George Lankford (Sharp et al. 2011), took care not to assume that the effigy bottles and figurines we were cataloging, describing, and analyzing were ceramic figurations of the supernatural personage long identified with nineteenth-century Siouan tribes: i.e., Old Woman Who Never Dies. Thus, we compiled our corpus, and as the number of examples accumulated beyond our expectations, we tried not to begin our analysis with any urgency to claim that "we know who this must be." The purpose behind our restraint was to respect that, while there are doubtless important deities, supernatural personages, culture heroes, and other-than-human characters depicted in the art of the Mississippian world that scholars have already identified, there may also be local, iconographical manifestations of such subjects that deserve to be studied free of any rush to judgment about their identity, function, or meaning (Knight 2013). That the ceramic effigy bottles and figurines at the center of our iconographical analysis were deemed female and produced in surprising quantity made the necessity of restraint even more critical, in precisely the way that studies by various feminist scholars have made clear. Consider, for example, this prudent advice from Sarah Milledge Nelson:

> To begin with, it is important to recognize that there is not just one "mother goddess" as an eternal representation of the feminine. In the same way that women are different within and between cultures, the

> statues are diverse, not only from different times and places but also in form, size, realism, and many other characteristics. Some of them probably had multiple meanings for the cultures in which they were made and used. To generalize about them through time and space is to deny their diversity and by extension to deny diversity to women. Just as all female figurines are not the same, representations known to be goddesses also differ widely. (Nelson 2004: 123)

In this chapter, I want to reexamine the ceramic female effigy bottles and figurines from the Middle Cumberland region (MCR) within a larger context of the materialization of female figures in other media and forms in the Mississippian era. As the number of relevant examples has increased and other examinations have brought forth evidence that has helped shape new hypotheses and interpretations (e.g., Bengtson 2017; Boles 2017, 2020; Claassen 2011, 2016; Dye 2012, 2015; Emerson 2015; Mueller and Fritz 2016; Sharp 2019, 2021; Sharp and Smith 2015; Sharp et al. 2020; Smith 2016, 2018; Smith and Sharp 2014; Weeks et al. 2015), it is clear that the depiction of female supernatural personages deserve further consideration. I also feel that it is imperative to examine the changes that occurred over time in the depiction of female figures that we *believe* materialize supernatural deities or transcendent beings. Certainly, given that the MCR has been recognized as one of the few centers of production of ceramic human effigies, along with southeast Missouri and northeast Arkansas (Holmes 1886: 422–426; Phillips et al. 2003 [1951]: 163–165, Tables 2 and 10), shifts in the manner of representation may reflect attention to attributes that distinguish one community from another. Laden with meanings that are understood by their makers and by others within a particular community, changes in style, technique, or form may point to the arrival of new members or the exercise of their influence.

When they sought to understand differences in the mortuary practices revealed at two Late Mississippian sites in East Tennessee and investigated the relationship between cultural identity and social practices, Lynne Sullivan and Michaelyn Harle (2010: 236) recognized that we can all manage to be "a member of a distinct community or enclave within [a] larger cultural tradition." So, as we examine what I perceive to be the contribution of Mississippian women in shaping beliefs and expressing those beliefs through the production of female effigy bottles and figurines and other related artifacts and then incorporating those material goods in rituals conducted in their households and communities for the care of their children, let us try "to identify [those] classificatory or cultural distinctions that prehistoric peoples perceived segregated themselves from other peoples, to the extent that these differences created perceptions of distinct identities" (Sullivan and Harle 2010: 236). The differences that we can observe in the fashioning, detailing, and ornamenting of ceramic figurines and human effigy bottles in the MCR may not take us directly to the ideology shared by their makers or to the differences intended by their makers in expressing their personal identities, but the effort to illuminate such characteristics will surely bring us closer to understanding those broad cultural shifts that are sometimes revealed by powerful artists who undertake to materialize beliefs about the sacred.

Stone Statuary of the Tennessee–Cumberland Region

From the evidence provided by dozens of anthropomorphic stone statues that have been unearthed over the past 150 years, principally in the Cumberland River valley of Middle Tennessee and secondarily in northwest Georgia, the Native inhabitants of this region were responsible for producing one of the few indigenous styles of artistic sculptural representation in the pre-contact era in the Eastern Woodlands (Smith and Miller 2009). According to Smith and Miller (2009: 7), "the overwhelming majority of the statues were discovered by farmers plowing their fields or through the unsystematic 'digging' of collectors and antiquarians during the eighteenth and nineteenth centuries." Although some pieces of Tennessee-Cumberland statuary are known to be no longer extant, and the reports of others have proved to be unverifiable, the works cataloged by Smith and Miller (2009: Tables A.1 and A.2) number nearly ninety:

> The statues classified in the Tennessee-Cumberland style include realistic portrayals of sitting or kneeling human or near-human figures sculpted from locally available stones. . . . In our definition, the Tennessee-Cumberland style images include two different (but probably interrelated) types of statues: (1) males and females created in pairs representing real or mythological lineage ancestors, and (2) depictions of an ancient, widespread, and complex supernatural female figure known historically across North America by various names such as Old Woman, Old Woman Who Never Dies, Grandmother, Corn Mother, and Earth Mother (among others). (Smith and Miller 2009: 31)

The more numerous of the two types of statues that constitute the focus of their study are the "ancestral pairs," works that have been interpreted to represent either those responsible for creation or, more likely, the founders of a chiefly lineage or of a community itself. This subset of ancestral couples includes perhaps the most widely exhibited and most frequently reproduced work of pre-contact Native American art: the kneeling male figure discovered in Wilson County, Tennessee, in 1939, on the Sellars Farm (Smith and Miller 2009: 39–41, Figs. 3.8–3.13; see also King 2004: 155, Fig. 7). The Tennessee-Cumberland ancestral pairs also include the well-known seated male and kneeling female figures sculpted in marble and excavated in North Georgia at Etowah in 1954 (Smith and Miller 2009: 99–105, Figs. 4.6–4.11; see also King 2004: 153–156, Fig. 6). The male figure found at the Link Farm site in Humphreys County, Tennessee, in 1895 also deserves to be mentioned here, although the female sculpture that it was discovered with may no longer be extant and certainly has not been publicly exhibited or published since the 1930s. The largest member of the Tennessee-Cumberland statuary corpus, this statue, along with its mate, was found beneath an extraordinary cache of forty-six ceremonial flint bifaces (Dye 2021). While the cache long ago entered the collections of the McClung Museum, Knoxville, the male resides in the Metropolitan Museum of Art, New York (accession no. 1979.206.476).

In addition to these notable ancestral pairs recovered from mound sites, others have been recovered from settlements without mounds. One such pair was plowed up in the spring of 1905 from the Martin Farm in Riddleton, Tennessee, and they display attributes that make them seem to have been carved by the same artisan, who chose somewhat different blocks of sandstone and produced a female shorter and darker than her companion (Figure 8.1; Smith and Miller 2009: 67–68, Figs. 3.30–3.34). Another such male-and-female pair appears to have been found on the Frost Farm in Williamson County, Tennessee. Discovered some thirteen years apart and held in different collections since being plowed up in the nineteenth century, this is the only pair in which both members display the raised right knee and lower leg, the significance of which remains open to discussion (Figure 8.2; Smith and Miller 2009: 77–80, Figs. 3.39–3.40).

Ironically, although the kneeling male statue from Sellars would quickly make its way into the collections of the University of Tennessee, Knoxville, together with a female figure discovered shortly after it, unbeknownst to all, the male had already been separated from its real mate, a darker and somewhat shorter female figure that had been plowed up perhaps a year earlier and taken into a private collection (Smith and Miller 2009: 42–50, Figs. 3.5–3.7). As a direct and fortuitous outcome of an exhibition at the Tennessee State Museum in Nashville in 2015–2016 (Weeks et al. 2015), however, this kneeling female figure—skirted and exhibiting a number of characteristics that convincingly support its attribution to the same artist who carved and ornamented the male—was purchased for the McClung Museum, where the ancestral pair were reunited.[1]

Figure 8.1. Ancestral pair of male and female figures, stone; Martin Farm site, Riddleton, Smith County, Tennessee. *Left,* male, h. 38 cm; private collection; *right,* female, h. 33 cm; National Museum of Natural History, Smithsonian Institution (334009). Photograph by David H. Dye.

Figure 8.2. Ancestral pair of male and female figures, stone; Frost Farm, near Brentwood, Williamson County, Tennessee. *Left,* male, h. 34 cm; National Museum of the American Indian, Smithsonian Institution (007277); *right,* female, h. 31 cm; Gates P. Thruston Collection, Tennessee State Museum (82.100.1091). Photograph by David H. Dye.

Given the evidence of even the few surviving examples of wooden figures of comparable scale and posture that have been recovered from a cave in Bell County, Kentucky (Pepper 1921; Smith and Miller 2009: 19, Fig. 2.3), from the Craig Mound at Spiro, Oklahoma (Brown 1985: 137–138, Pls. 95–96), and from what we can glean from the early post-contact–era reports of statuary "idols" in temple settings, there is every reason to believe that a sculptural tradition of anthropomorphic figures in wood and perhaps other perishable material existed prior to the appearance of stone statuary in the Tennessee-Cumberland region and may even have continued alongside it (Brown 2001). Certainly, among the early sources on European contact with Native "idols," several document both male and female statuary, about which Brown (2001: 77) notes that "in the context of the mortuary temple, these figures constitute a material embodiment of the venerated ancestors."

In his remarks in 1730 on the Natchez "temple filled with Idols," the Jesuit priest Mathurin le Petit documented both male and female effigies. He noted the placement on shelves of "cane baskets of an oval shape, and in [which] are enclosed the bones of their ancient Chiefs" (Le Petit 1925); nearby were the bones of those of their retinue who were sacrificed "to follow their masters into the other world. Another separate shelf supports many flat baskets [that are] very gorgeously painted, in which they preserve their Idols. These are figures of men and women made of stone and baked clay, the heads and the tails of extraordinary serpents, some stuffed owls, some pieces of crystal, and some jaw-bones of large fish" (Le Petit 1925). From his description, these basketed collections suggest an assemblage of sacred bundles, which are known to have contained anthropomorphic effigies, animal pelts, claws, beaks, skulls, and other powerful elements such as crystals, white sage, gourd rattles, as well as seeds, ear(s) of corn, and similar items (Bowers 1992 [1963]; Peters 2000 [1995]; Richert 1969).

While the burial of the Etowah marble statues in Mound C has been dated to the late Wilbanks phase (AD 1325–1375; King 2004), Smith and Miller (2009: 99)—knowing that these images of the ancestors would have been venerated and protected for a period of time as temple statuary prior to burial—have estimated the date of the creation of this pair of guardians to be between AD 1250 and 1325. Although the earliest occupation of Mississippian peoples at the Sellars site may have occurred by AD 1000, recognizing that the site may have been abandoned and later reoccupied (Beahm 2013: 69–74, Table 4.8), Smith and Miller (2009: 157–164) have estimated that the creation and deposition of the Sellars statues took place between AD 1200 and 1350.

The Cahokia Style of Flint-Clay Figurines and Figural Pipes

In defining what characterizes the Tennessee-Cumberland style of stone statuary, Smith and Miller (2009) enumerate the attributes that distinguish these works from the figurines and figural pipes fashioned from Missouri flint-clay as much as a century earlier, during the Stirling phase (AD 1100–1200) at Cahokia. Although not alone in their efforts to document, analyze, and interpret the Cahokian flint-clay figures, for the past four decades Thomas Emerson and his colleagues at the Illinois State Archaeological Survey and the University of Illinois at Urbana-Champaign have generated a distinguished body of research devoted to these figures, their sourcing and production, the contexts of their discovery, and their meaning and significance (e.g., Alt and Pauketat 2007; Boles 2014, 2020, 2022; Emerson 1982, 1983, 1989, 1997, 2003, 2015, 2022; Emerson and Boles 2010; Emerson and Girard 2004; Emerson and Hughes 2000; Emerson et al. 2002, 2003; Emerson and Jackson 1984; Farnsworth and Emerson 1989; Fortier 1992).

According to the most complete tally to date (Boles 2020: Table 3.1a), the Cahokia-style flint-clay corpus includes thirty-nine anthropomorphic figures, many of them made as or modified to be used as pipes: nine female figures and twenty-one males, whole or fragmentary. Nine other anthropomorphic figures or fragments thereof are indeterminate in regard to their sex. In addition, fifteen animals are also represented in the existing corpus; three-quarters of these are frogs, while the others depict raptors, a squirrel, and a crayfish, the most recent addition to this body of works (Boles 2017). Boles (2020) has also carefully cataloged an additional fifty-nine fragments from twelve separate locations, mostly from habitations at or near Cahokia.

What makes the Cahokian flint-clay corpus so compelling and its emergence in the Stirling phase so striking is the application of imaginative and artistic talent to the production of anthropomorphic figures in the extremely receptive medium of Missouri flint-clay, whose material composition lent itself to carving with stone tools and the rendering of fine details unachievable in sandstone. Artists at Cahokia produced a varied, animated, and original body of figurative images: one small kneeling female holding forth a conch-shell cup (Exchange Avenue figurine); another kneeling female hoeing the broad back of an immense, puma-headed serpent with a bifurcated tail that sprouts squashes or gourds (Birger figurine; Prentice 1986); another kneeling female leaning slightly forward with one of her hands at rest on the lid of a sizable sacred bundle basket, while the other grasps a plant stalk (Keller figurine). Other females, even several fragmentary ones, seem almost in an intimate embrace of serpents or hold forth to us—emerging from the palms of her hands—cane stalks or sunflower stalks whose mature seed heads rest upon her back (Sponemann, Willoughby, West, and Westbrook figurines). Time and again, on these flint-clay females we see pouches or twined bags that may be seed containers, as well as sacred bundle baskets made of woven lengths of split cane.[2]

While the crafting of the male figure pipes displays an equal richness of imagination and quality of sculptural ability, on the whole, the male flint-clay works present a somewhat different story. The female figures have been found in the vicinity of Cahokia in nearby shrine contexts (viz., BBB Motor site, Sponemann site, and East St. Louis), and only twice in burials—both times well removed from Cahokia. The males, however, already more than twice the number of females, have been found broadly distributed across the South from Oklahoma to eastern Tennessee and in burials or burial mounds the majority of times. These differences in archaeological context, function, and deposition suggest that the two groups of statuettes and pipes satisfied the ritual needs of distinct groups, perhaps serving entirely separate cults.

The difference in subject matter exemplified by the female and male flint-clay figurines and effigy pipes from Cahokia has been remarked upon by various scholars (Boles 2020; Brown 2011; Emerson 1997, 2015; Mueller and Fritz 2016; Prentice 1986) and is central to Kent Reilly's (2004) thesis regarding "People of Earth, People of Sky." The cluster of associations that directly pertain to the female figurines—serpents, both feline-headed and rattle-tailed; sacred bundle baskets and seed bags; a marine shell cup; plant stalks issuing from her palms and vines growing alongside her, both yielding their fruit: squashes and sunflower pods; her explicit act of hoeing the serpent/earth—these actions and attributes are symbols, and not simple ones. They are complex, overlapping, and synecdochic: individually and collectively they stand for the entire realm that the Earth Mother oversees. The watery Beneath World, from which comes the source that sustains the fertility of all vegetation, is but the most immediate of her domains. Recognizing her as "the progenitor of all living things" (Hultkrantz 1983: 202), Hultkrantz (1983: 206) can affirm that the mother goddess "who rules the plants is in charge of the germinating powers of the underworld and the subterranean realm of the dead." Given the nine flint-clay female figurines that have been discovered, we can see that the sum of their combined symbolic and individual artistic statements is startlingly coherent. Although they vary in size and modeling and exhibit little evidence that they are from the hand of a single artist, nor part of any set of figures created for a single tableau, their closely related content strongly suggests that their Stirling-phase makers shared—within their community—some well-established religious beliefs and ritual practices (Alt 2020; Alt and Pauketat 2018; Emerson 2015).

And this difference in subject matter between the male and female flint-clay statuettes and figure pipes is perhaps what we should expect, given the triad of cult institutions that Brown (1985) and Knight (1986) articulated as coexisting in Mississippian societies. Brown's (1985) definition of cult—"a formalized set of rites dedicated to the veneration or propitiation of specific individuals, spirits, or forces" (103)—remains a useful one, whether we are talking about an ancestor, warfare, or fertility cult. We must recognize that the symbolic consistency that has been noted in the corpus of female flint-clay figures is not accidental: instead, that iconographical coherence is the direct result of the actions conducted within small communities of individuals responsible for the rites and ceremonial practices that sustain the proper relationship with, in this case, the Earth Mother. Among the deities or supernatural beings of the Mississippian cosmology—a small number that includes the Earth Mother, the Great Serpent, and the Hero Twins—she is the guardian of life-generating forces (Dye 2012, 2015; Emerson 2015; Sharp 2007, 2019; Sharp et al. 2020). If, as Emerson (2015: 58–59) has stated, "The BBB Motor and Sponemann sites are archetypal examples of Cahokian temple complexes dedicated to fertility, death and life renewal ceremonialism, and Earth Mother," then I want to assert that those exercising responsibility over these temples and assembling and managing the requisite sacred paraphernalia, including the crafting and materializing of images of the principal deity, must almost certainly have been Mississippian women, conscious of the breadth and variety of the Earth Mother's realm. Expanding on her earlier study with Natalie Mueller (Mueller and Fritz 2016), Gayle Fritz (2019) has articulated an important understanding of the role of women at Cahokia, and clarified that the agents responsible for the flint-clay figures need not have been members of a politically powerful priestly elite; instead, they may have been part of a women's sodality such as "the historical Hidatsa and Mandan Goose Society—consisting of married women in their childbearing years who were the primary farmers" (Fritz 2019: 113). Thus, she continues, "If their supernatural patroness was a figure who survived into modern times as Old Woman Who Never Dies, we can interpret sacred Cahokian precincts as places where rituals invoking this Earth Mother were performed, and where images of her were honored and ultimately buried" (Fritz 2019: 113).

The Subset of Earth Mother Figures in the Tennessee-Cumberland Stone Statuary

What now seems apparent is that within fifty to one hundred years after the Stirling-phase production of flint-clay effigy figurines and the related suite of figure pipes at Cahokia, another sculptural tradition of anthropomorphic figures in stone made its appearance in the Middle Tennessee region.[3] As Smith and Miller (2009) have established, the Tennessee-Cumberland ancestral pairs appear to have been in use as temple statuary or shrine sacra by the middle of the thirteenth century and continued for another hundred years (Smith and Miller 2009: 157–163; Smith and Sharp 2018). Materially, archaeologically, and stylistically, the two groups display important fundamental differences. Whereas the Cahokia-style corpus, both male and female, are carved of the same material, the Tennessee-Cumberland group are made of varied, locally available types of stone (Bow 2020) and appear not to have moved far from where they were materialized. While I have already described the rich variety of actions in which the flint-clay figures are engaged, the often intriguing array of iconographical elements associated with them, and the fine detail of their execution, the Tennessee-Cumberland figures have been sculpted in only a few positions, all of which display a formal reserve, with primary attention to the face and hairstyle sufficient to distinguish them by sex according to a few conventions of representation (Smith and Miller 2009: 14–16). Nonetheless, though dramatically simpler in detail, they are significantly larger than the flint-clay pieces, and at their best these stone sculptures surely engaged the viewer's attention and gave assurance of their attention to prayers and entreaties.

What I have not addressed thus far, however, is the second subset of Tennessee-Cumberland-style stone statuary that Smith and Miller cataloged and that set in motion something profoundly new and revelatory in Mississippian art. In addition to presenting a number of ancestral pairs, the exhibition at the Tennessee State Museum (TSM) mentioned above (Weeks et al. 2015) afforded visitors an opportunity to study a small sample of the dozen or so female figures that, while also perhaps used as shrine sacra, appear to have been sculpted with no male counterpart. While Smith and Miller throughout their monographic study generally chose to describe these figures under the rubric of Old Woman (Smith and Miller 2009: 31–36), I have selected one of their several other frequently given identifiers, Earth Mother, judging it to be less restrictive than more widely cited nineteenth-century terms such as Old Woman Who Never Dies or Our Grandmother, and possibly more attentive to diverse, local identities (Colvin 2012; Diaz-Granados 2004; Duncan and

Diaz-Granados 2004; Koehler 1997; Prentice 1986; Weeks et al. 2015). Smith and Miller (2009: 33) define the conditions that distinguish this second group: "A subset of the statues in our survey is interpreted as representing a theme distinct from that of ancestral pairs. While sharing most of the characteristics marking female gender, these statues include two additional traits that appear to significantly set these apart from the statuary pair females: (a) hands resting on an often projecting abdomen; and/or (b) sculpting of the vulva."

As happened with the members of the ancestral pairs, these single females have by and large been plowed up since the second half of the nineteenth century, during the long period of intensifying settlement and the conversion of occupied land to Western agricultural purposes. Like them as well, the kneeling position in which these single females are shown is familiar, unsurprising, and universal. Yet, as Smith and Miller have shown us, all who study such collections as these must wrestle with the errors, confusions, and ravages caused by the accidental discovery of these sculptures and their unprofessional curation over time. Differences in description, identification, and interpretation will invariably result. Limitations in access to other pieces may have led to further misunderstanding. But from the dozen or so Earth Mother statues recorded in Smith and Miller (2009: Tables A.1 and A.2), seven figures appear to this author to have their hands across the abdomen; five reveal their genitalia. And at least two of the females in the group appear to have been associated with burials.

Dr. Joseph Jones, an antiquarian who published in 1876 one of the first studies of Native American art in Tennessee, had two of these female sculptures in his collection that were prominently featured in the Tennessee State Museum exhibition (Weeks et al. 2015). Found somewhere in the "Valley of the Cumberland River" (Jones 1876: 129, Figs. 67–68), one statue (Smith and Miller 2009: 203–204, Fig. B.1; CSS-045), now in the holdings of the Smithsonian's National Museum of the American Indian (NMAI, cat. 007276), is upright and straight-backed, and her vulva is clearly displayed. Her arms lie alongside her, her hands at her knees. She also exhibits the elongated hair bun that Middle Cumberland females most often display. A second stone statue, though plagued with contradictions about her place of origin, seems to have been dug up near McMinnville, Warren County, Tennessee (Smith and Miller 2009: 209–210, Fig. B.7; CSS-024). This sculpture depicts the other most frequent attribute of these single Earth Mother statues: with her arms bent at the elbow, her hands come together and rest against a noticeably swelling abdomen. This work also resides in the NMAI (cat. 210965).

Other important examples documenting the central place of these single Earth Mother sculptures in the shrine rituals could not be included in the

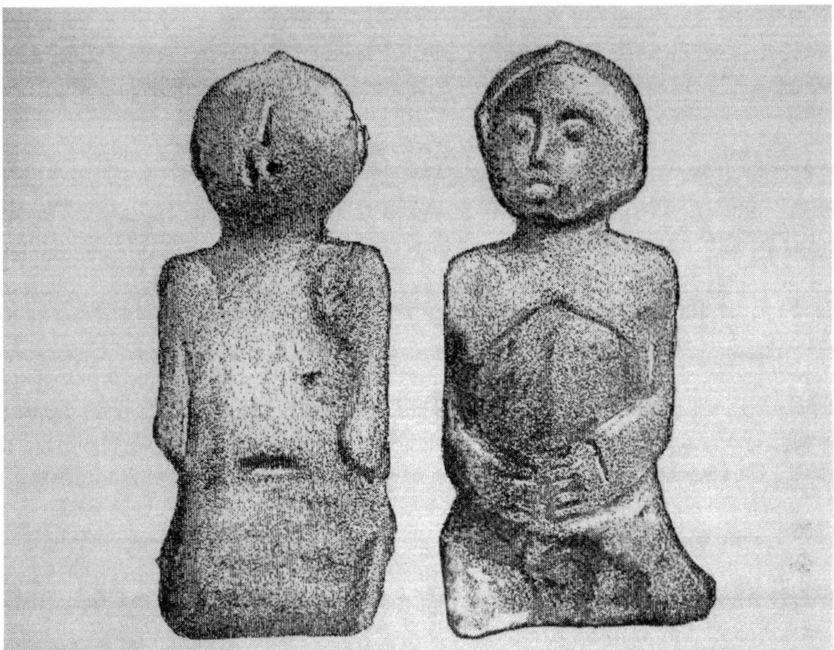

Figure 8.3. Female figure, stone; near Piper's Ford, Smith County, Tennessee; h. 38 cm; plowed up sometime prior to 1880, but later destroyed in William E. Myer's house fire. Illustration adapted from Thruston 1890: Fig. 28.

TSM exhibition because they are no longer extant or cannot be located. Tennessee archaeologist William Edward Myer had in his collection one statue (Figure 8.3; Smith and Miller 2009: 114–116; CSS-020) that was plowed up prior to 1880 near the Piper's Ford site in Smith County, near the confluence of the Caney Fork and the Cumberland River, but later destroyed in Myer's house fire. This kneeling female, upright and straight-backed as well, had an elongated and perforated hair bun and rested her hands against her abdomen. Following Thruston (1890: 107, Fig. 28), who illustrated this work from photographs Myer had supplied him, Smith and Miller (2009: 116) concur that this now-lost Earth Mother sculpture exhibited traces of a "garment . . . depicted across the front (similar to the hooded negative painted bottles)"—a significant detail as will soon become evident.

A second notable work (Figure 8.4; Smith and Miller 2009: 61–67; CSS-017) from the heartland of the Tennessee-Cumberland Earth Mother statuary is at present known only from a cast in the Smithsonian's National Museum of Natural History (cat. 61259). The record of attribution and location of the original sculpture is as knotted as these matters can get, all documented by

Figure 8.4. Female figure, stone; Beasley Mounds, Smith County, Tennessee, h. 32 cm; present location unknown; cast at National Museum of Natural History, Smithsonian Institution (61259). Illustration adapted from Thruston 1890: Plate 4.

Smith and Miller (2009). What's important for our purposes is that this kneeling female statue, probably from the Beasley Mounds site in Smith County, rests her hands at her knees and with her arms positioned to frame her midriff, as noted by Smith and Miller (2009: 63), "the protruding abdomen . . . appears to indicate pregnancy." This depiction of her condition will also take on additional importance.

Although others in the subset of single females may not be quite so uniform, the four stone figures I have discussed present a sharp contrast to any expectations one might have about a depiction of Old Woman: there is no evidence of advanced age and no sign of the humpbacked condition kyphosis commonly on elderly women and thought to characterize Mississippian female effigies (Sharp et al. 2011: 186). At this moment in the known sculptural corpus of Earth Mother, the depiction of her is, in this respect, largely uniform across all three sets of figures, whether in Missouri flint-clay from Cahokia, or as one of an ancestral pair from the Tennessee-Cumberland region, or from the somewhat more limited number of single female statues. There are, among the ancestral pairs, figures such as the Sellars male and Sellars female that may appear to be older, or display signs of advancing age: in addition to a furrowed brow or wrinkles at the outside corner of their eyes, there is on each a sagging fold of skin running down the center of the neck as well as the presence of nasolabial folds, which become more pronounced with age and that may therefore signal that they are recognized as the ancestors responsible for the founding of the chiefly lineage or at the very least revered elders of the community.[4]

Then what are we to say about these single females, each one sculpted by a different artisan it would seem, but sharing critical elements of form and made in such a way that all four emphasize their upright, emphatically straight-backed youthfulness—and showing, on close to half of the entire subset of *unpaired* females, the very evident statement of their sex. What happens next in the Middle Cumberland region sometime around AD 1250 is, I believe, directly related to the compelling presence, formal qualities, and mortuary associations of these stone statuary females, and the preponderance of evidence suggests that the contributions of Mississippian women had a determining influence on the material culture and mortuary practices that emerged in the late thirteenth century.

Women's Ritual Sodalities and the Emergence of Female Effigy Bottles in the MCR

While the few examples of stone female figures recovered from mortuary contexts at various sites in the Middle Cumberland River valley are exceptions to the larger body of ancestral pairs that, whether reported as dug up or plowed up, are *not* associated with graves, a rapid and radical change took place in the material culture and ritual practices of the MCR, significant enough to be distinct from the treatment accorded the ancestral couples: that is, beginning around AD 1250, the creation of an untold number of female figures, now in the form of *ceramic* female effigy bottles that are almost without exception recovered from burials. When they first appear, in the second half of the thirteenth century, these ceramic females are not just comparable in form to the stone examples I have shown and discussed above: they are, if not replicas, then closely modeled on them, reproduced at a slightly smaller scale, but in much greater quantity, and ultimately deposited as burial objects. The striking similarities between the youthful, straight-backed stone statues that were probably shrine sacra and the comparable ceramic examples may suggest to some simply the continuance of religious devotion to a female deity such as Earth Mother in the more widely available medium of clay, but I contend that what the ceramic examples illustrate is the emergence of a new way of visualizing and materializing this supernatural personage, the veneration of whom was shared by members of a religious sodality dedicated to her (Dye 2012, 2015, 2020; Sharp 2019; Sharp et al. 2020).

I recently addressed the available evidence for this argument (Sharp 2019), and some essential points are critical in this discussion. First, at least sixteen ceramic female effigies—kneeling and often tightly skirted—have been identified from sites across the MCR from Stewart County in the west to Smith County in the east that bear a strong stylistic resemblance not only to each other but to the four stone female statues discussed above (Figures 8.3 and 8.4). Second, in addition to having their hands held against the abdomen or resting alongside their thighs, these ceramic examples (Figures 8.5 and 8.6) show sufficient evidence of having been negative-painted with a design that represents a negative-painted shawl wrapped around the female—thus the appellation "Woman in the Patterned Shawl" (Sharp et al. 2011). Although most textiles do not survive long in burials, the record of their fabrication can often be gleaned from fabric-impressed sherds and from images such as these ceramic figures that show textiles being worn. Penelope Drooker's (1992) study of Mississippian textiles and her examples of hand-twined openwork fabrics and ceremonial garments that may be the inspiration for what has been negative-painted on these ceramic figures provided an important contribution to our interpretation. In addition to the long-established consensus that women are the principal potters in eastern North America, Sarah M. Nelson's (1997: 109, 2004: 84) assessment that textiles are likewise the product of women's labor brings us even closer to understanding the levels of both ritual engagement and artistic responsibility exemplified by these ceramic effigies that would support an argument that their potters were Mississippian women.

Third, the significance of the physical and material characteristics shared by these ceramic examples is especially strengthened when the mortuary context of these effigies is factored into this entire equation: ever since Kevin Smith's (1992: 270–274, Fig. 69) tabulation that ceramic effigy bottles are most often buried in the graves of infants, children, and other subadults in the MCR, additional examples, whenever the context of their discovery is known, have confirmed Smith's tally. Thus, in addition to consistency of subject and ornamentation—i.e., youthful female figures depicted as wearing textiles that display the same negative-painted design—the context of their discovery in the graves of children provides critical support for the belief that the makers of these ceramic figures were women, and, in this case, sixteen different women who shared with each other not only the skills to make such effigy bottles and to adorn them by means of a technique restricted in knowledge and circulation, but also shared an understanding of the meaning of the negative-painted

Figure 8.5. Female effigy bottle with negative-painted ornamentation; from a bluff shelter on the Cumberland River, near Beasley's Bend, Smith County, Tennessee; ceramic, h. 22.9 cm. Private collection. Photograph by David H. Dye.

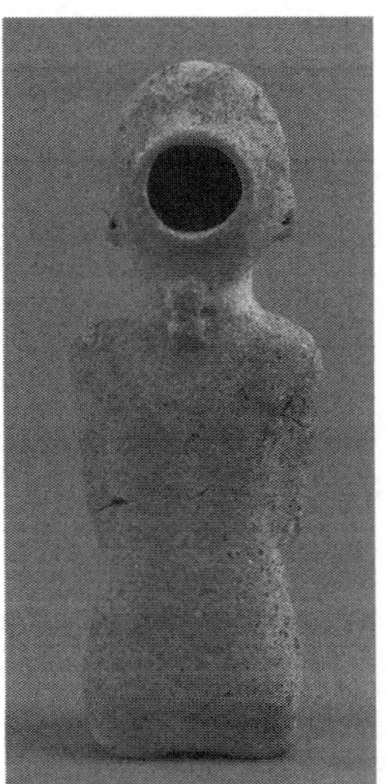
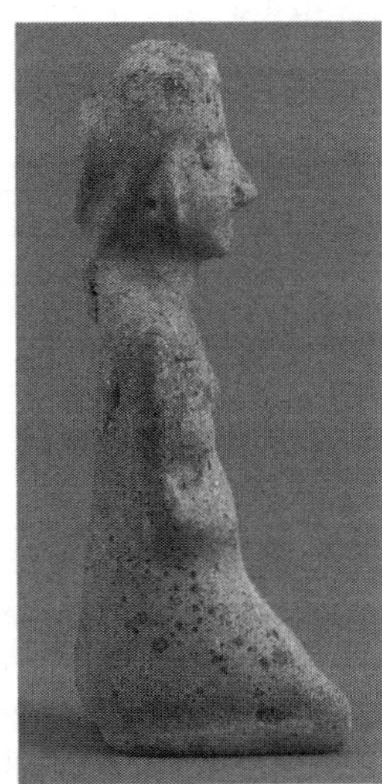

Figure 8.6. Female effigy bottle; Stewart County, Tennessee; ceramic, h. 19 cm. Private collection. Photograph by David H. Dye.

design, why it was appropriate for the Earth Mother to display it, and what was intended or expected by its ultimate deposition in the grave of a child.

Fourth, fragments of similar negative-painted female effigy bottles have been found in non-mortuary contexts at the Castalian Springs site in Sumner County, and one of these fragments, recovered during an archaeological field school conducted by Kevin Smith and Emily Beahm in 2011, has been radiocarbon dated to AD 1275–1319 (Smith et al. 2012). Castalian Springs was also the site of the discovery of a hollow ceramic figurine of a kneeling female bearing the complete pattern negative-painted around her. This figurine was in the collection of archaeologist William Edward Myer, who published it (1917 and 1928), identified it as a rattle, and noted that it was not removed from a grave. Fragments of other negative-painted females recovered at Castalian Springs have given support to a belief that the earliest appearances of ceramic female effigy bottles and figurines may not only have spread across the MCR by the mid-thirteenth century but also have been centered at Castalian Springs as the homeland for the first wave of this artistic expression (Smith and Beahm 2010).

Finally, the design replicated on the cloak-like garments that the ceramic female figures are depicted as wearing has been shown to be one illustrated on a shell cup recovered from the Craig Mound at Spiro (Sharp 2007, 2019: 22–24, Fig. 17). The replication of that design was undertaken multiple times by and among a sizable network of women who fashioned these ceramic figures and ornamented them in the same manner by sharing the coveted knowledge of the process of negative painting and the meaning of the design itself and, ultimately, its connection to mythic narratives about the Earth Mother, of course, but also the Hero Twins and their involvement in rebirth and reincarnation (Sharp et al. 2020: 327–332, Figs. 15.1–15.3). Certainly, knowledge of the engraved shell cup demonstrates that communities across the MCR received at least part of the migration of people leaving Cahokia around 1200 (Sharp et al. 2020). But the rapid spread of this new mortuary practice across the Middle Cumberland region, the consistency of representation of the kneeling female figure, the uniformity of design applied to the negative painting by the various women artists who shared in this belief system—these are the hallmarks of a religious sodality responding to the influx of new ideas and demonstrating its responses visually, materially, and rapidly. Ann Thrift Nelson (1976) has documented Native American women's sodalities responsible for ritual fertility ceremonies, curing, and "the complex of associations between women and agriculture, women and fertility, women and birth and growth" (Nelson 1976: 56–57). But sodalities can transcend kinship and local residence, and as Elman Service observed (1963: xxii), "unify persons who belong to different residential groups." John Ware (2014: 34) notes that "sodalities in western North America are invariably legitimized by their connection to the supernatural world and almost always have a sacred history in which various spirits brought medicine, rain, and health to the community through the intercession of the association." Ware (2014: 35) also consolidated information from several studies that suggest that sodalities "may become very important during times of ethnic mixing, migration, and other unstable social conditions," all of which would appear to apply to the MCR in the late twelfth century and the early thirteenth.

Archaeological reports have consistently acknowledged the influx of nonlocal people into the western periphery of the Middle Cumberland region that began around AD 1000 (Eckhardt and Guidry 2018; Moore et al. 2006; Moore and Smith 2001, 2009, 2012 [2009]; Smith and Moore 1999; Spears et al. 2008). We have already seen that the nature of the response of Middle Cumberland women to the religious and cosmological ideas and ritual practices brought into the MCR during the early part of the Moorehead phase (AD 1200–1300) was never wholesale adoption. Certainly, the depictions of the Earth Mother by Middle Cumberland women do not resemble the known corpus of the nine flint-clay female statuettes made at Cahokia. The conscious decisions of Middle Cumberland women to focus on particular aspects of the Earth Mother that were relevant to them and to materialize their own personal images of her—the deity they envisioned, venerated, and solicited for aid and health and care—are noticeably different from those of the artisans whose figures were recovered from the shrines at the BBB Motor and Sponemann sites. Yet, while it might appear that there are on the Middle Cumberland ceramic female figures no apparent serpents, no bundle baskets, no shell cups, and no plant stalks, such as we have seen in Cahokia, nonetheless, important aspects of their ideology and religious beliefs are still being communicated, principally through their adoption of the uniform negative-painted pattern (Sharp 2008, 2009, 2019, 2021; Sharp et al. 2020; Smith and Sharp 2014). Clearly, the women artists of the MCR, whether working in locally available types of stone or in negative-painted ceramics, produced figures that were substantially different from those at Cahokia: their own images are kneeling in repose, arms at rest, as we have seen, or held against the abdomen, possibly as an assurance—if the ultimate deposition of the figures in the graves of children can be invoked—of their fertility, if not an indicator of pregnancy itself.

I recognize that an argument for attributing the sculpting of stone statues to women has not, to my knowledge, been made about these figures, and that in doing so, I am extending to Mississippian women an additional area of responsibility and artistic expression as well as an expanded role of influence within their communities. Joan Gero's (1991) "genderlithics" analysis, however, drew significant attention to the involvement of women in stone tool production when they have access to locally available raw materials with which to work. That fact, coupled with Gero's insistence (1991: 186) that we not "assume a simple correspondence between one productive process and one sex," seemed to open an opportunity to examine the very close correspondence in form and intent between the subset of single stone figures and the new and much larger corpus of ceramic effigies that women artists began to produce in the mid-thirteenth century, without necessarily having to attribute the entire body of Tennessee-Cumberland statuary to them. To have attributed everything to them would have been an act of "gender polarization," precisely the type of judgment about the division of labor and assumptions about artistic responsibility for the figuration of females that Nelson (1997, 2004) and others (Claassen 1992; Gero and Conkey 1991; Joyce 2008) have sought to correct.

The Role of Middle Cumberland Women in the Representation of a Mississippian Deity

Issues such as fertility and pregnancy are critical for an understanding of the role of Middle Cumberland women not only in creating stone statues of their principal deity in the mid-thirteenth century, but also then essentially adapting that form, preserving its posture and solemnity, and transferring those qualities to the medium of clay in order to extend its application to mortuary rites devoted to infants and children. The production of ceramic female effigy bottles in the MCR remains one of the signal achievements in the material culture of Mississippian peoples. What appears to have begun around AD 1250 in the MCR with the crafting of these ceramic effigies lasted until the large-scale evacuation of the region around AD 1450–1475 (Krus and Cobb 2018). David Dye (2015, 2020) has made a strong case that the use of ceramic female effigy bottles continued even longer—until the middle of the seventeenth century—in other parts of the Southeast, notably, in the Tunican homeland in northeast Arkansas and other areas of the Lower Mississippi Valley. Dye argues that local, spatially distinct styles displaying remarkable uniformity—such as the "open-topped" female effigy bottles from sites in the Pemiscot bayou of Missouri, including Brooks (23PM56) and Campbell (23PM5) and others such as Crosskno in northeast Arkansas (3MS18)—exemplify the type of sustained production under the control of religious sodalities to serve as personal guardian spirits for Tunican women.

What happened in the MCR prior to the abandonment of the area, however, involved notable changes, as the materialization of beliefs—in this case, the actual form, posture, and use of hooded bottles in the shape of female figures—continued to evolve in the fourteenth century, a period that has been well documented through the efforts of the Tennessee Division of Archaeology in salvage excavations at sites such as Gordontown (40DV6; Moore and Breitburg 1998; Moore et al. 2006) and Rutherford-Kizer (40SU15; Moore and Smith 2001). Furthermore, the Brentwood Library site (40WM210; Moore 2005) triggered a major reexamination of the excavations that had been conducted between 1877 and 1884 at numerous sites in Middle Tennessee by the Peabody Museum of Harvard University (Moore and Smith 2009, 2012 [2009]). Moore and Smith's reassessment yielded a landmark contribution to Middle Cumberland archaeology, without which such studies as the present one would be greatly handicapped. The ceramics recovered during the Peabody excavations—especially at such places as the Cain's Chapel site adjacent to the Noel Farm cemetery (40DV3) and the Gray Farm site (40WM11)—document the continued production of female effigy bottles and the continuance of the mortuary rites that included the deposition of ceramic female figures in the graves of children throughout the fourteenth century and right up to the period of exodus in the mid-to-late fifteenth century, as confirmed, for example, by excavations at the Averbuch site (40DV60; Cobb and Butler 2002; Klippel and Bass 1984; Krus and Cobb 2018; Moore and Smith 2007; Sharp et al. 2011). While a certain number of the changes that occurred in the fourteenth century are quite evidently stylistic ones, they should not distract us from principal features that display a surprising adherence to the larger symbolic and purposive import of the female effigy bottles.

Building on the work of Ian Brown (1990, 2006), who cataloged the human effigy bottles and figurines removed from burials during the Peabody Museum excavations, I have proposed the identification of several individual women artists responsible for the production of negative-painted ceramic female effigy bottles in the MCR and have attributed specific groups of examples to these women artists (Sharp 2011, 2019; Smith and Sharp 2014). Among the artist-potters identified are two in particular believed to have been responsible for more than two dozen female effigy vessels almost evenly divided between them (Figure 8.7; see Sharp 2019; Sharp et al. 2011). Although a complete examination of the evidence for these attributions cannot be provided in this chapter, there are several essential points that must be included here. First, 80% of the twenty-six female effigy vessels attributed to the two female potters are provenienced at the county level: 77% to known sites, all in the heartland

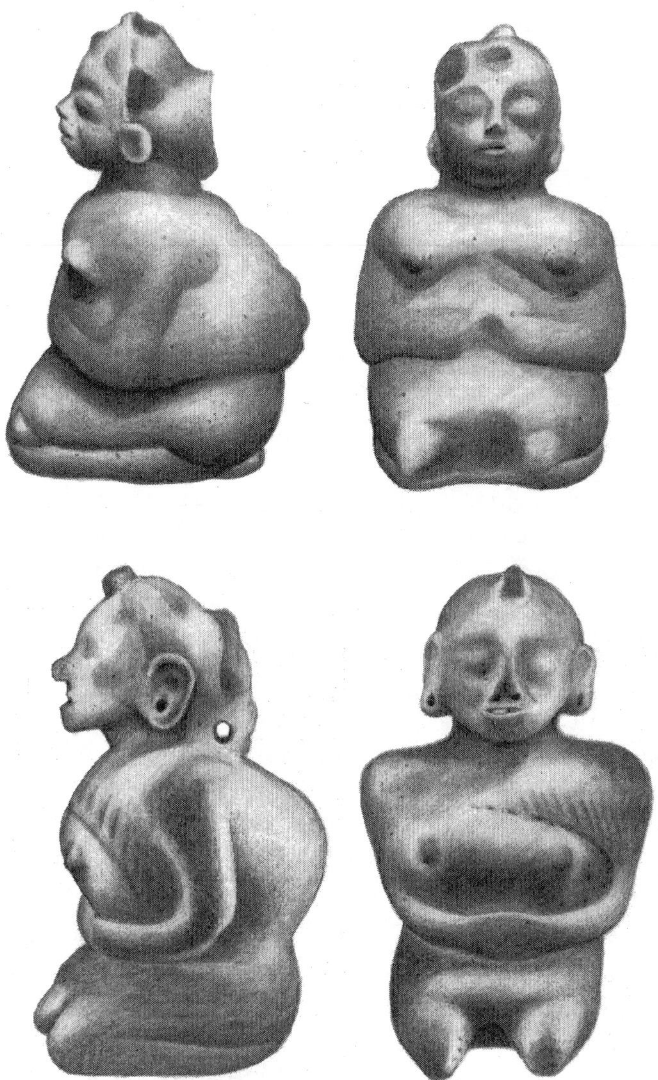

Figure 8.7. Comparison of two female effigy bottles; Averbuch site, Davidson County, Tennessee; *top,* profile and front views of bottle 362, ceramic, h. 17.7 cm; *below,* profile and front views of bottle 237, ceramic, h. 15.1 cm. Illustration © 2019, by Patricia J. Wynne. These two female effigy bottles from Averbuch represent the work of two different artist-potters, each of whom is credited with the crafting of a dozen or more similar pieces, distributed across the Middle Cumberland region.

of the Middle Cumberland region in Davidson, Robertson, Sumner, and Williamson counties. In many cases, of course, the knowledge that a particular effigy vessel was recovered from the Noel Farm cemetery, Rutherford-Kizer, the Gray Farm, or Averbuch will enable scholars to draw upon other information about burial assemblages from these sites for an enhanced understanding of context, relationships with other artifacts, a more accurate estimate of their period of use, and more.

Second, as was the case with the earliest female effigy bottles discussed above, while the technique of negative painting is known to be impermanent and highly perishable, whether applied directly to the surface or on top of a prepared slip of clay, wherever evidence of negative painting survives on these female effigy bottles, even in modest traces, the design originally applied to these vessels is the same one. These two women, the artist-potters of a dozen or more examples each, replicated the same design each time and circulated their effigy bottles to contacts in scattered communities across the MCR for the same apparent purpose each time.

Third, the design employed by these two artist-potters, who were master artisans in the craft of negative painting, would later be discovered on one or possibly two engraved shell cups removed from the Craig Mound at Spiro in the mid-1930s after having been deposited there sometime around AD 1400 (Phillips and Brown 1978: plate 2; Sharp 2019: Figure 17). The means by which this design was communicated and the direction of its movement from its place of origin remains a subject of speculation and study.

Fourth, in stark contrast to the "first wave" of production of the sixteen negative-painted female effigy bottles, all erect and straight-backed in their morphology and posture, made by perhaps as many as sixteen different women potters, in the "second wave" of ceramic human effigy bottles (perhaps AD 1300–1450), we see for the first time in the MCR the sudden appearance of *humpbacked* female effigy bottles and figurines. Furthermore, during this period, the two artist-potters responsible for their production created both straight-backed and humpbacked examples, all wearing the same type of garment, emblazoned with the same negative-painted pattern. In 2011 my colleagues and I (Sharp et al. 2011) judged that the figure we dubbed "Woman in the Patterned Shawl" depicted the same supernatural personage, regardless of whether she was shown straight-backed or humpbacked, because all of her other aspects or characteristics—e.g., hairstyle, facial structure, overall physique, etc.—as depicted by each artist, remained remarkably constant.

In 2014 Kevin Smith and I proposed a new title to acknowledge the alterations in her physique over time, "Middle Cumberland Changing Woman":

> We suggest that in the Middle Cumberland region . . . the specific lore focused on a Changing Woman: a deity who represented the female generative lifeforce, the ability to give birth; and a deity who reflected the changing face, body, and role of women over the course of their lives, a life cycle that included death and rebirth . . . . In the form of a negative-painted female effigy bottle, we interpret her as one part of the paraphernalia for a ritual associated with the curing and/or death of children and the protection of their free souls on the Path of Souls and their ultimate reincarnation as new members of their town. (Smith and Sharp 2014)

Conclusion

It should be clear by now that the earliest examples of ceramic female effigy bottles in the MCR (Figures 8.5 and 8.6), like the stone figures that they were first modeled after, are so upright and relatively slender that it is difficult not to identify them as youthful, especially in the context of the graves of infants and children, when it seems natural to interpret the combination of their form and their placement in burials as a statement of fertility, whether of a desire for new birth or a belief in rebirth (Hultkrantz 1953, 1967; Mills and Slobodin 1994). What I want to reexamine and refine is a judgment expressed in 2011 that the female figure represented in some of the fourteenth-century effigy bottles and figurines, even when they are "stout or even somewhat bloated through the midsection," were not intended to represent pregnant females, as "they certainly show no indication of the full or extended belly of a woman carrying a child late in her term" (Sharp et al. 2011: 179–180). Given how emphatic, how unmistakable, the condition of being humpbacked was made to appear, our first effort was focused on keeping readers from interpreting the straight-backed and humpbacked figures as two different personages. What Kevin Smith and I (Smith and Sharp 2014) posited was a revision that called attention to the changes that occur in us over time and that must be accepted and embraced as part of the larger cycle of life and death.

What I propose here is a slightly different interpretation of the emphatic statement of the humpbacked spinal condition that these women artist-potters are bestowing on their hand-modeled, negative-painted female effigies. For nearly two centuries, the women artists of the MCR, working within religious sodalities dedicated to the veneration and supplication of a female deity, retained a figural representation of that female deity whom they envisioned wearing a garment such as the artists themselves almost certainly wore, with a wrap-around emblem that meant something, as noted above

(Sharp 2019; Sharp and Smith 2015; Sharp et al. 2020; Smith and Sharp 2014), a motif included in a larger scene that invokes the exploits of the Hero Twins and their involvement with death and resurrection (Smith et al. 2018, 2019)—one element of the sacred narratives about these culture heroes that would be worthy of being engraved on large shell cups and carried off to Spiro.

There are Mississippian images of full-term pregnancies, of course: one can see them in the female effigy bottle from the Obion site in Henry County, Tennessee (Garland 1992: Fig. 54), or in a female effigy bottle in the Gilcrease Museum (5425.1333). Other Mississippian women made them, of course, but not Mississippian women from the communities we have been examining from the MCR. On these two images from the Obion site and in the Gilcrease collection, their arms are bent at the elbow so that their hands can cradle their abdomen, a natural gesture that we have already seen on a subgroup of the stone statues and a significant number of the earliest ceramic female effigies. It must be noted, however, that both of these females shown very evidently pregnant are also emphatically straight-backed. Therefore, the representational statement that we are to understand about them is that they are young and pregnant; or at least not so old as to be humpbacked. If that judgment is correct, then what interpretive changes are we to make when we see that two very productive artists in the fourteenth century have held constant the placement of the hands on the abdomen, have also held constant the negative-painted design on the garment that the figures are wearing, and have held constant the ultimate placement of the effigy vessel in the grave of a child, but have chosen to make the females emphatically humpbacked? All three physical aspects are symbolic: first of all, the hands on the abdomen may be a sign that the female depicted is conscious of her (pregnant) condition or aware of its potential importance, but in either case may also be aware of the risks she may face during pregnancy and childbirth and of her need for whatever protection she can receive against those risks. Second, it is now clear that the garment she wears declares her knowledge that it connotes the Hero Twins' mastery over death and their ability to be reincarnated (Sharp 2019; Sharp et al. 2020). And, third, that the addition of a humpback, acknowledged as a sign of advanced age, may, in combination with the first two, communicate that the woman who made this effigy bottle believes that the fertility granted to women by the Earth Mother and her tutelary role in their lives has been with them for a very long time.

If these symbolic elements have been accurately interpreted, then the contextual information gathered from site after site across the entire region—that the mortuary practice of placing these effigy bottles with the remains of children was sustained in the MCR for possibly two centuries—confirms the potency of these ceramic vessels, the heritage of the stone shrine sacra that first inspired them, and the critical role played within the larger community by the women who made them. The participation of these artist-potters in the mutually supportive environment of religious sodalities made them part of a broad network of like-minded women who sought to use these effigy bottles and figurines because these artistic materializations strengthened their own beliefs about the aid and comfort they would receive from the Earth Mother. As Iain Morley (2007: xxi) has stated, "material representations can permit the development of more explicit and precise concepts about the spiritual, and be seen to be directly connected with supernatural entities." In return, these Mississippian artists, as part of what Sullivan and Harle (2010: 236) call "culturally distinct units," are themselves strengthened, for, as Robert Hinde (2007: 323) explains, "belief in an unverifiable deity provides a feeling of affinity for others who share the belief, and thus provides a sense of community." Hinde continues, "Sometimes mystical powers are seen to reside in the material image, and sometimes the image is seen as providing access to the powers of the deity. . . . [B]elief in the power of an image is usually acquired as part of a world-view in a culture in which any distinction between sacred and secular is muted or absent, and religious beliefs are assimilated along with everyday aspects of the culture" (Hinde 2007: 324). As I believe we have now begun to see, these Middle Cumberland women, in addition to crafting negative-painted female effigy bottles, attempted further applications of their skills in the production of the entire range of other negative-painted ceramic vessels in the form of owl effigy bottles, Great Serpent bottles, and both Janus-faced bottles and human-head hooded bottles visualizing and materializing the Hero Twins (Smith et al. 2018, 2019). The achievement of these Middle Cumberland women artists is nothing less than the material culture we esteem and respect for its ability to illuminate their beliefs.

Acknowledgments

I wish to thank Rachel Briggs, Michaelyn Harle, and Lynne Sullivan for inviting me to submit a chapter to this volume, especially given that I was unable to participate in the initial Southeastern Archaeological Conference session that launched this project on Mississippian women. I want to acknowledge the unwavering support of David Dye and Kevin Smith in this and other undertakings. Finally, I am grateful to two anonymous reviewers for comments and queries that helped me strengthen this chapter.

Author's Note

No new data was collected specifically for this chapter. Some of the specific statuary discussed in the chapter are from private collections from private properties. While the claim status of others is unknown, they may be subject to the Native American Graves Protection and Repatriation Act.

Notes

1 Since the completion of this manuscript, I have learned that these sculptures and perhaps the cache as well have been removed from view, pending a claim made for their repatriation.
2 See also the excellent summary prepared by Mueller and Fritz (2016: Table 4.2), which is devoted expressly to the female flint-clay figures.
3 These works are distinct from the fluorite human figures found at sites ranging from Cahokia through southern Illinois and Indiana to western Kentucky and Tennessee (Boles 2014; Emerson 1982; Moorehead et al. 2000 [1929]; Smith and Miller 2009: 144–156; Wolforth and Wolforth 2000). But as these roughly half-dozen figures almost surely represent male figures exclusively, they will not figure further in this discussion, except to note that they too were apparently created after the flint-clay corpus was completed. The best-known example, from the Angel site in southern Indiana, was buried in Mound F probably sometime after its construction around 1250 and not later than 1350 (Smith and Miller 2009: 151–152, 159, Figs. 6.7–6.8; CSS-054).
4 All four stone sculptures that have been found on the Sellars Farm were exhibited in the *Ancestors* exhibition at the Tennessee State Museum (Weeks et al. 2015), and the ancestral pair (Smith and Miller 2009: CSS-002 and CSS-003) were later installed together at the McClung Museum of Natural History and Culture, University of Tennessee, Knoxville. Since the completion of this manuscript, I have learned that these sculptures have been removed from view, pending a claim made for their repatriation.

References Cited

Alt, Susan M.
2020 The Implications of the Religious Foundations at Cahokia. In *Cahokia in Context: Hegemony and Diaspora*, edited by Charles H. McNutt and Ryan M. Parish, pp. 32–48. University of Florida Press, Gainesville.

Alt, Susan M., and Timothy R. Pauketat
2007 Sex and the Southern Cult. In *Southeastern Ceremonial Complex: Chronology, Content, Context*, edited by Adam King, 232–250. University of Alabama Press, Tuscaloosa.
2018 The Elements of Cahokian Shrine Complexes and the Basis of Mississippian Religion. In *Religion and Politics in the Ancient Americas*, edited by Sarah B. Barber and Arthur A. Joyce, pp. 51–74. Routledge, New York.

Beahm, Emily L.

2013 Mississippian Polities in the Middle Cumberland Region of Tennessee. PhD dissertation, University of Georgia, Athens.

Bengtson, Jennifer D.

2017 Infants, Mothers, and Gendered Space in a Mississippian Village: Revisiting Wilkie's House 1 at the Hunze-Evans Site. *Childhood in the Past* 10(2): 102–121.

Boles, Steven L.

2014 Supernaturals in the Confluence Region. Paper presented at the 71st Annual Meeting of the Southeastern Archaeological Conference, Greenville, South Carolina.

2017 Earth-Diver and Earth Mother: Ancestral Flint Clay Figures from Cahokia. *Illinois Archaeology* 29: 127–146.

2020 Tracking Cahokians through Material Culture. In *Cahokia in Context: Hegemony and Diaspora*, edited by Charles H. McNutt and Ryan M. Parish, pp. 49–86. University of Florida Press, Gainesville.

2022 Cahokia's Wandering Supernaturals: What Does it Mean When the Earth Mother Leaves Town? In *Archaeologies of Cosmoscapes in the Americas*, edited by J. Grant Stauffer, Bretton T. Giles, and Shawn P. Lambert, pp. 47–65. Oxbow Books, Havertown, Pennsylvania.

Bow, Sierra May

2020 Characterizing Late Pre-Contact Mississippian Paint Recipes in the Southeastern United States. PhD dissertation, University of Tennessee, Knoxville.

Bowers, Alfred W.

1992 [1963] *Hidatsa Social and Ceremonial Organization*. Bulletin 194, Smithsonian Institution, Bureau of American Ethnology, Washington, D.C. Reprint. University of Nebraska Press, Lincoln.

Brown, Ian W.

1990 Catalog of the Human Effigy Vessels in the Collections of the Peabody Museum of Archaeology and Ethnology, Harvard University. Unpublished paper.

2006 The Hunchbacks of Tennessee: Ceramic Human Effigy Vessels in the Collections of the Peabody Museum of Archaeology and Ethnology, Harvard University. Unpublished manuscript.

Brown, James A.

1985 The Mississippian Period. In *Ancient Art of the American Woodland Indians*, edited by David S. Brose, James A. Brown, and David W. Penney, pp. 93–140. Harry N. Abrams, New York, in association with the Detroit Institute of Arts.

2001 Human Figures and the Southeastern Ancestor Shrine. In *Fleeting Identities: Perishable Material Culture in Archaeological Research*, edited by Penelope Ballard Drooker, pp. 76–93. Occasional Paper No. 28. Center for Archaeological Investigations, Southern Illinois University, Carbondale.

2011 The Regional Culture Signature of the Braden Art Style. In *Visualizing the Sacred: Cosmic Visions, Regionalism, and the Art of the Mississippian World*, edited by George E. Lankford, F. Kent Reilly III, and James F. Garber, pp. 37–63. University of Texas Press, Austin.

Claassen, Cheryl

2011 Rock Shelters as Women's Retreats: Understanding Newt Kash. *American Antiquity* 76(4): 628–641.

2016 Native Women, Men, and American Landscapes: The Gendered Gaze. In *Native American Landscapes: An Engendered Perspective*, edited by Cheryl Claassen, pp. xiii-xxxv. University of Tennessee Press, Knoxville.

Claassen, Cheryl, ed.

1992 *Exploring Gender through Archaeology: Selected Papers from the 1991 Boone Conference.* Monographs in World Archaeology No. 11. Prehistory Press, Madison, Wisconsin.

2016 *Native American Landscapes: An Engendered Perspective.* University of Tennessee Press, Knoxville.

Cobb, Charles R., and Brian M. Butler

2002 The Vacant Quarter Revisited: Late Mississippian Abandonment of the Lower Ohio Valley. *American Antiquity* 67(4): 625–641.

Colvin, Matthew H.

2012 Old-Woman-Who-Never-Dies: A Mississippian Survival in the Hidatsa World. Master's thesis, Department of Anthropology, Texas State University, San Marcos.

Diaz-Granados, Carol

2004 Marking Stone, Land, Body, and Spirit. In *Hero, Hawk, and Open Hand: American Indian Art of the Ancient Midwest and South*, edited by Richard F. Townsend and Robert V. Sharp, pp. 139–149. The Art Institute of Chicago and Yale University Press, New Haven, Connecticut.

Drooker, Penelope B.

1992 *Mississippian Village Textiles at Wickliffe.* University of Alabama Press, Tuscaloosa.

Duncan, James R., and Carol Diaz-Granados

2004 Empowering the SECC: The "Old Woman" and Oral Tradition. In *The Rock-Art of Eastern North America: Capturing Images and Insight*, edited by Carol Diaz-Granados and James R. Duncan, pp. 190–215. University of Alabama Press, Tuscaloosa.

Dye, David H.

2012 Mississippian Religious Traditions. In *The Cambridge History of Religions in America; Vol. 1, Pre-Columbian Times to 1790*, edited by Stephen J. Stein, pp. 137–155. Cambridge University Press, New York.

2015 Earth Mother Cult Ceramic Statuary in the Lower Mississippi Valley. Paper presented at the 72nd Annual Meeting of the Southeastern Archaeological Conference, Nashville.

2020 Anthropomorphic Pottery Effigies as Guardian Spirits in the Lower Mississippi Valley. In *Cognitive Archaeology: Mind, Ethnography, and the Past in South Africa and Beyond*, edited by David S. Whitley, Johannes H.N. Loubser, and Gavin Whitelaw, pp. 201–223. Routledge, London.

2021 The Link Farm Cache: Invoking the Ancestors and Supplicating the Hero Twins.

In *Mississippian Culture Heroes, Ritual Regalia, and Sacred Bundles*, edited by David H. Dye, pp. 161–210. Lexington Books, Lanham, Maryland.

Eckhardt, Sarah Levithol, and Hannah Guidry

2018 The Copper Creek Site (40SU317): A Multicomponent Mortuary Site in Goodlettsville, Sumner County, Tennessee. *Tennessee Archaeology* 9(2): 135–155.

Emerson, Thomas E.

1982 *Mississippian Stone Images in Illinois.* Circular No. 6. Illinois Archaeological Survey, Urbana.

1983 The Bostrom Figure Pipe and the Cahokian Effigy Style in the American Bottom. *Midcontinental Journal of Archaeology* 8(2): 257–267.

1989 Water, Serpents, and the Underworld: An Exploration into Cahokian Symbolism. In *The Southeastern Ceremonial Complex: Artifacts and Analysis; The Cottonlandia Conference*, edited by Patricia Galloway, pp. 45–92. University of Nebraska Press, Lincoln.

1997 Cahokian Elite Ideology and the Mississippian Cosmos. In *Cahokia: Domination and Ideology in the Mississippian World*, edited by Timothy R. Pauketat and Thomas E. Emerson, pp. 190–228. University of Nebraska Press, Lincoln.

2003 Materializing Cahokia Shamans. *Southeastern Archaeology* 22(2): 135–154.

2015 The Earth Goddess Cult at Cahokia. In *Medieval Mississippians: The Cahokian World*, edited by Timothy R. Pauketat and Susan M. Alt, pp. 55–60. School for Advanced Research Press, Santa Fe, New Mexico.

2022 Interpreting Context and Chronology of Cahokia-Caddo Mythic Female Stone Figures. *Southeastern Archaeology* 41(4): 203–215.

Emerson, Thomas E., and Douglas K. Jackson

1984 *The BBB Motor Site.* American Bottom Archaeology: FAI-270 Site Reports, Vol. 6. University of Illinois Press, Urbana, for the Illinois Department of Transportation, Springfield.

Emerson, Thomas E., and Jeffrey S. Girard

2004 Dating Gahagan and Its Implications for Understanding Cahokia-Caddo Interactions. *Southeastern Archaeology* 23(1): 57–64.

Emerson, Thomas E., and Randall E. Hughes

2000 Figurines, Flint Clay Sourcing, the Ozark Highlands, and Cahokian Acquisition. *American Antiquity* 65(1): 79–101.

Emerson, Thomas E., and Steven L. Boles

2010 Contextualizing Flint Clay Cahokia Figures at the East St. Louis Mound Center. *Illinois Archaeology* 22(2): 473–490.

Emerson, Thomas E., Randall E. Hughes, Mary R. Hynes, and Sarah U. Wisseman

2002 Implications of Sourcing Cahokia-Style Flint Clay Figures in the American Bottom and the Upper Mississippi River Valley. *Midcontinental Journal of Archaeology* 27: 309–338.

2003 The Sourcing and Interpretation of Cahokia-Style Figures in the Trans-Mississippi South and Southeast. *American Antiquity* 68(2): 287–314.

Farnsworth, Kenneth B., and Thomas E. Emerson

1989 The Macoupin Creek Figure Pipe and Its Archaeological Context: Evidence for

Late Woodland–Mississippian Interaction beyond the Northern Border of Cahokian Settlement. *Midcontinental Journal of Archaeology* 14: 18–37.

Fortier, Andrew C.

1992 Stone Figurines. In *The Sponemann Site 2: The Mississippian and Oneota Occupations (11-Ms-517)*, edited by Douglas K. Jackson, Andrew C. Fortier, and Joyce A. Williams, pp. 277–303. American Bottom Archaeology: FAI-270 Site Reports, Vol. 24. University of Illinois Press, Urbana, for the Illinois Department of Transportation, Springfield.

Fritz, Gayle J.

2019 *Feeding Cahokia: Early Agriculture in the North American Heartland.* University of Alabama Press, Tuscaloosa.

Garland, Elizabeth Baldwin

1992 *The Obion Site: An Early Mississippian Center in Western Tennessee.* Cobb Institute of Archaeology, Report of Investigations No. 7, Mississippi State University, Mississippi State.

Gero, Joan M.

1991 Genderlithics: Women's Roles in Stone Tool Production. In *Engendering Archaeology: Women and Prehistory*, edited by Joan M. Gero and Margaret W. Conkey, pp. 163–193. Basil Blackwell, Oxford.

Gero, Joan M., and Margaret W. Conkey, eds.

1991 *Engendering Archaeology: Women and Prehistory.* Basil Blackwell, Oxford.

Hinde, Robert A.

2007 The Worship and Destruction of Images. In *Image and Imagination: A Global Prehistory of Figurative Representation*, edited by Colin Renfrew and Iain Morley, pp. 323–331. McDonald Institute of Archaeological Research, Cambridge, England.

Holmes, William Henry

1886 *Ancient Pottery of the Mississippi Valley.* Bureau of American Ethnology, Annual Report 4, pp. 361–436. Government Printing Office, Washington, D.C.

Hultkrantz, Ake

1953 *Conceptions of the Soul among North American Indians: A Study in Religious Ethnology.* Monograph Series, Publication No. 1. The Ethnographical Museum of Sweden, Stockholm.

1967 *The Religions of the American Indians.* Translated by Monica Setterwall. University of California Press, Berkeley.

1983 The Religion of the Goddess in North America. In *The Book of the Goddess, Past and Present: An Introduction to Her Religion*, edited by Carl Olson, pp. 202–216. Crossroad, New York.

Jones, Joseph

1876 *Explorations of the Aboriginal Remains of Tennessee.* Smithsonian Contributions to Knowledge No. 259. Smithsonian Institution, Washington, D.C.

Joyce, Rosemary A.

2008 *Ancient Bodies, Ancient Lives: Sex, Gender, and Archaeology.* Thames and Hudson, New York.

King, Adam

2004 Power and the Sacred: Mound C and the Etowah Chiefdom. In *Hero, Hawk, and Open Hand: American Indian Art of the Ancient Midwest and South*, edited by Richard F. Townsend and Robert V. Sharp, pp. 151–165. The Art Institute of Chicago and Yale University Press, New Haven, Connecticut.

Klippel, Walter E., and William M. Bass, eds.

1984 *Averbuch: A Mississippian Manifestation in the Nashville Basin.* 2 vols. Department of Anthropology, University of Tennessee, Knoxville.

Knight, Vernon James, Jr.

1986 The Institutional Organization of Mississippian Religion. *American Antiquity* 51(4): 675–687.

2013 *Iconographic Method in New World Prehistory*. Cambridge University Press, New York.

Koehler, Lyle

1997 Earth Mothers, Warriors, Horticulturists, Artists, and Chiefs: Women among the Mississippian and Mississippian-Oneota Peoples, A.D. 1000 to 1750. In *Women in Prehistory: North America and Mesoamerica*, edited by Cheryl Claassen and Rosemary A. Joyce, pp. 211–226. University of Pennsylvania Press, Philadelphia.

Krus, Anthony M., and Charles R. Cobb

2018 The Mississippian Fin de Siècle in the Middle Cumberland Region of Tennessee. *American Antiquity* 83(2): 302–319.

Le Petit, Father Mathurin

1925 Letter to Father D'Avaugour (1730). In *The Jesuit Relations and Allied Documents; Travels and Explorations of the Jesuit Missionaries in North America (1610–1791)*, edited by Edna Kenton, pp. 406–428. Boni, New York.

Mills, Antonia, and Richard Slobodin, eds.

1994 *Amerindian Rebirth: Reincarnation Belief among North American Indians and Inuit.* University of Toronto Press, Toronto.

Moore, Michael C., ed.

2005 *The Brentwood Library Site: A Mississippian Town on the Little Harpeth River, Williamson County, Tennessee.* Tennessee Department of Environment and Conservation, Division of Archaeology, Research Series No. 15. Nashville.

Moore, Michael C., and Emanuel Breitburg, eds.

1998 *Gordontown: Salvage Archaeology at a Mississippian Town in Davidson County, Tennessee.* Tennessee Department of Environment and Conservation, Division of Archaeology, Research Series No. 11. Nashville.

Moore, Michael C., and Kevin E. Smith

2007 Mississippian Mortuary Pottery from the Nashville Basin: A Reanalysis of the Averbuch Site Ceramic Assemblage. Paper presented at the 64th Annual Meeting of the Southeastern Archaeological Conference, Knoxville, Tennessee.

2009 *Archaeological Expeditions of the Peabody Museum in Middle Tennessee, 1877–1884.* Tennessee Department of Environment and Conservation, Division of Archaeology, Research Series No. 16. Nashville.

2012 [2009] *Archaeological Expeditions of the Peabody Museum in Middle Tennessee, 1877–1884.* Revised electronic edition. Tennessee Department of Environment and Conservation, Division of Archaeology, Research Series No. 16. Nashville.

Moore, Michael C., and Kevin E. Smith, eds.
2001 *Archaeological Excavations at the Rutherford-Kizer Site: A Mississippian Mound Center in Sumner County, Tennessee.* Tennessee Department of Environment and Conservation, Division of Archaeology, Research Series No. 13. Nashville.

Moorehead, Warren K., Jay L. B. Taylor, Morris M. Leighton, and Frank C. Baker
2000 [1929] *The Cahokia Mounds.* University of Illinois Press, Urbana. Reprint edited by John E. Kelly. University of Alabama Press, Tuscaloosa.

Moore, Michael C., Emanuel Breitburg, Kevin E. Smith, and Mary Beth Trubitt
2006 One Hundred Years of Archaeology at Gordontown: A Fortified Mississippian Town in Middle Tennessee. *Southeastern Archaeology* 25(1): 89–109.

Morley, Iain
2007 Material Beginnings: An Introduction. In *Image and Imagination: A Global Prehistory of Figurative Representation*, edited by Colin Renfrew and Iain Morley, pp. xvii-xxii. McDonald Institute of Archaeological Research, Cambridge, England.

Mueller, Natalie G., and Gayle J. Fritz
2016 Women as Symbols and Actors in the Mississippi Valley: Evidence from Female Flint-Clay Statues and Effigy Vessels. In *Native American Landscapes: An Engendered Perspective*, edited by Cheryl Claassen, pp. 109–148. University of Tennessee Press, Knoxville.

Myer, William Edward
1917 The Remains of Primitive Man in Cumberland Valley, Tennessee. In *Proceedings of the 19th International Congress of Americanists, Washington, 1915*, pp. 96–102. Washington, D.C.
1928 Pictograph Slabs of America. In *Annaes do XX Congresso Internacional de Americanistas, Rio de Janeiro, 1922,* vol. 2, pp. 97–105. Rio de Janeiro, Brazil.

Nelson, Ann Thrift
1976 Women in Groups: Women's Ritual Sodalities in Native North America. *The Western Canadian Journal of Anthropology* 6(3): 29–67.

Nelson, Sarah Milledge
1997 *Gender in Archaeology: Analyzing Power and Prestige.* AltaMira Press, Walnut Creek, California.
2004 *Gender in Archaeology: Analyzing Power and Prestige.* 2nd ed. AltaMira Press, Walnut Creek, California.

Pepper, George H.
1921 A Wooden Image from Kentucky. *Indian Notes and Monographs* 10(7): 63–82.

Peters, Virginia Bergman
2000 [1995] *Women of the Earth Lodges: Tribal Life on the Plains.* Reprint. University of Oklahoma Press, Norman.

Phillips, Philip, and James A. Brown
1978 *Pre-Columbian Shell Engravings from the Craig Mound at Spiro, Oklahoma,* Part 1. Peabody Museum Press, Cambridge, Massachusetts.

Phillips, Philip, James A. Ford, and John B. Griffin
2003 [1951] *Archaeological Survey in the Lower Mississippi Alluvial Valley, 1940–1947.* Papers of the Peabody Museum of Archaeology and Ethnology, vol. 25. Reprint. University of Alabama, Tuscaloosa.

Prentice, Guy

1986 An Analysis of the Symbolism Expressed by the Birger Figurine. *American Antiquity* 51(2): 239–266.

Reilly, F. Kent, III

2004 People of Earth, People of Sky: Visualizing the Sacred in Native American Art of the Mississippian Period. In *Hero, Hawk, and Open Hand: American Indian Art of the Ancient Midwest and South*, edited by Richard F. Townsend and Robert V. Sharp, pp. 125–137. The Art Institute of Chicago and Yale University Press, New Haven, Connecticut.

Richert, Bernhard E., Jr.

1969 Plains Indians Medicine Bundles. Master's thesis, Department of Anthropology, University of Texas, Austin.

Service, Elman R.

1963 *Profiles in Ethnology.* Harper and Row, New York.

Sharp, Robert V.

2007 Iconographical Investigation of a Female Mortuary Cult Figure in the Ceramics of the Cumberland Basin. Paper presented at the 64th Annual Meeting of the Southeastern Archaeological Conference, Knoxville, Tennessee.

2008 Mississippian Regalia: From the Natural World to the Beneath World. Paper presented at the 65th Annual Meeting of the Southeastern Archaeological Conference, Charlotte, North Carolina.

2009 Clothed in the Serpent Robe: Mississippian Female Effigies and the Lords of the Beneath World. Paper presented at Texas State University, San Marcos.

2011 Effigy Styles of the Middle Cumberland Region. Paper presented to the Middle Cumberland Archaeological Society, Nashville.

2019 Our Lady of the Cumberland: Styles, Distribution, and Community. *Tennessee Archaeology* 10(1): 7–37.

2021 Earth Mother in the Middle Cumberland, Beneath World Powers, and a Portal to the Otherworld. In *Mississippian Culture Heroes, Ritual Regalia, and Sacred Bundles*, edited by David H. Dye, pp. 211–270. Lexington Books, Lanham, Maryland.

Sharp, Robert V., Vernon James Knight, Jr., and George E. Lankford

2011 Woman in the Patterned Shawl: Female Effigy Vessels and Figurines from the Middle Cumberland River Basin. In *Visualizing the Sacred: Cosmic Visions, Regionalism, and the Art of the Mississippian World*, edited by George E. Lankford, F. Kent Reilly III, and James F. Garber, pp. 177–198. University of Texas Press, Austin.

Sharp, Robert V., and Kevin E. Smith

2015 The Mother of Us All: Earth Mother and Her Children in the Ceramic Effigies of the Mississippian Period. Paper presented at the 72nd Annual Meeting of the Southeastern Archaeological Conference, Nashville, Tennessee.

Sharp, Robert V., Kevin E. Smith, and David H. Dye

2020 Cahokians and the Circulation of Ritual Goods in the Middle Cumberland Region. In *Cahokia in Context: Hegemony and Diaspora*, edited by Charles H. McNutt and Ryan M. Parish, pp. 319–351. University of Florida Press, Gainesville.

Smith, Kevin E.

1992 The Middle Cumberland Region: Mississippian Archaeology in North Central Tennessee. PhD dissertation, Vanderbilt University, Nashville.

2016 There and Back Again: The Path of Souls and Reincarnation Themes in Middle Cumberland Mississippian Iconography. Paper presented to the Middle Cumberland Archaeological Society, Nashville.

2018 Tennessee Scalloped Triskele Gorgets. *Central States Archaeological Journal* 65(4): 204–207.

Smith, Kevin E., and Emily L. Beahm

2010 Reconciling the Puzzle of Castalian Springs Grave 34: Scalloped Triskeles, Crested Birds, and the Classic Braden Gorget. Paper presented at the 75th Annual Meeting of the Society for American Archaeology, St. Louis, Missouri.

Smith, Kevin E., and James V. Miller

2009 *Speaking with the Ancestors: Mississippian Stone Statuary of the Tennessee-Cumberland Region.* University of Alabama Press, Tuscaloosa.

Smith, Kevin E., and Michael C. Moore

1999 "Through Many Mississippian Hands": Late Prehistoric Exchange in the Middle Cumberland Valley. In *Raw Materials and Exchange in the Mid-South: Proceedings of the 16th Annual Mid-South Archaeological Conference, Jackson, Mississippi, June 3–4, 1995*, edited by Evan Peacock and Samuel O. Brookes, pp. 95–115. Mississippi Department of Archives and History, Jackson.

Smith, Kevin E., and Robert V. Sharp

2014 The Middle Cumberland "Changing Woman" and the Path of Souls. Paper presented at the 71st Annual Meeting of the Southeastern Archaeological Conference, Greenville, South Carolina.

2018 Four Mississippian Stone Statues from Sellars Farm State Archaeological Area, Wilson County, Tennessee. *Central States Archaeological Journal* 65(4): 182–185.

Smith, Kevin E., Emily L. Beahm, and Michael K. Hampton

2012 The Castalian Springs Mounds Project 2011: Investigations of Mound 3. Paper presented at the 24th Annual Meeting of Current Research in Tennessee Archaeology, Nashville.

Smith, Kevin E., Robert V. Sharp, and David H. Dye

2018 "Bloody Mouth": A Distinctive Variety of Negative-Painted Effigy Bottle from the Middle Cumberland Region of Tennessee. Paper presented at the 75th Annual Meeting of the Southeastern Archaeological Conference, Augusta, Georgia.

2019 Iconographic Depictions of the Middle Cumberland "Hero Twins." Paper presented at the 31st Annual Meeting of Current Research in Tennessee Archaeology, Murfreesboro, Tennessee.

Spears, Steven W., Michael C. Moore, and Kevin E. Smith

2008 Evidence for Early Mississippian Settlement of the Nashville Basin: Archaeological Explorations at the Spencer Site (40DV191). *Tennessee Archaeology* 3(1): 3–24.

Sullivan, Lynne P., and Michaelyn S. Harle

2010 Mortuary Practices and Cultural Identity at the Turn of the Sixteenth Century in Eastern Tennessee. In *Mississippian Mortuary Practices: Beyond Hierarchy and the Representationist Perspective*, edited by Lynne P. Sullivan and Robert C. Mainfort, Jr., pp. 234–249. University Press of Florida, Gainesville.

Thruston, Gates P.

1890 *The Antiquities of Tennessee and the Adjacent States.* Robert Clarke, Cincinnati, Ohio.

Ware, John A.

2014 *A Pueblo Social History: Kinship, Sodality, and Community in the Northern Southwest.* School for Advanced Research Press, Santa Fe.

Weeks, William Rex, Jr., Kevin E. Smith, and Robert V. Sharp, curators

2015 *Ancestors: Ancient Native American Sculptures of Tennessee.* An exhibition at the Tennessee State Museum, Nashville, October 29, 2015–May 15, 2016.

Wolforth, Thomas R., and Lynne Mackin Wolforth

2000 Fluorite Figurines from the Midcontinent. In *Mounds, Modoc, and Mesoamerica: Papers in Honor of Melvin L. Fowler*, edited by Steven R. Ahler, pp. 455–467. Illinois State Museum Scientific Papers Series, Vol. 28. Illinois State Museum, Springfield.

9

Gender, Craft Production, and Emerging Power in Mississippian Hierarchical Societies

Maureen S. Meyers

The emergence of hierarchy usually coincides with an increase in craft production that culminates in the development of craft specialization in state societies (Brumfiel and Earle 1987; Costin 1998). Although craft specialization has been examined cross-culturally, this research has tended to focus on the organization of production and its role in contributing to leadership or state power. However, unless the gender of the craft specialists is known, it is rarely discussed; instead, the focus has been on the organization of production or the distribution of crafted items. Yet craft specialization is an intensification of craft production. Craft production is present in all societies, and in pre-state societies, these crafts are produced in the domestic household by women. This can include crafts such as pottery and fiber production but also the production of certain foods for feasts (Dietler 2001). The long history of women making crafts at a domestic level would suggest that as the scale of production changed and craft specialization emerged, women were a fundamental part of this production and played key roles in the emergence of power that accompanied craft specialization. In the Mississippian Southeast, there is evidence for craft specialization at larger sites such as Cahokia and probably Moundville and Etowah, although most Mississippian sites lack such evidence. Instead, there is evidence at many sites of intense craft production. One of these sites is located at a Mississippian frontier area, and craft production may have been fundamental to the emergence of power there. This chapter examines the role gender may have played in the intensification of craft production and likewise in the emergence of power in some Mississippian societies.

Craft Production, Craft Specialization and Gender

Although the debates about craft production vs. craft specialization (and, related to this, attached vs. independent crafting, full and part-time crafting, etc.) are in part a result of the imposition of archaeologists using admittedly biased capitalist systems onto the past, a history of that debate is presented here with an acknowledgment of its limitations. Craft specialization has traditionally been viewed as a hallmark of hierarchical societies (Costin 1998). I define it as the full-time employ of skilled crafts persons by a leader in an institutionalized hierarchy (following Meyers 2011, 2014). Craft specialization can emerge in large chiefdoms, and it is certainly present in states. The full-time craft specialist works for the political leader and in return is supported by them. That is, there is enough surplus generated by the populace who also work for the political leader to support the craft specialist full time. At the same time, the items created by the specialist are used by the political leader to increase their own power, either through trade of these items or through possession of them. This is especially true if the items are sacred, and therefore possession of them increases a leader's power. Craft specialists actively work to increase the leader's power, both by generating symbols of authority (Earle 1996) and also by serving as symbols themselves of the leader's wealth (Helms 1992).

One critical question in the emergence of craft specialization is whether it is a cause of chiefly power or an outgrowth of it. It is likely both. In some emerging hierarchies, crafts played a larger role in chiefly power at the beginning of emergence, and in others it became more important after power was established. A materialist perspective views it as a secondary or ancillary part of power where the surplus of a food source is usually seen as that which allows the craft specialist to be supported full time by the political leader. It is not usually viewed as a key factor in the emergence of hierarchy. By contrast, an ideological perspective might point to its importance as a symbol of religion tied to political power, and in this way may be seen as more primary to the emergence and maintenance of political power.

Craft specialization can take many forms. It can include (but is not limited to) the creation of shell goods like beads (Claassen 2019; Feinman and Nicholas 2007; Ridout-Sharpe 2017); the creation of finely made ceremonial blades of stone or metal; and the creation of cloth, which includes spinning, weaving, sewing, dying, and ornamentation (Drooker 1992). It can also include more consumable items, such as feasts where special foods or drinks require certain knowledge (DeBoer 2001; Dietler 2001). Craft specialists have knowledge of how to create and work with items, and likely were trained since childhood by other craft specialists. Like all artists, they must master the skill while also being able to innovate with new methods, materials, and designs. This innovation can add prestige to both the leader they are attached to but also the craft specialists themselves (Helms 1992). Also, while many craft specialists may have been known for their expertise in working with one material type or the creation of one item, this knowledge likely entailed knowledge of the creation of other items. For example, crafting shell beads required knowledge of stone drill production as well as shell sources for procurement of raw materials (Feinman and Nicholas 2007). Crafting items for special use also involved special knowledge of rituals, ritual use, ritual power, and the role such items played in political power. Leaders may have also provided crafters with raw materials, a further indication of the complex relationship between craft items, crafters, and political power (Pauketat 1997). Helms (1993) discusses skilled crafting, where the power of the object comes in part from the knowledge and ability of the crafter to travel to distant or little-known locations tied to the cosmos and powerful deities to obtain materials which in turn required special knowledge to properly handle and create. Skousen (2020) finds evidence of skilled crafters at the Fingerhut site near Cahokia, which was restricted to certain households and done by elites. Knight (2010) also finds evidence of skilled crafting at Mound Q at Moundville.

In contrast to craft specialization, craft production entails the part-time making of crafts (Meyers 2014) that was not necessarily controlled by another individual, although in hierarchical societies, it is probable that the political leader benefited in some way from the production of crafts (Meyers 2015: 82). It was likely done as part of other tasks. As Meyers states, "craft production entails decreased control by a central leader and increased control by individuals or households" (Meyers 2015: 82–83). Similar to Blitz's (1993) idea that in some Mississippian chiefdoms, the chief was simultaneously a leader and an active, participating member of the chiefdom, craft production could have been a way for leaders of emerging chiefdoms to gain power. It can lead to craft specialization, but Meyers (2015: 83) suggests it should also be viewed as "another way of making goods" and she uses it to better understand variation within Mississippian chiefdom organization. The full-time nature of craft specialization often results in its activity in a separate location. This can be attached to the political leader's household or in a special area, such as Mound Q at Moundville. By contrast, craft production is more likely to be present within households because it is an extension of daily household tasks. As such, it is of course also present in non-hierarchical societies.

One issue rarely discussed is the gender identity of the craft specialist. Exceptions to this exist in studies of crafters of Peru and Maya (Inomata 2001; Ramirez 2001; Isbell 2001), some of which have written records to clarify the gendered organization of craft production in these societies. It has been assumed, and sometimes this is supported by ethnohistoric evidence, that most leaders in institutionalized hierarchies are male. Some craft specialists are assumed to be male. For example, creating stone tools, either for ceremonial purposes or as a means to a final product, is assumed to be a male task, although this may be based more on modern gender constructions unless ethnohistoric or comparable ethnographic data is present. Because craft production is present in households, and because many of the crafts produced and identified above are household tasks done by women, it is likely that craft producers were women. This is not to say that men were not craft producers; however, craft production is done in households, and ethnohistorically households were women's domains in the Southeast (Sullivan 2001, 2006; Swanton 1928, 1946; Hudson 1976). Further, many of the crafts made—pottery, fabric production and ornamentation, and the making of food for feasts—all relate to tasks done by women. Associated craft items, like bone needles and dye pots, were also likely created by women. Indeed, craft production can be seen as the extension of women's household tasks but at a different level, where utilitarian items take on additional symbolic meanings or representations (although, to be fair, there is no strict dichotomy in most societies between utilitarian and symbolic uses of items).

Mississippian Societies, Crafts, and Gender

In the Mississippian world, evidence of crafting at the larger chiefdoms, namely Cahokia, Etowah, and Moundville, has been uncovered. Of all Mississippian sites, Cahokia had the largest range and quantity of craft production. Shell bead crafting is well documented (Kozuch et al. 2017; Kozuch 1998), mainly at Cahokia proper, but also at contemporaneous sites in East St. Louis and the Janey B. Goode site (Boles et al. 2018). Boles et al. (2018: 413–414) document not only the hundreds of hours it would have taken for skilled artisans to make beads, but also the distance the raw material traveled, most from the Gulf Coast of Florida. In addition to shell beads, of which tens of thousands were made, there was also a Stirling phase pipestone workshop and other workshops for copper working and galena bead making. Holder (Pauketat 1993) found evidence of a craftsperson's residence under the Kunneman Mound at Cahokia. Other exotica include the presence of shark teeth, some of which were found by Perino in a wooden club (Boles et al. 2018). Other items came from the Plains to the west, and other distant regions. At Moundville, Knight (2004, 2010) found evidence of craft production associated with Mound Q. In fact, this proposed craft workshop area appears to have been the main activity atop Mound Q, suggesting a clear link between crafting and political power. At Etowah, the presence of copper *repoussé* plates suggests highly skilled artisans working on material that may have originated from either the Lake Superior region or the closer Duck Town region in eastern Tennessee (King 2003; Goad 1980), while other materials including shell originated in the Gulf Coast (Brown 1983) and chert "flint swords" that was quarried in Tennessee (Larson 1971) were found. In addition, all three sites are known for their fine pottery, although this was a craft particular to Moundville, where animal effigies and painted pots are more predominant. Lesser-known sites of crafting include Pearson's (2019; Garland et al. 2021; Pearson and Cook 2012) work on a shell workshop site on the coast of Georgia and Connaway's (2019) work on shell beads from the Northern Yazoo basin. Both of these works focus on the late pre-contact period, whereas Claassen's work has examined the importance of shell beads during the Archaic period (Claassen 2010, 2015) and specifically at the Indian Knoll site (Classen 2019).

There has been much debate about the presence or absence of craft specialization during the Mississippian period, and this contributed to a debate on precolumbian states in the Southeast (Pauketat 2007). His evidence includes population size, levels of administrative bureaucracy present, and the presence of craft specialization. It should be noted, though, that the argument for statehood is made only for Cahokia and no other Mississippian societies, which are clearly viewed as chiefdoms or more generally as institutionalized hierarchies.

Specific to craft specialization, Muller (1984, 1987) has argued that craft specialization did not exist in the Mississippian world, contra to Yerkes (1983, 1989), who argues that it did. Again, most of their examples are specific to Cahokia, particularly in the case of Yerkes, or the larger American Bottom region, particularly for Muller. Yerkes argues that the presence and quantity of standardized drills at Cahokia, combined with the quantity and standardization of shell beads and the presence of clear workshop areas is evidence of craft specialization. By contrast, Muller (1984) looks specifically at the evidence for salt-making in the Mississippian world and finds evidence that it was done at a household rather than a larger political level. Because it was not controlled by the ruling hierarchy, it fits into the definition of craft production rather than craft specialization. Cobb (2000) examined the manufacture and distribution of Mill Creek hoes during the Mississippian period, and suggests that while these were standardized, they are found close to the source of material and manufacturing location, following a traditional fall-off curve away from the source. He suggests this is evidence of a lack of specialization as well. Overall, there is far greater evidence for craft production rather than craft specialization within Mississippian chiefdoms.

Less researched in the literature on Mississippian crafting is the gender of the crafters themselves (whether producers or full-time specialists). Gougeon (2002) examined household production at the Mississippian Little Egypt site and identified patterns of behavior tied to gender. Based on ethnohistoric evidence (e.g., Swanton 1946), women were the primary ceramicists in the Southeast (Hudson 1976), and there is evidence of women weaving fabric (Drooker 1992). Gougeon (2012: 1248 Table 5.2) identifies household activities by gender, based on work by Smith (1978b) and Swanton (1946). It is likely that the gender of craft producers reflected the way the division of labor was gendered within the household. That is, men likely created fine stone tools for ceremonial uses in much the same way as they crafted stone tools for utilitarian purposes. At the same time, women likely created ceremonial ceramics such as effigy vessels while also making utilitarian vessels for their own households. There were likely tasks that entailed men and women working together in some way—for example, the creation of drills by men and the making of shell beads by women. Indeed, this complementarity may have reflected notions of complementarity of genders within the universe, and/or the presence of moieties, or other ideologies (see Edwards 2018). Sullivan suggests as much when she notes that while men are buried in the mounds and women in the villages, we should see these areas as complementary to one another rather than ranked.

If women were the crafters of at least some of the valued non-utilitarian goods that chiefs used to attain and maintain power, then it would follow that women could use crafting to elevate their status and their own power within chiefdoms. If, as at Cahokia and possibly Moundville and Etowah, some Mississippian chiefdoms had craft production whose scale changed as hierarchy became more institutionalized, that is, if craft production in some chiefdoms was beginning to resemble craft specialization, then that suggests both men and women could become craft specialists. In some regions where agriculture was not the primary economic means of livelihood, other economic means, like craft production, may have been more important and therefore could have offered women an additional opportunity to attain power.

Frontiers, Crafting, and Power

Frontier areas in the Southeastern Mississippian cultural world are places where agriculture may not have been the primary subsistence source because they were not ideal environments for maize (for example, like those described by Smith [1978a] for the Lower Mississippi River valley). Instead, people in some frontier areas subsisted on a combination of hunting, gathering, and horticulture, and this could vary by region. In the southern Appalachian region, nuts and deer may have played a more prominent role in subsistence (Jefferies et al. 1996), whereas in coastal Florida and Virginia, fishing may have been more important (Gallivan 2016). In addition to a mixed subsistence economy, other ways to procure food, such as the production and trade of goods, may have been used. One result may have been that craft production played a more dominant role in frontier economies (Meyers 2011, 2017; Thomas 1996).

In the Mississippian Southeast, examinations of crafting have been most extensively examined in areas of large chiefdoms, like Cahokia (Kozuch 1998) and Moundville (Knight 2010), with some examination of less centralized areas, such as coastal Georgia (Pearson 2019) and the Northern Yazoo basin (Connaway 2019). Crafting at Cahokia, as discussed above, has been the subject of a debate about the presence of specialization, and certainly existed at a different economy of scale than most other chiefdoms, with the probable exceptions of Moundville and Etowah. In frontier areas, evidence for crafting is less documented. Rather, Thomas (1996) examined the distribution of finished shell beads to better understand their social context, particularly with regard to the degree of interaction between Mississippian groups and those on their eastern fringe located in the North Carolina Mountain and Piedmont regions. She found that shell beads were used in a similar way by both men and women in these regions. If, as she posits, shell beads represent social roles and statuses held by individuals, this suggests that "women and men could fill many of the same roles and equally hold status, prestige, and power within society" (Thomas 1996: 39); however, other ways to denote status tied to gender likely existed as evidenced by the presence of filed incisors among women and cranial modification among men in the Mountain region.

Studies of gender in the frontier region have noted the presence of shell predominantly in women's burials (Eastman 2001; Sullivan 2001). Thomas (1996) and others (Claassen 2019; Hall 1989) have suggested that shell beads are tied to women's fertility and are symbols of whiteness, where white was an important color in Southeastern Mississippian societies, denoting among other things, moiety affiliation. Thomas also notes (1996: 40; see Hammell 1983) that shell beads "have been metaphorically equated with berries" which were believed to be a protection against disease and therefore may have been worn by individuals as a protective measure against illness. Considering the multiple layered meanings of shell, they were likely worn as an outer layer expressing status, gender, and well-being.

More specific to gendered labor divisions in households, Thomas (2001) suggests that to understand exchange, we should examine households, because "the specific allocation of labor to various household tasks had implications for the organization of production for exchange" (Thomas 2001: 28). Using Swanton, she notes that there were specific tasks tied to men and women in the Southeast. Men's contributions to subsistence were focused on hunting and fishing (Thomas 2001: 32), whereas women's contributions were focused on plant production and collecting. Women also "contributed to Mississippian economies through the production of utilitarian goods" (2001: 33), including textile and basketry production, preparing skins, and making ceramics. Men were engaged in woodworking. Thomas notes (2001: 33) that "ethnohistoric sources are largely silent on the issue of flint knapping in the Southeast" but cites Swanton in stating that men were likely the primary producers of stone tools but that women "undoubtedly made and used a variety of expedient and formal tools for their daily tasks" (Thomas 2001: 33). At the Toqua site in east Tennessee, Sullivan (2001: 126 Note 1) notes that one elderly female burial was found in association with "two collections of objects, including various animal bones." Scott and Polhemus (1987:420) state that these were found "concentrated behind the back in two clusters which may represent bags or other containers." Other similar tool concentrations were found with elderly female burials at Toqua.

Thomas (2001) further compares hoe production at Dillow's Ridge with salt production at the Great Salt Springs site and finds that both were produced at a low level of intensity. The household economies between the two differed, though; hoe production was done by resident artisans on a part-time basis, whereas salt production was done by visitors to the salt springs over a few days. Thomas's work suggests that variations in gender roles may better explain variations in Mississippian economies. Sullivan (2001, 2006) suggests that we should reexamine our belief that mounds represent the only place of power within Mississippian societies. She compares burials of men and women and finds that women, especially older women, are more likely to be buried in the village and near their houses, and suggests that in these matrilineal societies, households functioned as domains of power for women just as mounds represented a more public sphere and were domains of power for men. In particular, she notes that post-menopausal women cross-culturally "often acquired increased prestige and/or special status, and sometimes participated with men in political and religious activities from which younger women were excluded" (Sullivan 2001: 107; see Crown and Fish 1996).

In sum, crafting has not been explicitly examined at Mississippian frontiers, except by Meyers (2011, 2014). Here, the crafting of shell was clearly important (see below). What has been examined are gender roles in the Southeast, how these roles are expressed in burials, and what those expressions might mean. Shell is more likely associated with women as a sign of fertility. Women are more likely buried in non-mound household or village contexts, and in at least a few instances at the Toqua site, were found with possible tool bags. Finally, post-menopausal women likely had more power and authority in these households.

Crafting at a Mississippian Frontier

The Carter Robinson site was occupied during the fourteenth century and is located in present-day Lee County in southwestern Virginia. It was a frontier of contemporaneous Mississippian sites in eastern Tennessee (Meyers 2011, 2014, 2017). Inhabitants of the Norris Basin moved up the river valley around AD 1250 into a part of Virginia inhabited by the Radford culture, a heterarchical society that relied on a combined hunting/gathering and agricultural subsistence strategy and who had limited interactions with Mississippian groups in Tennessee and North Carolina. The site consists of a mound surrounded by a plaza and a small village. Excavations there uncovered the remains of six structures spanning three 50-year-long occupations (Figure 9.1). During each period, evidence of craft production was present in at least one house, although the type and scale of that production changed over time. Initially, occupants made items like pendants out of cannel coal, a more malleable coal that crops at the surface and is both easily mined and worked.

The uncovered household remains appear to be *in situ* house floors. House floors were found at depths between 30–35 centimeters below ground surface. Plowzone was present from ground surface to a depth of 30 centimeters. Below this depth, postholes were apparent and often extended an additional depth of 10–30 centimeters into sterile subsoil. Artifacts were present on the household floor, which varied in depths between 5 and 15 centimeters before a sterile clay subsoil was encountered. In the southern half of the house, a large (5-meter wide) area of burned daub, as well as the presence of a hearth below the plowzone were further indicators of the presence of an intact house floor. These household floors were excavated in 10-centimeter levels using a

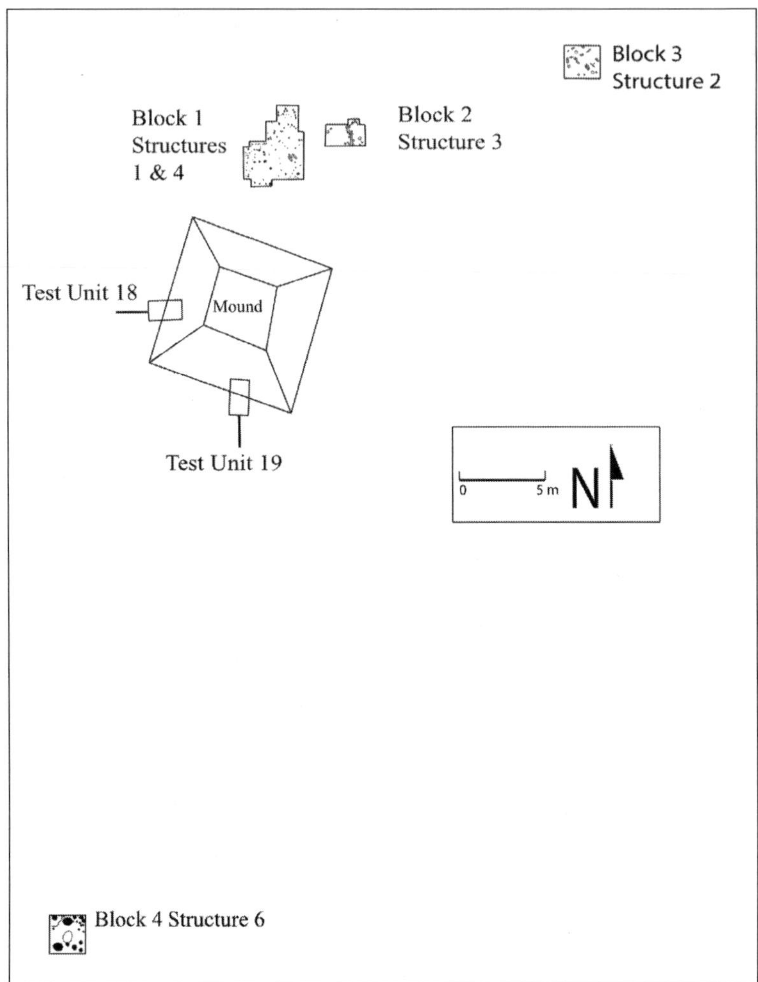

Figure 9.1. Location of structures at Carter Robinson mound site.

1 × 1-meter grid and screened through ¼″ hardware cloth. Features were excavated in stratigraphic zones. Provenience of artifacts was recorded by grid location and depth. Soil from many features as well as samples of the household floor were removed for flotation. Radiocarbon dates from Structure 1 date the house floor to the end of the thirteenth century (Meyers 2011: 254).

This production was centered in Structure 3, an early wall-trench structure. During the middle part of occupation, Structure 1 was built near the mound. This large structure lacked a hearth and may have been open on one side, suggesting it was a communal area rather than the location of a household. An area attached to and directly north of Structure 1, the Structure 1

Extension Area, contains extensive evidence of shell bead production. Finally, during the last part of site occupation, shell bead production continued in Structure 1, but it was also present in Structure 2 located east of the mound. Structure 2 had been built, burned, buried, and rebuilt twice and possibly three times, but only its third upper house layer contains evidence of some shell bead production. However, production here is not at the same scale as that seen in Structure 1. Because the production is so extensive in Structure 1, analyses of craft production at the site are focused here.

Amount and Distribution of Shell

Over 2.4 kg of shell were recovered in Structure 1 and Structure 1 Extension Area. Most of the shells were gastropod (83%; n=6357) (*Io fluvialis*), with mussel (16%; n=1341) making up most of the remaining amount, with minor (less than 1%) amounts of more exotic shell. These include four marginella beads and shell fragments not yet identified to species. The shell was concentrated in the Structure 1 Extension Area, but over time it expanded into Structure 1 proper and also into an area east of the extension area. During the beginning of occupation, the shell was concentrated in a small (2 × 3-meter) area. Within a short time, the amount of shell increased greatly—between three to five times as much shell was found in Level 2 as compared to the earlier Level 3. By the end of occupation, the number of shells in the later Level 1 is double that found in Level 2, and it is at this point that the working of shell expands into Structure 1 and east of the extension area.

As shell production increases over time, so does the mound. Remains of a structure, including postholes and a hearth, were found on the southern edge of the mound and analysis of ceramics as well as radiocarbon dates place the occupation of this house to about the same time as the founding of the site. Within about fifty years, the house was replaced by the initial mound layer, and it was at the same time that Structure 1 was built and shell production began. As shell production increases, another mound layer is added and Structure 4, a typical Mississippian domestic structure, was built east of, and next to, Structure 1.

Types of Production

Most of the production does not appear to be related to making beads. About 50 beads were recovered, in all stages of production, but as stated, over 2.4 kg of shell were recovered, which would be an inordinate amount of shell waste for 50 beads. If the beads were being made for trade, it's not surprising to find few finished beads in the production area. However, the beads present at the site are made of mussel shell, although gastropod far exceeds mussel shell at the site. Most of these gastropod shells are too small to be made into beads, but 99% of it is modified. An examination of the modifications on the 6300 gastropod shells identified four patterns of modification: whorl cut, base cut, whorl and base cut, and shell frames. Whorl and base cut gastropod were the most common found (n=1900), followed by 800 shell frames, 500 whorl cut only, and 36 base cut only. In addition, six unmodified shells were recovered.

I suggest the range of cuts present represent different stages of production, from whole shell to whorl or (less frequently) base cut, and finally whorl and base cut and shell frames. Modifying the shell in this way is evidence that the gastropod was intentionally selected and modified to sew onto fabric as decorations, similar to what is seen on the seventeenth-century Powhatan's Mantle from coastal Virginia. The large amount of shell frames suggests some shell was either overly modified or too fragile for use and discarded. It could have been used for another purpose, such as tempering ceramics. Both fiber and ceramic production have been identified as women's crafts in the pre-contact Southeast (Gougeon 2012: 148 Table 5.2; Smith 1978b; Hudson 1976). Note that the frequencies of the four types of shell modification increase over time, suggesting craft production of the shell increased at the same rate over time. This evidence of shell adornment production as a primary type of craft production, and shell bead production as a secondary type of production, suggests an efficient and innovative use of materials in a frontier region.

Shell in a Larger Context

The shell craft production that was located in Structure 1 is evidence of gendered craft production. As discussed above, shell is associated with women. As stated, Structure 1 lacks a hearth and may have been open on one side. This open side faced the plaza, indicating it was not used as a household structure. Based on the large amount of shell production debris and associated tools, it was likely a craft production area. It was located next to two other structures. One was the mound, a traditional seat of power primarily associated with men, which was located a few meters southwest of the entrance to Structure 1. The second is Structure 4, the traditional Mississippian domestic house located next to Structure 1 that contained a central hearth, entrance, and four corners. This follows other examples in Mississippian culture where specialization occurs in or near domestic settings, or in workshops. Following Sullivan, such a house (Structure 4) should be viewed as a seat of power for women. Structure 1's craft production is located directly between these two areas. The presence of stone tools in the same area may represent associated craft production activities by men. That is, this house could straddle the domain of men and women in its physical location and in the work that was done in it. At a frontier, in which labor is scarce but land is abundant, the negotiation of gender roles for survival and success are more likely and I argue the evidence of that negotiation is present in this structure.

A second possibility is that women were the only producers of crafts in Structure 1. In light of what we know of Southeastern gender roles, this makes more sense. That is, women and men worked and largely lived separately with their own genders. If this is the case at Carter Robinson, it suggests a difference is present in the way women could obtain power at the frontier. That is, because land is abundant but labor is scarce, skilled craftspersons of any gender might be able to use their skill as a way to increase their power in Mississippian chiefdoms (Parker 2006; Nyerges 1992). However, that prompts the question—how do we know this was not the norm? The overview of craft production evidence in the Southeast discussed above shows that most studies of craft production omit a discussion of the gender of crafters. Considering that (1) craft production and specialization are avenues of power; (2) most crafts done in the Southeast were done by women in and for the household; and (3) craft specialization is an intensification of craft production; it would be logical that most craft specialists were women. It may be that at this frontier site, where other avenues to power are emphasized, the ability of women to change or emphasize pre-existing roles are more pronounced.

Conclusion

Craft production in pre-state societies is traditionally done by women, although this is often not acknowledged or discussed in research on craft production. Craft production in some Mississippian chiefdoms played a critical role in the emergence of power, particularly at frontier sites because of the decreased role of corn agriculture in these societies. Because this production was done by women, it is likely that women held power in these societies. The shell production at Carter Robinson provides an example of the relationship between increased power and increased craft production. However, that increased power was likely reflected there in both traditional male seats of power—mounds—and female seats of power—households. The location of Structure 1 between these two seats of power may represent a negotiation of gender roles at a frontier site. However, I think it may just be more visible at this frontier site because of the focus on shell, a craft item traditionally associated with women in the Southeast, and such negotiations and expressions of power by both genders are likely visible at many Mississippian sites. The evidence from Carter Robinson is a good example of the complex relationship between power, gender, and crafts and suggests that focusing on materials and production is a useful method for examining this relationship.

References Cited

Blitz, John

1993 Big Pots for Big Shots: Feasting and Storage in a Mississippian Community. *American Antiquity* 58: 80–96.

Boles, Steven L., Tamira K. Brennan, Laura Kozuch, Steven R. Kuehn, and Mary L. Simon

2018 Crafting and Exotica at the East S. Louis Precinct. In *Revealing Greater Cahokia, North America's First Native City: Rediscovery and Large-Scale Excavations of the East St. Louis Precinct*, edited by Thomas E. Emerson, Brad H. Koldehoff, and Tamira K. Brennan, pp. 387–423. Illinois State Archaeological Survey Studies in Archaeology No. 12. The Archaeology of the New Mississippi River Bridge, Illinois Department of Transportation.

Brown, James A.

1983 Spiro Exchange Connections Revealed by Sources of Imported Raw Materials. In *Southeastern Natives and Their Pasts: A Collection of Papers Honoring Dr. Robert E. Bell*, edited by Dan G. Wyckoff and J.L. Holman, pp. 129–162. Studies in Oklahoma's Past No. 11. Oklahoma Archaeological Survey, Norman.

Brumfiel, Elizabeth, and Timothy Earle

1987 Specialization, Exchange, and Complex Societies: An Introduction. In *Specialization, Exchange, and Complex Societies*, edited by Elizabeth Brumfiel and Timothy K. Earle, pp. 1–9. Cambridge University Press, Cambridge.

Claassen, Cheryl

2010 *Feasting with Shellfish in the Southern Ohio Valley: Archaic Sacred Sites and Rituals.* University of Tennessee Press, Knoxville.

2015 *Beliefs and Ritual in Archaic Eastern North America: An Interpretive Guide.* University of Alabama Press, Tuscaloosa.

2019 The Beads of Indian Knoll. *Southeastern Archaeology* 38(2): 95–112.

Cobb, Charles

2000 *From Quarry to Cornfield: The Political Economy of Mississippian Hoe Production.* The University of Alabama Press, Tuscaloosa.

Connaway, John

2019 Shell Beads from Mississippian Sites in the Northern Yazoo Basin, Mississippi. *Southeastern Archaeology* 38(2): 113–126.

Costin, Cathy Lynne

1998 Introduction: Craft and Social Identity. In *Craft and Social Identity*, edited by Cathy Lynne Costin and Rita P. Wright, pp. 3–16. Archaeological Papers of the American Anthropological Association No. 8, Washington, D.C.

Crown, Patricia L., and Suzanne K. Fish

1996 Gender and Status in the Hohokam Preclassic to Classic Transition. *American Anthropologist* 98: 803–17.

DeBoer, Warren R.

2001 The Big Drink: Feast and Forum in the Upper Amazon. In *Feasts: Archaeological and Ethnographic Perspectives on Food, Politics, and Power*, edited by Michael Dietler and Brian Hayden, pp. 215–239. The University of Alabama Press, Tuscaloosa.

Dietler, Michael

2001 Theorizing the Feast: Rituals of Consumption, Commensal Politics, and Power in African Contexts. In *Feasts: Archaeological and Ethnographic Perspectives on Food, Politics, and Power*, edited by Michael Dietler and Brian Hayden, pp. 65–114. The University of Alabama Press, Tuscaloosa.

Drooker, Penelope

1992 *Mississippian Village Textiles at Wickliffe.* University of Alabama Press, Tuscaloosa.

Earle, Timothy

1996 *How Chiefs Come to Power: Political Economy in Prehistory.* Stanford University Press, Stanford.

Eastman, Jane

2001 Life Courses and Gender among Late Prehistoric Siouan Communities. In *Archaeological Studies of Gender in the Southeastern United States*, edited by Jane M. Eastman and Christopher B. Rodning, pp. 57–76. University Press of Florida, Gainesville.

Edwards, Tai

2018 *Osage Women and Empire: Gender and Power.* University Press of Kansas, Lawrence.

Feinman, Gary M., and Linda M. Nicholas

2007 Craft Production in Classic Period Oaxaca: Implications for Monte Albán's Political Economy. In *Craft Production in Complex Societies*, edited by Izumi Shimada, pp. 97–119. Foundations of Archaeological Inquiry. The University of Utah Press, Salt Lake City.

Gallivan, Martin D.

2016 *The Powhatan Landscape: An Archaeological History of the Algonquian Chesapeake.* University Press of Florida, Gainesville.

Garland, Carey J., Brandon T. Ritchison, Bryan Tucker, and Victor D. Thompson

2021 A Preliminary Consideration of Craft Production and Settlement Expansion on Ossabaw Island, Georgia, USA. *The Journal of Island and Coastal Archaeology.* DOI: 10.1080/15564894.2021.1962436.

Goad, Sharon I.

1980 Chemical Analyses of Native Copper Artifacts from the Southeastern United States. *Current Anthropology* 21: 270–271.

Gougeon, Ramie

2002 Household Research at the Late Mississippian Little Egypt Site (9Mu102). Unpublished PhD dissertation, Department of Anthropology, University of Georgia, Athens.

2012 Activity Areas and Households in the Late Mississippian Southeast United States: Who Did What Where? In *Ancient Households of the Americas*, edited by

John G. Douglass and Nancy Gonlin, pp. 141–162. University Press of Colorado, Boulder.

Hall, Robert L.

1989 The Cultural Background of Mississippian Symbolism. In *The Southeastern Ceremonial Complex: Artifacts and Analysis*, edited by Patricia Galloway, pp. 239–278. University of Nebraska Press, Lincoln.

Hammell, George

1983 Trading in Metaphors: The Magic of Beads, Another Perspective upon Indian-European Contact in Northeastern North America. In *Proceedings of the 1982 Glass Trade Bead Conference*, edited by C. Hayes, pp. 5–28. Rochester Museum and Science Center Research Records 16, Rochester, New York.

Helms, Mary W.

1992 Long-Distance Contacts, Elite Aspirations, and the Age of Discovery in Cosmological Context. In *Resources, Power, and Interregional Interaction*, edited by Edward M. Schortman and Patricia A. Urban, pp. 157–174. Plenum Press, New York.

1993 *Craft and the Kingly Ideal: Art, Trade, and Power.* University of Texas Press, Austin.

Hudson, Charles

1976 *The Southeastern Indians.* University of Tennessee Press, Knoxville.

Inomata, Takeshi

2001 Classic Maya Elite Competition, Collaboration, and Performance in Multicraft Production. In *Craft Production in Complex Societies*, edited by Izumi Shimada, pp. 120–136. Foundations of Archaeological Inquiry. The University of Utah Press, Salt Lake City.

Isbell, William H.

2001 A Community of Potters or Multicrafting Wives of Polygynous Lords? In *Craft Production in Complex Societies*, edited by Izumi Shimada, pp. 68–96. Foundations of Archaeological Inquiry. The University of Utah Press, Salt Lake City.

Jefferies, Richard, E. Breitburg, J. Flood, and Margaret Scarry

1996 Mississippian Adaptation on the Northern Periphery: Settlement, Subsistence, and Interaction in the Cumberland Valley of Southeastern Kentucky. *Southeastern Archaeology* 15: 1–28.

King, Adam

2003 *Etowah: The Political History of a Chiefdom Capital.* The University of Alabama Press, Tuscaloosa.

Knight, Vernon James

2004 Characterizing Elite Midden Deposits at Moundville. *American Antiquity* 69(1): 304–321.

2010 *Mound Excavations at Moundville: Architecture, Elites, and Social Order.* University of Alabama Press, Tuscaloosa.

Kozuch, Laura

1998 Marine Shells from Mississippian Archaeological Sites. PhD dissertation, Department of Anthropology, University of Florida, Gainesville.

Kozuch, Laura, Karen J. Walker, and William H. Marquardt
2017 Lightning Whelk Natural History and a New Sourcing Method. *Southeastern Archaeology* 36(3): 226–240.

Larson, Lewis H.
1971 Archaeological Implications of Social Stratification at the Etowah Site, Georgia. In *Approaches to the Social Dimensions of Mortuary Practices*, edited by James A. Brown, pp. 58–67. Society for American Archaeology Memoir 25. Washington, D.C.

Meyers, Maureen S.
2011 Political Economy of Exotic Trade on the Mississippian Frontier: A Case Study of a Fourteenth-Century Chiefdom in Southwest Virginia. Ph.D dissertation, Department of Anthropology, University of Kentucky, Lexington.
2014 Shell Trade: Craft Production at a Fourteenth-Century Mississippian Frontier. In *Trends and Traditions in Southeastern Zooarchaeology*, edited by Tanya M. Peres, pp. 80–104. University Press of Florida, Gainesville.
2015 The Role of the Southern Appalachian Mississippian Frontier in the Creation and Maintenance of Chiefly Power. In *Archaeological Perspectives on the Southern Appalachians*, edited by Ramie S. Gougeon and Maureen S. Meyers, pp. 219–244. University of Tennessee Press, Knoxville.
2017 Social Integration at a Frontier and the Creation of Mississippian Social Identity in Southwestern Virginia. *Southeastern Archaeology* 36(2): 144–155.

Muller, John
1984 Mississippian Specialization and Salt. *American Antiquity* 49: 489–507.
1987 *Mississippian Political Economy.* Plenum Press, New York.

Nyerges, A. Endre
1992 The Ecology of Wealth-in-People: Agriculture, Settlement, and Society on the Perpetual Frontier. *American Anthropologist* 94(4): 860–881.

Parker, Bradley J.
2006 Toward an Understanding of Borderland Processes. *American Antiquity* 71(1):77–100.

Pauketat, Timothy
1993 *Temples for Cahokia's Lords: Excavations of the Kunnemann Mound.* Memoir 26. University of Michigan Museum of Anthropology at Ann Arbor.
1997 Specialization, Political Symbols, and the Crafty Elite of Cahokia. *Southeastern Archaeology* 16: 1–15.
2007 *Chiefdoms and Other Archaeological Delusions.* AltaMira Press, Lanham.

Pearson, Charles E.
2019 Prehistoric Shell Beads on the Georgia Coast. *Southeastern Archaeology* 38(2):95–112.

Pearson, Charles E., and Fred C. Cook
2012 The Bead Maker's Midden: Evidence of Late Prehistoric Shell Bead Production on Ossabaw Island, Georgia. *Southeastern Archaeology* 31(1): 87–102.

Ramirez, Susan E.
2001 It's All in a Day's Work: Occupational Specialization on the Peruvian North Coast, Revisited. In *Craft Production in Complex Societies*, edited by Izumi Shi-

mada, pp. 262–280. Foundations of Archaeological Inquiry. The University of Utah Press, Salt Lake City.

Ridout-Sharpe, Janet

2017 Shell Ornaments, Icons, and Other Artefacts from the eastern Mediterranean and Levant. In *Molluscs in Archaeology: Methods, Approaches and Applications*, edited by Michael J. Allen, pp. 290–307.

Scott, Gary, and Richard Polhemus

1987 Mortuary Patterns. In *The Toqua Site: A Late Mississippian Dallas Phase Town*, edited by Richard R. Polhemus, pp. 378–431. University of Tennessee Department of Anthropology Report of Investigations 41, Knoxville.

Skousen, B. Jacob

2020 Skilled Crafting at Cahokia's Fingerhut Tract. *Southeastern Archaeology*. DOI: 10.1080/0734578X.2020.1782665.

Smith, Bruce D.

1978a *Mississippian Settlement Patterns*. Smithsonian Institution Press, Washington, D.C.

1978b *Prehistoric Patterns of Human Behavior: A Case Study in the Mississippi Valley*. Academic Press, New York.

Sullivan, Lynne S.

2001 Those Men in the Mounds: Gender, Politics, and Mortuary Practices in Late Prehistoric Eastern Tennessee. In *Archaeological Studies of Gender in the Southeastern United States*, edited by Jane M. Eastman and Christopher B. Rodning, pp. 101–126. University Press of Florida, Gainesville.

2006 Gendered Contexts of Mississippian Leadership in Southern Appalachia. In *Leadership and Polity in Mississippian Society*, edited by Brian M. Butler and Paul D. Welch, pp. 264–288. Center for Archaeological Investigations, Occasional Paper No. 33. Southern Illinois University, Carbondale.

Swanton, John R.

1928 *Aboriginal Culture of the Southeast*. Smithsonian Institution, Bureau of American Ethnology Annual Report 42: 673–726. Washington, D.C.

1946 *The Indians of the Southeastern United States*. Smithsonian Institution, Bureau of American Ethnology Bulletin 137, Washington, D.C.

Thomas, Larissa

1996 A Study of Shell Beads and Their Social Context in the Mississippian Period: A Case from the Carolina Piedmont and Mountains. *Southeastern Archaeology* 15(1): 29–46.

2001 The Gender Division of Labor in Mississippian Households: Its Role in Shaping Production for Exchange. In *Archaeological Studies of Gender in the Southeastern United States*, edited by Jane M. Eastman and Christopher B. Rodning, pp. 27–56. University Press of Florida, Gainesville.

Yerkes, Richard

1983 Microwear, Microdrills, and Mississippian Craft Specialization. *American Antiquity* 48: 499–518.

1989 Mississippian Craft Specialization on the American Bottom. *Southeastern Archaeology* 8: 93–106.

10

Women and Power at Joara, Cuenca, and Fort San Juan

Christopher B. Rodning, Rachel V. Briggs, Robin A. Beck, Gayle J. Fritz, Heather A. Lapham, and David G. Moore

Women practiced several forms of power within Mississippian societies of the American South, and the roles of women in politics, economic spheres, and social networks shaped the course of encounters and entanglements between Native American groups and European explorers and colonists. However, the impact of this power on the direction and outcome of the interactions between Indigenous groups of the upper Catawba Valley and surrounding areas with the mid-sixteenth-century Spanish entradas led by Hernando de Soto (1539–1543) and Juan Pardo (1566–1568) (Figure 10.1; Bauer 2022; Beck 1997, 2013; DePratter and Smith 1980; Edelson 2021; Hudson 1976, 2005, 2018; Hudson et al. 2008; Levy et al. 1990; Sampeck et al. 2015) is poorly understood. Primary historic sources emphasize activities and perspectives of Spanish men, but we try here to discern some of the gender dynamics underlying them, and to identify some of the ways Indigenous women may have shaped the course of events recorded in these documentary sources and that are manifested archaeologically at one particular site in western North Carolina.

This chapter considers several forms of power associated with women in the province of Cofitachequi in the Wateree Valley of South Carolina; and the community known to Soto as "Xuala," and known to Pardo as "Joara," and the province that encompasses the Berry site, the location of Pardo's colonial outpost of Fort San Juan and its associated town of Cuenca (Beck and Moore 2002; Beck et al. 2006, 2011, 2016a, 2016b, 2016c, 2017, 2018; Moore et al. 2005, 2017). Documentary evidence about those women offers insight into the lives of women and gender dynamics as they impacted the fortunes and misfortunes of Soto's exploration of and Pardo's attempted settlement of the northern borderlands of the Mississippian Southeast and the Spanish colo-

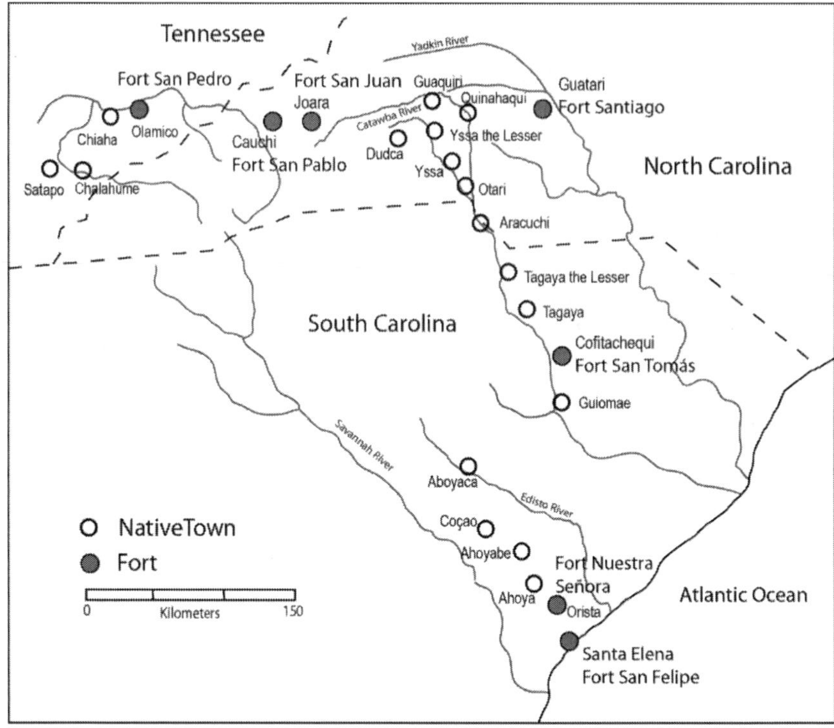

Figure 10.1. Map of Native American towns and Spanish forts associated with the mid-sixteenth-century expeditions of Hernando de Soto and Juan Pardo.

nial province of *La Florida.* It is our hope that this chapter will inspire further research into the contributions Native women made to the course of the sixteenth-century Spanish enterprises and failures in the Southeastern United States.

Documentary Evidence of Native Feminine Power

Power is a dynamic element of interpersonal relations that results in the ability to influence and impact the lives of others through everyday practice. Indigenous women had particularly important impacts in aspects of politics, foodways, and kinship that affected the lives and livelihoods of the men who participated in the Soto and Pardo expeditions. Spaniards were dependent upon Native women for sustenance, and this dependency conferred power to Indigenous women. The importance of women in kin networks and community leadership roles also put them in positions to affect the ways in which Indigenous groups engaged with Spanish colonists and the encampments and fledgling settlements they sought to establish in northern *La Florida* during the mid-sixteenth century. In other words, Indigenous women were not only influential in their own societies but were also influential in Spanish enterprises as well (even if their influence was not explicitly recognized by Spanish men).

The Chiefly Power of Tali Mico

Much of what we know about chiefly leadership in Mississippian societies derives from ethnographic cases of chiefly politics and leadership in other world areas; evidence of mortuary practices at Mississippian and post-European contact sites; and eighteenth-century written sources, which postdate the European slave trade, the deerskin trade, and other episodes of European-catalyzed culture change in the Native American South (Ethridge 2010). Though written accounts by European colonists reflect male-centric biases, and though the slave trade and deerskin trade greatly altered gender dynamics in the Native American South and the statuses of women (Beck 2013), evidence of mortuary practices indicates that there were distinct but generally complementary roles for women and men in pre- and post-European contact community leadership (Eastman 2001; Rodning 2001, 2011; Sullivan 2001; Sullivan and Harle 2010; Sullivan and Rodning 2001, 2011). Written accounts of the Pardo expeditions refer to several leadership titles, including *caciques grandes* (paramount chiefs), *micos* (regional chiefs), *oratas* (local chiefs), *mandadores* (war chiefs), *ynahaes* (mediators), *yatikas* (speakers), and others (Hudson 2005: 61–67). Except for war chiefs—which were often males following established gender roles later recorded by Europeans (e.g., Hudson 2005: 66, 2018: 17)—gender associations with leadership roles were likely non-existent (Trocolli 2006). However, members of Spanish entradas (mostly men themselves) probably had more insight into the lives and leadership roles of men than of women, and very likely over-valued the leadership of men while undervaluing that of women.

The political and military power of women leaders is very apparent in written accounts about interactions between Soto and Tali Mico. During April 1540, Soto and his men traveled north from the province of Ocute, in the Oconee River Valley, through uninhabited wilderness (*despoblado*) in areas of Georgia and South Carolina that had been densely populated by Mississippian towns and chiefdoms up to the point of regionwide abandonments in the late fifteenth century. They eventually arrived at the town of Hymahi, near the confluence of the Wateree and Congaree rivers. Several days later, with most of his men staying put, Soto and a detachment traveled north and upstream along the Wateree for a day, then encamped along its west bank, across from the main town of Cofitachequi on the other side of the river. They then crossed the river, and they stayed in several houses in the town. Rodrigo Rangel, secretary of the Soto expedition, wrote that the headman of the town of Altamaha, one of the towns in the orbit of the chiefdom of Ocute, always had his weapons nearby because he felt constantly threatened by Cofitachequi, though the enemy chief and chiefdom was some 125 miles east of the Oconee Valley and the province of Ocute; this persistent alertness on the part of Ocute speaks to the persistent fear of military violence that radiated from the chiefdom of Cofitachequi.

Chroniclers of the Soto expedition generally referred to the province and chiefdom of Cofitachequi as one of the most prosperous and powerful in all the areas they traversed en route to the Mississippi River valley. The Spanish were impressed with Tali Mico and the power she commanded; likely, she was a regional chief with a position akin to that of a mico (DePratter 1989, 1994; Hudson et al. 2008). Tali Mico was carried on a litter by a company of her principal men for her first encounter with Soto. She received tribute from surrounding towns and provinces, and there were large amounts of material wealth kept within temples on earthen mounds at major towns, wealth that she presented Soto with on numerous occasions as an attempt at diplomacy and later placation. Soto and his men witnessed and confiscated large amounts of mica, copper, pearls, deerskins, weaponry, and even metal goods and glass beads (the European items presumably salvaged from the attempted settlements by Lucas Vázquez de Ayllón in coastal South Carolina dating from 1521 through 1526) in the main town of Cofitachequi and the nearby town of Talimeco (likely, Tali Mico's birth town) (DePratter 1989: 134–135; Hudson 2005: 63–64; Snyder 2009).

From what we know, Tali Mico never attempted to mount a military response to Soto, though this would not have been beyond her power. Her authority undoubtedly stemmed from her birth into a high-status lineage (traced through her mother) but would have been bolstered by merit-based achievements in her lifetime. For some women, these achievements were militaristic (such as the "female warrior" at the King site [Hally 2008]), but for most, their burials suggest their social power was conferred through more common Indigenous feminine routes (Sullivan and Rodning 2001). Regardless of the source of her achieved power, Tali Mico, as chief, was owed the spoils of warfare, which included the incredible wealth witnessed by Soto and his men as well a number of enslaved war captives, many of whom may have been taken in military skirmishes with Ocute (Snyder 2009).

Tali Mico's status was revered among her people. Several days after the arrival of Soto to Cofitachequi, Tali Mico fled to Talimeco, likely in response to the demands and needs of the Spanish entrada. Soto dispatched one of his lieutenants to take a young warrior as a guide to retrieve the chief from her hiding place, but on the way, the warrior removed an arrow from his quiver and plunged it into his own heart rather than reveal her location. Tali Mico was eventually recaptured, and along with a retinue of female attendants, was forced to accompany Soto to the limits of her chiefdom. Was it possible for Tali Mico to escape? Could Tali Mico have asked her people to fight for her release? Very likely so. Christina Snyder (2009) proposed that Tali Mico understood the need to remove Soto from her province, but also understood the potential devastation that a direct confrontation with Soto could produce. To that end, she allowed Soto to use her power and influence to secure food supplies from the towns they encountered, moving him closer and closer to the limits of her domain. Finally, at the town of Guasili, located on the eastern side of the Appalachians, she and her retinue, accompanied by several enslaved men, fled the expedition and returned to the province of Joara (or Xuala), which was under her influence (Snyder 2009: 22). It was rumored that after their escape, she and one of the escaped enslaved men became lovers and planned to return to her capital. These references to the political power and influence wielded by Tali Mico, the material wealth concentrated in several towns within her territory—including in temples atop earthen mounds—and the food surpluses accessible to her in main towns and other settlements in her province, all point to her exceptional status within the Mississippian world (DePratter 1989; Hudson 2005: 68–83, 2018: 172–184), on par with the status of the paramount chief and chiefdom of Coosa (Hally 1994; Hudson 2005: 101–108, 2018: 214–217; Smith 1987, 2000).

The Native Women of the Pardo Expedition: Fort San Juan, Joara, and Guatari

One generation later, both Cofitachequi and Coosa were still important chiefdoms, but neither were as powerful nor as prosperous as they had been during the era of the Soto entrada; Joara (Xuala), on the other hand, was in ascendance. Though Soto and his men recognized the promise and potential of the province of Xuala, they did not stay long, and they soon departed for the mountains and the path to Chiaha (Beck 1997). Nearly thirty years later, Pardo and his men were favorably impressed with the polity of Joara, and they proclaimed the land of the province as fine as the farmlands of the Guadalquivir River in Spain. Pardo chose Joara as the setting for his colonial outpost of Fort San Juan and its supporting town of Cuenca, which Pardo named after his own hometown in Spain (Hudson 2005: 25, 146).

Interactions and diplomatic relations between Pardo and Joara were critical to the success of Spanish colonial enterprises in northern *La Florida* (Beck et al. 2011; see also Smith and Hally 1992). Upon the initial founding of Fort San Juan and Cuenca, Captain Juan Pardo placed his sergeant, Hernando Moyano, in charge of the fort, which was garrisoned with 30 men. This number varied at various points in 1567 and early 1568 depending on the comings and goings of Pardo himself and the men traveling with him on unauthorized "forays" by Moyano and men from Cuenca and Joara to conduct raids on Chisca villages in the mountains, and on periodic prospecting excursions involving Andres Suarez and others in search of sources of metals and gemstones.

After having established an early iteration of Fort San Juan and Cuenca at Joara by early 1567, Pardo marched eastward to Guatari. The chief of Joara was masculine, but the principal chief of Guatari was feminine and given the same title (*mico*) as the chief of Joara; written accounts of the Pardo expeditions hint at some amount of rivalry between these neighboring chiefdoms, suggesting that the chiefdom of Guatari was a threat. The chief of Guatari evidently held power and received tribute from other groups, as was the case within the chiefdom of Joara, though it was not on the same scale as the polities and provinces of Cofitachequi and Coosa (northwest Georgia) during the era of the Soto expedition. Guatari mico was not alone in her feminine leadership—the local chief (*orata*) within her own village was also a woman. During Pardo's first visit to Guatari in early 1567, as many as 39 chiefs owed tribute and deference to her. While these are the only two feminine chiefs recorded by Pardo, it is entirely possible women were chiefs in other areas of the Southeast, perhaps not recognized or recorded as such by the chroniclers of Spanish entradas, and it is likely that those chroniclers had imperfect knowledge of gender dynamics within Mississippian chiefdoms, broadly speaking (e.g., Trocolli 2006).

During his second visit in late 1567, Pardo assembled chiefs from the province of Guatari, gave them metal goods and other gifts, and asked that they help him build a fort, which was completed in early 1568, and which Pardo named Fort Santiago. The fort was built with *bastardos* (bastions of logs and earth) and *cavalleros* (tall log posts and earthen embankments). Pardo then rechristened the settlement with the town name of Salamanca. Pardo deputized Lucas de Caniçares to take charge of the fort and the 16 soldiers garrisoned there; he forbade his men from bringing women from Guatari into the fort after dark, and he gave Caniçares the charge of ensuring that his men would treat the people of Guatari well. The specific instructions to his men to treat Native people well and not to bring Native women into the fort after dark may have been given in deference to commands given to Pardo by Pedro Menéndez de Avilés, the aspiring colonial governor of *La Florida,* and in deference to the resident chaplain. It is likely these instructions also reflect problems that had arisen in the treatment and mistreatment of the community and women of Joara by Pardo's men during the preceding year, threatening the diplomatic relations Pardo was carefully crafting.

Written accounts of the Soto and Pardo entradas do not specify but do hint at potentially important kinship connections between the chief of Cofitachequi in 1540 and the chief of Joara in 1566. As stated above, in 1540, Tali Mico was a young woman (Hudson 2018: 174–175; Snyder 2009) who, after greeting the Spanish in the town of Cofitachequi, was forced to travel with the entrada until she escaped along with a slave owned by one of Soto's men as Soto's expedition set out from Xuala (Joara) to traverse the mountains en route to Chiaha. Together, they stayed for some time in the province of Xuala where they were said to have lived as wife and husband (DePratter 1989: 135–136; Snyder 2009: 21–22). In 1540, the province of Xuala may have been one of the areas associated with the paramount chiefdom of Cofitachequi, but one generation later, Joara had eclipsed Cofitachequi, which by then was known as Canos (Hudson 2005: 69–70). Important as well, when Pardo arrived at Joara in 1566, he encountered an "old cacica" to whom he gifted a Biscayan axe. While only speculative, there is the possibility that the chief of Joara who met Pardo in 1566 was a male relative of the "old cacica" and perhaps a relative as well of the enslaved West Indian or African man who was said to have become connected with Tali Mico in 1540 after departing from the Soto entrada in the territory of Xuala. Indeed, Tali Mico's status and authority would have been recognized at Joara when she passed through with Soto, and though she intended to return to her capital, it may be that after Soto depleted her chiefdom of needed food supplies and sacred items, Joara was the best place to recuperate her status (Snyder 2009: 22). Regardless of whether we can resolve the genealogical relationships between the leadership of Cofitachequi in 1540 and Joara in 1566, it is clear that the power of women shaped the structure and history of these chiefdoms in important ways.

Pardo attempted to situate himself as recipient of the food surplus tribute payments collected by the chiefs of Joara and Guatari through diplomatic maneuvering and gifting. In several instances, Pardo gave diplomatic speeches at Native settlements, asking Indigenous groups to build houses for him and his men, asking for stores of food to be set aside for them, and he gave leaders of Native groups gifts such as metal goods, glass beads, and cloth. Pardo asked people to bring tribute to him at his towns, although sometimes he also asked them instead to maintain traditional practices to preserve geopolitical stability when it may have served his own interests and agendas. In each of these scenarios, Pardo was calling upon the surplus tribute payments produced by Indigenous women. Further, once stores of food were available, Pardo required the labor of skilled Indigenous women to prepare meals for his soldiers, further fostering dependence on Indigenous women and their labor. Again and again, Pardo was asking for the help of women to care for his soldiers, and Indigenous women, in turn, responded by provisioning and cooking for his men.

By June of 1568, news reached Santa Elena that warriors had attacked Fort San Juan, and that all six of Pardo's outposts in northern *La Florida* had been abandoned. The nature of those attacks and abandonment events, and the reasons for the attacks themselves, are difficult to discern from firsthand written accounts, although there are some clues as to the sources of tensions and hostilities at Fort San Juan. The emphasis by Pardo on preventing mistreatment of women at Guatari and at forts founded in late 1567 and early 1568 indicates that mistreatment of Native women was one problem during the first nine months of the short life of Fort San Juan. Additionally, Pardo had intended to return quickly to Joara after his departure for Guatari in early 1567, but it was nine months later when he made it back. Pardo arrived at Joara during his second expedition and encountered signs of instability and unrest, and he soon learned that Moyano and the men he took with him on raids against the Chiscas (and probably some illicit prospecting activity) were hiding out and under some threat of attack at a makeshift fort in the town of Olamico, in the province of Chiaha, in eastern Tennessee. Clearly, there were sources of tension in the fall of 1567, and those simmered through the winter, undoubtedly contributing to hostilities in the spring of 1568.

Meanwhile, oral testimony recorded years later sheds further light on the sources of these tensions and hostilities. A soldier named Jaime Martínez, drawing upon testimony from Juan Martín de Badajoz, specifically reported that food demands were one of the primary reasons for the attacks on Pardo's forts in 1568, and he hinted that the Natives enticed Pardo's men outside of the relative refuge of the forts themselves, making the Spaniards vulnerable (Hudson 2005:176). Excessive food demands would have taxed the ability of women to produce food.

There are indications that there were prolonged and persistent droughts in much of *La Florida* during the mid-sixteenth century (Anderson et al. 1995), and those conditions could have diminished the capacity of Joara and other communities to feed their households, let alone contribute to the Mississippian tributary economy that was used to meet the demands for food by

Spanish colonists. A woman from Joara, identified and perhaps "renamed" by Spaniards as Teresa Martín, reported in testimony given in 1600 that the people of Joara were upset that Pardo did not return to Joara as soon as promised (Hudson 2005: 176), reflecting local concerns that the stream of gifts and relations of reciprocity that Pardo started upon his first arrival to Joara had run dry.

The lives and testimonies of Native women married to Spanish men add yet another interesting dimension to the story of Mississippian women in *La Florida*, and the importance of women within kinship structures and social networks. When news reached Santa Elena of the attacks on Fort San Juan and Pardo's other outposts, only three of Pardo's men stationed in the interior when the attacks unfolded are known to have survived (both Pardo and Moyano had returned to Santa Elena, and the chaplain Sebastian Montero abandoned his post at Guatari either before or after the uprisings): Juan Martín de Badajoz, stationed at Fort San Juan and husband of Teresa Martín; Juan de Ríbas, husband to the Native woman known as Luisa Mendez; and a "Flemish fife" married to a Native woman at Canos (Worth 2016). It seems likely that some other men did escape, or escaped before the attacks, but we currently do not know about such cases. Instead, what is apparent is that these three survivors were all married to Native women. In each case, it is not clear whether they became husband and wife before the conquest of Fort San Juan, or at some point afterward, but their survival must be related in some way to their relationships with Native women.

In the case of Juan Martín de Badajoz, about whom we know more than the others, perhaps he was warned of the attack by Teresa Martín herself, or by one or some of her male relatives who were involved in the attack. Perhaps he knew because of his close association with Teresa Martín that plans were afoot, perhaps even with ritual preparations for warfare. Indeed, perhaps he was allowed to live, and was even guided back to Santa Elena, solely because of his relationship with Teresa Martín. For whatever purpose and to whatever end, it is very likely that his connection to a woman from the local Native community was the key to his survival. Although somewhat speculative, marrying Native women likely gave Spanish men a social existence within their wives' communities, making their lives (and their deaths) more consequential within Indigenous towns. Such a conclusion is consistent with the general importance of women across the Native American South as lynchpins within social networks, kinship structures and matrilineal descent groups, and matrilocal households (see Briggs, this volume; Sullivan, Chapter 6 in this volume).

The Women of Fort San Juan: Archaeological Evidence

The Berry site, located in the upper Catawba Valley of western North Carolina, represents the principal town of Joara and Pardo's outpost of Fort San Juan (Figure 10.2). Excavations in 1986 targeted areas of the site associated with the earthen mound—formerly 15 feet tall when first recorded by the Smithsonian Institution in the late nineteenth century (Thomas 1891: 151)—and pit features and large post emplacements near the mound (Moore 2002). Geophysical surveys starting in 1997 and ongoing excavations starting in 2001 have focused on areas in and around the mound; in an area southeast of the mound where we have unearthed the remnants of a moat and other features and deposits associated with the fort itself, as well as remnants of structures that seem to predate and postdate the fort; in an area northeast of the mound and 20 meters north of the fort that represents the Spanish domestic compound, where the 30 men garrisoned at Fort San Juan were housed, in at least five structures, all of which show signs of having been burned down; and in an area southwest of the mound where we have recently begun unearthing remnants of what look like aboriginal structures and pit features that may represent a late stage of settlement at the site, postdating the conquest of the fort and its abandonment (Figure 10.2). There are numerous pits and posthole patterns in the areas of the fort, the mound, and the domestic compound that are not yet fully understood, but we do have some ideas about the history of settlement at the site, and patterns of change within the domestic compound itself.

It is not entirely clear what the settlement looked like before the arrival of the Pardo expeditions. The surface scatter of potsherds and projectile points diagnostic of the Burke phase (AD 1400–1600; Beck and Moore 2002) covers an area of five hectares along the western bank of Upper Creek, not far upstream from its confluence from Irish Creek, and some 10 kilometers upstream from the confluence of Warrior Fork with the Catawba River. Despite efforts to identify concentrations of domestic structures and features at the south end of the site, we have not (yet) found them, but we have unearthed considerable evidence about the structures and features associated with the Spanish domestic compound at the northern end of the site.

We have identified two major phases of occupation and construction activity within the Spanish domestic compound: during the first, three structures (1, 3, and 4) were built in a slightly curving arc generally following the course of the creek; and during the second, two additional structures (2 and 5) were built, farther away from the creek (Beck et al. 2016b). The first phase of construction activity corresponds to Pardo's original arrival at Joara in De-

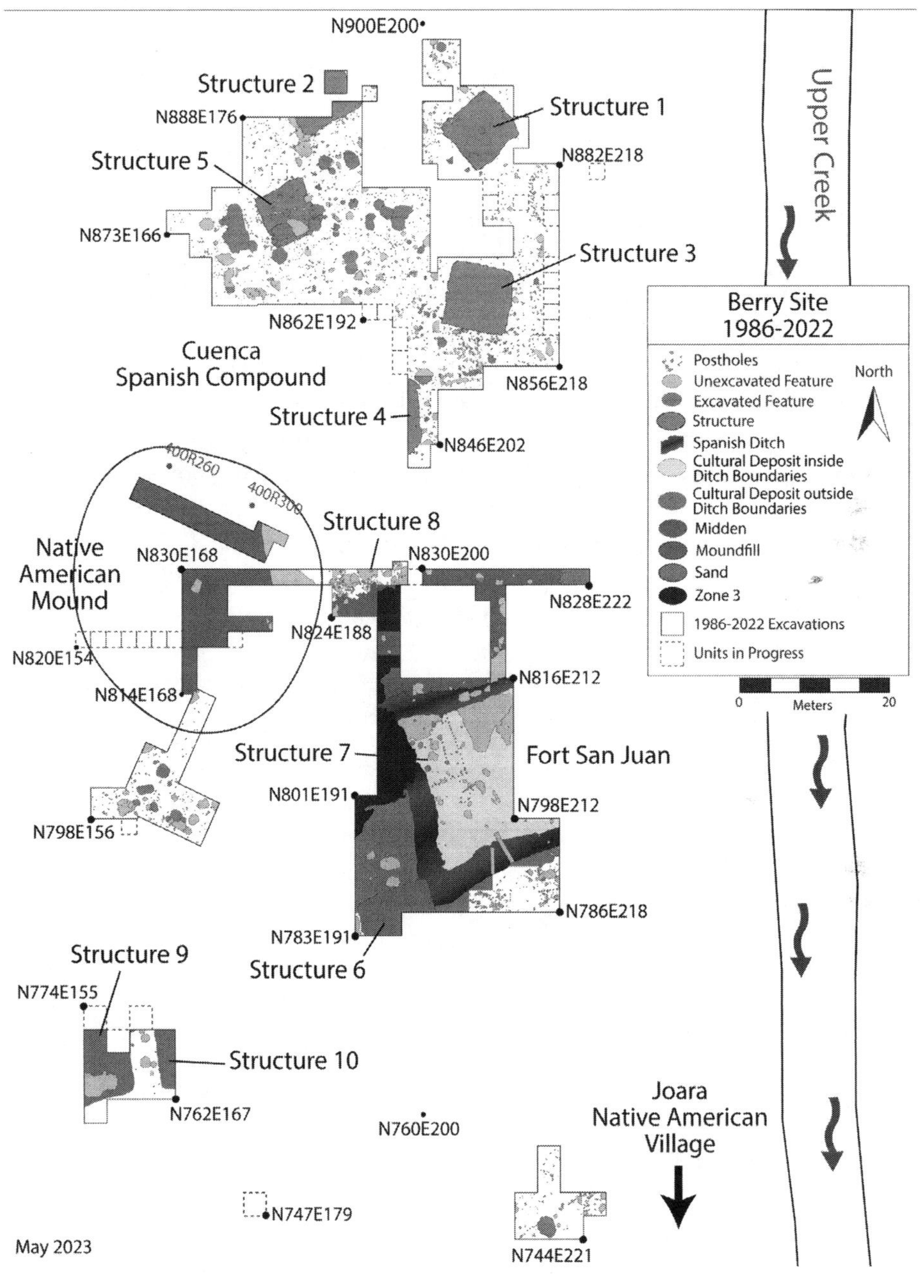

Figure 10.2. Excavation map of the Berry site, located in the upper Catawba River valley, western North Carolina.

cember 1566 and Pardo's efforts to build Fort San Juan and establish his town of Cuenca. The second phase of construction activity took place several months later, perhaps in association with Pardo's arrival and more prolonged stay at Fort San Juan during his second expedition, which was launched in September 1567. Evidence about the first phase of construction and occupation of the domestic compound gives indications of cooperation and favorable interaction among Pardo and his men and the people of Joara. Consistent with documentary evidence, remnants from the second phase hint at strained relationships between Joara and the colonists residing at Cuenca (Beck et al. 2016b).

Structures associated with the first phase of Spanish occupation look like typical Native American structures from this period in the greater southern Appalachians, although with some hints of European carpentry and construction practices. Structures 1 and 3 represent the same kind of domestic architecture as that seen at Mississippian and post-European contact Cherokee sites in southwestern North Carolina, and at Mississippian sites in northern Georgia and eastern Tennessee (Dickens 1976; Hally 2008; Keel 1976; Moore 2002; Rodning 2002, 2009, 2015; Schroedl 1998; Steere 2017; Sullivan 1987, 1995; Ward and Davis 1999). Both were built in basins (as may also be the case for Structure 4)—typical of South Appalachian Mississippian architecture—and the earth excavated in digging those basins was likely heaped up to create embankments around post-in-ground and wattle-and-daub walls and perhaps earthen coverings added to bark or thatch roofs. Some wooden timbers from Structure 1 show signs of having been cut with metal tools, and some show signs of having possibly been pierced by metal nails, which we interpret as evidence of participation of at least some of Pardo's men in building or maintaining this structure, and we know that Pardo's expedition had a carpenter and at least one metal saw. Structures 1 and 3 were built on relatively "clean" and "empty" surfaces—there are no signs of pit features, structures, or other occupational surfaces underneath them. Several pits west of Structures 1 and 3 were probably dug during this first phase of occupation of the domestic compound, perhaps in many cases to create pits for daub processing, which were then utilized for trash disposal, including fragments of Native American pottery, stone tools and debitage, and stone and clay pipes, as well as Spanish colonial items like olive jar fragments, glass beads, lead shot, wrought iron nails, and cuprous metals. One of the features in this area of the site, Feature 76, is a circular hearth, which we interpret as a cooking hearth associated with an open-air kitchen space.

Structures and features associated with the second phase of occupation of the Spanish domestic compound at Berry reflect continuing influences from and even the presence of Native peoples in this space, but in different circumstances than the favorable relations from early stages in the history of Fort San Juan. Structures 2 and 5 were built along an axis about 15 to 20 meters west of Structures 1, 3, and 4, and there is evidence of remodeling the central hearth and floor of Structure 1, perhaps in preparation for the second winter. Structures 2 and 5 were both built on surfaces in which pit features were already present, associated with early stages in the occupations of Structures 1, 3, and 4, and while Structure 2 appears to have been built in a basin like Structure 1, that is not the case for Structure 5, which seems to have been built at or close to the ground surface, perhaps in a shallow basin, but perhaps not. Within Structure 1, the largest and deepest posts are the four central roof support posts, which form a square around a central hearth, as is typical for South Appalachian Mississippian architecture, broadly speaking. Within Structure 5, there are not four clearly defined central roof supports, and postholes around the hearth are not as deep as some of the wall posts, and some postholes appear to have been dug with metal shovels and packed with yellowish clay around the posts themselves, in contrast to the South Appalachian Mississippian practice of ramming log posts straight into the ground, creating archaeologically visible postholes that are the same diameter as the associated posts and postmolds. Structure 1 looks like it was built by people who knew what they were doing; Structure 5 looks like it was built by people who knew what such houses should look like but did not have the expertise or skill sets to build them. Structure 5—more expediently built than Structure 1—seems to represent a formal kitchen (*cocina*) that replaced the open-air kitchen associated with Feature 76. Structure 5, like kitchens at other Spanish colonial settlements, was adjacent to several trash disposal pits and a large area of sheet midden that we have referred to collectively as the "western pits" (west of the "central pits" associated with the first stage of occupation in the compound). Large amounts of pottery, plant remains, and animal bone are all associated with these central and western pits. These finds offer insights into the ways in which food and foodways structured colonial entanglements at Joara, Cuenca, and Fort San Juan.

We presume that much of the food that Pardo and his men ate was prepared by and came from the women of Joara or from other Native groups, including, perhaps, the contingents of people from places and provinces near and far who traveled to Fort San Juan to meet with Pardo and form diplomatic relations with him. Given widespread evidence of the roles of men as hunters and warriors and women as farmers and cooks in Mississippian societies across the Southeast, we interpret the bones of bear (a feasting food for honored guests) and deer (a more "everyday" form of meat) to reflect provisioning by men—although women and children may well have been involved in processing and cooking such meats (Beck et al. 2016a; Lapham 2016, 2020). It is interesting to note that during the first phase of occupation by the garrison at Fort San Juan (the "honored guests" phase), large amounts of bear meat were presented to and eaten by the Spaniards, but bear is much less prevalent in zooarchaeological assemblages from the "western pits" and other deposits associated with later stages of occupation (the "outstayed-their-welcome" phase) (Lapham 2016).

Given the widespread association between women and growing, grinding, processing, and cooking maize, Chenopodium, beans, squash, and other plants, we interpret remnants of these foods as exclusive evidence of women's work and women's provisioning, probably often through activities that took place within the Spanish compound itself. Spatial and temporal patterns in the presence of these prepared foods illustrates how gender-mediated relations between Native people and the Spanish soldiers who were garrisoned at or who periodically visited Fort San Juan. Most if not all the men who traveled with Pardo had only barely reached America after sailing across the ocean from Iberia in 1566 before they marched inland to Joara. It is unlikely they would have become skilled at finding or growing much food on their own within a period of less than 18 months, and few would have had the skills necessary to cook those foods they found. There are no references in accounts of the Pardo expeditions to transporting Old World cultigens to northern *La Florida,* and no indications that they engaged in farming of any kind. On the other hand, there are many references in accounts of the Soto and Pardo expeditions to some foods transported by the expeditions, and strategies by which Soto, Pardo, and others sought to acquire—forcefully in Soto's case and somewhat more diplomatically in Pardo's case—food from Native groups.

During the occupation of the Spanish domestic compound associated with Fort San Juan, the most common foods consumed were maize, nuts (including acorn and hickory), and fruits (including passion fruit), and while not present in large amounts within archaeobotanical assemblages, there are specimens representing beans and squash (Fritz 2016). This profile of plant foods closely resembles the suites of plant foods found in the mound area at Berry (see Gremillion's analysis in Moore 2002: 299–313), and at other sites in the greater southern Appalachians and Piedmont (Gremillion 1993, 2002; Melton 2018; VanDerwarker 1999; VanDerwarker and Detwiler 2000, 2002; VanDerwarker et al. 2013). This evidence indicates that Mississippian women were preparing the same kinds of foods for Pardo and his men that they would have prepared for their own families. Further, there are some hints of attempts to reproduce European meals at the Berry site—turtle stews, for example, may have been known among Indigenous groups, but were consumed in greater abundance at the site (Lapham 2016). Such dishes may have been made by Pardo's men or may have been requested to be made for them. Regardless, the evidence indicates that Pardo's men consumed Indigenous meals and dishes that were dictated by the rules of Indigenous cuisines and prepared mostly with typical Mississippian food production practices, including those associated with maize-based and nut-based dishes.

When comparing plant foods present in deposits associated with early and late phases of occupation of the Spanish domestic compound at the Berry site, there are overarching similarities, indicating that women made and served similar kinds of foods throughout these phases. One exception to this general continuity is an apparent temporal shift to an increase in hickory nuts as ingredients of soups and stews. Within the "central pits" associated with the early phase of occupation, acorn nutshell fragments were more common than hickory in archaeobotanical assemblages collected through flotation. Within the "western pits" associated with the later phase of occupation, acorn forms 10% of the total count of all plant food specimens—considerably less than 27% in the "central pit" assemblage—and hickory is the most common nut species present in the "western pit" assemblage (Fritz 2016: 260). Acorn and hickory nuts are used in different culinary capacities in US Southeastern Indigenous meals—acorns were primarily used to create a kind of porridge to which fats (like bear oil) and meats (like venison) were added. Hickory nuts, on the other hand, were prized for their fat content, and shelled hickory nut meat added to pots of simmered carbohydrates like acorn porridge or hominy. However, comparing acorn and hickory counts demonstrates an increased use of hickory in dishes later in the fort's occupation.

One possible explanation of this trend is that it reflects changing food preferences by Pardo's men, and alterations by women from Joara in the ingredients or techniques of cooking meals for them. Acorns were considered a lower-class food in Iberian cuisine, and a shift away from acorn-based dishes may have been driven by Iberian tastes (Fritz 2016). Another possibility—and one consistent with archaeological evidence and documentary sources—is that Spanish meals changed because the women who prepared the food early in the history of Pardo's garrison were culturally distinct from the women who made the food later on. We see that the early provisioning by women from Joara reflects local "Burke-phase" foodways and culinary practices and preferences. We argue that the later provisioning of the garrison instead reflects "Pisgah-phase" foodways, which involved many of the same dishes and food combinations as those of the Burke phase but were prepared in vessels made in different styles and are associated with women who either came with or who were forcibly brought back to Cuenca after Moyano's raids against Native American villages in the Blue Ridge Mountains northwest of Joara.

Not long after Pardo christened Fort San Juan and departed Cuenca and Joara en route to Guatari, his sergeant, Hernando Moyano, led 15 of his men and a contingent of warriors from Joara to raid a Chisca village, evidently an enemy of Joara. Juan de Ríbas reported in 1602 that Moyano told him—sometime between 1571 and 1579—that Moyano was paid to help an Indian chief defeat a rival (Hudson 2005: 27–29). Following this attack, an Indian chief—probably from a Chisca village—threatened to kill Moyano and all of Pardo's men and to eat Moyano's dog, probably making a reference to a mastiff like those that Spanish conquistadors sometimes kept for threatening or committing violence against Indians. Moyano had written to Pardo about his first attack, and after receiving this threat, he did not wait at Joara for a reply. He took 20 of his men and presumably another contingent of Joara warriors to attack the stoutly stockaded settlement, probably located in the Nolichucky Valley in northeastern Tennessee, possibly at the Plum Grove site (Whyte and Boyd 2019). During the course of these attacks, unknown numbers of women were taken by Moyano and brought back to Joara. Eight of those women are known to have been taken as slaves to Santa Elena, where they were later freed that same year. Others of those women probably stayed at Fort San Juan, and we propose it is they who came to provision Pardo's men during later stages in the history of Cuenca's garrison.

Supporting evidence for this interpretation comes from Feature 112 at the Berry site, located just outside the southwestern corner of Structure 5. As already noted, we interpret Structure 5 (and Structure 2) as part of a late stage of renovating the domestic compound in which soldiers garrisoned at Fort San Juan were housed (Beck et al. 2016a, 2016b), whereas Structure 1, 3, and 4 were part of the original residential compound built when Pardo and his men first arrived at Joara and established the fort. The proximity of Feature 112 to Structure 5, and lack of evidence for either intruding into the other, leads us to conclude that Structure 5 and Feature 112 are broadly contemporaneous. Feature 112 is a circular pit that is nearly 2 m in diameter and 80 cm deep. It was unusual both for its extraordinary quantity of hickory nuts (Fritz 2016), and for its unique assemblage of Pisgah pottery. The core area of the Pisgah phase is located in the Appalachian Summit to the west and northwest of the Berry site (Dickens 1976; Keel 1976; Ward and Davis 1999; Whyte 2017), and Pisgah-phase pottery differs markedly from Burke-phase pottery that is more common in the upper Catawba Valley (Beck and Moore 2002; Moore 2002). Burke pottery, which is typically soapstone-tempered, includes curvilinear complicated stamped and burnished jars with everted and notched rim strips, as well as incised cazuelas with burnished surfaces and incised designs near carinated rims (Figure 10.3). Pisgah pottery, which is typically grit-tempered, includes rectilinear complicated stamped jars with filleted rims, with notched or punctate patterns on those rim fillets (Figure 10.4). Sherds from at least eight Pisgah cooking jars were recovered from Feature 112. While most of the sherds from the Berry site are attributable to the Burke series, we do occasionally find Pisgah potsherds, which are also present at other sites in the upper Catawba Valley. Villages attacked by Moyano are likely to have been Pisgah-phase sites, and he traversed areas of Pisgah-phase settlements between Joara and Chiaha. We therefore interpret the Pisgah cooking jar pottery from Feature 112 as an indication of the presence of Pisgah women in the Spanish domestic compound at the Berry site. It seems unlikely that the pots themselves could have been filled with appropriated foodstuffs taken from the towns that Moyano attacked—though the pots bear all markers of Pisgah-phase pottery, they were made with pastes with soapstone temper, a tradition typical and exclusive of the Burke phase.

If this is accurate, then it suggests two things: first, that Pisgah women interacted with local Burke phase, or Joaran women, learning soapstone paste recipes from them, but, second, chose to continue high-visibility Pisgah-style traditions. Ceramic studies suggest that high-visibility stylistic choices, like pot shape and decoration, are more likely to change than tempering traditions (Worth 2016); that the paste composition changed while the shape and design of the Pisgah cooking pots remained the same is telling. First, it strongly suggests that these relocated women were interacting with women from Joara, engaging in local ceramic-making traditions and frequenting local ceramic-making locations. Second, it suggests that these women were somewhat welcomed into the town of Joara, either because they were women, or because they were associated with Cuenca in some way, perhaps through networks of kinship or other forms of affiliation.

Despite their welcome by local women, we believe that the act of taking Pisgah women to provision the Spanish compound contributed to the fall of the fort. If these women were captives of Chisca communities who were enemies of Joara, as was the case when warriors from Joara and the detachments led by Moyano attacked them just a few months prior, would the presence of "enemy women" have sparked animosity between Joarans and Chiscas? If these women provisioned Pardo's men (or Moyano's men), whether willingly or not, did that activity undercut the status of Joaran women as agents of Native engagement with the Spanish colonial presence at Fort San Juan? If women from Joara reached a point of wanting to "starve out" the Spaniards at Cuenca—not by taking food away, but just by not investing effort and re-

Figure 10.3. Pisgah pottery from Feature 112 at the Berry site.

Figure 10.4. Burke pottery from Structure 1 at the Berry site.

sources in feeding or provisioning them any further—and if Chisca women instead helped Moyano and Pardo sustain the Spanish colonial presence at Fort San Juan, did that contribute to tensions that eventually led to the attack on the fort?

And what happened as local tensions between Joara and Cuenca simmered and worsened? Relations had begun favorably, but they grew worse. Bringing captive women to Cuenca may have displaced the provisioning power and kinship power of the women of Joara; it may have alienated women (and probably men) of Joara. And by doing so, this may have cut the Spanish off from the provisioning support from Joaran women that sustained them early on, leaving the men of Fort San Juan vulnerable. And what if Chisca women, who may have been welcomed into the feminine networks at Joara, aided in the preparations for the attacks against the Spanish? In other words, a move to strengthen their position at Cuenca, through the use of enslaved Native female labor, may have actually accomplished the opposite, sealing their fate. It is possible there were not major tensions between local women (from Joara) and non-local women (from Chisca villages), and it is possible that close relationships formed between women from these groups, but we think that gender dynamics related to these developments contributed in some way to the eventual attacks on Fort San Juan, and the agency of women is therefore an important force in these developments.

The Power of Mississippian Women

Outcomes of colonial entanglements among Europeans and Native peoples of the Americas are often framed as contacts between colonists and Native groups. Another way to frame our understandings of these episodes is to consider them as interactions among diverse groups of women and men (and children, for that matter), people from diverse cultural backgrounds, and people from different religious traditions. The case of the Berry site in western North Carolina, situated at the northern edge of the mid-sixteenth-century Spanish colonial province of *La Florida,* helps us to understand the power of Mississippian women, and the ways in which enactments of power by Mississippian women shaped the course of Spanish colonial history in the American South. It was a male chief who welcomed Pardo and his men to Joara, and perhaps it was a contingent of mostly male warriors who attacked Fort San Juan and dispatched the garrison, but they likely only did so with urging or support from the women of the community—the same women from this community and others who did much of the work to provision the Spaniards residing at Fort San Juan and at Pardo's other outposts. One of the major material components of diplomacy and interaction between Pardo and Native people and polities, including Joara, was food, the growing and gathering of which was and is today closely associated with women across the Native American South. Food surpluses enabled diplomatic engagements between Pardo and Joara and other Native groups, and thus they supported efforts by the leadership of Joara to cultivate that alliance. The availability or lack thereof of indigenous food provisioning, and adherence to or breaches of protocols about accessing indigenous foods, proved critical to the success or failure of Spanish colonial outposts at the northern edge of the Mississippian world. Put another way, women were important power brokers within Mississippian societies and in Mississippian engagements with Spanish conquistadors and colonists. In some cases, women made it possible for early European settlements to sustain themselves, but with that support withdrawn, those settlements, and even the individuals they were entangled with, could not and did not last.

Acknowledgments

We are grateful to the many supporters of and participants in our past and ongoing investigations at the Berry site in western North Carolina. Thanks to contributions to our Berry site excavations by David Anderson, Scott Ashcraft, Megan Best, Annie Blankenship, Johanna Bray, Charlie Cobb, David Cranford, Steve Davis, Kathleen Deagan, Chester DePratter, Merritt Eller, Charlie Ewen, Andrea Fink, Lotte Govaerts, David Hally, Tom Hargrove, Crickett Hefner, Liz Horton, Tim Horsley, Meg Kassabaum, Caroline Ketron, Heather Lapham, Abra Meriwether, Lee Newsom, Emma Richardson, Gerald Schroedl, Sarah Sherwood, Vin Steponaitis, Jason Ur, Greg Waselkov, and John Worth. We acknowledge and appreciate the Berry family for stewardship of the site, and for providing us access to the site for fieldwork and public events. Thanks for contributions from Sheila Bird and Lynne Sullivan as discussants for the "Mississippian Women" symposium at the annual Southeastern Archaeological Conference in 2018, and comments by Brooke Bauer in the symposium about the archaeology of the Catawba and Wateree valleys at the same SEAC.

References Cited

Anderson, David G., Malcolm K. Cleaveland, and David W. Stahle
1995 Paleoclimate and the Potential Food Reserves of Mississippian Societies: A Case Study from the Savannah River Valley. *American Antiquity* 60(2): 258–286.

Bauer, Brooke M.
2022 *Becoming Catawba: Catawba Indian Women and Nation-Building, 1540–1840.* University of Alabama Press, Tuscaloosa.
Beck, Robin A.
1997 From Joara to Chiaha: Spanish Exploration of the Appalachian Summit Area, 1540–1568. *Southeastern Archaeology* 16(2): 162–169.
2013 *Chiefdoms, Collapse, and Coalescence in the Early American South.* Cambridge University Press, Cambridge.
Beck, Robin A., and David G. Moore
2002 The Burke Phase: A Mississippian Frontier in the North Carolina Foothills. *Southeastern Archaeology* 21(2): 192–205.
Beck, Robin A., Christopher B. Rodning, and David G. Moore
2011 Limiting Resistance: Juan Pardo and the Shrinking of Spanish *La Florida,* 1566–1568. In *Enduring Conquests: Rethinking the Archaeology of Resistance to Spanish Colonialism in the Americas,* edited by Matthew Liebmann and Melissa S. Murphy, pp. 19–39. School for Advanced Research Press, Santa Fe, New Mexico.
Beck, Robin A., Christopher B. Rodning, and David G. Moore, eds.
2016c *Fort San Juan and the Limits of Empire: Colonialism and Household Practice at the Berry Site.* University Press of Florida, Gainesville.
Beck, Robin A., David G. Moore, and Christopher B. Rodning
2006 Identifying Fort San Juan: A Sixteenth-Century Spanish Occupation at the Berry site, North Carolina. *Southeastern Archaeology* 25(1): 65–77.
Beck, Robin A., David G. Moore, Christopher B. Rodning, Sarah Sherwood, and Elizabeth Horton
2016b The Built Environment of the Berry Site Spanish Compound. In *Fort San Juan and the Limits of Empire: Colonialism and Household Practice at the Berry Site,* edited by Robin A. Beck, Christopher B. Rodning, and David G. Moore, pp. 87–149. University Press of Florida, Gainesville.
Beck, Robin A., David G. Moore, Christopher B. Rodning, Timothy J. Horsley, and Sarah C. Sherwood
2018 A Road to Zacatecas: Fort San Juan and the Defenses of Spanish *La Florida. American Antiquity* 83(4): 577–597.
Beck, Robin A., Gayle J. Fritz, Heather A. Lapham, David G. Moore, and Christopher B. Rodning
2016a The Politics of Provisioning: Food and Gender at Fort San Juan de Joara, 1566–1568. *American Antiquity* 81(1): 3–26.
Beck, Robin A., Lee A. Newsom, Christopher B. Rodning, and David G. Moore
2017 Spaces of Entanglement: Labor and Construction Practice at Fort San Juan de Joara. *Historical Archaeology* 51(2): 164–193.
DePratter, Chester B.
1989 Cofitachequi: Ethnohistorical and Archaeological Evidence. In *Studies of South Carolina Archaeology: Essays in Honor of Robert L. Stephenson,* edited by Albert C. Goodyear III and Glen T. Hanson, pp. 133–156. Anthropological Studies 9, South Carolina Institute of Archaeology and Anthropology, Columbia.
1994 The Chiefdom of Cofitachequi. In *The Forgotten Centuries: Indians and Europe-*

ans in the American South, 1521–1704, edited by Charles Hudson and Carmen Chaves Tesser, pp. 187–226. University of Georgia Press, Athens.

DePratter, Chester B., and Marvin T. Smith

1980 Sixteenth Century European Trade in the Southeastern United States: Evidence from the Juan Pardo Expeditions (1566–1568). In *Spanish Colonial Frontier Research*, edited by Henry F. Dobyns, pp. 67–77. Center for Anthropological Studies, University of New Mexico, Albuquerque.

Dickens, Roy S. Jr.

1976 *Cherokee Prehistory: The Pisgah Phase in the Appalachian Summit Region.* University of Tennessee Press, Knoxville.

Eastman, Jane M.

2001 Life Courses and Gender among Late Prehistoric Siouan Communities. In *Archaeological Studies of Gender in the Southeastern United States*, edited by Jane M. Eastman and Christopher B. Rodning, pp. 57–76. University Press of Florida, Gainesville.

Edelson, S. Max

2021 Searching for Cofitachequi: How English Colonizers Mapped the Native Southeast before 1700. *XVII–XVIII* 78. DOI: 10.4000/1718.7383.

Ethridge, Robbie

2010 *From Chicaza to Chickasaw: The European Invasion and the Transformation of the Mississippian World, 1540–1715.* University of North Carolina Press, Chapel Hill.

Fritz, Gayle J.

2016 People, Plants, and Early Frontier Food. In *Fort San Juan and the Limits of Empire: Colonialism and Household Practice at the Berry Site*, edited by Robin A. Beck, Christopher B. Rodning, and David G. Moore, pp. 237–270. University Press of Florida, Gainesville.

Gremillion, Kristen J.

1993 Adoption of Old World Crops and Processes of Cultural Change in the Historic Southeast. *Southeastern Archaeology* 12: 15–20.

2002 Human Ecology at the Edge of History. In *Between Contacts and Colonies: Protohistoric Archaeology in the Southeastern United States*, edited by Mark A. Rees and Cameron B. Wesson, pp. 12–31. University of Alabama Press, Tuscaloosa.

Hally, David J.

1994 The Chiefdom of Coosa. In *The Forgotten Centuries: Indians and Europeans in the American South, 1521–1704*, edited by Charles Hudson and Carmen Chaves Tesser, pp. 227–253. University of Georgia Press, Athens.

2008 *King: The Social Archaeology of a Late Mississippian Town in Northwestern Georgia.* University of Alabama Press, Tuscaloosa.

Hudson, Charles

1976 *The Southeastern Indians.* University of Tennessee Press, Knoxville.

2005 [1990] *The Juan Pardo Expeditions: Explorations of the Carolinas and Tennessee, 1566–1568.* Revised edition. University of Alabama Press, Tuscaloosa.

2018 [1997] *Knights of Spain, Warriors of the Sun: Hernando de Soto and the South's Ancient Chiefdoms.* Revised edition. University of Georgia Press, Athens.

Hudson, Charles, Robin A. Beck, Chester B. DePratter, Robbie Ethridge, and John E. Worth
2008 On Interpreting Cofitachequi. *Ethnohistory* 55(3): 465–490.

Keel, Bennie C.
1976 *Cherokee Archaeology: A Study of the Appalachian Summit.* University of Tennessee Press, Knoxville.

Lapham, Heather A.
2016 Fauna, Subsistence, and Survival at Fort San Juan. In *Fort San Juan and the Limits of Empire: Colonialism and Household Practice at the Berry Site,* edited by Robin A. Beck, Christopher B. Rodning, and David G. Moore, pp. 271–299. University Press of Florida, Gainesville.
2020 In Feast and Famine: New Perspectives on Black Bears in the Southern Appalachians and Piedmont, AD 1000–1800. In *Bears: Archaeological and Ethnohistoric Perspectives in Native Eastern North America,* edited by Heather A. Lapham and Gregory A. Waselkov, pp. 160–192. University Press of Florida, Gainesville.

Levy, Janet E., J. Alan May, and David G. Moore
1990 From Ysa to Joara: Cultural Diversity in the Catawba Valley from the Fourteenth to the Sixteenth Century. In *Columbian Consequences, Volume 2: Archaeological and Historical Perspectives on the Spanish Borderlands East,* edited by David Hurst Thomas, pp. 153–168. Smithsonian Institution Press, Washington, D.C.

Melton, Mallory
2018 Cropping in an Age of Captive Taking: Exploring Evidence for Uncertainty and Food Insecurity in the Seventeenth-Century North Carolina Piedmont. *American Antiquity* 83(2): 204–223.

Moore, David G.
2002 *Catawba Valley Mississippian: Ceramics, Chronology, and Catawba Indians.* University of Alabama Press, Tuscaloosa.

Moore, David G., Robin A. Beck, and Christopher B. Rodning
2005 Pardo, Joara, and Fort San Juan Revisited. In *The Juan Pardo Expeditions: Explorations of the Carolinas and Tennessee, 1566–1568.* Revised edition by Charles M. Hudson, pp. 343–349. University of Alabama Press, Tuscaloosa.

Moore, David G., Christopher B. Rodning, and Robin A. Beck
2017 Joara, Cuenca, and Fort San Juan: The Construction of Colonial Identities at the Berry Site. In *Forging Southeastern Identities: Social Archaeology, Ethnohistory, and Folklore of the Mississippian to Early Historic South,* edited by Gregory A. Waselkov and Marvin T. Smith, pp. 99–116. University of Alabama Press, Tuscaloosa.

Rodning, Christopher B.
2001 Mortuary Ritual and Gender Ideology in Protohistoric Southwestern North Carolina. In *Archaeological Studies of Gender in the Southeastern United States,* edited by Jane M. Eastman and Christopher B. Rodning, pp. 77–100. University Press of Florida, Gainesville.
2002 The Townhouse at Coweeta Creek. *Southeastern Archaeology* 21(1): 10–20.
2009 Domestic Houses at Coweeta Creek. *Southeastern Archaeology* 28(1): 1–26.
2011 Mortuary Practices, Gender Ideology, and the Cherokee Town at the Coweeta Creek Site. *Journal of Anthropological Archaeology* 30(2): 145–173.

2015 Native American Public Architecture in the Southern Appalachians. In *Archaeological Perspectives on the Southern Appalachians: A Multiscalar Approach*, edited by Ramie A. Gougeon and Maureen S. Meyers, pp. 105–140. University of Tennessee Press, Knoxville.

Sampeck, Kathryn, Jonathan Thayn, and Howard H. Earnest, Jr.

2015 Geographic Information System Modeling of de Soto's Route from Joara to Chiaha: Archaeology and Anthropology of Southeastern Road Networks in the Sixteenth Century. *American Antiquity* 80(1): 46–66.

Schroedl, Gerald F.

1998 Mississippian Towns in the Eastern Tennessee Valley. In *Mississippian Towns and Sacred Spaces: Searching for an Architectural Grammar*, edited by R. Barry Lewis and Charles B. Stout, pp. 64–92. University of Alabama Press, Tuscaloosa.

Smith, Marvin T.

1987 *Archaeology of Aboriginal Culture Change in the Interior Southeast: Depopulation During the Early Historic Period.* University Press of Florida, Gainesville.

2000 *Coosa: The Rise and Fall of a Southeastern Mississippian Chiefdom.* University Press of Florida, Gainesville.

Smith, Marvin T., and David J. Hally

1992 Chiefly Behavior: Evidence from Sixteenth Century Spanish Accounts. In *Lords of the Southeast: Social Inequality and the Native Elites of Southeastern North America*, edited by Alex W. Barker, pp. 99–109. Archeological Papers of the American Anthropological Association 3, Washington, D.C.

Snyder, Christina

2009 The Lady of Cofitachequi: Gender and Political Power among Native Southerners. In *South Carolina Women: Their Lives and Times, Volume 1*, edited by Marjorie Julian Spruill, Valinda W. Littlefield, and Joan Marie Johnson, pp. 11–25. University of Georgia Press, Athens.

Steere, Benjamin A.

2017 *Archaeology of Houses and Households in the Native Southeast.* University of Alabama Press, Tuscaloosa.

Sullivan, Lynne P.

1987 The Mouse Creek Phase Household. *Southeastern Archaeology* 6(1): 16–29.

1995 Mississippian Community and Household Organization in Eastern Tennessee. In *Mississippian Communities and Households*, edited by J. Daniel Rogers and Bruce D. Smith, pp. 99–123. University of Alabama Press, Tuscaloosa.

2001 "Those Men in the Mounds": Gender, Politics, and Mortuary Practices in Late Prehistoric Eastern Tennessee. In *Archaeological Studies of Gender in the Southeastern United States*, edited by Jane M. Eastman and Christopher B. Rodning, pp. 101–126. University Press of Florida, Gainesville.

Sullivan, Lynne P., and Michaelyn S. Harle

2010 Mortuary Practices and Cultural Identity at the Turn of the Sixteenth Century in Eastern Tennessee. In *Mississippian Mortuary Practices: Beyond Hierarchy and the Representationist Perspective*, edited by Lynne P. Sullivan and Robert C. Mainfort Jr., pp. 234–249. University Press of Florida, Gainesville.

Sullivan, Lynne P., and Christopher B. Rodning

2001 Gender, Tradition, and the Negotiation of Power Relationships in Southern Appalachian Chiefdoms. In *The Archaeology of Traditions: History and Agency Before and After Columbus*, edited by Timothy R. Pauketat, pp. 107–120. University Press of Florida, Gainesville.

2011 Residential Burial, Gender Roles, and Political Development in Late Prehistoric and Early Historic Cherokee Cultures of the Southern Appalachians. In *Residential Burial: A Multi-Regional Exploration*, edited by Ron Adams and Stacie King, pp. 79–97. American Anthropological Association, Archeological Papers 20, Arlington, Virginia.

Thomas, Cyrus

1891 Catalogue of Prehistoric Works East of the Rocky Mountains. Bureau of American Ethnology Bulletin 12: 1–246, Smithsonian Institution, Washington, D.C.

Trocolli, Ruth

2006 Elite Status and Gender: Women Leaders in Chiefdom Societies of the Southeastern U.S. PhD dissertation, Department of Anthropology, University of Florida, Gainesville.

VanDerwarker, Amber M.

1999 Feasting and Status at the Toqua Site. *Southeastern Archaeology* 18(1): 24–34.

VanDerwarker, Amber M., and Kandace R. Detwiler

2000 Plant and Animal Subsistence at the Coweeta Creek Site (31MA34), Macon County, North Carolina. *North Carolina Archaeology* 49: 59–77.

2002 Gendered Practice in Cherokee Foodways: A Spatial Analysis of Plant Remains from the Coweeta Creek Site. *Southeastern Archaeology* 21(1): 21–28.

VanDerwarker, Amber M., Jon B. Marcoux, and Kandace R. Hollenbach

2013 Farming and Foraging at the Crossroads: The Consequences of Cherokee and European Interaction through the Late Eighteenth Century. *American Antiquity* 78(1): 68–88.

Ward, H. Trawick, and R. P. Stephen Davis Jr.

1999 *Time Before History: The Archaeology of North Carolina.* University of North Carolina Press, Chapel Hill.

Whyte, Thomas R.

2017 Household Ceramic Diversity in the Late Prehistory of the Appalachian Summit. *Southeastern Archaeology* 36(2): 156–164.

Whyte, Thomas R., and C. Clifford Boyd Jr.

2019 Dating the Native Plum Grove Site (40WG17), Washington County, Tennessee. In *Archaeological Adaptation: Case Studies of Cultural Transformation from the Southeast and Caribbean*, edited by C. Clifford Boyd Jr., pp. 67–82. University of Tennessee Press, Knoxville.

Worth, John E.

2016 Recollections of the Juan Pardo Expeditions: The 1584 Domingo de León Account. In *Fort San Juan and the Limits of Empire: Colonialism and Household Practice at the Berry Site*, edited by Robin A. Beck, Christopher B. Rodning, and David G. Moore, pp. 58–80. University Press of Florida, Gainesville.

11

Fort Walton Women

NANCY MARIE WHITE

Hard evidence is meager for identifying women's roles in the prehistoric Southeast. Archaeological, ethnographic, and historical data we *do* have suggest complementary political and social power and labor for Mississippian women and men (and additional-gender individuals) in native societies. Fort Walton archaeological culture is the Mississippian variant in the northwest Florida/southeast Alabama/southwest Georgia region where I work. It provides distinctive ceramics, high-status burials, and other ways to interpret–and imagine–women's lifeways.

The Fort Walton Region, Culture, and Antecedents

The extent of Fort Walton material culture is shown on the map in Figure 11.1. Fort Walton diagnostic artifacts may occur beyond this (somewhat fluid) boundary, but they are usually mixed with ceramics and other materials representing very different, contemporaneous archaeological manifestations (Pensacola culture to the west and southwest, Lamar to the north and northeast, and Safety Harbor to the southeast). Fort Walton extends from about 50 river/navigation miles up the lowest part of the lower Chattahoochee River and some 25 miles up the Flint River all the way down to the Gulf Coast, and from the eastern edge of Choctawhatchee Bay to somewhere between Tallahassee and the St. Johns River on the east. Sites range from small, presumed farmsteads to typical large Mississippian villages, many with flat-topped temple mounds, and there is good evidence for maize cultivation. But Fort Walton ceramics, while sometimes displaying typical Mississippian shapes, are *not* shell-tempered, and also include some unusual forms such as the 6-pointed open bowl (Willey 1999 [1949]). Also, in contrast to most other Mississippian burial programs, Fort Walton mortuary practices seem to focus as much attention upon elite women as upon men (Marrinan 2012; White et al. 2012).

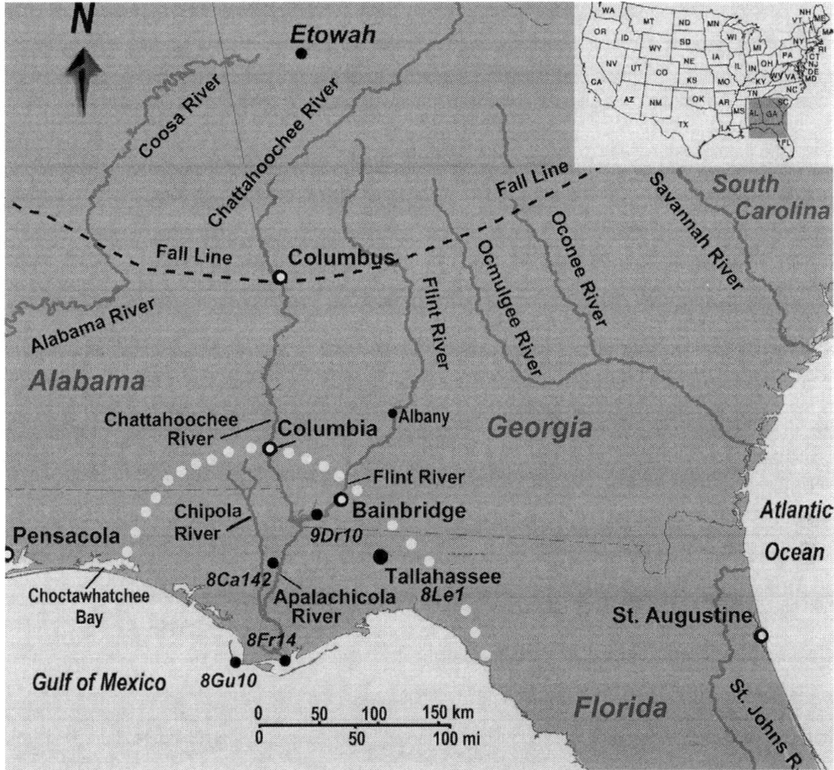

Figure 11.1. Map showing extent of the Fort Walton culture area in the Southeast, (dotted white line) and locations of archaeological sites discussed in this chapter.

The matrilineal societies first observed by Old World invaders were already impacted and altered by European contact by the time they were historically recorded, with huge population losses caused by the Spanish entrada. Chroniclers of the early expeditions, from male-dominated European societies, said far less about women than men. But some women must have been powerful enough to be targets of the violence of the conquistadores. Garcilaso de la Vega (1993[1605]: 101,106) described the expedition led by Panfilo de Narváez in 1528 along Florida's central and northern Gulf Coast. Narváez met Safety Harbor people upon landing on the coast of Tampa Bay, just southeast of the Fort Walton region. About the first thing he did was to cut off the nose of the male chief. Then, when the chief's mother protested, Narváez had his war dogs tear her apart to keep her from rallying resistance. The suppression of native women by Europeans continued, as missionaries and other colonials quickly forced them to wear more clothes, stay in the house, and do more domestic chores, changing their lives profoundly.

We know women were the farmers, and work, ritual, social, and leisure activity can be inferred from ethnographies of matrilineal societies and southeastern Indian history. Skeletal indicators do show that Mississippian women had increased upper arm strength, probably from pounding/grinding more grain with intensification of maize agriculture, or digging, hoeing, and other field tasks, while men had greater musculature of the legs, possibly tied to bow-hunting, playing the ball game, and/or warfare (Bridges 1989). Still, some early post-contact images, though flawed and Eurocentric, do give clues about the invisible roles of Fort Walton women, and show us that essentialist gender models (such as, women obtain plants and men obtain animals) are inadequate. Major sources are Theodor de Bry's copies of the paintings of Jacques le Moyne de Morgues, who recorded Indian life during the French expeditions to the Florida Atlantic coast in the middle 1500s. Among these are illustrations of men and women working together on subsistence-related projects. One picture depicts a scene of natives depositing crops in storage buildings in which the women are sitting back in the canoe and the men are paddling. Another scene portrays women planting maize with digging sticks while men chop up the soil with hoes (Florida Memory 2019: Plates XXII, XXI; Lorant 1946: 77, 79).

Women were not necessarily the nurturers. The Europeans described "curly-haired hermaphrodites" or "berdaches" or third-gender individuals (Callender and Kochems 1983; Lorant 1946: 69, 81), who carried heavy burdens of food to storage houses, supplies to battle, and the wounded and sick off the battlefield on litters to care for them or bury the dead (Florida Memory 2019: Plate XVII). (Many Native American societies once recognized additional genders beyond "male" and "female" though they may not be easy to identify archaeologically [Hollimon 2006], and multiple genders are known worldwide, many in matrilineal cultures [e.g., Davies 2007; Nanda 1999, 2004]).

In late pre-contact times, some Fort Walton women must have enjoyed distinguished status and power. We see indications as early as the Middle Woodland period in the region, when burials of women seem to have as many elaborate grave goods as those of men and children, and women may be portrayed in ceramic images as much as men. Figure 11.2 shows a ceramic effigy of a woman from the Pierce Mounds complex (8FR14 and other numbers) near the mouth of the Apalachicola River. This site has at least a dozen mounds, with seven arranged in an oval. The mounds on the west arc of the oval are mostly Early to Middle Woodland in age, and those on the east side are Fort Walton (White 2013). Collected in the mid-nineteenth century (and now displayed at the Florida Museum of Natural History), this vessel could

Figure 11.2. Ceramic effigy of a kneeling woman, from Pierce Mounds (8FR14 and other numbers) at the mouth of the Apalachicola River; recovered sometime in the nineteenth century and donated to the Florida Museum of Natural History, where it is on display, it could be from either the Middle Woodland or the Mississippian (Fort Walton) component of the site (photo by N. White, 2005).

be either Middle Woodland or Fort Walton, as its portrayal of a kneeling figure with folded arms resembles everything from Hopewellian figures to the painted marble statue of a woman (found with a similar one of a man) from a log-lined tomb within Mound C at Etowah, in northwest Georgia (King 2003). Notable are the protruding but small breasts, one of the few ways of telling the sex of such pre-contact human images.

The Late Woodland riverine shell midden site of Montgomery Fields (9DR10), on the Flint River, dug in 1953 by Carl Miller, was never reported, but documented in Smithsonian Institution archives. Miller was a River Basin Surveys field archaeologist who was moved from project to project in those days, with little time to write up his findings. Researching his materials and notes in the Smithsonian, I reconstructed the site map (White 2019). It shows numerous structure patterns under the plow zone, indicated by curved and straight lines of postmolds all over the place, and one can find many ways of connecting these dots to imagine building shapes. But in the west-center of the site, a relatively small, very clear circular pattern of nine postmolds, 2.1 m diameter, is apparent. Based on its size and unusual shape, Miller (1953) said it must have been "either a sweat lodge or a menstrual hut"; another such pattern of the same size, though not quite as discernible, was just to the east. Though the site had no Fort Walton component, Late Woodland was the time of the earliest experiments with cultivation of maize just before the expansion into Mississippian-style agricultural societies. Galloway (1997) has called out southeastern archaeologists for being too squeamish to suggest small or unusual structures as potential menstrual huts. Unlike elsewhere in the world, for southeastern Indians, menstrual huts were places where women, at a time when they had powerful, potentially dangerous magic, were isolated and required to rest and take a break from chores (!) for the benefit of the whole society. We can credit Carl Miller with being a guy ahead of his time for considering this interpretation, though whether menstrual huts would be close to the middle of the settlement is another question. But in the big picture, seldom do we see any attention paid to specific material signatures that indicate women, so we must keep on looking, especially when intra-site settlement patterns and other evidence are available to test real hypotheses. A probable 600 to 700-year-old Native American menstrual or menarche hut has been identified in the Pacific Northwest; it is almost 3 m in diameter and located away from other structures at the site (Carney et al. 2019).

Burial Ritual and Exotic Grave Goods

Fort Walton ceremonialism at the famous Lake Jackson mounds (8LE1) in Tallahassee highlights elite women. The high-status burials in Mound 3, salvaged by Calvin Jones and thoroughly researched by Rochelle Marrinan, are somewhat atypical for Mississippian times. Graves were placed in deep pits dug into the temple-mound summits and down through successive building floors. The dead were clearly important individuals, interred with abundant Southeastern Ceremonial Complex (SECC) mortuary goods, including ceramics; pipes; shell cups, beads, pendants, and engraved gorgets; copper-inlaid bone hairpins; pearls; spatulate stone celts, a chert core, tools, points, and debitage; stone discoidals; objects of sharktooth, lead, mica, possibly anthracite, graphite, steatite, limestone, and copper; red and yellow ocher pigment; fragments of woven cane matting, cloth, and leather coverings wrapping the copper objects; and even a wooden pole fragment that suggested a litter burial. The copper artifacts ranged from headdress spangles and hair ornaments to pendants, axes, and plates, which were decorated (cut out and engraved or repoussé) and plain (Jones 1982). Apparently, all three of the copper repoussé plates with complex raptor-bird iconography were buried with mature women, estimated to be age 49 or older (Marrinan 2012).

The women in Burials 7 and 16 had copper plates depicting bird-dancer figures usually interpreted as men; however, maybe they are not. These figures have bent legs, are wearing shell beads, feathered capes, and other items, including elaborate headdresses, and are holding various objects, including trophy heads. The Burial 7 plate image has a strong indication of a protruding breast, and both Burial 7 and Burial 16's plates show shell pendants on the humanoid figures. Burial 10's skeleton is variably interpreted as male or female, but Marrinan (2012: 222–223) notes how in its plates depicting a person and a falcon, the person may represent a man, but this burial lacks a copper axe as other burials of men in Mound 3 had. Copper plates of course occur at other famous SECC sites (Galloway 1989; King 2007). The Lake Jackson plates are similar to those from Etowah, Georgia (King 2003), which might even have been the place where they were manufactured. While some Etowah copper plates have straight torsos on the human-like figure, which is typically called a "bird-man," at least a couple also have small but protruding breasts (Strong 1989: 224–225). In fact, across the South, this feathered human figure can be seen elsewhere with protruding small breasts, such as on some carved Mississippian shell gorgets (King 2007: cover; Strong 1989: 227). Could these ceremonial feathered, apparently dancing figures sometimes be women? Yes, the breast is little but, as noted, other pre-contact Native American portrayals of women usually show small breasts. And even if most warriors were men, a religious specialist dancing with a trophy head need not be the person who acquired it.

Figure 11.3a shows a Reflectance Transformation Imaging (RTI) rendering of the original Lake Jackson Burial 7 plate as produced by Jeff Du Vernay's (2016) 3-D documentation and visualization project. RTI is a photographic method of seeing the surface of an artifact with lighting from any direction to enhance shapes and colors not always immediately visible (Cultural Heritage Imaging 2019). Du Vernay's research aimed to conserve as much information as possible about these famous and fragile artifacts (which are locked in a state vault requiring multiple persons with different keys to come together to open). The image is compared with the original drawing of the plate (Jones 1982: Figure 6b) based on the photo of the reverse side, that is, the back side from which the engraving or punching of the design was done. Both of these clearly show a triangular, protruding breast on the left center. Next to these images, in Figure 11.3c, is artist Theodore Morris's (1991) reconstruction of

Figure 11.3. Bird-dancer figure on repoussé copper plate from Burial 7, Mound 3, Lake Jackson site, 8LE1, Tallahassee: *a,* RTI rendering of original plate by Jeff Du Vernay (2016); *b,* line drawing of image (adapted from Jones 1982: Figure 6b); *c,* artist's interpretation (adapted from Morris 1991); *d,* another artist's interpretation (adapted from drawing by Scott Mitchell in White 1999: Fig.15.2).

the ceremonial Fort Walton figure shown on this plate, made for the Florida Anthropological Society's official poster (which I have reversed to permit better comparison). A beautiful drawing, it is nonetheless of a muscular, young, attractive man who, by the way, is holding a stylized human head or even something resembling a doll head. Finally, for comparison, I present (again) the drawing I commissioned from artist/archaeologist Scott Mitchell (White 1999: Figure 15.2) for which I asked him to use the Lake Jackson and Etowah plates as a foundation but show the same bird dancer how it *could* look: as an older noblewoman or ritual practitioner, dancing with a real, recently severed trophy head. This picture is no more improbable than other reconstructions of the real humans represented on those plates and elsewhere in Mississippian iconography. Maybe they were women, celebrating with actual human heads. In fact, anthropologists have often noted how, in some indigenous American societies and many cultures elsewhere around the world, older women, after menopause, transform into a different gender, since they are no longer the childbearers, and take on powerful roles involving political positions, magic, and the supernatural (e.g., Hays-Gilpin 2008).

Therefore, we can ask if these older women with the plates at Lake Jackson were chiefs or clan matriarchs or religious practitioners (or all of these)? They must have been important if their graves included such prized artifacts, which were retired or taken out of circulation at their deaths. The plates were heirlooms, repaired often, with more copper fragments added for mending (you can see the rivets on the 3-D image and the drawing), and probably often polished to gleam in sunlight. Stylistic resemblances suggest the Lake Jackson plates were made at or distributed from Etowah, some 300 miles away. They must have been expensive and exotic, and their repaired/"gently used" state at burial suggests they were perhaps kept for generations as special, revered identity or status markers. Further, their rarity makes it truly extraordinary that they were retired in the first place, let alone retired with three older women. Maybe when these Fort Walton women died, their clan leadership symbols went with them. They were placed in deeper floors in Mound 3, estimated to date to around AD 1200. Later, elite graves in Mound 3 have abundant additional copper, buried with men, women, and kids.

In my research region of the Apalachicola-lower Chattahoochee valley, some 50 miles (80 km) west of Tallahassee and Lake Jackson, the Corbin-Tucker site (8CA142), on the middle Apalachicola, is of interest. Its village area was dated to cal. AD 770–1170, early in Fort Walton times. North of the village was a cemetery with elite fragmentary burials. A prominent one was the skull and one or two possible longbones of a woman. She had a copper disc in the middle of her forehead, a 5-lb (2.3 kg), foot-long (30 cm) greenstone celt under her chin, and sherds of Fort Walton Incised pottery, including a six-pointed open bowl, surrounding her remains. She also had the teeth of a child and three other individuals near her skull. Preservation conditions were awful, and gopher tortoises had burrowed into and churned up the graves. However, other remains, of skulls, longbones, and teeth were determined to represent a total of 10 to 19 individuals within the 3 square meters exposed. Other fancy grave goods within this cemetery included a copper-covered wood disc, a whelk shell cup, another greenstone celt, and a ceramic mushroom-shaped object, possibly a pottery trowel. One radiocarbon date on the cemetery was cal. AD 1440–1640 (intercept at 1480), but another was from the contact period in the 1600s, so groups in the same matrilineage may have returned to place the honored dead in this burial ground over the centuries. Though no post-contact artifacts were found, the woman's copper disk had small, raised bosses around the edge, which might indicate a contact-period style (White 1994; White et al. 2012). Meanwhile, we must stop interpreting high-status burials of women as somehow reflecting in the glory of their male family members and consider how men in rich graves might have been trophy husbands!

One additional source of direct data is the burial mound at Richardson's Hammock site (8GU10). At this large gastropod shell midden on St. Joseph Bay, at the bottom of the Apalachicola delta, the burial mound was looted 50 years ago (it was on private land) by collectors who recovered artifacts and some human skeletal remains. Now, one collector has accumulated others' materials and initiated scientific research on them. The human remains include skulls of at least eight individuals, both men and women, and some are clearly from Fort Walton times, but others are Middle Woodland; the later people placed their graves into the earlier existing mound. Most of the skulls have substantial fronto-occipital cranial modification, and the dead were buried with elaborate grave goods. At present, radiocarbon dating, strontium isotope analysis (to see diet and local vs. non-local origins), and ancient DNA studies are ongoing, but promising in terms of demonstration of matrilineal relationships among elite lineages, as discussed below. One of the Fort Walton burial offerings in this mound was a "spaghetti-style" carved shell gorget, and another is a fragment of a copper plate. The oldest of the minimum ten individuals known to have been placed in the mound was a woman in her 50s, with a heavily modified cranium and few to no teeth—possibly a clan mother herself. (With the Muscogee Nation of Florida Traditional Chief, a consultant in this work, we aim for reburial of the remains after completion of the research).

Ceramics, Subsistence, and Labor

Beyond graves, Fort Walton material culture suggests other aspects of women's lives. Pottery, assumed to have been produced by women, is notably different from that usually made in the Mississippian world. Forms are typical—jars with handles, cazuela bowls—but, as noted, vessels are not shell-tempered. Characteristic Mississippian jars, such as Bell Plain (Phillips et al. 1951), are reinterpreted without shell temper as Lake Jackson and Marsh Island Incised types (Willey 1999 [1949]), and Moundville (Heimlich 1952) or Dallas Incised (Lewis and Kneberg 1946) jars without shell are named Cool Branch Incised (Sears 1967). Besides distinctive temper, there is at least one unusual shape, the 6-pointed Fort Walton Incised open bowl (which also does occur in shell-tempered form farther west in the Pensacola culture). So, many ideas on how to be Mississippian filtered into the region, but Fort Walton women were shapers of identity, making ceramics with their own regional markers.

Subsistence and divisions of labor are other important areas in which to see women's activities and identities. We assume women cultivated fields; historically, southeastern women were the agriculturalists, and men resisted colonial efforts to put them to work picking crops. However, what about coastal Fort Walton fisherfolk, where it seems maize was not grown? Many want to see shell collectors as women, presumably while guys go after the rough stuff, perhaps huge fish or whales, but ethnographically this is not always the picture. Around St. Joseph Bay, at the bottom of the Apalachicola delta on the west side, Fort Walton sites such as Richardson's Hammock are large-gastropod shell middens. Since this bay is so salty, with few discharging freshwater streams, the faunal assemblages are dominated by lightning whelk and horse conch shells, with only a few oysters, but other saltwater fish species. Often, sites consist of individual shell piles with these large shells and some fish bones (White 2005). Who collected these resources at these short-term camps? It is so easy to wade into the shallow bay and pick them up that I am sure that the children did it, along with parents of both sexes. And in winter, the cold-stunning of sea turtles also meant easy harvest. When bay waters chilled, turtles instinctively swimming south become trapped in the bay and could easily have been grabbed for supper. Water temperatures below 40 degrees made them cold-stunned, immobilized (Summers et al. 2001), so maybe less dangerous for kids to drag up onto the beach. Other, less salty bays around the Apalachicola delta have similar zooarchaeological remains, oyster and clamshell middens indicating abundant fish and turtle harvests, with some procurement of terrestrial mammals. So far, there is no indication of agriculture on the coast, while interior riverine sites have charred maize remains. Were divisions of labor by sex and gender more relaxed among coastal Fort Walton communities because wild resources were easier to procure, and crops were not grown?

Turning to lithic materials, some interesting developments must have affected Fort Walton women. Mississippians probably still used both spears and atlatls, but only men? Many assume it was men since supposedly great upper body strength is needed to throw a spear. But the reason humans make tools is to enhance effort, and the atlatl certainly does that. By Late Woodland-early Fort Walton times, the bow and arrow appeared, which may have made a considerable difference in native life. Interestingly, Fort Walton lithic assemblages are known for being, well, pitiful. There is seldom much debitage and just a few small triangular points, presumably for arrows. Contemporaneous Mississippian cultures elsewhere, not to mention earlier and later indigenous peoples in this same region, had plenty of chipped-stone tools. Thus, explaining the scarcity of such a lithic record for Fort Walton is difficult. They may have made cane or bone arrow tips and other tools of perishable raw materials. Meanwhile, would the introduction of the bow have affected women, with their lesser upper body strength? The right *sized* bow *or* spear for the size of the user is the crucial element. Even if a woman archer can only pull 30–40 lbs (as is widely standard today), it is sufficient to kill a deer, since skill, silence, and strategy count as much as strength. Such an observation would be true no matter the hunting weapon. To put it in perspective, a YouTube video shows a 7-year-old bagging a deer with an atlatl and spear (Wide Open Spaces 2017), complete with music from the movie *Rocky*.

A bigger issue is that some see the bow and arrow as a new superior weapon for human conflict, leading to vast social inequality, with inter-group strife and warfare becoming endemic in the Mississippian South (Bingham et al. 2013; Blitz 1988; Blitz and Porth 2013; Grund 2017). Many interesting, complicated, and interrelated hypotheses about this technological change, which originally was probably for hunting, have yet to be evaluated in the light of hard evidence. However, in the Fort Walton region, we have so far none of the material indications supporting scenarios of frequent warfare: no mass graves, frequent skeletal wounds, buffer zones, or palisaded villages. To be fair, there has been far less wide-scale excavation in the region that would expand horizontally our views of whole sites, in order to see encircling palisades or large cemeteries with many skeletons showing arrow wounds or other indications of violence. But for this region, the so-called buffer zones may just be effects of sampling error, areas with little archaeological survey conducted (Marrinan and White 2007: 301). Even outside the Fort Walton region, places thought to have palisades, tracts of land surrounded by walls of posts, might not necessarily be for defensive purposes but perhaps sacred grounds set aside for ceremonial practice or group rites–maybe even dance floors!

While evidence of violence may turn up eventually in the Fort Walton area, it might have been individual conflict or feuds, not warfare. Gender equality and complementarity may have characterized Fort Walton culture more than perhaps other Mississippi-period groups. The hard-core feminist in me would love to see maize-goddess-worshipping peaceful Fort Walton matriarchies. However, in reality, anthropological research worldwide has never identified a true matriarchy, where women run absolutely everything, and really even very few total patriarchies are known (the tiny Vatican state being one still in existence). We need more research on matrilineal societies that are still extant, where, despite imposition of global western male-dominated capitalism, egalitarian roles and complementary power for men and women and other genders is common.

Matrilineal Societies

For example, the Minangkabau in Sumatra, Indonesia, possibly the largest matrilineal society left in the world, still have families dominated by the most senior woman, and men in the household serve mothers first, then wives (I like that idea). Gender equality and sharing of power and authority includes husbands moving into their wives' homes, women's ownership of the home and land and what is produced from it, and treasuring of female children to keep the family tradition alive. These exist within what is really a conservative society that originally held animist and Hindu beliefs before Islam took over centuries ago (Blackwood 2000; Shapiro 2017). In another case, the matrilineal Mosuo of southwest China have no real institution of marriage, with women-run households, brothers helping raise children, and men visiting women for sex and socializing, but then returning to their own family homes (Yuan and Mitchell 2000). Another example is an island in Melanesia, where the matrilineal Vanatinai people, like others with such kinship systems, have no gender-based words in their language for individual children, sorcerers, and other roles, and both women and men enjoy equal opportunities to attain power, prestige, and spiritual prowess (Lepowsky 1993). Old-fashioned ethnographies by male anthropologists who assumed men were always the dominant gender nonetheless faced the reality of matrilineal societies in which they were obliged to document lifeways that contradicted their assumptions. For example, among the Kaguru of East Africa, men prized sisters for providing them with heirs, and both men and women cleared land and did hoeing and harvesting (Beidelman 1971). Many other societies, matrilineal and not, have had no strict gender-based divisions of labor (e.g., Endicott and Endicott 2008).

However, Native Americans of the Southeast did have real divisions of labor according to gender. Historical, ethnographic, and biological research demonstrate differences in sex-based physical activities and types of power and prestige obtained by men and women. Women were the farmers and controllers of the land, household, and children, while men married *into* families and households but did not dominate them, and recognized women's complementary social power (e.g., Hudson 1976). Gender roles among the region's Aboriginal peoples were distinct but reciprocal, interdependent, and of equal status. As archaeologists, we must learn from ethnographic research as much as possible about potential lifeways in cultural groups organized around matrilineages. Only if we can logically hypothesize what women's (and men's and others') roles *could have been* can we then search for material correlates of these systems. Yet most books on southeastern US archaeology do not even have "matrilineality" or "matrilineal" in their indexes, let alone paying much attention to this type of social organization.

Other Research Avenues

More DNA and other archaeogenomic and biochemical study would shed light upon some of these issues. Stable isotopes in bone might show if women were local and men from elsewhere, or if each had different diets. Relationships among individuals with similar mitochondrial DNA could show hereditary elite burial within a female line, demonstrating matrilineal kinship systems of post-contact southeastern Indians traceable far back in time. In the Southwest, ancient DNA research on skeletal remains (Kennett et al. 2017) has documented at least three centuries of matrilineally based inherited leadership extending from AD 800–1139. Affirmation of geographical location or family affiliation centered around the female line might quell some of the improbable explanations often seen in southeastern US archaeological interpretation. For example, new ceramic styles are often attributed to wives taken from outside the group, when more likely husbands were brought *in* from elsewhere (maybe with pots of offerings from their moms?). My old professor Charlie Callender studied social relationships among many extant Native American groups. He explained to an amazed class that in matrilineal society, divorce was easy. If a man wanted a divorce, he packed his things and he left. If a woman wanted a divorce, she packed his things and he left!

Fort Walton material culture disappeared by about AD 1700, apparently due to pressure, conflict, and disease introduced by invading European colonial powers as well as other Native American groups. It is unknown whether the Fort Walton people themselves died out, left with the Spanish, or were absorbed into other groups such as Creeks. They probably did contribute to both the biological and the cultural heritage of later southeastern Native Americans. Even after a couple centuries of domination by colonial peoples from lands where only men ran things, and men only dealt with other men, women were important in the formation of the Creeks and the Seminoles, who came to inhabit the region. Women wanted from European traders many commodities such as cloth and other items, and told their leaders, by then all male in response to colonial standards, to go get these items. Male chiefs or others representing Creeks in meeting with the British wondered why no British women were present (Hudson 1976: 269). Women in matrilineal societies usually enjoyed great sexual freedom. Creek women may have chosen to mate with representatives of colonial British and Spanish powers for reasons of family and prestige. In matrilineal Indigenous groups, offspring of matings with foreign men were still Indians, but they were more able to move fluidly in European circles and learn those languages. In later post-contact times, many Creek leaders had American Indian mothers and European or African fathers or other mixed ancestry.

Until we can accumulate more direct scientific evidence, we must continue to imagine the kinds of powers, positions, and daily labors that Fort Walton women and people of so many other roles within southeastern native societies might have had. Even if my hypothesis that Fort Walton societies were more peaceful than most Mississippians could be supported with further research, women's roles in avoiding warfare would be far more difficult to establish. But, as noted, several Fort Walton women were accompanied in death by objects with powerful political and ideological symbolism. Further, if Fort Walton women's unusual Mississippian ceramics were specific to their region, archaeological analysis should begin with assumptions of matrilineal kinship and those potters controlling community production and providing the majority of the artifact record expressing regional identity. Even zooarchaeological remains and the paltry lithic assemblages at individual sites probably represent choices made by female lineage heads at least as much as by male leaders. Matrilineal family members would probably have had to do what Big Mama clan mother wanted. The old saying, "if mama ain't happy, ain't nobody happy," familiar from country songs and ubiquitous in the South, was probably true in pre-contact times as well. There was a lot of hard work done by everyone, especially women, but there was probably also a lot of dancing.

Acknowledgments

Thanks to Jeff Du Vernay for sharing his RTI images of the Lake Jackson plates; to Ted Morris for assuring me he always gives educators and students free access to his images; to Rochelle Marrinan for constant inspiration; and to Rachel Briggs, Michaelyn Harle, and Lynne Sullivan for inviting me to be a part of the original symposium and this book.

References Cited

Beidelman, T. O.

1971 *The Kaguru, A Matrilineal People of East Africa.* Hold, Rinehart and Winston, Inc., New York

Bingham, Paul M., Joanne Souza, and John H. Blitz

2013 Social Complexity and the Bow in the Prehistoric North American Record. *Evolutionary Anthropology* 22: 81–88.

Blackwood, Evelyn

2000 *Webs of Power: Women, Kin, and Community in a Sumatran Village.* Rowman & Littlefield Publishers, Inc., Lanham, Maryland.

Blitz, John Howard

1988 Adoption of the Bow in Prehistoric North America. *North American Archaeology* 9: 123–145.

Blitz, John H., and Erik S. Porth

2013 Social Complexity and the Bow in the Eastern Woodlands. *Evolutionary Anthropology* 22: 89–85

Bridges, Patricia

1989 Changes in Activities with the Shift to Agriculture in the Southeastern United States. *Current Anthropology* 30(3): 385–94.

Callender, Charles, and Lee M. Kochems

1983 The North American Berdache. *Current Anthropology* 24: 433–56.

Carney, Molly, Jade d'Alpoim Guedes, Kevin J. Lyons, and Melissa Goodman Elgar

2019 Gendered Places and Depositional Histories: Reconstructing a Menstrual Lodge in the Interior Northwest. *American Antiquity* 84: 400–419.

Cultural Heritage Imaging

2019 Reflectance Transformation Imaging (RTI). What is it? Electronic document, http://culturalheritageimaging.org/Technologies/RTI/, accessed August 18, 2019.

Davies, Sharyn Graham

2007 *Challenging Gender Norms: Five Genders among Bugis in Indonesia.* Thomson Wadsworth, Belmont, California.

Du Vernay, Jeffrey P.

2016 *The 3D Documentation and Visualization of the Copper Repoussé Plates from the Lake Jackson Site (8Le1), Florida.* Report submitted to the Florida Bureau of Archaeological Research, Tallahassee.

Endicott, Kirk M., and Karen L. Endicott.

2008 *The Headman Was a Woman: The Gender-Egalitarian Batek of Malaysia.* Waveland Press, Long Grove, Illinois.

Florida Memory

2019 [1562–1564] Theodor de Bry's Engravings of the Timucua. Electronic resource, https://www.floridamemory.com/collections/debry/, accessed July 14, 2019.

Galloway, Patricia K.

1997 [1998] Where Have All the Menstrual Huts Gone? The Invisibility of Menstrual Seclusion in the Late Prehistoric Southeast. In *Women in Prehistory: North America and Mesoamerica*, edited by C. Claassen and R. Joyce, pp. 47–64. University of Pennsylvania Press, Philadelphia. Reprinted in *Reader in Gender Archaeology,* edited by K. Hays-Gilpin and D. Whitley, pp. 197–211. Routledge, New York.

Galloway, Patricia K., ed.

1989 *The Southeastern Ceremonial Complex: Artifacts and Analysis.* University of Nebraska Press, Lincoln.

Garcilaso de la Vega, the Inca

1993[1605] *La Florida.* In *The De Soto Chronicles,* volume II, edited by Lawrence A. Clayton, Vernon James Knight, Jr., and Edward C. Moore, pp.25–560. University of Alabama Press, Tuscaloosa.

Grund, Bridget Sky

2017 Behavioral Ecology, Technology, and the Organization of Labor: How a Shift from Spear Thrower to Self Bow Exacerbates Social Disparities. *American Anthropologist* 119: 104–119.

Hays-Gilpin, Kelley

2008 Archaeology and Women's Ritual Business. In *Belief in the Past: Theoretical Approaches to the Archaeology of Religion*, edited by David S. Whitley and Kelley Hays-Gilpin, pp. 247–258. Left Coast Press, Walnut Creek, California.

Heimlich, Marian Dunlevy

1952 *Guntersville Basin Pottery.* Geological Survey of Alabama Museum Paper 32. University of Alabama, Tuscaloosa.

Hollimon, Sandra E.

2006 The Archaeology of Nonbinary Genders in Native North American Societies. In *Handbook of Gender in Archaeology*, edited by Sarah Milledge Nelson, pp 435–450. AltaMira Press, New York.

Hudson, Charles

1976 *The Southeastern Indians.* University of Tennessee Press, Knoxville.

Jones, B. Calvin

1982 Southern Cult Manifestations at the Lake Jackson Site, Leon County, Florida: Salvage Excavation of Mound 3. *Midcontinental Journal of Archaeology* 7: 3–44.

Kennett, Douglas J., Stephen Plog, Richard J. George, Brendan J. Culleton, Adam S. Watson, Pontus Skoglund, Nadin Rohland, Swapan Mallick, Kristin Stewardson, Logan Kistler, Steven A. LeBlanc, Peter M. Whiteley, David Reich, and George H. Perry

2017 Archaeogenomic Evidence Reveals Prehistoric Matrilineal Dynasty. *Nature Communications* 8(4115). Electronic document, DOI:10.1038/ncomms14115, accessed May 5, 2017.

King, Adam
2003 *Etowah: The Political History of a Chiefdom Capital.* University of Alabama Press, Tuscaloosa.

King, Adam, ed.
2007 *Southeastern Ceremonial Complex: Chronology, Content, Context.* University of Alabama Press, Tuscaloosa.

Lepowsky, Maria
1993 *Fruit of the Motherland: Gender in an Egalitarian Society.* Columbia University Press, New York.

Lewis, Thomas M. N., and Madeline Kneberg
1946 *Hiwassee Island: An Archaeological Account of Four Tennessee Indian Peoples.* University of Tennessee Press, Knoxville.

Lorant, Stefan
1946 *The New World: The First Pictures of America.* Duell, Sloan and Pearce, New York.

Marrinan, Rochelle A.
2012 Fort Walton Culture in the Tallahassee Hills. In *Late Prehistoric Florida: Archaeology at the Edge of the Mississippian World*, edited by Keith Ashley and Nancy Marie White, pp. 186–230. University Press of Florida, Gainesville.

Marrinan, Rochelle A., and Nancy Marie White
2007 Modeling Fort Walton Culture in Northwest Florida. Southeastern Archaeology 26(2):292–318.

Miller, Carl
1953 9Dr10 Field Notebook and correspondence. Boxes 595–597, Jim Woodruff Reservoir, Flint River Aspect, Georgia, 1953. River Basin Surveys Papers, Anthropological Archives, Smithsonian Institution Museum Resource Center, Suitland, Maryland.

Morris, Theodore
1991 The FAS "Florida Indians" Poster. *Florida Anthropologist* 44: 99.

Nanda, Serena
1999 *Neither Man nor Woman.* Wadsworth Publishing, Belmont, California.
2004 Multiple Genders among North American Indians. In *The Kaleidoscope of Gender*, edited by Joan Z Spade and Catherine G. Valentine, pp. 64–70. Thomson Wadsworth, Belmont, California.

Phillips, Philip, James A. Ford, and James B. Griffin
1951 *Archaeological Survey in the Lower Mississippi Alluvial Valley, 1940–1947.* Papers of the Peabody Museum of American Archaeology and Ethnology, Harvard University, Volume 25.

Sears, William H.
1967 The Tierra Verde Burial Mound. *The Florida Anthropologist* 20: 25–73.

Shapiro, Danielle
2017 Indonesia's Minangkabau: The World's Largest Matrilineal Society. *Daily Beast,* July 13, 2017. Electronic document, https://www.thedailybeast.com/indonesias-minangkabau-the-worlds-largest-matrilineal-society?ref=scroll, accessed August 8, 2019.

Strong, John A.

1989 The Mississippian Bird-Man Theme in Cross-Cultural Perspective. In *The Southeastern Ceremonial Complex: Artifacts and Analysis*, edited by Patricia Galloway, pp. 211–237. University of Nebraska Press, Lincoln.

Summers, Tammy Mae, Tony Redlow, Alley Foley, Karrie Singel, Jennifer Blackwelder, and Carla Boyce

2001 Hypothermic Stunning of Sea Turtles in St. Joseph Bay, Florida. Poster report, Apalachicola National Estuarine Research Reserve, Eastpoint, Florida.

White, Nancy Marie

1994 *Archaeological Investigations at Six Sites in the Apalachicola River Valley, Northwest Florida.* National Oceanic and Atmospheric Administration Technical Memorandum, NOSSRD 26. U.S. Department of the Interior, Washington, D.C.

1999 Reflections and Speculations on Putting Women into Southeastern Archaeology. In *Grit-Tempered: Early Women in Southeastern U.S. Archaeology*, edited by Nancy Marie White, Lynne P. Sullivan, and Rochelle A. Marrinan, pp. 314–336. University Press of Florida, Gainesville.

2005 Archaeological Survey of the St. Joseph Bay State Buffer Preserve, Gulf County, Florida. Report to the Apalachicola National Estuarine Research Reserve, Eastpoint, Florida, and the Division of Historical Resources, Tallahassee. Department of Anthropology, University of South Florida.

2013 *Pierce Mounds Complex: An Ancient Capital in Northwest Florida.* Report to George Mahr, Apalachicola, and the Florida Division of Historical Resources, Tallahassee.

2019 The Montgomery Fields Site on the Lower Flint River. *Early Georgia* 47(1&2): 27–42.

White, Nancy Marie, Jeffrey P. Du Vernay, and Amber J. Yuellig

2012 Fort Walton Culture in the Apalachicola Valley, Northwest Florida. In *Late Prehistoric Florida: Archaeology at the Edge of the Mississippian World*, edited by Keith Ashley and Nancy Marie White, pp. 231–274. University Press of Florida, Gainesville.

Wide Open Spaces

2017 Impressive 7-Year-Old Hunter Kills Deer with Atlatl on Video. Electronic resource, https://www.wideopenspaces.com/impressive-7-year-old-hunter-kills-deer-atlatl-video/, accessed July 14, 2079.

Willey, Gordon R.

1999 [1949] *Archeology of the Florida Gulf Coast.* Smithsonian Miscellaneous Collections 113. Washington, D.C. Reprinted by University Press of Florida, Gainesville.

Yuan, Lu, and Sam Mitchell

2000 Land of the Walking Marriage. *Natural History* 109(9): 58–65.

12

Learning About and From Mississippian Women

Lynne P. Sullivan

Mothers, leaders, farmers, crafters, providers, teachers, healers, wives, and warriors—these are just a few of the many roles of women in Mississippian societies, and indeed in many human societies. As the chapters in this volume demonstrate, Mississippian women were not powerless laborers. They made decisions and controlled resources—from agricultural production to the use of foodways to integrate communities and to influence diplomacy with Spanish conquistadors, to their skills as crafters and artisans, to the power of female fertility to create life and spiritual regeneration, and to the significant roles of women in kin group leadership and regional political integration.

Nonetheless, it has taken concerted effort by a slowly increasing number of scholars to make the case that the lives and contributions of Mississippian women were significant to the communities in which they lived and beyond. For a variety of reasons, research regarding women of the Mississippian period has lagged behind research about women in other ancient cultures (e.g., *Ancient Maya Women* [Ardren 2002]). These reasons range from:

the male-centric accounts of Spanish conquistadors who wanted to impress their king with accounts of conquests of powerful leaders, and who only recognized powerful women (or nonbinary leaders) as those few carried on litters (Clayton et al. 1993; Driskill 2016; Welch and Butler 2006: 1–2);

the "petticoat government" insults of the English that forced native peoples to send only men to negotiations so as to be taken seriously (Perdue 1998: 56);

European priests who endeavored to overturn the traditional control of agriculture by Indigenous women and to force men to do and manage this work (Perdue 1998: 116–134);

male ethnohistorians who did not have much access to, or apparently do much to seek, information from and about women (Swanton 1946);
male-dominated archaeological scholarship that built upon Spanish accounts of powerful chiefs and dominated women to standardize and stereotype the chiefdom model (Sullivan 2009) and incorrect bioarchaeological assessments that correlated males with "well-endowed" mound burials (e.g., Mound 72, Cahokia, see Emerson et al. 2016; Lake Jackson, see White, this volume);
and the context of limited roles and opportunities accessible to modern women as professional archaeologists, especially in academia (White et al. 1999; Sullivan 2014).

In addition to these formidable obstacles, the limited communication between native peoples and archaeologists, especially about gender roles, allowed misinformed assumptions about women's roles in native societies to persist until feminist-informed research began to take a new and closer look, and the federal Native American Graves Protection and Repatriation Act (NAGPRA) as well as the National Historic Preservation Act (NHPA) began to require more consultation (Watkins 2000).

There is still much to learn and understand about Mississippian women. The first part of this chapter examines themes that thread through the preceding chapters, including women as producers and providers; as community connectors and leaders; and women as ideological and iconographic beings. These themes are familiar ones among the women of ancient America (Bruhns and Stothert 1999). The second and last part of the chapter examines some new directions that research about Mississippian women should take.

Learning About Multifaceted Mississippian Women

The studies in this volume demonstrate that archaeological evidence combined with ethnographic and historical accounts suggests that in at least some areas, Mississippian women, men, and nonbinary individuals participated in complementary political and social power and work roles (see White, this volume; also, Rodning 2011; Sullivan 2006; Sullivan and Rodning 2001, 2011). The foundations of feminine power that are highlighted in the preceding chapters are in fact multifaceted, and echo or support the "balance" that is discussed by Cooper (2022: 9) in Cherokee culture: "Women lived among equals since male and female realms balanced each other in respectful accord."

In some cases, the work of Indigenous women has been degraded because of differences in how this work is perceived by Western cultures. For example,

Sheila Bird of the United Keetoowah Band has noted that providing food is an act of power and an honor for Cherokee women—not an act of subjugation (personal communication 2018; Bird, this volume). As Rodning, Briggs, Beck, Fritz, Lapham, and Moore (Chapter 10) have explained, the mistake of the Spaniards in not recognizing the agency of the mid-sixteenth-century Joaran women who provided them with food may have even led to the Spaniards' demise (see also Beck et al. 2016).

Another significant point is that control of the major mode of agricultural production and processing certainly would have been a basis for economic power for women, and also set the stage for women to influence the power of men, such as refusals to provision warriors for raids if the women did not agree with what was proposed (Sattler 1995: 222). Fritz (Chapter 2) points out that the food production role of women at Cahokia and other Mississippian sites in the region corresponded with the importance of women as economic decision makers over a diverse agricultural system, in which Eastern Agricultural Complex crops persisted as staples along with maize (*Zea mays* ssp. *mays*). This intensive agriculture system existed throughout the height of Cahokia's population density.

More feminine power related to food is discussed by Briggs (Chapter 3). She suggests that an influx of maize-growing, hominy-making women was instrumental in establishing the social identity necessary for the emergence of Moundville, the second-largest Mississippian center in the Eastern Woodlands. Her interesting corollary idea that men with skills for building wall-trench structures came later than the corn-growing, hominy-cooking women deserves more investigation. Envisioning scenarios under which those sorts of movements might have happened would be an informative exercise in thinking about mate exchange and how that process could have played a role in the distribution of technology. Relating mate exchange to gendered production activities, as a visible archaeological signature of such movements, is particularly insightful.

Craft production at a Mississippian mound site in southwestern Virginia is the subject of Meyers's chapter (Chapter 9). Her "Martha effect" is reminiscent of a museum exhibit that showed how ancient Indigenous peoples used every part of a deer. This economy of production likely is a characteristic of many preindustrial people, as well as the "waste-not, want-not" ethic of later generations who grew up during hard times, such as the Great Depression. Household production of crafts, rather than crafts commissioned from a stable of specialists supported by a powerful overlord, would seem to be the most natural way craft production would have happened in Mississippian societies. Meyers describes how an archaeologically observed crafting area may have been developed by a feminine community of practice as an efficient and economical way to carry out complex, but related tasks for fabric production, and in so doing, collectively increasing their productive capacity.

Gougeon (Chapter 7) examines households and domestic spaces to discover the nature of gendered workspaces in Late Mississippian communities in North Georgia. Building upon his earlier work, he broadens the perspective to add both spatial and human dimensions with a taskscape perspective. This approach enlivens the household as a place where multiple generations of (mostly) women gathered, worked (and likely also played) together with children, elders, and other kin, and where knowledge was shared, both formally and through informal observation. Although not exclusively occupied by women and children, these matrilineal and matrilocal places were managed and controlled by women, and also were the places where most of the education and enculturation of Mississippian women happened, including skills that promoted social integration.

Harle, Betsinger, and Sullivan (Chapter 4) examine this educational and enculturation process over the life courses of Mississippian women in the Upper Tennessee Valley. Evidence for changing roles and contributions is evident in mortuary practices for different age groups, as females transitioned from children to adults, and from young mothers to grandmothers. Women's prestige and influence increased with age as they became heads of matrilineal households and kin groups. But even at a young age, girls began to participate in community ceremonies, as evidenced by the shell rattles interred with many of them. If females survived the childbearing years, they seemed to live longer than males and attained high social standing and possibly leadership positions later in life.

As Briggs and Harle (Chapter 1) and also Rodning et al. (Chapter 10) mention, there is solid evidence of Mississippian feminine leaders on the Carolina piedmont during the contact period—more than just at Cofitachequi (e.g., DePratter 1989, 1994; Hudson et al. 2008; Trocolli 1999, 2002, 2006). White (Chapter 11) also notes the presence in the Fort Walton area of adult females who were buried in mounds with similar funerary associations as those with adult males who are presumed to be leaders. But Indigenous women were not only in positions of leadership that were highly visible to outsiders, their interactions through kinship networks across communities likely provided stability and strong social ties across the region. The kinship networks suggested by pottery attributes, in my study of Late Mississippian communities in East Tennessee (Sullivan Chapter 6), show highly interactive and tightly knit communities in this region. This connective web woven by women provided the structure for both social and political relationships, and the ability of women to use these connections for political influence also should not be underestimated.

The depiction of women in the art of the Mississippian world illustrates the multiple connections among women's powers and abilities as mothers, providers, artisans, and social connectors. Sharp's (Chapter 9) overview of portrayals of women in Mississippian carvings and his research into the female effigy bottles of the Middle Cumberland region pulls together many of these threads. Of particular interest are his insights about how the effigy bottles may be part of the work of a sodality of women potters, and also that the use of this pottery is typically in mortuary contexts for children. These contexts mirror the findings in Chapter 6 concerning the cosmos jars in the Upper Tennessee Valley, and perhaps show similar social processes, but using different iconography.

The connections Sharp makes of the effigy bottles with female fertility and children also segue into Bengtson and Alexander's (Chapter 5) research on a rather amazing structure filled with objects related to female fertility at the Hunze-Evans site in southeastern Missouri. Their analysis of the contents of this structure, including a unique effigy bottle depicting a nursing mother, explores the many dimensions of female fertility and how it may have been experienced by these Mississippian women–from corporeal, emotional, to ideological. The location of the structure within a Mississippian village is particularly interesting because, as the authors note, this location would not have provided privacy for menstrual or birthing rituals. Continued investigation of the site should provide some contextual information to help spatially situate this very interesting building.

Learning from the Experiences of Mississippian Women

We turn now from studies in this volume about the multifaceted roles of Mississippian women to some reflections about what might be learned from Mississippian women that could contribute more broadly to knowledge of the experiences of women. As a beginning, comparisons among Mississippian subregions across time could reveal variations in women's lives in differing cultural contexts. Discovering such nuances and differences could enrich our understanding of women's roles, identities, and power across the Mississippian world. For example, Ashmore (2002: 232) points out that in the Maya region, such variation can extend to differences in class and social standings, as well as in the supernatural and worldly realms.

Serving as cultural mediators was a particularly important role that Indigenous women in North America took on from the time of European contact to the nineteenth century (Kidwell 1992). There is potential to learn about how Mississippian women also may have served as mediators during the migrations that occurred from ca. AD 1200 to 1400 (Cook and Comstock 2022). People in the midcontinent were on the move as population dispersed from the great city of Cahokia and into other areas. A series of serious droughts, one of the possible factors in this dispersal, pushed people out of the Mississippi and Ohio river valleys, and eventually, out of the Middle Cumberland region in central Tennessee (Bird et al. 2017). The construction of fortifications and consolidation of formerly dispersed, small settlements into larger villages surrounded by these palisades took place in many areas of the larger Mississippian region. Studies in Ohio have shown conclusively that people bearing Mississippian technology, material culture, and with biological ties to the Middle Cumberland region moved into villages of the Fort Ancient culture during this time (Cook 2017; Cook and Aubry 2014). Briggs's (Chapter 3) observation that Mississippian women came first (before men) into the Moundville area is potentially related to such movements. In the Upper Tennessee Valley, palisade construction was underway at multiple settlements by AD 1300, followed by major changes in material culture, including architecture and mortuary practices. Constructions on platform mounds changed from multiple smaller buildings to one large building similar to historically known meeting houses (Sullivan 2018). Objects from other areas, especially the Middle Cumberland region and northern Georgia, also become more common at some sites with platform mounds at this time (Sullivan et al. 2022).

Were Mississippian women instrumental in mediating the tensions created during this turbulent time? If so, did their efforts create cultural coalescences that eventually led to the tribes encountered by Europeans some two centuries later? Studies from other areas suggest that sodalities "may become very important during times of ethnic mixing, migration, and other unstable social conditions" (Ware 2014: 35). These conditions certainly would apply to much of the "Mississippian world" between ca. AD 1200–1400.

Sharp (Chapter 8) discusses the formation of such sodalities of women surrounding the female effigy bottles in the Middle Cumberland region. The tightly woven networks among potters in the Upper Tennessee Valley, identified in Chapter 6, also might be interpreted as such. How might archaeological research help to better understand how, and if, women's networks may have helped foster this dramatic cultural change and new traditions during times of strife and upheaval? Relevant to this discussion is White's (Chapter 11) observation that in the Fort Walton area, where there is evidence of women who likely were important leaders, there are no palisaded villages or other signs of warfare.

While much of what we are learning about Mississippian women is positive and empowering, there also were substantial hardships. Mortality from childbirth was high, as was the death rate for infants (e.g., Harle 2003). The inter-group conflict that was elevated during the Mississippian period in much of the region put everyone at risk for attack, especially when away from a palisaded village (Milner et al. 1991). Evidence for such attacks on both women and men is widespread. Milner (1999; Milner et al. 1991) notes that women's work groups away from the village could be targets of ambushes and disturbing evidence of such attacks is indicated by graves containing several women whose remains show clear documentation of violent attacks, including decapitation.

Similar treatment of war captives and slaves, both male and female, is depicted in Mississippian iconography (e.g., gorget designs with figures holding severed heads and displaying scalps) and reported in historical accounts (Brown and Dye 2007; Chacon and Dye 2007; Milner 1999). Burials of skulls, headless individuals, and human remains with evidence of scalping, are known from Middle Cumberland (Hodge et al. 2010) and Tennessee River sites, and elsewhere (Chacon and Dye 2007). Some of these individuals are reported as female (e.g., Jacobi 2007: 312). At Cahokia, a mass grave that was a final phase (ca. AD 1100) to Mound 72 contained an estimated 39 individuals, both females and males, whose remains showed clear evidence of violent deaths, including decapitations (Fowler et al. 1999: 70). Biological and chemical analyses of these individuals showed that they were derived from a single population that was different from other individuals in the mound, suggesting they were not from Cahokia (Thompson et al. 2015: 353).

Incidents of women being forced into slavery or intentionally killed by captors also are documented post-European contact. For example, as Rodning et al. discuss in Chapter 10, the Qualla women who likely served the Spanish soldiers at Fort San Juan in the latter part of occupation were reportedly kidnapped and involuntarily forced into slavery. Jacobi (2007:299) recounts that in 1811, the Shawnee chief Tecumseh, during a visit with the Chickasaw and Choctaw, stated in his talks to tribal councils that "the Indian custom of killing women and children in war" should end (Halbert and Ball 1969:44). "This custom they should renounce, and henceforth, in all wars, the lives of women and children should be spared" (Halbert and Ball 1969:44).

Ritual acts were another context in which Mississippian women could meet their death at the hands of other humans. Mound 72 at Cahokia also provides an example, as well as extreme contrasts, in the mortuary treatments of females. In addition to female individuals in or associated with the central beaded burial (Emerson et al. 2016), there are four mass graves with a sum total of 118 individuals, primarily adolescent and young adult females (Fowler et al. 1999; Thompson 2013; Thompson et al. 2015). The demographics and careful placement of these individuals in the mass burial features within the context of the mound further suggested that these young females represent the ritual sacrifice of deliberately selected individuals from outlying communities (Fowler et al. 1999). But contrary to this initial interpretation, new biological and chemical analyses indicate these individuals likely were from the Cahokia area (Thompson et al. 2015).

The significance of these mass burials, or indeed of the entire mound, is not clear, however, the distinct differences in the mortuary treatments of females, from the beaded burial to the mass graves, reflect the fact that the power, agency, and prestige discussed in many chapters in the volume may not have been accessible to all Mississippian women. Just as today, age, class, ethnicity, and other aspects of individual identity likely structured the social positioning and privileges of individuals. Such intersectionality in the ancient Southeast is a topic that has not been explored in the lived experiences of women, men, or nonbinary individuals.

The mass graves also remind us that Mississippian women, sadly, like women elsewhere, and regardless of their value and contributions to their families and communities, could suffer deadly harm at the hands of other human beings. Sacrifice of young females was done by many ancient cultures worldwide, from Greece to Peru (Bruhns and Stothert 1999: 181). Such violence can be motivated by religious ritual or political power (Martin and Harrod 2015).

Le Page Du Pratz's 1725 account (published 1774) of the death of the Natchez chief Tattooed Serpent and the female sacrifices made at his funeral have heavily influenced previous interpretations of the mass graves at Cahokia, as have mythic male–warrior heroes such as Red Horn (e.g., Brown 2003, 2010). In contrast with single event interpretations such as the funeral of a chief, more recent information on dating of the Mound 72 features indicates that a sequence of events took place, likely over a number of years. The male warrior interpretation is countered by Emerson et al. (2016) who suggest the presence of females and underworld/water symbols (e.g., shells) may correlate with fertility, creation, and world renewal themes associated with the Earth Mother-Grandmother figure representation of early Cahokia. Alt (2020:47) notes that Cahokian shrines were closed with water and a human sacrifice burial. How these themes may be compatible with mass sacrificial deaths of females is yet to be understood.

What is puzzling about the Cahokia case is that the sacrificed young females were members of the community, a community that relied on women to manage the agricultural production that sustained the society. Also, given the high mortality of young women from childbirth, the sacrifices of these young lives were extremely costly, not only to the individuals who lost their lives but to the greater community. What desperate circumstances would lead a community to commit such acts? Alt (2020: 47) makes the case that cultural changes that led to Cahokia's rise were rooted in new and deeply influential religious beliefs and practices. A better understanding of these beliefs and knowledge of the political and other circumstances of Cahokia at that time might lead to new discoveries about the reasons these violent acts toward women were carried out. The severe droughts beginning by AD 1200 and their potential correlation with water and human sacrifices are tempting to invoke as a context, but the dating for the mass graves is between AD 1050 to 1150 (Emerson et al. 2016: 407).

Some less-disturbing contexts in which learning about and from Mississippian women could enrich knowledge and respect for women's experiences and contributions include women's roles in medicine and health care, such as care of the infirm and elderly (e.g., DiGangi et al. 2009), the rearing and teaching of children, and in ceremonial and political life, to name a just a few. There are many fresh perspectives that could focus on the ancient women who lived in, supported, and helped to construct their communities that today are marked by platform mounds and plazas as the most visible reminders of this ancient past.

Mississippian Women: Their Lives Matter

A big question for the future is: what can and should be studied and learned about Mississippian women? The information presented in this volume is based on data resulting from many years of archaeological research, much of it collected with limited collaboration with Indigenous peoples. Although this is the case, as White (Chapter 11) points out, the kinds of evidence for understanding the lives of women in the pre-contact Southeast are meager. Ethnographic and historical data provide some clues, but as in every part of the world, cultures change over centuries and there can be surprises and new information about how life was many centuries ago.

"Traditional" archaeological evidence that can provide new information about women in the past comes from things associated with women, including objects women made or used, or the patterns, both intentional and unintentional, left on their physical remains by repetitive activities potentially performed by women (e.g., maize grinding, weaving, etc., see Bridges 1989, 1991), as well as childbearing, illness, injury, or cultural standards of appearance and beauty (e.g., dental modifications, foot binding, intentional cranial modification, etc.). Chapters in this volume illustrate how things associated with women are important for understanding women's roles. Examples of questions significant to using material culture to study ancient women (and indeed all genders) include: where are the things associated with women's work and roles found; were different types of work performed in individual households or in multi-household, collaborative settings; were certain types of things made by specialists or for special uses; were there special places used only by women, such as places to give birth or to hold ceremonies; were women buried in different places than men, and if so, why; did some women receive different mortuary treatments because of their roles or status?

If the traditional sources of information collected and used by archaeologists are no longer available because of cultural concerns, how can information be collected that can teach about the lives and accomplishments of these ancient women? Is such information even seen as desirable to know by present-day Indigenous peoples? If such research is to continue, a younger generation of Indigenous peoples and archaeologists will need to work together to sort out how and if research concerning the lives of women and other underrepresented groups in the past is indeed important and if it should and can be conducted.

What will not change is the need to promote respect and admiration for these ancient women who did so much more than for what they have been credited. A better understanding of the lives of these remarkable women could inform much more than the contributions they made to their own cultures. A better understanding of the societies of the Mississippian era also could advance knowledge of matrilineal societies and the ways in which they shape human lives in different ways than the European-style patrilineal societies that now dominate North America. Most importantly, the lives of Mississippian women are significant to the diversity of lived experiences of people who have been lost to history. Their lives did and do still matter.

References Cited

Alt, Susan M.

2020 The Implications of the Religious Foundations at Cahokia. In *Cahokia in Context: Hegemony and Diaspora*, edited by Charles H. McNutt and Ryan M. Parish, pp. 32–48. University of Florida Press, Gainesville.

Ardren, Traci, ed.

2001 *Ancient Maya Women*. AltaMira Press, Walnut Creek, CA.

Ashmore, Wendy

2002 Encountering Maya Women. In *Ancient Maya Women*, edited by Traci Ardren, pp. 229–246. AltaMira Press, Walnut Creek, CA.

Beck, Robin A., Christopher Bernard Rodning, David G. Moore, eds.

2016 *Fort San Juan and the Limits of Empire: Colonialism and Household Practice at the Berry Site*. University Press of Florida, Gainesville.

Bird, Broxton W., Jeremy J. Wilson, William P. Gilhooly III, Byron A. Steinman, and Lucas Stamps

2017 Midcontinental Native American population dynamics and late Holocene hydroclimate extremes. *Scientific Reports (Nature Research)* 7: 41628. DOI: 10.1038/srep41628

Bridges, Patricia S.

1989 Changes in Activities with the Shift to Agriculture in the Southeastern United States. *Current Anthropology* 30(3): 385–394.

1991 Degenerative Joint Disease in Hunter–gatherers and Agriculturalists from the Southeastern United States. *American Journal of Physical Anthropology* 85(4): 379–391.

Brown, James A.

2003 The Cahokia Mound 72-Sub 1 Burials as Collective Representation. *The Wisconsin Archeologist* 84: 81–98.

2010 Cosmological Layouts of Secondary Burial as Political Instruments. In *Mississippian Mortuary Practices: Beyond Hierarchy and the Representationist Perspective*, edited by Lynne P. Sullivan and Robert C. Mainfort, Jr., pp. 30–53. University of Florida Press, Gainesville.

Brown, James A., and David H. Dye

2007 Severed Heads and Sacred Scalplocks: Mississippian Iconographic Trophies. In *The Taking and Displaying of Human Body Parts as Trophies by Amerindians*, edited by Richard J. Chacon and David H. Dye, pp. 278–298. Springer, New York, NY.

Bruhns, Karen Olsen, and Karen E. Stothert

1999 *Women in Ancient America*. University of Oklahoma Press, Norman.

Chacon, Richard J., and David H. Dye, eds.

2007 *The Taking and Displaying of Human Body Parts as Trophies by Amerindians*. Springer, New York.

Clayton, Lawrence A., Edward C. Moore, and Vernon James Knight, Jr., eds.

1993 *The De Soto Chronicles: The Expedition of Hernando de Soto to North America in 1539–1543*, vol. 1 and 2. The University of Alabama Press, Tuscaloosa.

Cook, Robert A.

2017 *Continuity and Change in the Native American Village: Multicultural Origins and Descendants of the Fort Ancient Culture*. Cambridge University Press, Cambridge.

Cook, Robert A., and B. Scott Aubry

2014 Aggregation, Interregional Interaction, and Postmarital Residence Patterns: A Study of Biological Variation in the Late Prehistoric Middle Ohio Valley. *American Journal of Physical Anthropology* 154: 270–278.

Cook, Robert A., and Aaron R. Comstock, eds.
2022 *Following the Mississippian Spread: Using Biological and Archaeological Evidence to Measure Migration and Climate Change.* Springer Press, New York.

Cooper, Karen Coody
2022 *Cherokee Women in Charge: Female Power and Leadership in American Indian Nations of Eastern North America.* McFarland & Company, Incorporated Publishers, Jefferson, North Carolina.

DePratter, Chester B.
1989 Cofitachequi: Ethnohistorical and Archaeological Evidence. *Anthropological Studies* 9:133.
1994 The Chiefdom of Cofitachequi. In *The Forgotten Centuries: Indians and Europeans in the American South, 1521–1704*, edited by Charles Hudson and Carmen Chaves Tesser, pp. 197–226. University of Georgia Press, Athens.

DiGangi, Elizabeth, Jon Bethard, and Lynne P. Sullivan
2009 Differential Diagnosis of Cartilaginous Dysplasia and Probable Osgood-Schlatter's Disease in a Mississippian Individual from East Tennessee. *International Journal of Osteoarchaeology* 20(4): 424–444.

Driskill, Qwo-Li
2016 *Asegi Stories: Cherokee Queer and Two-Spirit Memory.* University of Arizona Press, Tucson.

Emerson, Thomas E., Kristin M. Hedman, Eve A. Hargrave, Dawn E. Cobb, Andrew R. Thompson
2016 Paradigms Lost: Reconfiguring Cahokia's Mound 72 Beaded Burial. *American Antiquity* 81(3): 405–425.

Fowler, Melvin L., Jerome Rose, Barbara VanderLeest, Steven R. Ahler
1999 *The Mound 72 Area: Dedicated and Sacred Space in Early Cahokia.* Illinois State Museum Reports of Investigations, No. 54, Springfield.

Harle, Michaelyn S.
2003 A Bioarchaeological Analysis of Fains Island. Master's thesis, Department of Anthropology, University of Tennessee, Knoxville.

Halbert, Henry S., and Timothy H. Ball.
1969 *The Creek War of 1813 and 1814.* Southern Historical Publications No. 15, edited by Frank L. Owsley, Jr. University of Alabama Press, Tuscaloosa.

Hodge, Shannon C., Michael K. Hampton, and Kevin E. Smith
2010 Ritual Use of Human Skulls at Castalian Springs, Tennessee. Paper presented at the 67th annual meeting of the Southeastern Archaeological Conference, Lexington, KY.

Hudson, Charles, Robin A. Beck Jr., Chester B. DePratter, Robbie Ethridge and John E. Worth
2008 On Interpreting Cofitachequi. *Ethnohistory* 55(3):465–490.

Jacobi, Keith P.
2007 Disabling the Dead: Human Trophy Taking in the Prehistoric Southeast. In *The Taking and Displaying of Human Body Parts as Trophies by Amerindians*, edited by Richard J. Chacon and David H. Dye, pp. 299–338. Springer, New York.

Kidwell, Clara Sue
1992 Indian Women as Cultural Mediators. *Ethnohistory* 39(2): 97–107.
Le Page du Pratz, AntoineS.
1774 *The History of Louisiana.* London, England: T. Becket. [French version published in 1763]
Martin, Debra L., and Ryan P. Harrod
2015 Bioarchaeological Contributions to the Study of Violence. *American Journal of Physical Anthropology* 156 (S59): 116–145.
Milner, George R.
1999 Warfare in Prehistoric and Early Historic Eastern North America. *Journal of Archaeological Research* 7: 105–151.
Milner George R., Eve Anderson, and Virginia G. Smith.
1991 Warfare in Late Prehistoric West-Central Illinois. *American Antiquity* 56:581–603.
Perdue, Theda
1998 *Cherokee Women: Gender and Culture Change, 1700–1835.* University of Nebraska Press, Lincoln.
Rodning, Christopher B.
2011 Mortuary Practices, Gender Ideology, and the Cherokee Town at the Coweeta Creek Site. *Journal of Anthropological Archaeology* 30: 145–173.
Sattler, Richard A.
1995 Women's Status among the Muskogee and Cherokee. In *Women and Power in Native North America*, edited by Laura F. Klein and Lillian A. Ackerman, pp. 214–29. University of Oklahoma Press, Norman.
Sullivan, Lynne P.
2006 Gendered Contexts of Mississippian Leadership in Southern Appalachia. In *Leadership and Polity in Mississippian Society*, edited by Paul Welch and Brian Butler, pp. 264–285. Southern Illinois University Press, Carbondale.
2009 Deposing the Chiefdom Model "Monster-God." *Native South* 2: 88–97.
2014 What I Believe: Taking Up the Serpents of Social Theory in Southeastern Archaeology. In thematic section "Taking Stock of Social Theory in Southeastern Archaeology," edited by V. James Knight. *Southeastern Archaeology* 33(2): 238–245.
2018 The Path to the Council House: The Development of Mississippian Communities in Southeast Tennessee. In *The Archaeology of Villages in Eastern North America*, edited by Jennifer Birch and Victor Thompson, pp. 106–123. University of Florida Press, Gainesville
Sullivan, Lynne P., and Christopher B. Rodning
2001 Gender, Tradition, and Social Negotiation in Southern Appalachian Chiefdoms. In *The Archaeology of Historical Processes: Agency and Tradition Before and After Columbus*, edited by Timothy R. Pauketat, pp. 107–120. University Press of Florida, Gainesville.
2011 Residential Burial, Gender Roles, and Political Development in Late Prehistoric and Early Cherokee Cultures of the Southern Appalachians. In *Residential*

Burial: A Multi-Regional Exploration, edited by Ron Adams and Stacie King, pp. 79–97. AP3A Series, American Anthropological Association. Washington D.C.

Sullivan, Lynne P., Kevin E. Smith, Shawn Patch, Sarah Lowry, John Jacob Holland-Lulewicz, and Scott Meeks

2022 Heading for the Hills: New Evidence for Migrations to the Upper Tennessee Valley. In *Following the Mississippian Spread: Climate Change and Migration in the Eastern U.S. (ca. AD 1000–1600)*, edited by Robert A. Cook and Aaron R. Comstock, pp. 227–256. Springer Nature, Switzerland.

Swanton, John R.

1946 *Indians of the Southeastern United States.* Bureau of American Ethnology, Bulletin 137, Smithsonian Institution, Washington D.C.

Thompson, Andrew

2013 Odontometric Determination of Sex at Mound 72, Cahokia. *American Journal of Physical Anthropology* 151(3): 408–419.

Thompson, Andrew, Kristin Hedman, and Philip Slater

2015 New Dental and Isotope Evidence of Biological Distance and Place of Origin for Mass Burial Groups at Cahokia's Mound 72. *American Journal of Physical Anthropology* 158(2): 341–357.

Trocolli, Ruth

1999 Women Leaders in Native North American Societies: Invisible Women of Power. In *Manifesting Power: Gender and the Interpretation of Power in Archaeology*, edited by Tracy L. Sweely, pp. 49–61. Routledge, London.

2002 Mississippian Chiefs: Women and Men of Power. In *The Dynamics of Power*, edited by Maria O'Donovan, pp. 168–87. Center for Archaeological Investigations, Southern Illinois University Carbondale.

2006 Elite Status and Gender: Women Leaders in Chiefdom Societies of the Southeastern U.S. PhD dissertation, Anthropology Department, University of Florida, Gainesville.

Ware, John A.

2014 *A Pueblo Social History: Kinship, Sodality, and Community in the Northern Southwest.* School for Advanced Research Press, Santa Fe.

Watkins, Joe

2000 *Indigenous Archaeology: American Indian Values and Scientific Practice.* AltaMira Press, Walnut Creek, CA.

Welch, Paul D., and Brian M. Butler

2006 Borne on a Litter with Much Prestige. In *Leadership and Polity in Mississippian Society*, edited by Paul D. Welch and Brian M. Butler, pp. 1–15. Southern Illinois University Press, Carbondale.

White, Nancy M., Lynne P. Sullivan, and Rochelle A. Marrinan, eds.

1999 *Grit-Tempered: Early Women Archaeologists in the Southeastern United States.* Florida Museum of Natural History, Ripley P. Bullen Series, University Press of Florida, Gainesville.

CONTRIBUTORS

Toni Alexander is professor of geography at Southeast Missouri State University. Her research interests are in cultural and historical geography of socially and spatially marginalized groups.

Robin A. Beck is professor of anthropology and curator of Eastern North American Archaeology at the Museum of Anthropological Archaeology, University of Michigan. Beck is the author of *Chiefdoms, Collapse, and Coalescence in the Early American South*, editor of *The Durable House: House Society Models in Archaeology*, and coeditor of *Fort San Juan and the Limits of Empire: Colonialism and Household Practice at the Berry Site*. He has published numerous book chapters and articles in journals such as *Current Anthropology, American Anthropologist, American Antiquity, Historical Archaeology, and Southeastern Archaeology.*

Jennifer Bengtson is professor of anthropology at Southeast Missouri State University. Her research interests include Mississippian and Oneota archaeology, gender, infancy, and childhood.

Tracy K. Betsinger is professor of anthropology at SUNY Oneonta. Her bioarchaeological research focuses on the relationships of age, gender, mortuary pattern, and status with various aspects of health, including disease, trauma, and diet. Some of her notable publications include *The Bioarchaeology of Urbanization: The Biological, Demographic, and Social Consequences of Living in Cities* (with Sharon N. DeWitte), *The Odd, the Unusual, and the Strange: Bioarchaeological Explorations of Atypical Burials* (with Amy B. Scott and Anastasia Tsaliki), and *The Anthropology of the Fetus: Biology, Culture, and Society* (with Sallie Han and Amy B. Scott).

Shelia Bird is a member of the United Keetoowah Band of Cherokee Indians, a descendant of the Keetoowah Nighthawks and a member of the Paint Clan. She is a former Tribal Historic Preservation Officer (THPO) for the Cherokee Nation, and served as the Environmental Director, THPO and Native American Graves Protection Repatriation Act Representative for the United Keetoowah Band. She is now the Principal Consultant at Nighthawk Consulting of Kituwah Nighthawk, LLC and the host of "THPO Talk, An Indigenous Podcast."

Rachel V. Briggs is teaching assistant professor of anthropology and the curriculum in archaeology at the University of North Carolina-Chapel Hill. Briggs has published several book chapters and articles on American Indian food and gender roles in journals such as *American Antiquity, American Anthropologist,* and *Native South,* and is currently working on her manuscript *Meals of the Southeastern American Indians.*

Gayle J. Fritz is professor emerita of anthropology at Washington University in St. Louis. She is an environmental archaeologist and paleoethnobotanist with special research interests in Native American foodways and the origins and spread of agriculture who has participated in excavations and studied archaeological plant remains from sites across the southeastern and midwestern United States and from the US Southwest/Mexican Northwest. Fritz is engaged in a decades-long research agenda focused on plants belonging to the Eastern Agricultural Complex. Fritz also studies foodways resulting from interactions between Native Americans and European colonizers. Her recent book, *Feeding Cahokia: Early Agriculture in the North American Heartland*, takes a broad look at farming before and after the intensification of maize, with emphasis on the Native women who, because they were the farmers, were key agents of economic decision making and social integration.

Ramie A. Gougeon is professor and chairperson of the Department of Anthropology at the University of West Florida. He is coeditor of *Archaeological Perspectives on the Southern Appalachians.* Dr. Gougeon's research interests include houses and households, vernacular architecture, and the anthropological archaeology of the everyday.

Michaelyn S. Harle is archaeologist at the Tennessee Valley Authority. Her research interests include Mississippian archaeology, gender, identity, bioarchaeology, and New Deal Archaeology.

Heather A. Lapham is associate director of the Research Laboratories of Archaeology and adjunct associate professor of anthropology and the curriculum in archaeology at the University of North Carolina-Chapel Hill. She is author of *Hunting for Hides,* coeditor of *Bears,* and numerous articles and book chapters on human-animal relationships in the American Southeast and Oaxaca, Mexico.

Maureen S. Meyers is senior archaeologist with New South Associates, Inc., in Stone Mountain, GA. She has worked in Southeastern archaeology for over 30 years, with a focus on Native American mound sites in southwestern Virginia, seventeenth-century Westo in Virginia and South Carolina, and identifying and decreasing the rate of sexual harassment in the field. Her work in Virginia focuses on fiber production, ceramics, and shell beads, and the role of women's labor in Mississippian societies. She is a past winner of the Southeastern Archaeological Conference Rising Scholar Award, former president of the Southeastern Archaeological Conference, and former associate professor at University of Mississippi.

David G. Moore is professor emeritus of anthropology at Warren Wilson College, in Asheville, North Carolina. He is the author of numerous book chapters and articles for peer-reviewed journals as well as the books *Catawba Valley Mississippians: Ceramics, Chronology, and Catawba Indians* and *Fort San Juan and the Limits of Empire: Colonialism and Household Practice at the Berry Site* along with Christopher Rodning and Robin Beck.

Christopher B. Rodning is professor of anthropology at Tulane University, New Orleans, Louisiana. He is coeditor with Robin A. Beck and David G. Moore of *The Limits of Empire: Household Archaeology at the Berry Site*, coeditor with Jane M. Eastman of *Archaeological Studies of Gender in the Southeastern United States*, and author of *Center Places and Cherokee Towns: Archaeological Perspectives on Native American Architecture and Landscape in the Southern Appalachians*. His interests include culture contact and colonialism, the archaeology of landscape and built environment, and the archaeology of ritual.

Robert V. Sharp is an independent scholar based in Chicago. He received his BA and MA degrees in English literature from Saint Louis University and Vanderbilt University, respectively. Now retired from the Art Institute of Chicago after more than thirty years as an editor and publisher of exhibition catalogs and books on the museum's permanent collections, he pursues his interests in iconography, Mississippian mortuary practices, and the representation of the human figure in prehistoric Native American ceramic art.

Lynne P. Sullivan is adjunct professor of anthropology and emerita curator of archaeology at the McClung Museum of Natural History and Culture at the University of Tennessee. Her primary research is the Mississippian period in the Upper Tennessee Valley, an area on which she has published extensively. Her publications include *The Prehistory of the Chickamauga Basin in Tennessee* (editor and compiler), *Mississippian Mortuary Practices* (with Robert C. Mainfort Jr.), *Archaeology of the Appalachian Highlands* (with Susan C. Prezzano), as well as numerous articles and book chapters on gender roles in Mississippian societies.

Nancy Marie White is professor of anthropology at the University of South Florida. Her books include *Archaeology for Dummies, Late Prehistoric Florida* (with Keith Ashley), *Gulf Coast Archaeology, the Southeastern United States and Mexico* and *Grit-Tempered: Early Women Archaeologists in the Southeastern United States* (with Lynne Sullivan and Rochelle Marrinan). Current work is an archaeological synthesis of the Apalachicola-lower Chattahoochee valley region, from Paleo-Indian through the present.

INDEX

Page numbers followed by the letters *f* and *i* indicate figures and tables.

Ripley P. Bullen Series

Florida Museum of Natural History

Tacachale: Essays on the Indians of Florida and Southeastern Georgia during the Historic Period, edited by Jerald T. Milanich and Samuel Proctor (1978)

Aboriginal Subsistence Technology on the Southeastern Coastal Plain during the Late Prehistoric Period, by Lewis H. Larson (1980)

Cemochechobee: Archaeology of a Mississippian Ceremonial Center on the Chattahoochee River, by Frank T. Schnell, Vernon J. Knight Jr., and Gail S. Schnell (1981)

Fort Center: An Archaeological Site in the Lake Okeechobee Basin, by William H. Sears, with contributions by Elsie O'R. Sears and Karl T. Steinen (1982)

Perspectives on Gulf Coast Prehistory, edited by Dave D. Davis (1984)

Archaeology of Aboriginal Culture Change in the Interior Southeast: Depopulation during the Early Historic Period, by Marvin T. Smith (1987)

Apalachee: The Land between the Rivers, by John H. Hann (1988)

Key Marco's Buried Treasure: Archaeology and Adventure in the Nineteenth Century, by Marion Spjut Gilliland (1989)

First Encounters: Spanish Explorations in the Caribbean and the United States, 1492–1570, edited by Jerald T. Milanich and Susan Milbrath (1989)

Missions to the Calusa, edited and translated by John H. Hann, with an introduction by William H. Marquardt (1991)

Excavations on the Franciscan Frontier: Archaeology at the Fig Springs Mission, by Brent Richards Weisman (1992)

The People Who Discovered Columbus: The Prehistory of the Bahamas, by William F. Keegan (1992)

Hernando de Soto and the Indians of Florida, by Jerald T. Milanich and Charles Hudson (1992)

Foraging and Farming in the Eastern Woodlands, edited by C. Margaret Scarry (1993)

Puerto Real: The Archaeology of a Sixteenth-Century Spanish Town in Hispaniola, edited by Kathleen Deagan (1995)

Political Structure and Change in the Prehistoric Southeastern United States, edited by John F. Scarry (1996)

Bioarchaeology of Native American Adaptation in the Spanish Borderlands, edited by Brenda J. Baker and Lisa Kealhofer (1996)

A History of the Timucua Indians and Missions, by John H. Hann (1996)

Archaeology of the Mid-Holocene Southeast, edited by Kenneth E. Sassaman and David G. Anderson (1996)

The Indigenous People of the Caribbean, edited by Samuel M. Wilson (1997; first paperback edition, 1999)

Hernando de Soto among the Apalachee: The Archaeology of the First Winter Encampment, by Charles R. Ewen and John H. Hann (1998)

The Timucuan Chiefdoms of Spanish Florida, by John E. Worth: vol. 1, *Assimilation*; vol. 2, *Resistance and Destruction* (1998; first paperback edition, 2020)

Ancient Earthen Enclosures of the Eastern Woodlands, edited by Robert C. Mainfort Jr. and Lynne P. Sullivan (1998)

An Environmental History of Northeast Florida, by James J. Miller (1998)

Precolumbian Architecture in Eastern North America, by William N. Morgan (1999)

Archaeology of Colonial Pensacola, edited by Judith A. Bense (1999)

Grit-Tempered: Early Women Archaeologists in the Southeastern United States, edited by Nancy Marie White, Lynne P. Sullivan, and Rochelle A. Marrinan (1999; first paperback edition, 2001)

Coosa: The Rise and Fall of a Southeastern Mississippian Chiefdom, by Marvin T. Smith (2000)
Religion, Power, and Politics in Colonial St. Augustine, by Robert L. Kapitzke (2001)
Bioarchaeology of Spanish Florida: The Impact of Colonialism, edited by Clark Spencer Larsen (2001)
Archaeological Studies of Gender in the Southeastern United States, edited by Jane M. Eastman and Christopher B. Rodning (2001)
The Archaeology of Traditions: Agency and History Before and After Columbus, edited by Timothy R. Pauketat (2001)
Foraging, Farming, and Coastal Biocultural Adaptation in Late Prehistoric North Carolina, by Dale L. Hutchinson (2002)
Windover: Multidisciplinary Investigations of an Early Archaic Florida Cemetery, edited by Glen H. Doran (2002)
Archaeology of the Everglades, by John W. Griffin (2002; first paperback edition, 2017)
Pioneer in Space and Time: John Mann Goggin and the Development of Florida Archaeology, by Brent Richards Weisman (2002)
Indians of Central and South Florida, 1513–1763, by John H. Hann (2003)
Presidio Santa María de Galve: A Struggle for Survival in Colonial Spanish Pensacola, edited by Judith A. Bense (2003)
Bioarchaeology of the Florida Gulf Coast: Adaptation, Conflict, and Change, by Dale L. Hutchinson (2004; first paperback edition, 2020)
The Myth of Syphilis: The Natural History of Treponematosis in North America, edited by Mary Lucas Powell and Della Collins Cook (2005)
The Florida Journals of Frank Hamilton Cushing, edited by Phyllis E. Kolianos and Brent R. Weisman (2005)
The Lost Florida Manuscript of Frank Hamilton Cushing, edited by Phyllis E. Kolianos and Brent R. Weisman (2005)
The Native American World Beyond Apalachee: West Florida and the Chattahoochee Valley, by John H. Hann (2006)
Tatham Mound and the Bioarchaeology of European Contact: Disease and Depopulation in Central Gulf Coast Florida, by Dale L. Hutchinson (2007)
Taíno Indian Myth and Practice: The Arrival of the Stranger King, by William F. Keegan (2007; first paperback edition, 2022)
An Archaeology of Black Markets: Local Ceramics and Economies in Eighteenth-Century Jamaica, by Mark W. Hauser (2008; first paperback edition, 2013)
Mississippian Mortuary Practices: Beyond Hierarchy and the Representationist Perspective, edited by Lynne P. Sullivan and Robert C. Mainfort Jr. (2010; first paperback edition, 2012)
Bioarchaeology of Ethnogenesis in the Colonial Southeast, by Christopher M. Stojanowski (2010; first paperback edition, 2013)
French Colonial Archaeology in the Southeast and Caribbean, edited by Kenneth G. Kelly and Meredith D. Hardy (2011; first paperback edition, 2015)
Late Prehistoric Florida: Archaeology at the Edge of the Mississippian World, edited by Keith Ashley and Nancy Marie White (2012; first paperback edition, 2015)
Early and Middle Woodland Landscapes of the Southeast, edited by Alice P. Wright and Edward R. Henry (2013; first paperback edition, 2019)
Trends and Traditions in Southeastern Zooarchaeology, edited by Tanya M. Peres (2014)
New Histories of Pre-Columbian Florida, edited by Neill J. Wallis and Asa R. Randall (2014; first paperback edition, 2016)
Discovering Florida: First-Contact Narratives from Spanish Expeditions along the Lower Gulf Coast, edited and translated by John E. Worth (2014; first paperback edition, 2016)
Constructing Histories: Archaic Freshwater Shell Mounds and Social Landscapes of the St. Johns River, Florida, by Asa R. Randall (2015)
Archaeology of Early Colonial Interaction at El Chorro de Maíta, Cuba, by Roberto Valcárcel Rojas (2016)
Fort San Juan and the Limits of Empire: Colonialism and Household Practice at the Berry Site, edited by Robin A. Beck, Christopher B. Rodning, and David G. Moore (2016)

Rethinking Moundville and Its Hinterland, edited by Vincas P. Steponaitis and C. Margaret Scarry (2016; first paperback edition, 2019)
Gathering at Silver Glen: Community and History in Late Archaic Florida, by Zackary I. Gilmore (2016)
Paleoindian Societies of the Coastal Southeast, by James S. Dunbar (2016; first paperback edition, 2019)
Cuban Archaeology in the Caribbean, edited by Ivan Roksandic (2016)
Handbook of Ceramic Animal Symbols in the Ancient Lesser Antilles, by Lawrence Waldron (2016)
Archaeologies of Slavery and Freedom in the Caribbean: Exploring the Spaces in Between, edited by Lynsey A. Bates, John M. Chenoweth, and James A. Delle (2016; first paperback edition, 2018)
Setting the Table: Ceramics, Dining, and Cultural Exchange in Andalucía and La Florida, by Kathryn L. Ness (2017)
Simplicity, Equality, and Slavery: An Archaeology of Quakerism in the British Virgin Islands, 1740–1780, by John M. Chenoweth (2017)
Fit for War: Sustenance and Order in the Mid-Eighteenth-Century Catawba Nation, by Mary Elizabeth Fitts (2017)
Water from Stone: Archaeology and Conservation at Florida's Springs, by Jason O'Donoughue (2017)
Mississippian Beginnings, edited by Gregory D. Wilson (2017; first paperback edition, 2019)
Harney Flats: A Florida Paleoindian Site, by I. Randolph Daniel Jr. and Michael Wisenbaker (2017)
Honoring Ancestors in Sacred Space: The Archaeology of an Eighteenth-Century African-Bahamian Cemetery, by Grace Turner (2017; first paperback edition, 2023)
Investigating the Ordinary: Everyday Matters in Southeast Archaeology, edited by Sarah E. Price and Philip J. Carr (2018)
New Histories of Village Life at Crystal River, by Thomas J. Pluckhahn and Victor D. Thompson (2018)
Early Human Life on the Southeastern Coastal Plain, edited by Albert C. Goodyear and Christopher R. Moore (2018; first paperback edition, 2021)
The Archaeology of Villages in Eastern North America, edited by Jennifer Birch and Victor D. Thompson (2018)
The Cumberland River Archaic of Middle Tennessee, edited by Tanya M. Peres and Aaron Deter-Wolf (2019)
Pre-Columbian Art of the Caribbean, by Lawrence Waldron (2019)
Iconography and Wetsite Archaeology of Florida's Watery Realms, edited by Ryan Wheeler and Joanna Ostapkowicz (2019)
New Directions in the Search for the First Floridians, edited by David K. Thulman and Ervan G. Garrison (2019)
Archaeology of Domestic Landscapes of the Enslaved in the Caribbean, edited by James A. Delle and Elizabeth C. Clay (2019; first paperback edition, 2022)
Cahokia in Context: Hegemony and Diaspora, edited by Charles H. McNutt and Ryan M. Parish (2020)
Bears: Archaeological and Ethnohistorical Perspectives in Native Eastern North America, edited by Heather A. Lapham and Gregory A. Waselkov (2020)
Contact, Colonialism, and Native Communities in the Southeastern United States, edited by Edmond A. Boudreaux III, Maureen Meyers, and Jay K. Johnson (2020)
An Archaeology and History of a Caribbean Sugar Plantation on Antigua, edited by Georgia L. Fox (2020)
Modeling Entradas: Sixteenth-Century Assemblages in North America, edited by Clay Mathers (2020)
Archaeology in Dominica: Everyday Ecologies and Economies at Morne Patate, edited by Mark W. Hauser and Diane Wallman (2020)
The Making of Mississippian Tradition, by Christina M. Friberg (2020)
The Historical Turn in Southeastern Archaeology, edited by Robbie Ethridge and Eric E. Bowne (2020)
Falls of the Ohio Archaeology: Archaeology of Native American Settlement, edited by David Pollack, Anne Tobbe Bader, and Justin N. Carlson (2021)

A History of Platform Mound Ceremonialism: Finding Meaning in Elevated Ground, by Megan C. Kassabaum (2021)

New Methods and Theories for Analyzing Mississippian Imagery, edited by Bretton T. Giles and Shawn P. Lambert (2021)

Methods, Mounds, and Missions: New Contributions to Florida Archaeology, edited by Ann S. Cordell and Jeffrey M. Mitchem (2021)

Unearthing the Missions of Spanish Florida, edited by Tanya M. Peres and Rochelle A. Marrinan (2021)

Presidios of Spanish West Florida, by Judith A. Bense (2022)

En Bas Saline: A Taíno Town before and after Columbus, by Kathleen Deagan (2023)

Mississippian Women, edited by Rachel V. Briggs, Michaelyn S. Harle, and Lynne P. Sullivan (2024)